# RASHI

# THE LITTMAN LIBRARY OF
# JEWISH CIVILIZATION

*Dedicated to the memory of*
Louis Thomas Sidney Littman
*who founded the Littman Library for the love of God
and as an act of charity in memory of his father*
Joseph Aaron Littman
*and to the memory of*
Robert Joseph Littman
*who continued what his father Louis had begun*

יהא זכרם ברוך

*'Get wisdom, get understanding:
Forsake her not and she shall preserve thee'*

PROV. 4:5

*The Littman Library of Jewish Civilization is a registered UK charity
Registered charity no. 1000784*

# RASHI

◆

## AVRAHAM GROSSMAN

TRANSLATED BY JOEL LINSIDER

Oxford · Portland, Oregon
The Littman Library of Jewish Civilization

The Littman Library of Jewish Civilization

Chief Executive Officer: Ludo Craddock
Managing Editor: Connie Webber

PO Box 645, Oxford OX2 OUJ, UK
www.littman.co.uk
———

Published in the United States and Canada by
The Littman Library of Jewish Civilization
c/o ISBS, 920 NE 58th Avenue, Suite 300
Portland, Oregon 97213-3786

First published in Hebrew 2006 © The Zalman Shazar Center for Jewish History
English translation © 2012 The Littman Library of Jewish Civilization
First issued in paperback 2014
Paperback reprinted 2016

A catalogue record for this book is available from the British Library

The Library of Congress catalogued the hardback edition as follows:
Grossman, Avraham.
[Emunot ve-de'ot be-'olamo shel Rashi. English.]
Rashi / Avraham Grossman ; translated by Joel Linsider.
p. cm.
ISBN 978-1-904113-89-8
Includes bibliographical references and index.
1. Rashi, 1040-1105—Teachings.  I. Linsider, Joel A.    II. Title.
BM755.S6G7513 2012       296.1092—dc23 [B]        2011043861

ISBN 978-1-906764-61-6

Publishing co-ordinator: Janet Moth
Copy-editing: Mark Newby
Proof-reading: Bonnie Blackburn
Indexing: Bonnie Blackburn
Design and production: Pete Russell, Faringdon, Oxon.
Typeset by John Saunders Design & Production, Eastbourne
Printed in Great Britain on acid-free paper by
TJ Books Limited, Padstow, Cornwall

◆

*We sat, all of us, at the long table and studied ḥumash with Rashi—*
*The purity of our childhood restored, our innocence captured anew . . .*
*The words sparkled radiantly, blinding our eyes.*
*They shone with the light of Creation, a strange and distant glow . . .*
*Suddenly, a wonder! Of the opaque stones in the wall,*
*One was glowing and clear, like a sacred stone in the priestly breastplate . . .*
*This was your stone, grandfather Rashi, yours, the most precious of stones . . .*
*How we loved you, grandfather Rashi, how we embraced you! . . .*
*Flourish again, grand garden, refreshing Jewish children,*
*Bring forth your produce, wondrous orchard, reviving the dispersions of Israel.*

SAMSON MELTZER
*Ashirah lerashi* (Of Rashi I Sing)

◆

# Preface to the Hebrew Edition

RASHI, the post-biblical figure most highly regarded by Jews overall, left an indelible mark on Jewish culture, a mark greater than that left by anyone else since the completion of the Talmud. The present book examines his life, his oeuvre, his world-view, and his vast influence on Jewish culture. Although thousands of articles have been written, two key questions related to how we characterize him have scarcely been considered: 'Did he have a fully developed conceptual intellectual doctrine?' and 'Was he a revolutionary or a conservative?' A substantial portion of this book is devoted to those issues. Of course, these questions and others (such as the historical reasons for his vast influence) cannot be answered without first reviewing the course of his life, his defining character traits, his ties to the non-Jewish world, and his multi-faceted literary work.

The book forms part of the Zalman Shazar Center's series on 'Great Minds in Jewish Thought and Creativity'. Consistent with the series' character, it is not a typical scholarly study. Its scholarly apparatus is very limited, many subjects are discussed only briefly, and I had to refrain from referring to many studies of Rashi's oeuvre. The purpose of the series is to tell the life stories of these people while maintaining a suitable academic framework. But that goal, however worthy, cannot be attained in a study of Rashi, because we lack basic information on many subjects. It is enough to note in that regard that we know nothing of his childhood except the names of his father and his uncle. We know neither his mother's name nor whether he had siblings. The first confirmed information we have of him is that of his presence in the *beit midrash* in Mainz when he was 20 years old. Dozens of folk legends about his life are in circulation, but they have no historical value: all we can really learn from them is the esteem in which he has been held over the ages. Accordingly, I have made no use of those folk legends in studying the events of his life. Still, almost every subject considered in the book includes something new, especially with respect to his intellectual world.

It is my pleasant obligation to thank all those who helped me bring this work to its conclusion. Professor Aviezer Ravitzky, editor of the series, provided valuable advice on the policies governing the writing of the book. Mr Zui Yekutiel, the director of the Zalman Shazar Center, devotedly attended to the book's preparation, and the centre's staff helped see it through to publication. Avital Regev-Shoshani laboured to improve its prose and to ready it for printing. My wife Rachel worked devotedly to type the manuscript and improve its style. They all have my gratitude.

# Contents

## PART III
## RASHI'S WORLD-VIEW

## PART IV
## POSTSCRIPT

# Translator's Note

THIS volume quotes extensively from Rashi's writings and other primary sources, including classical Jewish texts, some of which are available in published English translations. Where such a translation is used, the source is given in the notes; in most instances, however, the translations are my own.

In translating biblical verses, I have relied primarily on the New Jewish Publication Society version (*The Tanakh*, Philadelphia, 1999: NJPS), but where the Old JPS version (*The Holy Scriptures*, Philadelphia, 1917: OJPS) was better suited to Rashi's understanding of the verse, I have followed that instead.

Some passages quoted from Rashi's commentary move back and forth between extracts from the biblical verse being interpreted and the interpretation itself. In these cases, I have adopted the convention of italicizing the extracts from the biblical verses.

Notes on particular points of the translation appear on the relevant page below the author's numbered footnotes.

J.L.

# Note on Transliteration

THE transliteration of Hebrew in this book reflects consideration of the type of book it is, in terms of its content, purpose, and readership. The system adopted therefore reflects a broad approach to transcription, rather than the narrower approaches found in the *Encyclopaedia Judaica* or other systems developed for text-based or linguistic studies. The aim has been to reflect the pronunciation prescribed for modern Hebrew, rather than the spelling or Hebrew word structure, and to do so using conventions that are generally familiar to the English-speaking reader.

In accordance with this approach, no attempt is made to indicate the distinctions between *alef* and *ayin*, *tet* and *taf*, *kaf* and *kuf*, *sin* and *samekh*, since these are not relevant to pronunciation; likewise, the *dagesh* is not indicated except where it affects pronunciation. Following the principle of using conventions familiar to the majority of readers, however, transcriptions that are well established have been retained even when they are not fully consistent with the transliteration system adopted. On similar grounds, the *tsadi* is rendered by 'tz' in such familiar words as barmitzvah. Likewise, the distinction between *ḥet* and *khaf* has been retained, using *ḥ* for the former and *kh* for the latter; the associated forms are generally familiar to readers, even if the distinction is not actually borne out in pronunciation, and for the same reason the final *heh* is indicated too. As in Hebrew, no capital letters are used, except that an initial capital has been retained in transliterating titles of published works (for example, *Shulḥan arukh*).

Since no distinction is made between *alef* and *ayin*, they are indicated by an apostrophe only in intervocalic positions where a failure to do so could lead an English-speaking reader to pronounce the vowel-cluster as a diphthong—as, for example, in *ha'ir*—or otherwise mispronounce the word.

The *sheva na* is indicated by an *e*—*perikat ol*, *reshut*—except, again, when established convention dictates otherwise.

The *yod* is represented by *i* when it occurs as a vowel (*bereshit*), by *y* when it occurs as a consonant (*yesodot*), and by *yi* when it occurs as both (*yisra'el*).

Names have generally been left in their familiar forms, even when this is inconsistent with the overall system.

## PART I

# RASHI AND HIS WORLD

# CHAPTER ONE

# The Social and Cultural Background of Rashi's Work

## The Jews' Political, Economic, and Social Status

Any enquiry into the significance of the work of an intellectual or community leader must begin with at least a brief examination of his or her social and cultural milieu. This background is especially important in Rashi's case, for he was active during a period of great change. According to evidence preserved in the literary accounts and archaeological findings that have come down to us, Jews began to settle in what is now France during Roman times, in the first century CE. That settlement continued uninterrupted until Rashi's time. During the Carolingian period (eighth to tenth centuries) the situation of the Jews—politically, socially, and economically—underwent marked improvement, as they played an important role in international trade. The end of the tenth century saw the Capetian dynasty rise to power, and its early years were characterized by a fragmented kingdom and a weak sovereign. Until the middle of the twelfth century and even beyond, each of the feudal states in France struggled with its own administrative problems, and all had only loose ties to the king.

In general, Jews continued to do well in France. Nevertheless, the weakness of the central government and the ascendancy of local fiefdoms meant that their social and political status differed in each of the feudal states that made up eleventh-century France, depending upon the good will of the local rulers.

Two developments during the eleventh and twelfth centuries influenced Jewish economic and intellectual life and the internal organization of the Jewish community: the growth of cities and the European intellectual renaissance. At the start of the Middle Ages cities went into decline, serving more as assembly points for ecclesiastical institutions than as regional economic centres. Only in the eleventh century did cities change, as they developed in the wake of increased commerce and overall economic growth. But while the process became evident during the eleventh century, cities did not really flourish until the twelfth and thirteenth centuries. Urban development was the primary agent of expanded Jewish settlement in France, and it influenced the internal organization of Jewish communities.

As Jews in northern France increased in number during the eleventh century and established new communities, their political and economic status changed in some respects. Although they played an important part in the economies of the renewed cities, their share in international commerce—in which many French and German Jews had made their livings during the ninth and tenth centuries—gradually declined, and more of them began to engage in local commerce and in money-lending to non-Jews. Their diminished role in international trade caused their ties to the Jewish centres in Babylonia and the Land of Israel to weaken somewhat, though links were maintained throughout the eleventh century.

Jews retained only limited agricultural holdings, primarily those granted to them by the rulers as fiefs. According to Haym Soloveitchik, Jews then—and later—played an important part in the production and sale of wine, and Rashi's responsa preserve several accounts of agricultural holdings devoted to viticulture. One concerns a couple who gave their son and his bride 'a large vineyard that they owned in the city' as a wedding gift. The bride testified that the gift had been granted in her name as well as her husband's from the outset. The mother is described as a substantial businesswoman, 'established in the city and known to the princes'. The newly married husband had gone on a long-distance business trip, and his fate was unknown.[1] This account, along with others, provides at least a partial picture of how Jews made their living and of their close commercial and social ties to the upper classes in northern France. It also sheds light on the place of Jewish women in maintaining those ties and in the economic life of their families.[2]

Another important change involved the increased power of the Church and the intensification of its anti-Jewish propaganda. Late in his life, Rashi could sense the growing hatred of Jews, fuelled by the accusation of deicide, by their rejection of the doctrine of the Trinity, and by their refusal to accept the principles of Christian belief. This hatred reached its peak with the First Crusade at the end of the eleventh century. France's lack of a central and authoritative royal government affected the status of the Jews, increasing their dependence on local rulers. A further change, this time within the Jewish community, involved the strengthening of France as a centre of Torah study at the end of the eleventh century and the diminution in its ties to and dependence on the more important Jewish centres in Germany.

## The Troyes Community and the Jewish Centre in Champagne

Rashi (Rabbi Shelomoh Yitshaki) was born, lived, worked, died, and was buried in Troyes, an important city in the Champagne region of northern France. Jews did

---

[1] *Tahtsul*, §§30–1; Rashi, *Responsa* (Heb.), ed. Elfenbein, §240. On the role of Jews in the non-Jewish wine trade, see Soloveitchik, *Their Wine* (Heb.), 31–9, 66–90.

[2] See Schwarzfuchs, *History of the Jews in Medieval France* (Heb.); Taitz, *The Jews of Medieval France*; Hallam, *Capetian France, 987–1328*.

not begin to arrive in the cities in this region in large numbers until the second half of the twelfth century when the region's markets flourished. In Rashi's time, the Jewish communities of northern France were small: a community that numbered one hundred Jewish families was considered quite large. However, local markets existed in Troyes as early as the second half of the eleventh century, and they formed an important source of income for the region's Jews.

Governance of the communities had not yet taken firm shape, and various sources clearly show a degree of social strain. One of the questions addressed to Rabbi Joseph ben Samuel Tov Elem (Bonfils) early in the eleventh century recounts how Troyes claimed primacy over the surrounding Jewish communities. In 1015 Jews from the community of Reims came to do business in the Troyes market. Several of them were arrested and imprisoned by the local feudal authorities. 'The philanthropists of Troyes' imposed a share of the ransom costs on the surrounding communities against their will, and it is hard to imagine they would have presumed to do so had it not been for Troyes' central economic standing.[3] More and more disputes arose during the first half of the eleventh century, and members of the community turned to sages in distant communities—especially that of Mainz, Germany—for help in resolving them. One of their questions, dating from the time of Rashi's youth in the mid-eleventh century, tells of a potential schism that threatened the Troyes community:

We warned them on several occasions not to behave in so abandoned a way, but they did not heed us. And when our community saw that to be the case, we withdrew from them. But the entire community feared that they would steal the Torah scrolls and other property of the community, for their house was near the synagogue, and they would not be prevented from bringing it wherever they wished. And they violated that decree [ban].[4]

The royal government at the time was weak, and the Jews were, as a practical matter, subject to the authority of local rulers, the feudal nobles. Rashi's responsa contain important accounts of that situation, including the Jews' economic ties to the nobility and their political standing. One of the questions addressed to Rashi mentions a Jewish woman who had received land in fief—a fact that attests to the integration of the Jews into the feudal regime and their good relationships with the ruler of Champagne and other feudal princes. Everyone is influenced by the circumstances of his or her youth, and Rashi's responsa and commentaries on the Bible and the Talmud show plainly the marks of his life in Troyes and his studies in Germany.

The numerous disputes within and between communities stemmed from the fact that many people had migrated to the area within a short period. Competition among community members pertained primarily to sources of livelihood. Members of distinguished families claimed privileges in their trade with non-

[3] Agus, *Responsa of the Tosafists* (Heb.), §§1, 39–40.    [4] *Kol bo*, §142.

Jews—in particular, they sought restraints on competition for their established clientele—but the new immigrants objected to that privilege. The community's trade was conducted largely with non-Jewish neighbours, rather than within the community itself. Restraints on competition mainly injured the non-Jewish consumers, while increasing the profits earned by the Jews. *Ḥerem hayishuv*—literally a 'ban on settlement', the right of a member of the community to veto the settlement within it of a new immigrant—was intended to serve the same purpose; that is, to prevent economic competition. Monopolists sought to bar competitors in the same line of trade from settling and joining the community.

The earliest Jewish sages and communal leaders in France and Germany—Rashi among them—saw the Jewish community and the enhancement of its strength as essential for the continued existence of the Jewish people. Given the community's weakness and limited size, the task was both urgent and daunting. The existence of public institutions and the power of the communal leadership—sometimes made up of common folk—to impose its will on the community as a whole were constantly being tested and were a serious bone of contention. Questions related to the level of taxes and the manner of their collection were another frequent source of conflict. Contemporary sources tell of varied economic interests, opposing cultural traditions, and struggles for power. The growth of Jewish communities in Christian Europe and the formation of their institutions of self-government took place side by side with the establishment of local Torah centres and the lessening of ties to the Babylonian yeshivas. The absence of a binding halakhic tradition concerning communal governance was among the factors that account for the extensive and contentious treatment of the issue in medieval rabbinic literature, especially the responsa literature. Rashi and most of the early Ashkenazi sages devoted considerable attention to the authority of the communal leadership.

These difficulties explain the use of varied enforcement mechanisms, such as fines, flogging, and bans. A ban was considered a particularly harsh penalty, for not only did it prohibit all social or commercial contact with the banned person, but it was also understood to mean that the offender had been banned by the heavenly court. The religious character of the ban made it frightening and intimidating, and communities used this weapon widely as they strove to impose their will on those who refused to heed their enactments and decisions. As early as the first half of the eleventh century, Rabbi Joseph Tov Elem noted that 'the wicked cannot be subdued nowadays except by bans and fines, and one who would abolish them would increase lawlessness in Israel'.[5] Rashi, too, made use of this severe enforcement mechanism.

---

[5]  Meir of Rothenburg, *Responsa* (Heb.), ed. Rabinowitz, §423.

# The Twelfth-Century Renaissance

To understand Rashi's literary work, one must be aware of the revival of intellectual life in Christian Europe in general and in France in particular during the eleventh and twelfth centuries. Any substantive enquiry into the writings of Rashi and his disciples and into the growth of Jewish exegetical literature during that period also requires consideration of the parallel developments in the surrounding society.

The eleventh century saw the start of an important intellectual awakening that reached its peak during the twelfth century and came to be known as 'the twelfth-century renaissance'. This renaissance left its mark on all areas of human life and creativity and profoundly affected people's perspective on the world. Studies written in the previous generation show that some glimmerings of this revival could already be seen during the second half of the eleventh century. This early dating is important for understanding the changes in the viewpoint and literary output of the Jewish sages in France and Germany at the time. Distinguished itinerant teachers, who went from town to town and from one *beit midrash* (study hall) to the next, played a crucial role in these developments. Some of the greatest contemporary Christian thinkers were active in France, among them Fulbert of Chartres (960–1028) and Berengarius of Tours (1010–88). Learned Jews and Christians attracted students from afar. All told, France became the most important centre for the intellectual revival that was under way. During the eleventh century, Italy and Germany had taken the lead in intellectual activity, but by the end of the century, it had shifted to France. This development had parallels with the changes that took place in Jewish society at the time.

Within Christian society there had long been two approaches to the interpretation of Scripture. Some favoured a textual method that focused on the literal meaning; others sought spiritual content by seeking out the implicit, conceptual meanings that emerged once the 'outer shell' had been peeled away. Advocates of the second method generally applied allegorical interpretations as they sought out the text's implicit, conceptual sense. Jerome—a Church Father who lived in the fourth century and profoundly influenced later Christian thinkers—called for both methods to be used together. Nevertheless, Christian scholars through the ages generally chose one or the other, and most of them favoured the second method, neglecting literal interpretation.

The second half of the eleventh century saw an important change, which reached its pinnacle in the scriptural interpretation pursued at the abbey of Saint-Victor in Paris. This exegetical school turned away from allegorical interpretation and preferred a literal approach, contending that the conceptual depths of the Bible could not be plumbed without first understanding the literal meaning of the texts.

Contemporary trends in the broader society—a general cultural revival; a great conceptual debate between faith and reason; issues related to the authority and interpretation of Scripture; the attendance of disciples on distinguished teachers, who encouraged them to take an active part in the intellectual debates of the time— all had interesting parallels in Rashi's *beit midrash* and the activities of his disciples. The parallels between the two groups extend even to literary activity itself, including examination of the literal meaning of the text, treatment of grammar, critical study (even if limited) of sacred Scripture, the search for reliable texts, allowing reason to be brought to bear on the study of the commandments' purposes, and committing the traditions and activities of distinguished teachers to writing.

This cultural development was marked primarily by the central position afforded to reason in intellectual activity, which led the way to a freer and more critical enquiry into the Hebrew Bible and the Gospels and even into some tenets of belief. Reason brought about greater openness in many areas, as thinkers sought to understand the laws of nature and developed a more powerful historical consciousness. The study of Scripture underwent a significant change, becoming more critical, and biblical commentators showed a growing degree of independence.

The similarities between the development of Jewish biblical interpretation in northern France and the parallel processes within Christian society are too great to be mere happenstance. The resemblances can be seen in several characteristics of the exegetical school that flourished in northern France, two such traits being particularly noteworthy: rejection of Midrash, together with pursuit of the plain meaning of the text, and an interest in philological matters, with primacy given to linguistic analysis.

There is, to be sure, no proof of direct influence. But intellectual movements are characterized by their tendency to create shared cultural platforms on which cultural activities and intellectual creativity can be pursued in different societies. The intellectual activity of Jewish sages in Germany and France is related to the general European renaissance in other areas of literary creativity as well, a phenomenon that began as early as the second half of the eleventh century with the activity of Rashi and his disciples. These areas include interpretation of the Talmud (this was when the Tosafot were written), interpretation of the liturgical poems (*piyutim*), the study of astronomy, and biographical study of the talmudic sages. The changes that took place in the thought of Jewish sages of the time—especially their deep-seated commitment to reason and rational enquiry in all areas of intellectual life—resemble the changes that were taking place around them. Pierre Riché described France during the second half of the eleventh century as a crossroads between the Carolingian past and the renaissance of the twelfth century. Rashi's *beit midrash* can likewise be seen as a point of encounter between the talmudic interpretation of the German yeshivas going back to the days of Rabbenu Gershom (Rabbi Gershom Me'or Hagolah (the light of the diaspora), *c.*960–1028) and his disciples and the new modes of analysis practised by the tosafists, which were developed primarily in northern France during the twelfth century.

During the second half of the eleventh century, then, France stood at the centre of a process of renewal and revival and at the focal point of conceptual disputes and literary creativity—in both Jewish and Christian society.

## The Jews' Social Ties to their Surroundings

The work of the earliest French sages, particularly Rashi, is of considerable importance in helping us understand the social and cultural ties between Jews and their surroundings during the period in question. By the twelfth century, the situation in Germany was noticeably different from that in northern France, but the differences had begun to emerge as early as Rashi's time. Jewish intellectual activity in Germany was not entirely disconnected from that of the surrounding society, but accounts of cultural exchange are far fewer than those of encounters between French Jews and their surroundings. These accounts, moreover, seem to reflect the actual situation. It is possible that the differences between France and Germany arose because schools in France had taken a leading role in the intellectual development of Christian Europe overall as early as the end of the eleventh century. More likely, however, the difference is attributable to the cultural isolation of Jewish society in Germany during the second half of the eleventh century and after the First Crusade.

The firm economic ties between Jews and their Christian neighbours and their close contact in many areas of life seem to have exerted an influence on the other connections between the two cultures. This was particularly so in France. Jews did business with their non-Jewish neighbours, employed non-Jewish servants in their homes, and were in regular daily contact with their surroundings, as is evident from various documents. These close contacts naturally generated attitudes of affinity and friendship. At the Church conclave in Metz in 888, a rule was adopted forbidding shared meals with Jews, and the adoption of the rule clearly shows the close relations between Jews and Christians and the concern they caused. At that time, French Jewry was still developing under the first Carolingian rulers. In criticizing a Jew who, in his view, had not behaved properly towards his wife, Rashi cited as a model the positive attitude of Christian noblemen towards their wives.[6]

The Jews of France, in both its northern regions and its central and southern regions, came into close contact with Christian culture. This was apparent in several areas: among the most prominent were religious disputations between Jews and Christians, links between the Jews and the twelfth-century cultural renaissance, and ties between Christian biblical exegesis of the school of Saint-Victor during the first half of the twelfth century and Jewish exegesis.

Jewish names of the period also attest to this socio-cultural influence. Many Jews—women especially, but also great sages—were known by non-Jewish names

---

[6]  *Taḥtsul*, §40.

or soubriquets. The phenomenon, equally evident in France and in Germany, was widespread during the tenth century; and even though it became less pronounced in the eleventh century, many Jewish women during the twelfth century and even later bore non-Jewish names. Many Jews lived outside the 'Jewish quarter', especially before the middle of the eleventh century, and that too contributed substantially to the development of social relations with Christians. Religious differences, of course, along with mutual animosity towards the other's religious symbols, meant that the contacts were confined to certain clearly defined areas, especially during the eleventh century. But the existence of religious conversions in both directions attests to the intensity of the sociocultural ties.

## Jewish–Christian Religious Polemics

The ties between the two societies were also influenced by frequent public religious disputations. Because of those disputations, both sides made efforts to learn about the opposing camp's viewpoints and texts. The disputations, both oral and written, began during the ninth century and continued throughout the Middle Ages. Most accounts come from France, with only a few from Germany or England, but the phenomenon seems to have been prevalent throughout Christian Europe. In any case, it is impossible to understand the biblical commentaries of Rashi and his disciples or Rashi's sense of mission without considering the importance of this polemic to his consciousness and his literary output.

Various accounts that have come down to us tell of the frequency of disputations and their importance to high-ranking Church authorities. This can be seen, for example, in the fact that Filbert of Chartres (early eleventh century) and Petrus Damianus (second half of the eleventh century) armed Christian participants with arguments to be pressed in their disputations with Jews. To this end they even compiled a guidebook for the use of Christian participants in disputations, in which they emphasized the importance of these polemics to the effort to convert Jews to Christianity.

Biblical exegesis stood at the centre of these disputations, but they also included discussion of other texts. The public challenge to Judaism compelled Jewish sages to participate in the debates in order to forestall their harmful effect on the Jewish masses. Evidence of this is preserved in the biblical interpretation of the early Franco-Jewish sages, especially Rashi. The commentaries of many biblical exegetes in twelfth-century France incorporate responses to Christian arguments and anti-Christian polemics. Moreover, in many cases where the commentators do not mention Christian arguments, an analysis of their comments clearly shows them to be meant as refutations. Without exception, this phenomenon appears in the work of every exegete of the plain-meaning school that developed among Jewish sages in northern France at the end of the eleventh century and throughout the twelfth. It is present in Rashi's writings and even more so in those of his successors, who brought the plain-meaning school to some of its exegetical pinnacles: Rabbi Joseph Kara (*c.*1065–*c.*1135), Rashbam (Rabbi Samuel ben Meir, *c.*1080–*c.*1155), Rabbi Joseph Bekhor Shor (twelfth century), and Rabbi Eliezer of Beaugency (twelfth century). Their indirect polemics against Christological interpretations are more extensive than previously described in the scholarly literature. It is likely that the polemics between Judaism and Christianity influenced not only the content of various commentaries but even some of the basic elements of the new plain-meaning approach, whose founders included Rashi.

These polemics indicate both the degree of Jewish concern over Christian propaganda and the Jews' familiarity with Christian arguments and the literature of Christian exegesis. The concern about propaganda grew out of the large number of converts—some from the families of sages—and the Jews' intense distress over their humiliating exile and the lack of any satisfactory explanation for their sorry state. Clear evidence of this appears in Jewish polemical works written in response to Christian arguments and presenting lines of counter-attack.

# CHAPTER TWO

# A Biographical Sketch

## Rashi's Life

### His Milieu and his Family

Rashi's childhood and youth are shrouded in mystery. He was born in Troyes in northern France, where he spent all his life except for the time he studied in Germany. The year of his birth is uncertain: some manuscripts report it as AM 4800 (1040 CE), but others—almost certainly more accurate[1]—give it as 4801 (1041). He died on Thursday, 29 Tamuz 4865 (1105). That date is mentioned in several manuscripts, such as Rashi's commentary on the Torah in MS Parma (De Rossi 175), and is derived from a report by Rashi's students, copied in 1305:

The holy ark, the holy of holies, the great rabbi Rabbenu Solomon, may the memory of the righteous be for a blessing, son of the holy Rabbi Isaac, may his memory be for a blessing, of France, was taken from us on Thursday, 29 Tamuz AM [4]865. He was 65 years old when he was summoned to the heavenly yeshiva.[2]

The twenty-ninth of Tamuz 4865 indeed fell on a Thursday, a fact that lends credibility to the date. We see from this that Rashi lived to the age of 65—relatively old for the time. Some scholars have argued that the extent of his oeuvre indicates that he was born earlier, in 1030, but that assumption lacks any basis, and it is his own students here who tell us his age. The expression 'was taken from us' likewise lends support to the premise that the passage was written by his disciples. As far as we can tell, Rashi died in Troyes and was buried there. His grandson, Rabbenu Tam (Rabbi Jacob Tam, *c.*1100–1171), called the city 'the place of our rabbi Solomon and

---

[1] Authors and copyists tended to round numbers. For a detailed discussion of Rashi's youth, his family, and his studies in Germany, together with documentation of the dates in printed texts and manuscripts, see Grossman, *The Early Sages of France* (Heb.), 121–31. I have revised and expanded some of the details in that account on the basis of sources I became aware of following its publication. On page 123, I cited the view of Victor Aptowitzer (*Introduction to Sefer Rabiah* (Heb.), 395) that Rashi had been born some ten years earlier, but I cannot agree with him. As for the soubriquet 'Rashi', it may first have been applied to him by his students, who used it as an abbreviation of 'our rabbi, may he live' (*rabenu sheyiḥyeh*). Later it came to be explained as an abbreviation for *rabi shelomoh yitsḥaki*, his name and patronymic.

[2] MS Parma, fo. 198*b*.

the city of our ancestors' graves'.[3] This supports the premise that Rashi—and, apparently, his ancestors—were buried in Troyes.

There are numerous folk legends about Rashi's birth, especially the miracles wrought for his mother during her pregnancy, and about his father and his father's journeys outside France and meetings with various sages, including Maimonides. None of these legends is reliably documented, however, and nothing can be gleaned from them about the events of Rashi's life. They grew as a result of the widespread reverence for Rashi and the luminous halo that became part of his image. They also reflect the cultural world of Jewish society in the late Middle Ages—a time that saw the composition, in Jewish circles as in Christian, of numerous hagiographical works recounting the miracles performed for holy men.

Reliable information about Rashi's parents likewise is lacking. He appears to mention his father once in his commentary on the Talmud: 'the words of my father and teacher, may his rest be honoured' (on *AZ 75a*, *vela peligei*; but it is uncertain whether Rashi wrote that himself or it was written by his grandson, Rashbam, who was referring to his own father, Rabbi Meir). Had Rashi's father been a great and renowned sage, Rashi might be expected to have mentioned him more often in his commentaries on the Bible and the Talmud and in his hundreds of responsa, as was the practice of the sages of the time. In the passage from MS Parma quoted above, Rashi's father is referred to as 'the holy Rabbi Isaac', but it is doubtful that this tells us anything about his character. Most likely he was so designated because he had a son as distinguished as Rashi. The writers appear to have been Rashi's students, as they call him 'the great rabbi [teacher]' rather than 'the great exegete', as he was known in later times, and it is possible that they were acquainted with his father and referred to him as 'the holy' because of his qualities. In one of his acrostic liturgical poems, Rashi refers to his father as *ribi yitshak* (Rabbi Isaac), lending further support—though hardly unambiguous proof—to the premise that he was a scholar. In any case, it is evident from the sources that Rashi was not a scion of one of the distinguished Ashkenazi families of the time. It may be assumed that his father was a poor man, for he does not appear to have supported his son, as he might otherwise have been expected to do, during the latter's studies in Germany. Rashi says he struggled for food and clothing for himself and his family, as we shall see below.

We have no information about Rashi's mother either. His considerable concern for the dignity and rights of women allows us to infer, however, that his mother was devoted to her son and that he loved and esteemed her.

Rashi's maternal uncle was a renowned scholar, whom Rashi referred to as 'Rabbi Simeon the Elder'. It is not known for certain who he was, but chronology makes it evident it was not Rabbi Simeon ben Isaac ben Abun, the greatest liturgical poet of early Ashkenaz. The uncle studied with Rabbenu Gershom in Mainz, Germany. Rashi relied on a halakhic work he had written and probably studied

---

[3] Rabbenu Tam, *Sefer hayashar*, ii: *Responsa*, §16.

with him. It is quite possible that the uncle's influence contributed to Rashi's decision to travel to Mainz and study in its yeshiva. Several other of Rashi's relatives
are mentioned in various manuscripts, but their identities are unclear.

No information on Rashi's wife has come down to us, and we do not even know
her name. In one responsum, he writes that she sent a messenger to the synagogue
on the eighth day of Passover to tell him that a non-Jew had sent him a gift of food.
It is not known whether she took an active part in supporting the family, as was the
practice of many Jewish women in Germany and northern France at the time. They
had three or four daughters, two of whom— Jochebed (known as 'the pious') and
Miriam—were married to great scholars. Jochebed married Rabbi Meir ben
Samuel, and their four sons, Rashi's grandsons, went on to become great scholars
too. Two of the grandsons—Rashbam and Rabbenu Tam—are among the leading
French tosafists. Miriam married Rabbi Judah ben Nathan (Rivan). The third
daughter, Rachel, was apparently married to a Rabbi Eliezer, of whom nothing else
is known, but they divorced after a brief while. There may have been a fourth
daughter who died in childhood.

Over the generations, Rashi's descendants played important roles in community leadership and were among the most prominent tosafists. Of particular note
is his great-grandson, Rabbi Isaac ben Samuel of Dampierre, known as Rabbi Isaac
the Elder (*hazaken*), who was the leading tosafist of the last quarter of the twelfth
century. The existence of families of scholars and communal leaders, whose descendants exercised multi-generational communal leadership, was widespread in other
Jewish centres in the Middle Ages and was also common within the Christian
world. The fame of Rashi's family and the esteem in which it was widely held led
many people over the ages to try to identify themselves with it. Many documents
attesting to that pedigree record unsubstantiated traditions and cannot be relied
upon.

## Studies in Germany

At about the age of 18, Rashi left France to study at the yeshiva in Mainz. The
yeshiva had attained considerable fame, due largely to the activity there two generations earlier of Rabbenu Gershom. Rashi held Rabbenu Gershom in great
esteem, referring to him as 'the great one of the world' and 'one who illuminates
the eyes of the exile'. As noted, Rashi's maternal uncle had also studied in this
yeshiva. No source has come down to us to document Rashi's feelings upon entering the yeshiva for the first time, but it is fair to assume the experience was an emotional one. He, a young man, had the privilege of standing next to Rabbenu
Gershom's chair, of holding commentaries on the Talmud that Rabbenu Gershom
had written with his own hand, of contemplating Rabbenu Gershom's writing, and
of drawing these pages close to his heart. He even held the Torah scroll from which
Rabbenu Gershom had read during worship. And if that were not enough, he con-

versed with Rabbi Jacob ben Yakar, one of the pre-eminent students of Rabbenu Gershom, who quickly became his honoured principal teacher. As we shall see, Rabbi Jacob was a unique and charismatic person, who made a powerful impression on all his students. Rashi's esteem for him is evident each time he is mentioned in his commentaries. This first encounter with the world of the yeshiva and its teachers left a strong impression on the young student.

At the time of his stay in Germany, Rashi was already married and a father, and his economic situation was extremely hard. He devoted his strength and energy primarily to his studies and had great difficulty supporting his wife and daughters. In a responsum written late in his life he mentioned the difficult times in Germany and added that he had not been able to devote his time exclusively to study because of the difficulty of making a living. He had trouble providing for even the minimal needs of himself and his family: 'For a lack of food and clothing were as a millstone around my neck, ruining the time I spent studying with my teachers.'[4] His concluding words express the powerful emotions evoked by his recollection of those times. Rashi's daughters—at least the eldest, Jochebed—appear to have been born while he was in Germany, as a letter from Rashi to his son-in-law, Rabbi Meir ben Samuel, who was studying in Worms with Rabbi Isaac Halevi, contains the blessing that he (Rabbi Meir) and his children (Rashi's grandchildren) should 'live forever'.[5] Rabbi Isaac died sometime between 1080 and 1085, and this shows that by that time Rashi's daughter was already a mother.

According to some accounts Rashi first studied in Worms, but that appears not to be the case. He began his studies at the yeshiva in Mainz and only later moved to Worms, where he remained for ten years. His studies in Germany had a substantial influence on his personality and world-view. Without the exegetical traditions he received from his teachers in Germany and from texts written in the two yeshivas and without his knowledge of the manuscripts possessed by those yeshivas, he could not have produced his impressive literary oeuvre. Rashi himself attested to the great effect of this period on his personality, particularly his studies in Mainz with his teacher, Rabbi Jacob ben Yakar. He studied with Rabbi Jacob for about six years and called him 'my venerable rabbi'.

Rabbi Jacob was a unique individual, and Rashi's stay with him left a lasting impression, as is evident from his comment late in his life: 'I am but a branch on a great tree, Rabbenu Jacob ben Rabbi Yakar. And even if I did not hear this point directly from him, nevertheless, *my heart, my reason, and my understanding all come from him.*'[6] The context of the comments suggests that Rashi believed his understanding of the Talmud was identical to Rabbi Jacob's. What Rashi meant by each of these terms ('heart', 'reason', and 'understanding') is not entirely clear, but it is apparent that they forcefully express his profound sense that not only his mode of

[4] Goldberg, *Ḥofes matmonim*, §1.    [5] Rashi, *Responsa* (Heb.), ed. Elfenbein, §58.
[6] Cited in Marmorstein, 'An Italian Sage and Decisor' (Heb.), 238, emphasis added.

study but even his personality traits ('my heart') were identical to those of his esteemed teacher. One of Rashi's notable characteristics was humility, a trait that likewise defined Rabbi Jacob. Rashi described him as one who shunned communal leadership and 'conducted himself as a doorsill, placing himself last of the last; he was not moved to claim the crowning glory he deserved, to innovate [in matters of halakhah] in his time'.[7]

*Sefer hahasidim* reports that it was the practice of Rabbi Jacob ben Yakar 'to sweep clean the area before the holy ark with his beard',[8] an act that demonstrates not only his humility but also the powerful religious feeling that suffused him. He would occasionally pray while barefoot in order to emphasize man's sinfulness and insignificance. The practice at that time was for students to remain with their teachers even outside the walls of the yeshiva and to learn from their overall conduct. From early times, this daily, unmediated contact was regarded by sages as extremely important, and it was already practised in the tannaitic and amoraic yeshivas, as is evident from dozens of reports preserved in the Talmud. In medieval Germany and France, the yeshivas were small and the phenomenon widespread. The atmosphere in the yeshiva was informal, even though distinguished ancestry was much esteemed in society as a whole. Teachers and their students enjoyed close and friendly relationships, and students stayed with their teachers even after official studies had ended for the day. There exist reports that Rashi accompanied Rabbi Jacob on his journeys from Mainz to other communities. But despite Rabbi Jacob's considerable influence on the formation of Rashi's character and on his intellectual and emotional world, Rashi did not follow his teacher in trying to avoid a role in communal leadership.

Rashi's studies with Rabbi Jacob included several tractates of the Babylonian Talmud as well as Scripture. At various points in his biblical commentary, Rashi mentions interpretations that he learned from Rabbi Jacob. Rashbam explicitly described Rabbi Jacob as Rashi's 'teacher of Talmud and Bible'. Rashi appears to have studied only the Talmud with his two other teachers.

After Rabbi Jacob's death in 1064 Rashi stayed on for a while at the yeshiva in Mainz and studied with Rabbi Isaac ben Judah, who was head of the yeshiva. He also studied with other sages in Mainz, especially Rabbi David Halevi. Rashi also referred to the latter as 'my teacher', and he continued to correspond with him after returning to France. But Rabbi Isaac ben Judah was relatively young and not equipped to fill Rashi's great intellectual expectations and needs.

At the same time, the yeshiva in Worms was flourishing under the leadership of Rabbi Isaac Halevi. That yeshiva did not have the lustre of its senior counterpart in Mainz, but it was distinguished by being less conservative. The Worms yeshiva reached the pinnacle of its development in the last thirty years of the eleventh

---

[7] *Sidur rashi*, §174.          [8] *Sefer hasidim*, §991.

century, and it attracted sages from distant parts. This appears to be why Rashi decided to move there too.

Rashi's stay in Rabbi Isaac Halevi's yeshiva seems to have lasted from three to five years, and his studies in Worms also had an important influence on his way of life and his thought. Rabbi Isaac Halevi, like Rabbi Jacob, is described as a man of profound religious feeling, and his contemporaries referred to him as 'the holy one'. But he differed from Rabbi Jacob in his great self-assurance, his willingness to break new ground in study, his attitude towards custom, and his style of communal leadership. He served not only as head of the yeshiva in Worms but as spiritual leader of that entire distinguished community, and he may even have acted as a representative for it to the non-Jewish authorities. In addition, he showed a willingness to change long-standing Ashkenazi custom on the basis of enquiries into how the underlying issues were treated in the Talmud itself—something at odds with the generally accepted practice in Mainz at the time.[9] It was Rabbi Isaac Halevi who inspired Rashi to innovate and to lead his community.

Rashi himself spoke of the differences between his two teachers. Later in the responsum referred to above, in which he described Rabbi Jacob as 'not moved to . . . innovate in his time', that is, not willing to undertake the role of community leader, he described Rabbi Isaac's very different approach: 'he was the spokesman and leader of the generation: by his word, people go and come'.[10] In Worms, Rashi became acquainted with another prominent scholar, Rabbi Solomon ben Samson, who headed the Worms yeshiva during the last quarter of the eleventh century, but they parted company, because Rabbi Solomon was very conservative and opposed innovation. Rashi pursued a different path, and the sources preserve evidence of tension between the two sages.

In his own personality, Rashi maintained a remarkably harmonious blend of the styles of his two great teachers. In his personal life, in dealings with students and other people, and even in his writing style, he adopted the humility and warmth of Rabbi Jacob ben Yakar. But in his leadership of the community and his readiness to struggle forcefully on behalf of the truth as he saw it and to introduce innovations, he followed the path of Rabbi Isaac Halevi.

Rashi's attitude to his ten-year period of study in Germany was ambivalent. On the one hand, he had the privilege of studying at the most important yeshiva in Christian Europe at the time and of learning Torah directly from a distinguished teacher; on the other, he struggled with economic deprivation to the point of lacking food and clothing for himself and his wife and children. It is hard to imagine that he did not consider giving up his studies and attending to the support of his family, but his love of Torah and strong sense of mission ultimately prevailed. As far as we can tell, his wife encouraged him to continue his studies despite the

[9] On R. Isaac Halevi, see Grossman, *The Early Sages of France* (Heb.), 282–8, 412–15.

[10] *Sidur rashi*, §174.

hardships the family endured. It is reasonable to assume that so sensitive a man would not have made such a decision on his own, without taking account of his family's needs. At the age of about 30, he returned to Troyes as a mature scholar and began to engage in literary production and community activity. Five years later he returned to Worms to visit Rabbi Isaac Halevi. According to Rashi's account, he engaged in forceful and self-assured debate with Rabbi Isaac, disagreeing with an interpretation presented by Rabbi Isaac when Rashi was studying with him. The teacher acknowledged his error and accepted his student's view.

Even after leaving Germany, Rashi maintained close ties with his teachers. He turned to them with questions and presented his innovations to them; they praised him generously in their letters and described him as a sage worthy of leading all the Jewish communities of France. The pre-eminent sages of Germany at the end of the eleventh century recognized his greatness. We see this in Rabbi Nathan ben Makhir, a great sage of illustrious lineage in Mainz during the final quarter of the eleventh century, directing questions to Rashi, and in Rabbi Isaac ben Asher Halevi, a pre-eminent sage of the Speyer community, coming to study with Rashi in Troyes.

Rashi's stay in Germany was influential in the following ways:

1. **Proximity to two distinguished teachers, Rabbi Jacob ben Yakar and Rabbi Isaac Halevi.** The two men left a deep impression on Rashi's personality. As mentioned, Rashi himself recognized as much. His close relationships with his own students and his style of communal leadership were also influenced by those teachers.

2. **Acquaintance with the grand and diverse tradition of talmudic interpretation that had developed in Germany.** In his commentary on the Talmud—based primarily on what he had learned at the yeshivas in Worms and Mainz—Rashi immortalized the teachings of the German sages. Many of Rashi's comments on the Talmud are derived from his teachers at the German yeshivas; that is true to a lesser extent of his biblical interpretations.

3. **Familiarity with the manuscripts held by the German yeshivas, especially that of Mainz.** They served as the basis for Rashi's interpretations of the Talmud, the Bible, and the liturgical poetry. That is true primarily with respect to the recension of the Talmud appearing in the books of Rabbenu Gershom, Rabbi Isaac ben Judah, and other sages, to which Rashi assigned great importance. The libraries of the German yeshivas were larger than those in France. Even after returning to France, Rashi asked people staying at the yeshiva in Mainz to check sources that he did not possess, even though his library was fairly well stocked.

4.  **Familiarity with intellectual, cultural, and literary traditions coming from various centres of Jewish life, especially Babylonia, the Land of Israel, and Italy.** The Jewish population of Germany at the time included immigrants from various places with different traditions. Many came from Italy, which followed the traditions of the Land of Israel, primarily with respect to the liturgy and the place within it of liturgical poems. However, Babylonian traditions also maintained a strong foothold. Rashi was thus familiar with diverse and varied traditions and used them in his own writing.

5.  **The formation of close personal ties to the greatest German sages of the second half of the eleventh century.** These ties continued even after Rashi returned to France. Of particular note are his ties with Rabbi Isaac ben Asher and Rabbi Nathan ben Makhir, who led the communities of Speyer and Mainz towards the end of the eleventh century.

6.  **Proximity to and greater familiarity with non-Jewish surroundings.** Worms and Mainz are situated in the Rhine Valley, in those days a great commercial centre. During his stay in those cities, Rashi maintained close ties with the surrounding world—learning about it and thus broadening his horizons. Among other things, he was familiar with the appurtenances of day-to-day life, as is evident from his commentaries on the Bible and the Talmud and his use of terms borrowed from German.

7.  **Closer familiarity with Jewish–Christian polemic.** The polemics became stronger during the course of the eleventh century and reached their peak in Germany with the edicts of 1096, representing the beginning of the First Crusade. They left a powerful mark on Rashi's biblical commentary and liturgical poetry.

## Community Activity in Troyes

There is very little information available regarding Rashi's personal life in Troyes. One obvious question is how he made a living. In Germany and France, sages were not paid for teaching in yeshivas. While various scholars have maintained that he made his living from viticulture, Haym Soloveitchik dissents, arguing that the agricultural conditions where Rashi lived were not suited to growing grapes. Apparently, he earned his living in commerce with non-Jews, as did most Jews in France and Germany. Several pieces of evidence support this. One of Rashi's students, probably Rabbi Shemayah, told of a transaction Rashi had entered into with a non-Jew. The latter claimed he had already paid his obligations in full, so Rashi demanded that he swear to that effect in a church, as was the accepted practice at the time, and pretended that he meant to enforce the oath. He did so because he believed that the threat of the oath would be intimidating enough to prevent the non-Jew from uttering a falsehood. But when it became evident at the last minute that the threat made no impression, Rashi withdrew the demand. We will return to this later.

MS Paris 380 tells of Rashi being in Russia. But, while there is evidence that Jewish merchants travelled as far as Russia, what is recounted in the manuscript does not pertain to Rashi:

And here are the words of Rashi of blessed memory: I, Solomon bar Isaac was in Russia, in Yoldmir. On the [fast of the] Ninth of Av, it happened that there was a circumcision, and Rabbi David bar Hisdai, Rabbi Abraham and Rabbi Sinai his son, Rabbi Samson, and Rabbi Joseph of Gush Halav were present, and they ruled, in the name of the early geonim, that the infant should not be circumcised in the morning, at the time the elegies are recited.[11]

The source of the error is a later copyist, who thought the 'Solomon bar Isaac' mentioned in the passage was Rashi and prefaced his statement with 'And here are the words of Rashi of blessed memory'. This is not the only case in which teachings reported in the name of sages called 'Solomon ben Isaac' were erroneously attributed to Rashi. For example, words of his great-grandson, who was named after him, have also been attributed to him.

Immediately upon his return from Germany, Rashi assumed a central position in the leadership of the small Troyes community. In the previous generation, numerous internal squabbles had broken out, and there was no spiritual leader who could impose his authority on all its members. They were unable to deal with the conflicts on their own, and they sought help from Rabbi Joseph Tov Elem, a native of Provence, and from Rabbenu Gershom, Rabbi Judah Hakohen, and Rabbi Eliezer the Great, all of Mainz. The residents of Troyes themselves attest to their internal weakness in describing a harsh internal squabble that threatened to split the community.

Recourse to sages outside the community ended with Rashi's return to Troyes. While still young, about 30 years old, he served as a member of the court in Troyes. He promulgated several enactments for the members of his community, and they were accepted by neighbouring communities. Only one generation earlier, those communities had declined to accept the authority of the sages of Troyes regarding redeeming captives, but they now acknowledged Troyes' supremacy. Rashi played an important part in setting the Jewish community of northern France overall on a stronger footing.

Another event, recounted in MS Schocken, apparently took place while Rashi was taking his first steps in Troyes, after returning from Germany:

And on the festival day itself, something took place involving a deceased [person] who was buried on the festival, and scholars were assembled at the burial, wondering what to

[11] MS Paris 380, fo. 25*b*.

do, whether or not to recite 'Tsiduk hadin' [a portion of the burial service omitted on some occasions]. And Rashi, of blessed memory, rose to his feet and recited 'Tsiduk hadin' himself, and no scholar disputed what he had done.[12]

This event could not have taken place in Germany while Rashi was studying there, for he would then have been acting improperly by issuing a ruling in the presence of his teachers; moreover, the custom in Mainz was different. But nor can the event be dated much later than his return to France, for once he had gained renown and assumed a senior position in his community, they would have turned to him directly for guidance on how to proceed. His status as a rising, but not yet established, force is evident also from the statement in *Maḥzor vitri* that some disagreed with Rashi and objected to reciting 'Tsiduk hadin'.[13]

Rashi's great self-confidence is evident in a modification he made to the text of an ancient blessing in his community's prayer book. To fully appreciate the significance of this action, one should recognize that few prayer books existed at the time. The one in question was written by hand and served, in effect, as the most important manual for public worship in the community's synagogue. It included not only prayers but also various laws and customs that provided guidance on fulfilling the commandments and living one's daily life. It may be said that the prayer book played the role then that the *Shulḥan arukh* and its commentaries play today. Yet Rashi, with his own hand, deleted the earlier version found in the prayer book, allowing himself to characterize the ancient custom as 'falsehood' and the ancient blessing as 'a blessing said in vain'. Another important aspect of his ruling here was that it assigned priority to the Babylonian Talmud as the source of halakhic rulings. In so doing, he differed from the accepted Ashkenazi practice, which still maintained a strong connection to the customs of the Land of Israel.

Additional evidence for the authority Rashi acquired in the communities of northern France soon after his return from Germany appears in the comments of his teachers in Germany, Rabbi Isaac Halevi and Rabbi Isaac ben Judah, who described him as the spiritual leader of all the communities in France. Particularly important are the comments of Rabbi Isaac Halevi. He lived only until 1080 (or 1085), and the numerous praises he showered on the head of his student were thus written only a few years after Rashi's return to Troyes. Rabbi Isaac wrote that Rashi's generation was not orphaned, for it had a leader who could be relied upon.

Rashi's speedy and impressive ascent to leadership and his abundant confidence in his ability and knowledge came to the fore in disagreements he had with these teachers—Rabbi Isaac Halevi and Rabbi Isaac ben Judah—when he was only about 35 years old. Particularly noteworthy is his dispute with them over the *kashrut* of an animal's lung, a dispute in which Rashi engaged forcefully.

Rabbi Meir ben Samuel, Rashi's son-in-law, was studying at the time in the

[12] MS Schocken 19523, fo. 244*a*.     [13] *Maḥzor vitri*, 244.

yeshiva at Worms, and Rashi wrote to him about the dispute. His words clearly show his confidence and his forcefulness when he believed his position was right:

I, Solomon, your beloved, tell you that I have not changed my mind nor will I change my mind. The words of my teachers do not make sense to me, and they have responded to my comments only superficially, and I still convey [my words] to my intimates. And but for the great trouble that has afflicted [them or us], I would convey it to them [too], even though they would not heed me.[14]

Rashi firmly stood his ground and noted that but for 'the great trouble' that occurred in Germany (it is not known what he was referring to), he would have sharpened the dispute further. Rabbi Shemayah, an outstanding student of Rashi's who assembled and edited these comments by his master, compared Rashi to a lion and summed up the polemic: 'come and see the might of the lion, Rashi of blessed memory'.

Rashi made use of numerous sources. It is not certain that all of them were in his personal library, though it was certainly well stocked: each source must be examined separately. We have no details about the disposition of his personal library after his death. Some later sages claimed to own works that had belonged to Rashi, but they did not explain how the texts had come into their possession. It may be assumed that Rashi's writings and books passed into the hands of family members, who loaned them to others.

## Rashi's Later Years

Very little information about Rashi's later years has come down to us, and my conclusions here rely more on reasonable inferences than on reliable sources. On the personal level, it is fair to assume that his later years, before he fell ill, were years of contentment. He had attained high status and wide renown. His greatness was universally recognized, and the leading sages of Germany addressed questions to his *beit midrash*. His students were among the elect in the various centres of European Jewry.

Rashi was privileged to see two of his sons-in-law—Rabbi Meir ben Samuel and Rabbi Judah ben Nathan—attain senior status among the Franco-Jewish sages of the time. He likewise saw his grandsons following his path. One of them, Rashbam, remained close to Rashi and studied with him. At a young age he was already a scholar, something that no doubt brought his grandfather great satisfaction.

Rashbam did not hesitate to disagree forcefully with Rashi and to insist on his views, and Rashi sometimes acknowledged that his grandson was right. When he formulated a linguistic rule related to biblical verses marked by a certain literary technique, Rashi named that type of verse after Rashbam: 'All this is from Rabbi

[14] MS Rab. 1087, Jewish Theological Seminary of America, New York, fo. 138b.

Samuel's treatise, and when Rabbi Solomon his grandfather came to one of those verses, he would refer to them as "Samuel verses", in his name.'[15] In other words, it appears that Rashi drew pleasure not only from Rashbam's talents but also from his wonderful blend of humility with forcefulness and pursuit of truth—the two qualities that characterized Rashi himself and which he saw as those to which all men should aspire. (The subject will be considered further in Chapter 9.)

Rashi no doubt felt great satisfaction when he completed his commentaries on the Bible and the Babylonian Talmud. Every work brings great joy to its creator, and that is a fortiori true when the creations are commentaries on the two most sacred Jewish texts and the writer is a Jew for whom the texts are spiritually as well as intellectually vital. He must likewise have derived satisfaction from his important and central role in Jewish–Christian religious polemics. In his biblical commentary, he described the leader's duty to stand at the head of his people and enlist in the struggle to protect them against hostile propaganda and the dangers of conversion (Rashi on S. of S. 7: 9). With respect to this task he stood in the first rank of Jewish sages and leaders in his time.

Two factors cast a shadow over the contentment of his old age: the edicts of 1096 and his failing health. Many Jews were killed in the pogroms carried out against the Jews of Ashkenaz by participants in the First Crusade, and the great yeshivas of Mainz and Worms, in which Rashi had studied only a generation earlier, were seriously damaged. The lists of those killed in the pogroms show that many of them were friends and colleagues from his yeshiva days. He told of his frail health in correspondence with other sages. As he described it, he suffered from a serious, long-term illness—an illness so harsh that he even lost the ability to write:

I, the undersigned young man [a term of humility] have been sentenced to the torments of illness, laid out on my deathbed. I must be inappropriately brief, for my strength is diminished and my hand cannot manipulate a scribe's pen. And I have spoken these lines to a member of my household and he has written them to my lord and master, the glory of the priesthood.[16]

My strength is diminished and my mouth is silenced, preventing me from telling of the hardships that sweep over me, wave after wave, as a result of which my hand is too weak to write in my own hand a response to my relative Rabbi Azriel and my dear friend Rabbi Joseph. I therefore say it to one of my brethren, and he writes [it down].[17]

## Character Traits

Rashi is renowned throughout the Jewish world not only for his wide-ranging literary productivity but also for his unique character. Five qualities stand out in his warm and radiant personality: humility and natural simplicity, pursuit of truth,

---

[15] MS Vienna 32; Poznański, *Introduction to the French Biblical Interpreters*, p. xxv.
[16] *Sefer ma'aseh hage'onim*, 11.        [17] *Taḥtsul*, §15.

concern for human dignity, great confidence in his own abilities, and a sense of mission as a community leader. These qualities are evident in his actions, his relations with other people, his ties to his students, his world-view, his scorn for arrogance, his love of peace, his literary output, and even in his writing style.

## Humility and Pursuit of Truth

Pursuit of truth and personal humility are traits that can be at odds with each other: it is difficult to behave humbly while struggling uncompromisingly for what one regards as the truth. Those who pursue the truth with all their might and refuse to compromise will quickly find themselves in personal conflict with those who disagree with them. It was not without reason that Rabbi Joseph ibn Kaspi, a fourteenth-century Jewish sage in Provence, argued that an intellectual's clash with other people attests to the primacy he assigns to truth: 'We have no alternative but to strive to mount the chariot of righteousness, to the point of being hated by the masses; and we have no better indicator of whether we are doing well than being hated by the masses.'[18] The point may be overstated, but it has a kernel of validity: a humble person will sometimes be willing to concede a point in order to avert conflict and will forgo struggling forcefully for the truth. In Rashi's case, however, the two characteristics coexisted in remarkable harmony. Humility came so naturally to him that he may not even have been aware of it. In his commentary on *Sanhedrin*, Rashi defined humbleness as something 'that a person practises without thinking' (on *San.* 19*b*, *tokpo shel yosef*), thereby unintentionally describing his own natural humility. He fully lived up to his own principles. These two qualities are evident in his actions and in his relations with other people, including his students. On the one hand, Rashi fought vigorously for his views and stood his ground even in the face of his great teachers in Germany; on the other hand, he was often prepared to forgo the honour due him.

In a responsum to the sages of another community, Rashi wrote: 'Heaven forbid that I claim renown and make myself into a prominent tribunal . . . who am I to claim renown in other parts, I, the poor and young one, whose hands are the orphans of orphans?'[19] When he found that people had erred, he did not confront them with their errors but would say something like 'my beloved did not intend his remarks'. But he was always quick to acknowledge his own errors, using such wording as 'until now, I had permitted this, but I was in error'; 'in any event, I erred in that interpretation'; 'I was mistaken, and I change my mind *ab initio*'. He would frequently write 'I do not understand' or 'I do not know'.[20]

His greatest self-effacement appears in his correspondence with members of the distinguished families of Ashkenaz. Those families at the time enjoyed a special social status, expressed, among other things, in the structure and routines of the

---

[18] Ibn Kaspi, 'Commentaries on the Book of Proverbs' (Heb.), 125; MS Munich 265, fo. 32*b*.
[19] *Tahtsul*, §22.     [20] See *Sefer hapardes*, 157; *Mahzor vitri*, 444; Lipschuetz, 'Rashi' (Heb.), 28–9.

yeshiva. In one of his responsa to Rabbi Nathan ben Makhir—a member of Rabbenu Gershom's family—Rashi went so far as to describe himself as a plant growing in murky wastewater ('a flowerbed planted by a spring used for laundry, muddy and murky . . . my fruit strays and its taste is inferior') and as 'a disappointing source, a dry stream'.[21]

A humble man like Rashi was ready to waive his honour and not be too harsh even on those who saw him as their enemy: 'Reuben, who wrote the enquiring letter, is someone I know, and I recognize his handwriting. And I fear to mention his name, for he suspects me of being his enemy. But I am not so within me, and his blessing will not remain with me unuttered. May he have blessings of good.'[22] Rashi's commitment to peace appears several times in his writings: for example, he begins a responsum to his student Rabbi Shemayah with a fourfold use of the word *shalom*: 'I, Solomon [*shelomoh*], who love you, enquire regarding your well-being [*shelomekha*], Shemayah my brother, and may He to Whom peace [*shalom*] belongs grant you the tranquillity from which to draw peace [*shalom*] and again rejoice over you for good.'[23]

The self-effacing and apologetic language Rashi used in addressing those who posed questions to him was not commonly employed by the early French and German sages, and it therefore should not be seen merely as conventional rhetoric. Still, it is hard to agree with E. M. Lipschuetz that 'one always feels that Rashi did not recognize his own greatness'.[24] Numerous sources show clearly that Rashi was aware of his worth and stature and had great confidence in his abilities as a decisor and a leader. As already noted, even in his youth he did not hesitate to debate forcefully with his great teachers, the heads of the renowned yeshivas of Mainz and Worms. When he was convinced that he was in the right, he took a firm stand in support of his position. In adjudication he showed no favour, and all his writings manifest his sense that the words of Torah are the truth and that no person should be unduly favoured over another. He had no qualms about sharply and forcefully attacking those who questioned the authority of community leaders, as we shall see below. His humility was genuine, and it did not flow from a failure to recognize his own ability and stature.

## Self-Confidence and Sense of Mission

Lipschuetz and others have taken the position that Rashi was afraid to issue halakhic rulings, but that premise likewise lacks any basis. In some instances, to be sure, it is expressly noted that Rashi 'said neither yes nor no' and that he declined 'to don a crown before us, determining the halakhah for the ages',[25] but he did so because he had not yet adopted a clear stance on the question or because the point at issue was one of long-established custom that he was reluctant to contravene or

---

[21] Goldberg, *Hofes matmonim*, §1.     [22] *Taḥtsul*, §84.     [23] MS Cambridge 667 Add.
[24] Lipschuetz, 'Rashi' (Heb.), 29.                                     [25] *Maḥzor vitri*, 39.

oppose unambiguously. This betokens not a fear of issuing rulings but a sense of respect for halakhah and custom. Rashi preferred not to issue a ruling until he had clarified the matter for himself, by examining the pertinent talmudic texts and later halakhic sources. In certain cases, he said that 'this matter should not be publicized', but even in those cases his rulings are anchored in the halakhah.

On most of the halakhic problems of the time, Rashi took a clear and unambiguous position, a position adopted with confidence and without hesitation. As noted, he differed forcefully and unhesitatingly with his teachers and frequently ruled leniently in disputes on doubtful matters that many had struggled with. As genuine as his humility was, it entailed not a scintilla of fear of issuing rulings or lack of confidence. To help us understand this aspect of Rashi's personality, let me offer two of the many illustrations that might be provided. First, the most renowned work of the Babylonian geonim on which the Ashkenazim drew was the *Halakhot gedolot*, a text that greatly influenced the halakhic rulings of Ashkenazi sages from the eleventh century onwards.[26] *Halakhot gedolot* established the rule that because 'in our time' (as distinct from the time of the Talmud), the sages are no longer expert in examining animals, uncertainties about the *kashrut* of an ill or injured animal should be resolved stringently. Rashi disagreed in principle with that idea and believed that the sages in all generations should rely on their own deliberations and discernment: 'It seems to me that he should rule only on the basis of what his eye sees and it is permitted to rely on that, as it is written, "unto the judge that shall be in those days" [Deut. 17: 9]; but he should act very carefully' (on *Ḥul. 52a, bitrei gapei*).

Decision-making of this sort—that is, audaciously disputing the ruling of the Babylonian geonim on a highly sensitive issue entailing a risk of eating non-kosher food—requires a great deal of courage and self-confidence. Can one taking such a position be fairly characterized as fearful of issuing halakhic rulings? This ruling gives clear expression to Rashi's determination: 'From the day I began to understand the words of the Talmud, my heart has been inclined to follow those who rule leniently.'[27]

Rashi's self-confidence and courage are also evident in his attitude towards custom. He attacked customs that had been accepted in Germany and France for generations if he believed them to have developed out of an error. One of the clearest illustrations is provided by his student, Rabbi Samuel ben Parigoros, who attests that Rashi, with his own hand, erased an early version of a blessing in the prayer book and proposed a different version instead (discussed further below in connection with Rashi's attitude towards custom).

[26] See the comment of R. Isaac Halevi, Rashi's teacher: 'The established *Halakhot gedolot*, which provides instruction to all Israel' (MS Adler, Jewish Theological Seminary of America, New York, cited in Marmorstein, 'An Italian Sage and Decisor' (Heb.), 236; see also Grossman, *The Early Sages of Askenaz* (Heb.), 290).        [27] *Taḥtsul*, §11.

Despite his extreme humility, Rashi broke new paths in his literary works and in defining the characteristics of his *beit midrash*, and he was prepared to take on the yoke of community leadership. All this flowed from his understanding that this was the duty of a scholar at all times, but particularly at a difficult time for the Jewish people. To understand Rashi's multifaceted activities and their motivation, one must recognize this weighty sense of mission that he felt. I consider this further at the end of Chapter 11.

## Pursuit of Peace and Human Dignity

Another notable facet of Rashi's character was his pursuit of peace. He called for internal peace among the members of the Jewish communities and saw it as a guarantee of external peace with the non-Jewish surroundings:

Now, you should direct your hearts to the pursuit of peace, and see that because of our sins, those who are around you have inflicted an incapacitating blow and the nations are about to consume you. But peace will provide you with help against the enemy, and Satan will be unable to prevail over you ... And he whose name and blessing are peace will set peace before you.[28]

Rashi practised what he preached. In one instance, he acted in a manner beyond the law's requirements, expressing his willingness to pay for a ring that had been loaned to his daughter, even though the law did not require him to do so:

Once, a certain woman loaned a ring to the underage daughter of our rabbi [Rashi], and she lost it. Our teacher said, as a matter of law, I need not provide compensation for something lost by my underage daughter ... but she was injured by my daughter, [and I will compensate her for] the value of the ring, but not more.[29]

Rashi was very attentive to the feelings of others. He found it difficult to witness human suffering without offering comfort. Thus, on the intermediate days of a festival, when condolences are not offered, he found a way to extend them to a bereaved person, through an exposition of words of Torah.[30] This is also the background to his attitude towards Jews who had been forced to convert. He insisted that they should not be dishonoured and that they should be lovingly accepted back into the community and its institutions. (This subject is considered further in Chapter 10.) For the sake of human dignity, moreover, he believed that the congregation should not pause in its prayers to await the return of one who has left the synagogue, even an important and honoured person.

Punctilious in observing the commandments, Rashi would not even hand his wife a key during the days of her menstrual impurity. He undertook personal strin-

[28] Ibid., §23.    [29] Rashi, *Responsa* (Heb.), ed. Elfenbein, §230.
[30] His treatment of the matter is quoted in Ch. 9, in the discussion of his teachings regarding human dignity.

gencies with respect to matters permitted by the law, and he took care that his rulings be precisely worded to avoid error. Rabbi Shemayah recounted how he would refrain from praying while he was ill, lest he be unable to muster the proper intention, and he so ruled for others too: 'Our rabbi would say that a sick person was forbidden to pray, for the weight of his illness distracts his mind and he cannot properly direct his attention when he is sick. He does not pray but only recites the Shema.'[31] It may be inferred from this that he routinely stressed proper intention in prayer. Similarly, he refrained from eating bread (that is, a full meal) for the third sabbath meal when he was still satiated, as would be the case during the winter, when afternoons were short: 'During the winter, when days were short, he would not dine with bread at the third sabbath meal, considering that to be gluttonous eating ... Rather, he would eat some sweets and thereby discharge his obligation.'[32] We may infer from this that he stressed eating the third sabbath meal solely for the sake of the commandment to honour the sabbath.

A manuscript from Moscow depicts Rashi as not being strict with respect to the commandment to don phylacteries, but the legend recounted there is late and must be considered a folk tale:

I also heard from a respectable student, who had heard from one of the great scholars of France, that a pious man, a *ba'al shem*,[a] was elevated in a dream to the heavenly yeshiva, where he saw great sages engaging in Torah with their students before them. He raised his eyes and saw an elder seated in the yeshiva with his head bent and eyes not raised. He asked the members of the yeshiva about him and they told him he was Rashi of France, may the memory of the righteous and holy be for a blessing, who illuminated the eyes of the diaspora with his commentaries, and because he was not punctilious about the commandment of phylacteries during his life, he was now ashamed before his colleagues. And that is why he is seated with great humility and bowed head.[33]

As far as we can tell, this legend was invented to encourage people to fulfil the commandment of phylacteries assiduously, donning a set that accords with the view of Rabbenu Tam as well as the usual set that accords with Rashi's view. (The two authorities differed with respect to the sequence of texts within the phylacteries.)

Along with his piety and his stress on the careful observance of the commandments, Rashi also found great joy in life. Lipschuetz has already noted this:

For all his extreme piety, he was not removed from life, and he had much practical wisdom. The yoke of heaven that he bore did not rest heavy on him, as it does on many. In everything he said or wrote, one can see evidence of a smiling, welcoming face, with heartfelt joy bursting forth from his words: 'If one's heart is content, every day is a banquet day'

[31] *Taḥtsul*, §60.      [32] MS Schocken 12141, fo. 32*c–d*.      [33] MS Moscow 924, fo. 174*a*.

[a] Literally 'a master of the [divine] name'.

[Rashi on Prov. 15: 15]; 'one who has a manly spirit, sensing that he is strong and not allowing worry into his heart, receives everything that comes upon him with happiness and love' [Rashi on Prov. 18: 14].[34]

Similarly, at several points in his commentary on Ecclesiastes, Rashi called for loving acceptance even of tribulations.

Mystical charms against demonic acts have been attributed to Rashi, as will be discussed below, but these too are late attributions, folk tales meant to associate the charms with a great man. Rashi did permit 'muttering over a wound' (that is, using spells to heal it) even in languages other than Hebrew, but that halakhah is based on a discussion in the Talmud and implies nothing about Rashi's ties to Jewish mysticism. Similarly we do not know for certain whether the various prayers and supplications attributed to him were, in fact, uttered by him or were attributed to him later because of his stature.

## Literary Style and Sensitivity

Rashi's writing style says much about his character, and some have attributed his great influence and wide acceptance throughout the Jewish world to it. It is a style marked by simplicity, refinement, sensitivity, clarity, beauty, linguistic riches, and wonder at the beauty of natural phenomena. Several scholars have already dealt with this subject: Lipschuetz, for example, wrote:

All his qualities are crystallized in his writing style. We never see him adorning himself with empty rhetoric, void of anything except adornment and able only to entice the reader's heart. The simplicity and clarity of his soul are reflected in the precision and lucidity of his style, within the understanding of the simplest folk . . . His style is pure, clear, and unpretentious, just like his pure heart, filled with humility. And as his style is pure, so is it precise . . . but its clarity does not suffer on account of its brevity. Rashi's style is not like one of the virtues associated with a great man; it is an important part of his greatness, flowing from the inwardness of his soul . . . Sometimes we see him season his words with a light rhetorical flourish, adorning his clear style. Sometimes he incorporated a biblical or mishnaic rhetorical flourish to beautify his simplicity.[35]

Despite his avoidance of rhetorical flourishes, Rashi's language is full and rich. I will consider this further in Chapter 5. His love of beauty is evident throughout his writing. An example is his comment on a verse speaking of the structure of the Tabernacle: 'the Torah taught proper conduct, that a man care for the beautiful' (Rashi on Exod. 26: 13). He manifests his linguistic riches in his formulation of ideas and his use of word pairs.

Rashi's confidence in his ability is shown by his taking the liberty to coin words and forms of writing. Isaac Avinery has already commented on this point:

---

[34] Lipschuetz, 'Rashi' (Heb.), 39.     [35] Ibid. 44.

Rashi's style [is] a direct continuation of the language of the talmudic sages. In that respect, it resembles [the style of] the tana'im more than that of the geonim who lived just before him. In his innovations, he neither breaches all bounds nor innovates solely for the sake of innovation, as did the composers of liturgical poems. (Only in the few penitential poems that he wrote did he follow this path.) But neither is he fervently devoted to the language of the generations that came before him, whether biblical or mishnaic, to the point of eschewing formal and substantive innovation . . . Who is as close to the early sources as he; who, like him, drew from the wellspring and gave drink to his brethren, slaking their thirst? But to be subservient—that was not for him.[36]

## Ties to his Non-Jewish Surroundings

Rashi was heavily involved in the Christian society within which he lived and worked, and he was familiar with its way of life and culture. In his commentaries, he treats in detail various aspects of everyday life—among others, coinage, glassmaking, military tactics, nature, bird hunting, agriculture, and raising animals. It is evident from his accounts that he was personally acquainted with these matters through his day-to-day contacts and that he was a pragmatic man who maintained friendships and commercial relations with non-Jews:

An incident occurred to me, Solomon the descendant of Isaac, in which a non-Jew sent me cakes and eggs on the eighth day of Passover. The non-Jew came into the courtyard and called to my wife, and my wife sent for me at the synagogue. I went and directed . . .[37]

The non-Jew had sent Rashi a gift, knowing Jewish halakhah and custom with regard to leaven at Passover. Rashi even entered into economic partnerships with non-Jews. In one such case, he had a serious dispute with his non-Jewish partner:

On one occasion, a non-Jew was obliged to take an oath for our teacher [Rashi], and [Rashi] led him to the entrance of a place of idolatry [a church], as if he meant to cause him to swear, but he did not intend to do so . . . and only wanted to give that appearance so [the non-Jew] would acknowledge [the obligation]. And they brought the rotting sacred relics, and the non-Jew placed a small coin on them, disgracefully, for the idol.[38] From that time on, Rashi undertook not to do business with a non-Jew on the basis of trust.[39]

An important source for understanding Rashi's attitude towards his non-Jewish neighbours is a ruling attributed to him that forbade giving 'gifts for the poor' on Purim to non-Jewish servants. In that ruling, Rashi expressed strong opposition to giving such gifts:

[36] Avinery, *Rashi's Palace* (Heb.), i. 103.  [37] Rashi, *Responsa* (Heb.), ed. Elfenbein, §114.
[38] That is, the non-Jew placed a monetary offering on the remains of the saint (*reliquiae*).
[39] Rashi, *Responsa* (Heb.), ed. Elfenbein, §180. On Rashi's attitude towards business dealings with non-Jews, see ibid., §§177–84. The Talmud prohibits a joint business venture with a non-Jew when it is possible that the non-Jew will take an oath by his idol (Mishnah *AZ* 1: 1; BT *San.* 63b; Tosafot ad loc., *asur*).

The matter was as harsh in Rashi's eyes as thorns ... And one who gives to non-Jews steals from the poor ... and Rashi applies to him the verse 'I ... multiplied unto her silver and gold, which they used for Baal' [Hos. 2: 10], for God gave Israel abundant gold, so it could be brought for the construction of the Tabernacle, but in the episode of the golden calf, 'all the people broke off the golden rings which were in their ears' [Exod. 32: 3]. It may be compared to a man who receives guests. Jewish guests came and he received them; non-Jewish guests came and he received them, thereby losing the merit of the prior act. And it is as they say of him—he is a fool, and that is his way. So, too, one who gives gifts to a non-Jew on Purim loses [the merit of] the gifts he gave to the poor, for his actions show that he did not do it for the sake of Heaven but only because it is his way to do so.[40]

It is, however, questionable whether that quotation in fact should be attributed to Rashi.[41] That Rashi was at ease in his surroundings may be evident in the comparison he drew between the ephod, a holy garment worn by the high priest, and the garments worn by French noblewomen of his day—a comparison drawn to clarify the nature of the ephod. It did not occur to him that there was anything wrong in drawing the comparison: 'Ephod—I have neither heard nor found anything in a *baraita*[b] to explain its composition. But my heart tells me that it is tied behind him ... as a sort of apron ... that princesses tie on when they ride on horseback' (on Exod. 28: 4).

Rashi dealt with several cases pertaining to economic relations between Jews and non-Jews. He sought to rule leniently, within the halakhic framework, with respect to commercial relations with non-Jews, relying on the Talmud's dictum: 'In the diaspora, we cannot refrain from commercial dealings with them, for we reside among them and derive our livelihoods from them' (Rashi on *AZ* 11b, *bagolah*). Elsewhere, he wrote that 'non-Jews today are not well versed in the nature of idolatry'.[42] As we shall see, he even sought ways to rule leniently, at least in part, with

[40] Rashi, *Responsa* (Heb.), ed. Elfenbein, §131.

[41] Elfenbein attributes the responsum to Rashi, because it appears, in the name of 'my rabbi', in books that originated in Rashi's *beit midrash* and is expressly ascribed to Rashi in two other sources (notes to Rashi, *Responsa* (Heb.), ed. Elfenbein, pp. 158–9). In other printed and manuscript sources, however, including *Sefer ma'aseh hage'onim* (46), the words are attributed to R. Kalonymus the Elder of Speyer. I elsewhere expressed my preference for the attribution to R. Kalonymus (*The Early Sages of Germany* (Heb.), 17), which is also the view of Shochetman ('On the Custom of Giving Gifts to Poor Non-Jews on Purim' (Heb.)). Nevertheless, the words appear in the earliest layers of text in R. Shemayah's prayer book (including the Jewish Theological Seminary's manuscript of *Maḥzor vitri*, MS Reggio, Mic. 8092), and we cannot say with confidence who authored them.

[42] Rashi, *Responsa* (Heb.), ed. Elfenbein, §327. An explicit responsum by Rashi on the subject appears in MS Bodleian 566, fo. 35a: 'You have already heard from me that I do not now mean to forbid deriving benefit from wine of non-Jews, for it is not their way to pour libations to idols; but I [do not] want to declare it vocally. Solomon ben R. Isaac, of blessed memory.' 'Of blessed memory' refers to Isaac, Rashi's father, or it might have been added by a copyist.

[b] A tannaitic tradition.

respect to non-Jewish wine. As a matter of principle, however, Rashi did not differentiate between Christians and the nations referred to in the Bible and the
Talmud, and he considered Christianity to be idolatry.[43] He feared that Christians,
because they did not understand the commandments, would accuse Jews of witchcraft. One of his students reported that Rashi had directed that the meat of a lamb
be buried, 'and he told them to do it in secret, so the non-Jews would not say they
were practising witchcraft'.[44]

Rabbi Solomon Luria (Maharshal), in his responsa,[45] wrote that Rashi had
composed the liturgical poem 'Titenem leḥerpah' ('Let Them Be Shamed') in
response to the edicts of 1096. It contains the cruellest curses invoked against
Christians of any medieval liturgical poem. Because of concern about harsh
Christian reactions, the poem was deleted from nearly every medieval Jewish
prayer book manuscript. The poem's curses evince the intense hatred and deep
loathing felt by Jews towards Christian society; they include:

> Let them be shamed, accursed, and destroyed . . .
> unleash the sword against them so that not one survives . . .
> cut off their progeny and cut off their memory and erase their name from
>      under the heavens . . .
> give them over to death and eternal disgrace . . .
> kill them with a bizarre death and vile epidemic, a death abject and raging.[46]

Were we certain that this poem was written by Rashi, it would provide persuasive
proof for the profound hatred that he felt towards his non-Jewish neighbours, perhaps
in the wake of the edicts of 1096, and that would be so even if he were simply following
the path of earlier liturgical poets. A. H. Freimann believed the attribution to Rashi
to be reliable, if not absolutely certain, while several other scholars believe the attribution to be in error. More recently, a manuscript has come to light in which the poem
is explicitly ascribed to Rashi, but questions still remain. The manuscript is relatively
late, and its writer may have been influenced by the comment of Rabbi Solomon Luria

---

[43]  Jacob Katz has already noted as much: 'Rashi's resort to talmudic terminology is not mere conservatism. When it came to Jewish misgivings about foreign faiths and beliefs, he saw no need to differentiate between Christians and the nations referred to in the Bible and, even more so, in the Talmud.
Israel alone was deemed to worship God; other nations, Christians included, were considered to be
idolaters. But while this generalization could be accepted easily in the area of faiths and beliefs, it was
subject to qualification in other areas of thought' (Katz, *Between Jews and Gentiles* (Heb.), 35).

[44]  Rashi, *Responsa* (Heb.), ed. Elfenbein, §182. On the concern in principle about witchcraft, especially on the part of Jews living near non-Jewish neighbours, see *Pes. 7a–b*; *SA*, 'Oraḥ ḥayim', 433: 7.

[45]  Luria, *Responsa* (Heb.), §29.

[46]  The poem was first published by Freimann, '"Let Them Be Shamed"' (Heb.), 70–1. For a detailed
discussion of the poem, see Yuval, *Two Nations in Your Womb*, 121–3, and the literature cited there. For
further discussion of the sources and manuscripts related to this text, see Grossman, *The Early Sages
of France* (Heb.), 144–5, esp. the literature cited in n. 83.

noted earlier, written during the thirteenth century, or by some similar tradition. It was not unusual in later times for prayers and charms that Rashi did not write to be attributed to him because of his great fame in order to augment their value.

## Attitude towards Communal Governance

Rashi played an important role in determining the basic elements of community rule in his time and he did much to establish it. In this capacity he was a man of ideas as well as of action. His goal was to establish a system of governance and bolster its power and authority. He ruled, for example, that obedience to the community's statutes was within the rubric of a biblical (as distinct from a merely rabbinic) commandment. Accordingly, an oath to refuse to conform to the community's statutes was invalid. Halakhically, it was a vain oath having no force: 'It thus seemed to me that one who took an oath to transgress community rules has taken an oath in vain ... for since his oath was to transgress the Torah, it is an oath to do something impossible, for he is already sworn from Mount Sinai [to heed the community's statutes].'[47]

Rashi's ruling that obedience to the community's rule was a biblical commandment had great importance in his time. Other decisors had already taken that position in principle, but Rashi's important innovation was to assign the local community the status of a 'prominent court' (*beit din ḥashuv*). Most Jewish sages took the view that the community derived its authority because it was regarded as a court, and Rashi concurred. That view, however, opened the door to challenges to its authority. Talmudic sources declared that a 'prominent court' or a 'proper court' (*beit din yafeh*) had greater power and authority than an ordinary court, and a person was permitted to demand that his case be heard before such a court. In some circumstances, then, those who wanted to avoid submitting to the authority of their local leaders (their 'court') could try to justify doing so and look to some other court instead, on the grounds that the other court was a superior one. Rashi ruled out that possibility:

Even if there are more prominent [judges] elsewhere, we have only the local court, for otherwise there would be no end to the matter, for there is no court so prominent that there is not another one more prominent somewhere in the world.[48]

Rashi's tendency to strengthen community rule is evident also in his recognition of the right of the majority to impose its view on the entire community. That was the practice in his time in Troyes and evidently in nearby communities.

Rabbi Shemayah, Rashi's devoted student, summed up his teacher's stance on the matter:

[Rashi] was asked about people who hasten to vow and swear not to heed and not to stand by the community's decree and coercion, or *even a case in which there are ten such people* and

---

[47] *Taḥtsul*, §24.　　[48] Ibid., §27.

the community thereafter issued a decree in the matter . . . [Rashi] replied . . . 'Woe to them, and they are as one who swears to annul a commandment . . . rather, they issue a decree against them, expel them, and encumber them; and there is no prohibition at all against doing so.'[49]

As Rashi saw it, even a large minority must yield to the majority. Most of the Jewish communities in France were small, and the opposition of 'ten such people' no doubt made a substantial impression. Nevertheless, Rashi stood by the fundamental right of the majority to impose its opinion.

As a natural corollary to his support for the community leadership, Rashi warned that it was important to preserve peace and unity, and he sharply attacked dissension. The many discussions of the issue show that the subject arose frequently. Rashi's enactments on community matters, most of which pertained to payment of taxes, were to become very important.

## Stance on Community Problems

Rashi's rulings on the organization of the Jewish communities in France offer one example of his involvement in community affairs. He took a firm stance on three additional weighty matters: the attitude towards converts (forced or voluntary), wine produced by non-Jews, and interest. He was lenient with respect to converts who wanted to return to Judaism, an issue to be considered in Chapter 10. His consideration of issues affecting the Jews' economic situation also manifests clear links to the circumstances of his time. In explaining one of his rulings, he wrote: 'It is difficult for me to do away with a Jew's wealth for a matter such as this, where it is clear and fitting on the basis of several proofs that one should rule leniently.'[50] This inclination to make it easier for the 'children of the covenant' to earn a living and to spare them monetary loss, as far as possible within the framework of halakhah, guided Rashi in dealing with other issues too, especially those directly related to the livelihoods of the community's members. This principle guided his decision, mentioned earlier, to reject the stringent ruling in *Halakhot gedolot* that forbade any food whose *kashrut* might be subject to doubt. Rashi also permitted various ways of lending to fellow Jews on interest, using a non-Jew as a 'straw man': 'As for what you have enquired about, know that it is permitted, and one who avoids doing so is a pious fool, as long as he does not intend in the first instance to do so.'[51] In another responsum, mentioned earlier, Rashi wrote of his lifelong inclination to rule leniently.

Rashi received numerous enquiries regarding *yayin nesekh*.[c] It was only natural

---

[49] MS Rab. 1077, Jewish Theological Seminary of America, New York, fo. 75*a*, emphasis added.
[50] Rashi, *Responsa* (Heb.), ed. Elfenbein, §69.
[51] *Sefer haterumot*, 80*b*; see Soloveitchik, *Halakhah, Economics, and Self-Image* (Heb.), 28–30.

[c] Literally 'libation wine'; the term originally referred to wine used in pagan rituals and hence forbidden but was extended, according to many halakhic views, to encompass all wine produced or handled by non-Jews.

that such questions would arise, for many Jews made their living in viticulture and employed non-Jewish workers, as Haym Soloveitchik has recently shown in his book, *Their Wine: Trade in Non-Jewish Wine and the Evolution of Halakhah in the Practical World* (Heb.). Rashi held, in principle, that 'non-Jews today are not well versed in the nature of idolatry, and they are as a new-born infant, whose touch does not make wine into *yayin nesekh*'. He therefore permitted drinking wine that had been touched by a non-Jew: 'his touch does not render it in any way forbidden, even for drinking'.[52] Rashi's lenient rulings on this issue—which ran contrary to the view of his teachers and colleagues in Germany, including Rabbi Isaac ben Judah, then head of the celebrated yeshiva in Mainz—had wide implications. He ruled that it was permitted to ship wine with non-Jews under 'only one seal', contrary to the explicit ruling of Rabbi Isaac ben Judah. Rashi's responsum on the subject to Rabbi Isaac ben Judah evinces Rashi's intense involvement with the realities of his day:

In our region, the early practice was to send wine under only one seal, and the people who did so included pious men and sages. For about the last ten or fifteen years [however] we have taken on greater stringency, and matters have been very difficult, for the roads are disorderly, and Jews do not come and go, and our wine is not suitable for *kiddush* and *havdalah*, so wine must be brought from afar.[53]

This passage provides important evidence of the lack of security in northern France during the 1080s. Rashi noted that the early sages in the region had ruled leniently, and he blamed himself for the more stringent recent practice. Most likely he would not have written 'we have taken on greater stringency' had the practice been instituted by his predecessors without his involvement, and we may assume that he instituted the more stringent practice upon his return from Germany, where he had been taught the need to do so. This view of the events gains further support from the discussion in *Sefer ha'orah*.[54] But Rashi now decided to restore the lenient practice.

Rabbi Solomon ben Samson, head of the yeshiva at Worms, attacked Rashi's lenient ruling sharply ('there is no prohibition more serious than this'), and the 'sons of Makhir' (descendants of Rabbenu Gershom's brother) likewise attacked Rashi, arguing that a specific ruling of his with respect to wine was in error: 'And those men whom you cite as great in Torah are, in this matter, insignificant. They have breached the fence to allow foxes into their vineyards.'[55] This was a clear and sharp allusion to 'the little foxes that spoil the vineyards' (S. of S. 2: 15).

---

[52] Rashi, *Responsa* (Heb.), ed. Elfenbein, §327.    [53] MS Bodleian 566, fo. 35a.
[54] See Grossman, *The Early Sages of France* (Heb.), 155–6. For detailed discussion of the development of Rashi's position on *yayin nesekh*, see Soloveitchik, *Their Wine* (Heb.), 51–9.
[55] *Sefer ma'aseh hage'onim*, 79.

## Attitude towards Custom

The scholarly literature for the most part portrays Rashi as assigning great importance to Jewish custom and subordinating himself to it. One study went so far as to link Rashi's attitude towards custom to his profound love for the Jewish people. This view is fundamentally correct, for custom played an important part in the halakhic rulings of the German and French sages, and Rashi was no exception. Nevertheless, he was less bound by custom than were many contemporary sages in Germany. His writings clearly manifest the attitude towards custom that appears more forcefully two generations later in the writings of his grandson, Rabbenu Tam. On this view, customs should not be taken as self-evidently valid; rather, their origins should be investigated and on occasion, when a custom is at odds with the Babylonian Talmud, it should be considered an 'erroneous custom' and rejected or altered. Rashi frequently followed this course, and to see how important it was to his approach, we need look no further than his rationale for rejecting the recitation of 'Yiru eineinu' as part of the evening prayer: '"Yiru eineinu" should absolutely not be recited, *for it is not set forth in the Talmud and it is a blessing said in vain*.'[56] This ruling demonstrates how widely Rashi's approach to custom differed from that of the German sages of his day, and recently discovered manuscripts provide further support for the view that this was Rashi's position.

Particularly impressive evidence is preserved in MS Vatican 318, which includes customs and rulings from Rashi's *beit midrash*. One of his students, Rabbi Samuel ben Parigoros, recounted how Rashi had changed the earlier local custom for separating *ḥalah*,[d] as it appeared in the town synagogue's prayer book:

The order for *terumah*[e] and separating *ḥalah* was written in the prayer books ... and our rabbi [Rashi] edited it, as I shall write for you below ... and he edited all this and erased it with his own hand and wrote: *'this instruction is false'* ... The practice in Troyes in earlier times had been to separate two *ḥalot* on the eve of Passover, and to recite over one the blessing for separating *ḥalah* and over the other the blessing for separating *terumah*. Rashi, may the memory of the righteous be for a blessing, voided the custom, on the grounds that it was a blessing recited in vain.[57]

This shows that Rashi adopted an independent course soon after his return from Germany, while still relatively young. It provides valuable evidence of his bold pursuit of truth, for he set out to change what had been the local practice 'in earlier times' even though it was set forth in the prayer books.

To understand the full significance of Rashi's actions, one must take into account the small number of prayer books in those days. The prayer book, written

---

[56] Rashi, *Responsa* (Heb.), ed Elfenbein, §91, emphasis added. There is some uncertainty about the authorship of this responsum.     [57] MS Vatican 318, fos. 291*b*–292*a*, emphasis added.

[d] A small portion of a batch of dough that is set aside before baking.
[e] A portion of agricultural produce set aside before the rest can be used.

by hand, effectively served as the most important tool and guidebook used by the community in its worship in the synagogue. It contained not only the prayers themselves but also various laws and customs that guided people in carrying out the commandments and living their day-to-day lives. One can go so far as to say that the prayer book at the time played the same part that the *Shulḥan arukh* and its commentaries play now. Against this background, Rashi's forceful rejection of the customary practice, described above, appears particularly bold. Another important aspect of his ruling was assigning the Babylonian Talmud pride of place as the source of halakhic decision-making.

As these and other instances show, Rashi was ready to examine things in depth and to reach decisions through rational deliberation instead of treating traditions and customs of doubtful origin as self-evident. That trait, more than anything else, attests to the great openness that marked him and his yeshiva. Pursuit of truth was the sole criterion that guided teacher and students alike, and Rashi therefore was not ashamed to acknowledge his own errors and change his mind—whether because of further analysis of the subject or in the wake of observations by his students during their deliberations. This is also what underlies the frequent statements in his commentaries on the Bible and the Talmud and even in his response: 'I do not know what this teaches us', 'I did not know', 'I did not understand', and so on. The pursuit of truth that guided Rashi and his actions is evident throughout his literary oeuvre, including his writings on custom.

Rashi's method, of examining the origins of a custom, was not accepted at the time in the great yeshiva of Mainz. In the mid-eleventh century an attitude of self-deprecatory deference to earlier generations began to develop there, an outlook that became stronger during the final third of the century and left a clear mark on the yeshiva's literary output. The teachers were all descendants of five distinguished families and were overshadowed by their illustrious ancestors. They saw their own generation as one of decline, whose task was to preserve the old traditions, not to innovate and create. They regarded 'the custom of the early ones' and 'the custom of the fathers' as binding and admitting of no deviance. Even an attempt to clarify the reason for a custom aroused the ire of Rabbi Nathan ben Makhir, a prominent sage in Mainz during the final quarter of the eleventh century: 'That was the reply of Rabbi Nathan to Rabbi Joshua ... and he admonished him, [asking] what need he had to examine the custom of holy communities, since the days of the holy ones.'[58] Custom was sanctified, and, in his opinion, any attempt to look into the origins of a custom was improper. The Worms yeshiva did not adopt this approach during the time of Rabbi Isaac Halevi, but a conservative strain also emerged there after his death, especially in the work of Rabbi Solomon ben Samson, and it gathered force at the end of the century.[59]

[58] *Sefer ma'aseh hage'onim*, 55.
[59] The developments are more broadly described in Grossman, *The Early Sages of Ashkenaz* (Heb.), 265–88.

As mentioned, Rashi differed. He did not see himself as bound by any sanctified earlier tradition from which one was not permitted to stray. In truth, it is questionable whether one can even speak of that sort of tradition in Troyes, although, as noted earlier, Rashi himself referred to 'sages and pious men' who preceded him in northern France. Certainly, Rashi assigned considerable importance to customs and preached in support of their preservation and observance—but only if they were not at odds with the Babylonian Talmud. If they clashed with the Talmud, they were to be declared invalid. This aspect of Rashi's halakhic work had a great effect on intellectual life in his yeshiva, for he taught his students to examine traditions by comparing them with the Babylonian Talmud even if they were venerable and widely invested with the sanctity of custom.

Haym Soloveitchik and Israel Ta-Shma have recently examined Rashi's attitude towards custom, and their conclusions, especially Soloveitchik's, differ somewhat from mine:

A detailed reconstruction based on texts incorporating Rashi's words shows that his writings constitute, to no less a degree, a defence of his local customs. Like any finely crafted work, Rashi's commentary has multiple aspects and layers. Here he moves in parallel on the plane of timeless interpretation and that of dealing with his own times. The commentary clarifies the [talmudic] passage in order to bolster it and simultaneously defends ancestral custom. In this, Rashi is both an exegete for the ages and a loyal son of the early Ashkenazi community.[60]

In Ta-Shma's view, Rashi's stance with respect to custom should be seen, in principle, as one of compromise:

As noted, Rashi was inclined to compromise; and even though he wanted to preserve the values of the old custom, and recommended to individuals that they diligently maintain it, he left much room to allow textual study and reason to serve as considerations warranting leniency with respect to taking on most of the recent customs. In that, as elsewhere, he was the herald of the great revolution that was to take place in the twelfth century, at the hands of the tosafists.[61]

His conclusions, as noted, differ somewhat from mine, and he assigns greater importance to Rashi's reservations. But Ta-Shma, too, emphasized the innovative nature of Rashi's stance compared to that of most of the Ashkenazi sages active in his time. Ta-Shma also considered Rashi's technique for dealing with customs that were accepted in the generations that preceded his:

There are other examples of how Rashi often attacked an established custom and called for its abolition, in cases where he had difficulty explaining it . . . In truth, Rashi did not hesitate to determine clearly that it was proper as a matter of law to adopt a halakhic prac-

---

[60]  Soloveitchik, 'Can Halakhic Texts Talk History?' (Heb.), 25.
[61]  Ta-Shma, *Early Franco-German Ritual and Custom* (Heb.), 53.

tice that treated something as permitted (and not merely after the fact) even if contrary to a generally accepted custom under which the item at issue was forbidden. One need not be concerned about the rule that 'something [legally] permitted that others have treated as prohibited may not be ruled permissible before them' . . . We have seen that Rashi, in order to undermine a bad custom, sought, in various ways, to find a historical explanation for it and thereby demonstrate its lateness. This method, of locating the roots of the error in a stringency within the [otherwise] correct tradition, can also be found in Rashi's straightforward exegesis.[62]

## Exegesis as a Reflection of Personality

Although Rashi's commentaries for the most part lack any personal tone, his literary output in all its forms reveals his world-view. In Chapters 8–10, I will describe Rashi's views on various subjects, primarily on the basis of his commentaries on the Bible and the Talmud. The question that then arises is whether one can draw inferences from his commentaries not only about his world-view but also about his character. I believe such inferences can be drawn not only from his commentary on the Bible but also from his commentaries on the Talmud and the liturgical poems. Rashi's character influenced his writing style, and anyone who reads him recognizes quickly his humility, his straightforwardness, and his clarity. At various points in this book, I consider his tendency to interpret biblical texts as referring to the demise of the Christian world, and it is clear that his biblical commentaries were meant to fortify his weaker brethren. On occasion, he couched this polemic in terms that show his own emotional involvement, investing it with a psychological force that reveals his agitated soul. A prominent example of this appears in his introduction to his comments on the Song of Songs, portions of which have a poetic quality: 'And he wrote this book with the holy spirit, in the voice of a rejected wife, a living widow, longing for her husband, fondly remembering her beloved, recalling the love of her youth . . . and he mentions the kindnesses of her youth, the loveliness of her beauty, and the skilfulness of her actions' (Rashi on S. of S., Intro.).

In her book *Rashi's Aggadah* (Heb.), Yosefa Rachaman offers an interesting suggestion regarding Rashi's writing style. In her view, it is not only through its content that Rashi's commentary on the Torah can serve as an important source for the study of his value system and conceptual world, but also in its style and the manner in which *midrashim* are worked into it. She argues that many of the changes he makes to the *midrashim* he cites can be explained in light of his conception of the world. She offers her suggestion cautiously, aware of the difficulty of relying on such fine distinctions whose causes are neither clear nor unambiguous.

Rachaman cites thirty-eight examples to support her idea—twenty-five that show 'a realistic understanding of the world', six that show 'an impressive moral approach', and seven that show 'complex thought about God's works and

---

[62] Ibid. 56–7.

conduct'.[63] Some of the examples are persuasive (assuming the texts are, in fact, authentic), but most remain rather speculative. It is possible that Rashi's reason for changing the Talmud's wording was stylistic. As we shall see below, he frequently altered the wording of the *midrash* for interpretative and stylistic reasons. Let me cite two of Rachaman's examples that seem to me to be close to the mark:

1.  In commenting on the verse 'male and female created he them' (Gen. 1: 27), Rashi writes: 'An aggadic *midrash* [relates] that He created it with two faces in the initial creation, and they thereafter divided.' The version in *Genesis Rabbah* reads 'When the Holy One, Blessed be He, created primeval Adam, He created him double-faced, and He cut him [in two] and made a back to one side and a back to the other.'[64] Rachaman concludes: 'With respect to the creation of man, whose body and skin are delicate rather than hard substances, the term cutting, associated with carpentry, is inappropriate. For that reason, it seems, Rashi changed it.'[65] What she says makes sense: the change followed from Rashi's concern for human dignity.

2.  Regarding the prohibition on eating flesh torn from a living animal, Rashi writes: 'He did not permit Adam and his wife to kill a created being and eat [its] flesh' (on Gen. 1: 29). The talmudic source reads: 'Primeval Adam was not permitted to eat flesh' (*San.* 59*b*), without the term 'created being'. Rachaman therefore concludes: 'The term "created being" in the context of killing sets the animal on the same level as man with respect to the essence of life, and attests to a profound religious-humanist concept of God's creations.' Here, too, she is persuasive.[66]

The reflection of Rashi's personality in his commentary on the Talmud is a more complex matter. There has been almost no reliance on the Talmud in the study of Rashi's personality, and that is understandable. My own view, however, is that, although there is less pertinent material in Rashi's talmudic commentary than in his biblical commentary, it does exist. Numerous examples appear below, in my discussion of Rashi's world-view (Chapters 8–10). Let me here cite just a few illustrations that are of methodological importance.

1.  **Care for the honour of the talmudic sages.** Towards the beginning of *Pesaḥim* (4*a*), sages speak in praise of those who do not report bad news directly, but allude to it indirectly. As an example, they cite the statement of the *amora* Rav, who hinted to Rabbi Hiya indirectly that Rav's parents (who were also members of Rabbi Hiya's family) had died. When Rabbi Hiya asked Rav if his father was still living, he replied that 'mother is living'; when he asked if his mother was still living, he replied that 'father is living'. Rashi commented that Rav

---

[63] Rachaman, *Rashi's Aggadah* (Heb.), 119, 141–7.   [64] *Genesis Rabbah* 8: 1.
[65] Rachaman, *Rashi's Aggadah* (Heb.), 119.   [66] Ibid., esp. 144–8.

voiced his words as questions, and then added: 'But some say that Rav was replying gently, speaking of the person who was not the subject of the question, so that he would understand from the overall context. But it is difficult for me to say that Rav would utter false words.' Only one whose beacon was truth would reject an interpretation suggesting that a prominent scholar such as Rav would allow a falsehood to pass his lips, even when the interpretation appears to be the plain meaning of the text in the Talmud and the circumstances are unusual ones in which the halakhah permits varying from the truth.

An additional illustration arises out of the consideration of Rabbi Papa's behaviour. Rashi rejected an interpretative tradition describing Rabbi Papa's improper conduct, maintaining that it was unreasonable to believe he had acted improperly—'in my eyes, it is difficult to say that' (Rashi on *Kid. 72a, ba'a minaihu*).

2.  **Great confidence in the force of his halakhic rulings.** In his comments on *Ḥulin*, Rashi attacked the determination reached in *Halakhot gedolot* and ruled that even in his day, one could rely on examination of slaughtered animals to ascertain whether there was any disqualification, and that it was not necessary to stringently reject the *kashrut* of the animal in any case of doubt.

3.  **Concern for women.** He ruled that the act of levirate marriage depended, as a practical matter, on the will of the woman subject to it, even though that is not the simple meaning of the text in the Talmud. The ruling arose from his concern about the woman's rights in the context of the harsh reality of his time. The issue is considered in detail at the end of Chapter 10, in the discussion of the status of women.

4.  **Esteem for the Land of Israel.** Rashi wrote: 'For outside the Land [of Israel] she has no right; rather, it is sinful to dwell there' (on *Ber. 57a, belo ḥet*). He took the rabbinic comment that one dwelling in the diaspora resembles 'one who has no God' (or resembles 'one who worships other gods') and rephrases it more sharply in determining that dwelling in the diaspora is itself a transgression.[67]

5.  **Concern for human dignity.** In *Ḥulin 6a*, a verse in Proverbs is interpreted to mean that one should not request interpretations from a teacher who 'does not know', and one should no longer turn to him. Rashi takes the verse to mean that the student must learn and understand on his own instead of directing questions to the teacher, lest he embarrass him. But the motif of embarrassment is not mentioned in the passage in the Talmud, and the call to avoid posing questions to the teacher can be understood as concern that the teacher may offer a faulty interpretation that the student will then follow. Rashi introduced the idea of embarrassment because of his concern about human dignity.

---

[67] See the discussion of the Land of Israel in Rashi's thought in Ch. 8 and compare his comment on *Yev. 64a, mikets eser shanim*: 'for the sin of [residing] outside the Land'.

A striking illustration of the use of Rashi's commentary on the Talmud as a basis for drawing inferences about his personality appears in Haym Soloveitchik's study of Rashi's stance on *yayin nesekh*.[68]

Rashi's commentaries on the liturgical poems, though few, also reveal aspects of his personality. I here offer just one example. A line alluding to a night-time assignation that appears in a poem by Eleazar Kallir ('Zekher tehilat kol ma'as') was interpreted by Rabbi Menahem ben Helbo—consistently, it seems, with the plain meaning—as referring to David's sin with Bathsheba. Rashi objected to that interpretation: 'But Rabbi Solomon ben Rabbi Isaac, may his rest be honoured, did not agree with his comment and said: Heaven forbid that the poet would say anything about David's iniquity.'[69] Whatever Rashi's comment may say about Kallir's poem, it says more about the love of Israel that resided in his heart. He believed it would make no sense to recall the past transgression of King David, the sweet singer of Israel and progenitor of the messiah, even though the offence is explicitly recounted in the Bible.

## Standing and Fame

### Rashi's Status in France and Germany

From a historical perspective, Rashi ranks among the greatest Jewish luminaries of all time. No other Jewish sage has been the subject of so extensive a literature by both traditional and academic scholars, and none rivals him in remaining a touchstone for scholars to this day. It is enough to note that his commentary on the Torah alone has been the subject of hundreds of studies and supercommentaries.[70]

I share the view of various scholars, E. E. Urbach among them, that, seen from a historical perspective, Rashi is known and appreciated throughout the Jewish world even more than Maimonides, the greatest Jewish scholar of the Middle Ages. It is no coincidence that many have claimed descent from Rashi's family. The extraordinary esteem in which he is held arises primarily out of his contribution to the study of the Talmud and the Bible, but the mark left by his universally beloved and admired personality is another important factor. The present context does not allow for detailed discussion of the historical evidence regarding his unique position, and I will limit myself to some of the major points. Were Rashi and his contemporaries aware of his greatness, or did recognition emerge only in later generations? And how did esteem for Rashi spread throughout the Jewish diaspora?

[68] Soloveitchik, 'Can Halakhic Texts Talk History?' (Heb.), 9–26; id., *Their Wine* (Heb.), 51–9.

[69] Abraham ben Azriel, *Sefer arugat habosem*, 6.

[70] Simeon Schwarzfuchs writes that 'there is no end to the studies devoted to or bearing on Rashi's work; they continue to be published almost daily' (*History of the Jews in Medieval France* (Heb.), 320). While 'no end' is a deliberate exaggeration, it conveys the remarkable extent to which Rashi's oeuvre has been the subject of study—more so than that of any other writer since the completion of the Talmud. This is further evidence of the unique force of the man and his work.

One of the communities in northern France sent a request, asking Rashi to find a way to revoke the ban that had been imposed on a member of the community because he had mentioned to another Jew that the latter had once converted to Christianity ('he had been drawn into the waters of apostasy'). Rabbenu Gershom had imposed a ban on anyone who referred to a forced convert's past once the convert had returned to Judaism, to spare the feelings of the individual concerned. The community asked Rashi, as the leading sage of his generation, to help revoke the ban on the basis of the talmudic rule that a court's decree may be revoked by a greater court. The request constitutes remarkable recognition of Rashi's greatness. Rashi, however, declined to revoke the ban, arguing that no one in his generation was qualified to revoke a ban imposed by Rabbenu Gershom ('for there is none as great as he, who could revoke'). He did not consider himself to be the greatest scholar of the age, worthy of being deferred to by other communities:

As for what you have written asking me to release the ban, Heaven forbid that I claim the renown to make myself a prominent court. Were I among you, I would vote with you to release it, but who am I to claim renown in other places, I, the poor and young one, whose hands are orphaned orphans? Let him subject himself to the rule, appease his fellow, and then release him [from the ban].[71]

The words of this responsum are not mere rhetorical flourishes; rather, they represent a self-assessment having practical consequences for a person's fate. It seems fair to me to assume that if this sort of request had been directed to Rashi's grandson, Rabbenu Tam—who saw himself as his generation's leader—he would have granted it.

During the last quarter of the eleventh century, Rashi's fame gradually grew—not only in France but also in Germany and the Slavic lands. The two most important accounts of how his greatness came to be recognized even during his lifetime involve sages in Germany. Rabbi Nathan ben Makhir, one of the great sages in Mainz during the last quarter of the eleventh century and scion of one of the most distinguished families in Germany, turned to Rashi with various questions. The questions pertained to liturgical matters or to clarification of biblical and talmudic interpretations rather than to practical halakhah, but the very fact that the questions were posed is quite significant, given the honour and esteem afforded by the German sages to the illustrious tradition of the Mainz community. Rashi, indeed, replied to Rabbi Nathan in deferential terms, referring to him with numerous honorific titles, and it is evident that he was surprised to have received the enquiry. But the fact remains that a prominent and distinguished sage of Mainz needed Rashi's advice. A little later, evidently after the edicts of 1096, the greatest sage of Speyer at the time, Rabbi Isaac ben Asher Halevi (Riva), came to study with Rashi. As far as we can tell, Rabbi Isaac spent only a brief time in Rashi's yeshiva in Troyes, as

[71] *Taḥtsul*, §22.

alluded to in Rabbi Solomon Luria's responsa: 'And Riva came to serve before him [as apprentice] *and returned home.*'[72] Still, Rabbi Isaac was the greatest German sage of the late eleventh and early twelfth centuries, and his going to Rashi's yeshiva was understood by the Jews of Germany and France as recognition of the yeshiva's primacy following the damage to the distinguished centres of Worms and Mainz. The author of the note mentioned by Rabbi Solomon Luria, who was describing the development of rabbinic literature in Germany, saw fit to mention this detail because he recognized its great historical importance.

By the middle of the twelfth century Rashi was regarded in many European Jewish centres as having made an important contribution to the study of the Talmud and the Bible. Naturally, his students treated him with great deference, as was the practice then, and addressed him with exaggerated and flowery honorific titles. Sages in Rashi's time likewise referred to him by a variety of soubriquets, such as 'the great tamarisk', 'illuminator of the eyes of the diaspora', 'light of the diaspora', 'lamp of Israel', 'our holy rabbi', 'the great scholar of the world', and 'the great teacher'. But these expressions and descriptions cannot themselves be relied on as evidence of his stature, for they are sometimes used simply as rhetorical flourishes or as honorific terms of address, and they were also applied to other Ashkenazi sages of the time.

That said, we have additional evidence of the high regard for Rashi during his lifetime. By the end of the eleventh century, he was recognized as one of the great scholars of the age, both inside and outside France. Students came to his yeshiva from various parts of Europe, and his relations with other great sages—including his teachers, Rabbi Isaac Halevi and Rabbi Isaac ben Judah—manifest the esteem in which he was held even when he was still in his forties. Still, not all late eleventh-century German sages saw him as 'the greatest scholar of the generation'. The sons of Makhir—among them, Rabbi Nathan, one of the great German sages of the time—engaged in polemic with him and treated him with ambivalence, finding it difficult to accept his willingness to deviate from time-honoured Ashkenazi customs. 'The received tradition of the sages' and 'the custom of the ancients' were turns of phrase regularly used by Rabbi Nathan ben Makhir and his brothers, especially Rabbi Menahem.

Remarkable admiration for Rashi is evident in the comments of Rabbi Eliezer ben Nathan (Raban), a leading sage in Germany during the first half of the twelfth century—the Germany whose pre-eminence Rashi had appropriated:

I saw wise men who came to prattle stuff and nonsense about the responsum of the elder, Rabbi Solomon, may his soul rest, from whose waters we drink and from whose mouth we live . . . and he who hears will hear and he who lives will direct his heart and understand the perfect Torah of our rabbi Solomon, who weighed, and probed, and made the Torah

---

[72] Luria, *Responsa* (Heb.), §29, emphasis added.

easier to grasp . . . And so, let the intelligent one be intelligent and the understanding one understand, and the one who lives direct his heart to the response of the great scholar [Rashi] and those who reply to him, and [let him] probe, and examine with precision and give thanks to his soul and acknowledge the truth; for the words of the great scholar make sense to one who understands and are righteous to one who knows. His lips preserve knowledge, and Torah is sought, renewed, and interpreted by his mouth. A Torah of truth was in his mouth; he walked in peace and righteousness and stabilized the world; he aggrandized and glorified the Torah.[73]

In many communities in Germany, prayers were recited for Rashi's soul for hundreds of years, and he was described as one who 'illuminated the eyes of the diaspora with his commentaries'. Indeed, since the twelfth century it has been impossible to imagine the study of the Bible and the Talmud, their exegesis, and the study of halakhic literature in general in the Ashkenazi communities without reference to Rashi's commentaries. The Tosafot, which were at the centre of Jewish scholarship and creativity in Germany, France, and England during the twelfth and thirteenth centuries, were themselves in part written with reference to Rashi's commentary,[74] and he serves as the point of departure or the basis for many of them. The vast influence of his commentary on the Torah is considered in Chapter 4 below.

## Rashi's Reputation in Spain

Although the Spanish Jewish heritage differed in many respects from that of northern Europe, Rashi attained considerable esteem in Spain—though he also had numerous critics there. The subject is an important one, but we cannot address it here in detail. Although his advocates in Spain gradually gained the upper hand over his critics, the process was slow, and Sephardi sages remained divided for many generations. In any event, the most important supercommentaries on Rashi's commentary on the Torah were written by sages of Spanish origin, including those whose ancestors had migrated to the Ottoman empire following the Expulsion from Spain.

Rabbi Joseph Halevi ibn Migash, who died in 1141, was not aware of Rashi's commentaries. He asked the sages of Provence to send him a commentary on *Zevaḥim*, and if he had had a copy of Rashi's commentary in his possession, he is unlikely to have disregarded it. Maimonides, too, did not explicitly refer to Rashi's commentaries, though he may well have been influenced by them. As far as we know, Rabbi Abraham ibn Ezra (1089–1164) was the first Spanish sage to refer to Rashi's commentary on the Torah, taking a critical stance towards it. In the intro-

---

[73] Eliezer b. Nathan of Mainz, *Sefer even ha'ezer*, §107.

[74] The tosafists' method began to be used in Germany while Rashi was still alive; one of its first proponents was Rabbi Isaac ben Asher Halevi. On the subject generally, see Grossman, 'The Origins of the Tosafot' (Heb.).

duction to his book *Safah berurah*, Ibn Ezra described the commentary as far removed from the plain meaning of the text: 'He thinks he is on the path of plain meaning, but his books lack even one plain-meaning [interpretation] out of a thousand; yet the sages of our generation glory in these books.' Later Sephardi sages—adherents of rationalism and devotees of Ibn Ezra and Maimonides—shared this view and took the lead among those who had reservations about the embrace of Midrash that marks Rashi's biblical commentary. But it is those very reservations that demonstrate Rashi's great and growing fame, alluded to in the remark that 'the sages of our generation glory in these books'. Ibn Ezra, in his biblical commentary, refers to Rashi's commentaries only rarely, and when he does, he does not explicitly mention Rashi. He did not consider Rashi a worthy opponent, believing him to lack expertise in Hebrew grammar.

In contrast to the reception afforded him by the rationalists, Rashi was highly regarded by the kabbalists—the leading opponents of philosophical learning—and by the conservative camp in general. First and foremost, one should mention Nahmanides (Rabbi Moses ben Nahman; 1194–1270), a prominent sage who stood at the head of the conservatives and kabbalists in Spain. In the introduction to his commentary on the Torah he described his attitude towards Rashi's commentaries:

> I will place as an illumination before me
> The lights of the pure candelabrum,
> The commentaries of our Rabbi Shlomo [Rashi],
> A crown of glory and a diadem of beauty,
> Adorned in his ways,
> In Scripture, Mishnah, and *Gemara*.
> The right of the firstborn is his.
> In his words I will meditate,
> And in their love will I ravish,
> And with them we will have
> Discussions, investigations and examinations,
> In his plain explanations
> And Midrashic interpretations,
> And every difficult aggadah.
> Which is mentioned in his commentaries.[75]

Nahmanides often disagreed with Rashi, but that does not detract from the high regard in which he held him. Renewed interest in Ibn Ezra's commentary during the fourteenth century revived criticism of Rashi in some circles. Among his harshest critics was the anonymous author of the treatise *Alilot devarim*, who maintained that Rashi lacked rational intellect and strayed far from the plain meaning of the text:

---

[75] Nahmanides, *Commentary on the Torah*, i, 5.

He put out the eyes of the righteous of God, bound them in fetters, and carried them to babble,[f] for most of his words are not interpretations but talmudic *midrashim* ... and he thought to explain Scripture that way, doing so because he lacked the science of grammar ... and this commentary of his came to every place where his name was mentioned and Jews remained bare of the plain meaning of the Torah and Scripture ... and this is the reason for blindness and babble [preventing] perfection of souls.[76]

This harsh criticism probably arose against the background of the wide dissemination of Rashi's commentary and great attention directed to it. Impressive evidence for that is the ruling by Rabbi Jacob, son of Rabbi Asher ben Jehiel (Rosh), in his *Arba'ah turim*, followed in Rabbi Joseph Caro's *Shulḥan arukh*, that the study of Rashi's commentary fulfils one's obligation to review the weekly Torah portion once in translation (as well as twice in Hebrew).

Further evidence of the wide dissemination of Rashi's commentary on the Torah is provided by the writing of supercommentaries on it in fourteenth-century Spain. It appears that Spanish sages of that time assigned Rashi the soubriquet *Parshandata*—that is, interpreter of the law, the Torah, and the instruction. The appellation is used in the second half of the fifteenth century by Rabbi Abraham ibn Zakut and Rabbi Moses ibn Danon, both students of Rabbi Isaac ibn Abohav, but it is earlier than that. Some attribute it to Ibn Ezra, but that is not established.[77]

Important evidence of the spread and popularity of Rashi's biblical and talmudic commentaries appears also in the attitude towards them shown by Rabbi Isaac ben Jacob Canpanton, who established a school for the study of Talmud in Spain in the fifteenth century. He advised his students to pay close attention to every word of Rashi, as one does in studying Torah and Talmud, and to apply the logical rules on which Rabbi Isaac based the study of Talmud in his yeshiva. In that way, even 'Greek wisdom' became a tool for the study of Rashi, something that must be seen as an ironic twist.

Rabbi Judah Kalatz, a Castilian sage of the second half of the fifteenth century, called for comprehensive and intense study of Rashi's commentary, for 'by reading him, not only does one gain an understanding of the plain meaning of the written Torah; one also learns from him how to understand languages; but that is if one studies him thoroughly'.[78] He similarly determined that 'even though Rashi, of

---

[76] *Alilot devarim*, 182.

[77] On Rashi's standing in Spain, see Gross, 'Spanish Jewry and Rashi's Commentary on the Pentateuch' (Heb.). On the subject in general, including the renewed interest in Ibn Ezra during the fourteenth century, see Grossman, *The Early Sages of France* (Heb.), 176–7 n. 195. On the soubriquet *Parshandata* bestowed on Rashi, including its attribution to Ibn Ezra, see Urbach, 'How Did Rashi Merit the Title *Parshandata*?'          [78] Kalatz, *Mesiaḥ ilmim*, 8.

[f] This is an elaborate play on 2 Kgs 25: 7, which describes the treatment of the last king of Judah at the hands of the Babylonian king Nebuchadnezzar's forces: 'They ... put out the eyes of Zedekiah [whose name can be read as 'the righteous of God'], and bound him in fetters, and carried him to Babylon.'

blessed memory, did not study logic, he without doubt thought clearly'. In other words, not only did Kalatz disregard the two primary grounds on which Rashi had earlier been attacked—his allegedly inadequate knowledge of Hebrew grammar and lack of rationality—but he turned them into important reasons for encouraging people to study his teachings. Kalatz regarded Rashi as the foremost Jewish biblical commentator in the Middle Ages and down to his own time:

The great luminary that can overpower the night of foolishness of those who walk in darkness . . . is none other than Rashi, known and renowned to all for his wisdom, the illuminator of the diaspora . . . And it is known that there has been none like him, interpreting words in accordance with the meaning of their speakers. And of him I say by way of jest that the word of the Lord is straight[g] and all his actions are done in faith . . . The last of the geonim but first among them in importance . . . Even if he had lived in the time of the ancients and the early geonim, he would have been their guide to understanding Scripture and Talmud; and a fortiori none like him has arisen since.[79]

Kalatz here speaks of Rashi's commentaries on the Bible and the Talmud without drawing any distinction between them. He believed that Rashi's interpretations surpassed even those of the Babylonian geonim—an assessment that would never have occurred to the earlier Spanish sages, whose literary oeuvre was based on the halakhic and cultural tradition of those geonim.

It is impossible to know whether this expression of high regard, which pertained, inter alia, to Rashi's biblical commentary, in fact reflected the opinion of many fifteenth-century Spanish sages, but it clearly shows the great change over the generations in how his commentaries were viewed in Spain. Among the kabbalists, the reception of Rashi's commentaries was much more straightforward, but even among the halakhists and talmudic interpreters, Rashi's commentaries held an important place from the time of Rabbi Meir Halevi Abulafia (Ramah, c.1170–1244) until that of the distinguished sages of the generation of the Expulsion. The comment of Rabbi Menahem ben Aaron ben Zerah (the son of a family that had come to Spain after being expelled from France) in praise of Rashi's talmudic commentary typifies the view of the halakhists: 'But for him, the way of the Babylonian Talmud would have been forgotten in Israel.' In the seventeenth century Rabbi David Conforte summed up the view of Rashi held by the descendants of the Jews expelled from Spain who had taken up residence in the Ottoman empire: 'And he is everywhere called the master, the leader of the interpreters, because the light of his Torah and the virtues of his wisdom were great in his interpretation of the Torah. By his teaching and wisdom the world stands.'[80] Other sages in Spain and the Muslim lands shared this esteem for Rashi, and we will return to this subject in discussing the spread and influence of Rashi's biblical and talmudic commentaries.

[79] Kalatz, *Mesiaḥ ilmim*, 8.        [80] Conforte, *Kore hadorot*, 9a.

[g] *Yashar*: an anagram of Rashi in Hebrew.

In Provence, too, Rashi's talmudic commentary became well known and highly esteemed. Rabbi Menahem Meiri, the greatest Provençal sage of the thirteenth and fourteenth centuries, offered this expression of regard:

Foremost among the treatises written by way of commentary are the commentaries of Rashi, of blessed memory. And if there are many who do battle against him, he is well armed; and his responses in what he has written are plain to one who understands. His virtue is recognized only by a select few; for he can sometimes encompass in a single word the responses to a bundle of questions. But he did not thereby mean to rule on halakhic matters.[81]

Another sage wrote:

A great light shone forth from France, illuminating the eyes like none seen before—namely, the great and pious rabbi, our Rabbi Solomon of Troyes, son of Rabbi Isaac. He received [the tradition] from our Rabbi Gershom and his yeshiva, and he interpreted all of the Torah, all the Prophets, all the Writings, and four orders of the Talmud, so that the reader may go through them fleet-footedly. He left nothing, whether great or small, without a full interpretation. And once the nature of his commentaries became known to the world, there was no rabbi or great [teacher] who taught halakhah without them, and they were known throughout the world, to every great scholar and rabbi. May the Lord grant him his reward.[82]

During the seventeenth century, Rabbi Joseph Sambari, an Egyptian sage, described Rashi as one who 'produced his commentary [on the Talmud] with the holy spirit that had alit on him'.[83] Beginning in the thirteenth century, learned Christians also found Rashi's commentaries to be of interest, and some of them were influenced by him following the polemic against the Talmud in 1240. Particularly noteworthy is Nicholas of Lyra (1270–1349), one of the most important Christian biblical exegetes of the Middle Ages. He had a thorough knowledge of Hebrew and was familiar with other Hebrew commentaries on the Bible. Some believe him to have been a descendant of a Jewish family. Nicholas relied extensively on Rashi and often cited him by name. The translation of Rashi into other languages—including German, Yiddish, English, and French—began during the seventeenth century.

---

[81] Meiri, *Seder hakabalah*, 131.    [82] Neubauer (ed.), *Medieval Jewish Chronicles* (Heb.), i. 84.

[83] Sambari, *Sefer divrei yosef*, 189. On the legend about Rashi's attitude to Rashbam's commentary on *Bava batra*, see ibid. 190: 'And they said that he [Rashbam], too, wrote a commentary on the entire Talmud, just as had his grandfather Rashi, of blessed memory, but it never saw the light of day and over time, all recollection of it was lost. He wrote a lengthy commentary, until he reached *Bava batra*, and he brought it to show to his grandfather Rashi, of blessed memory, so he would place his hands on it [that is, approve it], but he said to him: "My son, it is too heavy for my hands to encompass", by which he meant to say that he had written at excessively great length.'

## Legends, Traditions, Charms

Additional evidence for Rashi's fame and the esteem in which he was held can be found in the legends that grew up around him. The late legends describe the various stages of his life, from birth to death. They tell of Rashi 'meeting' with Abraham, Moses, and other figures—Jews and Christians alike—and with sages who lived after his time, and portray him as having wandered far and wide. Some of the legends even arose in eastern lands. The legends should be seen as a folk-cultural product of Jewish and non-Jewish society at the end of the Middle Ages. They were inspired by Rashi's charismatic image, but they have no historical value.[84]

A similar phenomenon can be seen in the Torah-related comments, prayers, protective charms, and recitations that have been attributed to Rashi. Here, too, it is hard to imagine that many of the items ascribed to him are, in fact, his work. Still, we cannot determine in each instance whether the tradition is authentic or whether it arose after his time and attributed some item or another to him in order to use his fame to enhance its value. One example:

The Rabbi [Rashi] does not recite 'Avinu malkenu'[h] on the sabbath; for we never recite on the sabbath a prayer in the manner of the 'Shemoneh esreh',[i] and 'Avinu malkenu' encompasses passages in the manner of the 'Shemoneh esreh'. Moreover, it happened after the death of Rabbi Solomon, may his rest be honoured, that they began to recite 'Avinu malkenu' on the sabbath, and a certain elderly man was present and said to them, 'Do you not recall that in the days of Rabbi Solomon, we would not say [it]?' and silenced them [that is, prevented them from reciting the prayer].[85]

Also indicative of the high regard for Rashi is the frequency with which people tended to claim affinity with his family. Notices to that effect began to appear several generations after Rashi lived, especially in manuscripts, and the claims continue to be made to this day: they can be identified even in recently published genealogical listings. There is a touch of irony in this, for Rashi himself was not from a distinguished lineage in Germany. Had he remained there, it is doubtful that he would have attained a senior position in any of its yeshivas. We have already

---

[84] In the introduction to his book *Rashi's Palace* (Heb.), Avinery lists some of the motifs in these legends, including the following: Rashi's birth, Elijah the prophet as Rashi's *sandek* (the person who holds an infant at his circumcision), the patriarch Abraham and Rashi, Moses and Rashi, Rashi and the nazirite, Rashi and Maimonides, Rashi and his neighbour in Paradise, Rashi foretelling the future, Rashi and his grandson, Rabbenu Tam, Rashi appearing in a dream to his grandson Rashbam. On the relationship between medieval Jewish folk legends and the historical reality generally, see Yassif, 'Rashi Legends and Medieval Popular Culture' and the literature cited there.

[85] MS Oxford 1160 and parallels in other manuscripts (MS Vatican 308, fo. 43*a*, reads 'silenced him').

[h] A prayer recited between Rosh Hashanah and Yom Kippur and on fast days.
[i] Literally 'eighteen', the central weekday prayer, originally comprising eighteen blessings.

seen how self-effacingly he behaved towards members of distinguished families, but after only two generations his own family became the object of adulation and honour. In Rashi's case, however, his descendants were honoured not only on account of their lineage but also on account of their achievements.

The sociological phenomenon of affinity with a known family is itself of interest. It is neither novel nor unique, and we find it in connection with Maimonides. Despite Maimonides' opposition to and disdain for outward signs of glory and familial distinction, his descendants, too, became objects of adulation.[86]

---

[86] On Maimonides' disdain for the pursuit of honorifics and familial distinction, see Maimonides, *Letters* (Heb.), 303.

# CHAPTER THREE

# Rashi's *Beit Midrash*

## Growth of the *Beit Midrash*

Soon after returning to Troyes, Rashi established a yeshiva there. It began with only a few students, but gradually grew as his fame spread. Students from outside the vicinity roomed and boarded in Rashi's house. These characteristics—small size and students boarding with the head of the yeshiva—were common in European yeshivas of the time, and they provide the background for the report in MS Bodleian 1147 regarding flour purchased by Rashi's maidservant 'for the young men' on a festival. As word of Rashi's reputation reached distant lands, students came to his yeshiva not only from France, but also from Byzantium, Germany, and the Slavic lands.[1]

Several factors contributed to the fame of Rashi's yeshiva and its attractiveness even to scholars from distant parts:

1. The growth, albeit gradual, in the Jewish population of Germany and northern France, including the Champagne region where Rashi was active, that took place during the eleventh century.

2. The 'twelfth-century renaissance', which effectively began in the middle of the eleventh century, and the increased importance of the individual in European society at the time (two factors that were considered in Chapter 1). The multi-pronged interpretative effort of Rashi and his students reflected the new atmosphere that encouraged people to work with greater openness and a more critical approach than in the past. This activity, which enabled more scholars to have access to ancient sources, had a democratic quality that suited the new atmosphere, as I pointed out when discussing Rashi's personality. These two developments—the renaissance and the increased importance of the individual—reached their peak only in the twelfth century, but it is hard to separate developments in the atmosphere and literary output of Rashi's *beit midrash* from the earliest sparks of the renaissance in Europe as a whole and France especially.

[1] Detailed support for the following discussion of Rashi's yeshiva and students appears in Grossman, *The Early Sages of France* (Heb.), 166–74, 580–4.

3. **France's ascent to pre-eminence in the intellectual life of Christian Europe at the end of the eleventh century and the beginning of the twelfth.** It is reasonable to assume that this development had an influence on the changes in intellectual life within Jewish society. The study of medieval Jewish culture in Muslim and Christian lands alike shows the close, if not absolutely direct, link between the development of Jewish society and the development of its non-Jewish surroundings.

4. **The strengthening of the ideal of Torah study within the Judaism of Germany and northern France during the second half of the eleventh century.**

5. **The decline in the political standing of the Jews of Germany, which reached its nadir with the edicts of 1096.** Those edicts resulted in the death of most of the sages of Worms and Mainz, and the two celebrated yeshivas of those communities were severely harmed. A new centre gradually developed in Speyer, but it never attained the stature of the two earlier ones.

To these external factors must be added three highly important internal ones:

1. **The openness of Rashi's yeshiva and its encouragement of creativity.** This was in contrast to the yeshivas at Mainz and Worms.

2. **Rashi's analytic thoroughness, great erudition, and multifaceted literary production, encompassing the Bible, the Talmud, halakhic decisions, and poetry.**

3. **Rashi's cordial and radiant personality and his warm attitude towards his students.**

## 'The Great Rabbi'

At the beginning of Chapter 2, I mentioned that Rashi's students referred to him as 'the great rabbi [teacher]'. Of all the soubriquets applied to him—'stabilizer [literally, 'third leg'] of the world', *Parshandata*, 'Rabbi of Israel' (*raban shel yisra'el*: the initial letters spell Rashi in Hebrew)—'the great teacher' is the one most appropriate to his activity in his *beit midrash*. He was not content simply to write commentaries whose excellent pedagogical technique would be instructive throughout the ages; he also took pains to prepare students who would follow his path, developing and expanding his methods. This was a highly important innovation in the nature of the *beit midrash*, an innovation that sprang from Rashi's sense of mission. In the present chapter I will describe the brilliant, varied, and impressive output of Rashi's students, some of it produced while its authors were still studying with him, but most of it after his death. The scope of this material, its variety, and the new paths it broke are remarkable, especially when compared to the relatively modest output of other centres, including the grand yeshivas of the Babylonian geonim. Although the Babylonian centre endured for some five hundred years, it did not produce a literature as broad in scope as that produced by Rashi and his students during one or two generations, a literature that also exceeds in quantity the works produced at that time in Germany and Spain.

What accounts for Rashi's success in producing this valuable material? Among the important factors, one may cite his openness, critical approach, encouragement of creativity, thorough analysis, and cordiality. The following story demonstrates the great teacher's modus operandi. Rashbam disagreed with Rashi about some issues even while Rashi was still alive. In one instance, when Rashbam was about 20 years old, Rashi acknowledged that his student was right, and even said that 'if [he] had the time' he would alter his commentaries.[2] As already noted, MS Vienna 32 and other manuscripts recount that after Rashbam had identified an important literary technique, Rashi was so impressed by the discovery that he named it after him, referring to the texts in which it appeared as 'Samuel verses'. Not only did the great teacher praise the young exegete for his accomplishment, he also ensured he would be remembered. A young student whose rabbi not only acknowledged publicly that he was right but even called certain verses by his name would be expected, of course, to feel a strong sense of satisfaction, and he and his fellow students would naturally be led thereby to pursue further discoveries that the teacher himself had not made. It is hard to imagine that Rashi acted towards Rashbam in this way only because he was his grandson or that he accorded him preferential treatment.

## Rashi's Close Relationships with his Students

One impressive quality of Rashi's yeshiva was the closeness between him and his students. These students recounted, orally or in writing, dozens of his actions, practices, ways of doing things, and thoughts, thereby preserving them for the ages. His students told of the food he ate, his bathing practices, his conduct at worship and at meals, his customs at the Passover *seder*, his manner towards others and towards his wife, and his sayings and ideas. These accounts show the close ties between Rashi and his students and their profound feelings of friendship for one another. In principle, this was nothing new. Similar relationships prevailed between teachers and students in the tannaitic and amoraic yeshivas and in the yeshivas of Ashkenaz, and Rashi witnessed this sort of study under Rabbi Jacob ben Yakar. Some of the most renowned teachers in European Christian society of the time likewise had close relationships with their students, and students in Christian schools would also record their teachers' actions. But the accounts of the relationships between Rashi and his students suggest an exceptional degree of closeness. It may simply be the number of such accounts that gives this impression, but the primary reason appears to be Rashi's cordial personality. Either way, this is one of his most prominent traits. For example, Rashi arranged a wedding ceremony at his home for one of his students,

---

[2] Reported by Rashbam on Gen. 37: 2.

and he accepted a bill of divorce on behalf of the bride of a student who was about to die.[3] This warmth is evident too in the marginal notes written by students on his halakhic rulings. As a result, minute details have been preserved of his actions and practices in many areas, which his students considered as precedents to be followed. It is no coincidence that *rabi* or *rabenu* stands at the centre of many works written by Rashi's students. That his students referred to him as 'the great teacher' was the product of this closeness, not only of his actual teaching in the yeshiva. From a broader historical perspective, Rashi deserved the title because of his wide-ranging exegetical oeuvre, which enabled many to study the sources on their own, and because of his establishment of worthy students, men of stature, builders and creators, who carried on his efforts in centres of Jewish life in France and beyond.

The students' participation in the literary effort is instructive. They assisted Rashi in various ways: checking his interpretations with him, copying his comments, completing them, and recording his actions and practices in writing.

As noted, the two principal characteristics of Rashi's *beit midrash* were openness and encouragement of creativity. Certainly, there was a glimmer of these traits in the German yeshivas, especially that of Worms, but they do not begin to compare to Rashi's *beit midrash*.

In *Sanhedrin 24a*, a comparison is drawn between the mode of study used by sages in the Land of Israel and that used by sages in Babylonia. The Talmud praises, in general terms, the manner of study in the Land of Israel—'they are pleasant to one another regarding halakhah'; 'they are easy-going towards one another regarding halakhah'. Rashi elaborated on these general words of praise: 'Residents of the Land of Israel are easy-going together, study together, correct one another, and the subject is illuminated.' In contrast, the Babylonian sages 'are not easy-going with one another, and they have a questionable grasp of what they are studying' (Rashi on *San.* 24*a, bo ure'eh*). It seems to me that Rashi here defined what he regarded as the desirable characteristics of a *beit midrash*, based on the reality of his own. He trained his students to learn with 'pleasantness' and with mutual love and 'to correct one another'.

Elsewhere, I have compared the Ashkenazi yeshiva to the yeshivas of the Babylonian geonim and concluded that the former were more democratic.[4] The Babylonian geonim refrained from writing comprehensive, systematic commentaries on the Talmud: such commentaries began to be written only at the end of the

---

[3] 'It happened that a certain young man married a woman and they set up his wedding canopy in the house of our Rabbi, may he live. Everything needed in connection with his wedding was prepared in another house, next door to it' (Rashi, *Responsa* (Heb.), ed. Elfenbein, §100). 'It happened that a certain young man who was dying in the house of R. [the abbreviation indicates either Rashi or Rabbi] had a betrothed and he requested R. to accept her bill of divorce [on her behalf]' (*Taḥtsul*, §16; see also Grossman, *The Early Sages of France* (Heb.), 168 nn. 160–1).

[4] Avraham Grossman, 'Social Structure and Intellectual Creativity in Medieval Jewish Communities (Eighth to Twelfth Centuries)'.

geonic period. The geonim sought to maintain their intellectual elitism, lest students who had not attained the proper level of competence attempted to decide halakhic questions from talmudic sources. They likewise sought to protect the centrality of their yeshivas. In general, the Babylonian yeshivas were characterized by conservatism and a sense of their own distinguished pedigree, expressed in trappings of royalty, grand ceremony, and a pronounced distance between teachers and students. In this regard, a striking detail pointed out by Louis Ginsburg is worth noting.[5] The Babylonian Talmud refers by name to hundreds of sages who played no official role in the yeshiva. In contrast, the geonic literature produced in Babylonia mentions by name only a handful of sages who did not serve as geonim. Of course, the two corpora differ in their literary qualities, but the absence of references to other sages is also evident in the letters written by the geonim. The writings of the German and French sages, like the Talmud, frequently refer by name to sages who played no official roles in the yeshivas.

In general, we find abundant evidence of democratic tendencies in the manner of study and in relations between teachers and students in the Ashkenazi yeshivas, especially Rashi's. Those tendencies are reflected in the willingness to write more detailed commentaries on the Talmud and to encourage students to pursue that path.[6]

## Openness and Productivity

This pedagogical revolution had been initiated in Germany two generations before Rashi by Rabbenu Gershom, but it was in Rashi's yeshiva that it was widely implemented. In Mainz, meanwhile—which had been home to Rabbenu Gershom's celebrated yeshiva—there was a degree of backpedalling. There are various accounts of the conservatism that prevailed in Mainz, in contrast to the openness in Rashi's yeshiva, which is especially evident when one compares the number of writers at each and the range of their works. Literary output in Mainz during the second half of the eleventh century was confined almost exclusively to annotating the Talmud and included no works in new areas.[7] In contrast, Rashi's *beit midrash* saw an efflorescence that was unprecedented in three respects: (1) the large number of sages

---

[5] Ginzberg, *Geonica*, i. 1–19.

[6] Ta-Shma generally agrees with this: 'This view is fundamentally correct, though it must be kept in mind that we are speaking of an extended process, not completed until the time of the tosafists in the middle of the twelfth century' (*Talmudic Commentary in Europe and North Africa* (Heb.), i. 45). I have dealt with the process that began in France (Grossman, *The Early Sages of France* (Heb.), 437–56).

[7] The book known as *Ma'aseh hamakhiri* can be identified as a new literary genre, as can R. Meshullam b. Moses' commentary on the liturgical poems. R. Meshullam's method, however, differs in a number of ways from that used by Rashi, R. Shemayah, and R. Joseph Kara. The yeshiva at Worms likewise tended towards a certain degree of conservatism (see the discussion in Grossman, *The Early Sages of Ashkenaz* (Heb.), 334–48). But for the important work of R. Kalonymus b. Shabbetai, who came from Italy bearing 'a breath of fresh air', the conservative tendency would have been even more prominent. On R. Kalonymus, see Grossman, *The Early Sages of Ashkenaz* (Heb.), 348–54.

engaged in writing, (2) the breadth of their literary output, and (3) its variety. It is evident that the students' wide range of activities was not a matter of happenstance; rather, it was planned and led by Rashi. All of these developments flowed from Rashi's sense of mission, which will be discussed in Chapter 11.

The table below identifies the areas Rashi's students worked in. The list is incomplete, for much of their output has been lost. The variety of their output should not mislead us: it was primarily commentaries and exegesis that were produced in northern France generally and in Rashi's *beit midrash* in particular. There are almost no ancient texts on which they did not write interpretative commentaries: Bible, Mishnah, Talmud, liturgical poems, and, to a degree, Midrash, for Rabbi Joseph Kara wrote a commentary on *Genesis Rabbah*. Moreover, he and Rabbi Shemayah dealt extensively with Midrash in the course of commenting on the liturgical poems As a practical matter, involvement in interpretation was so extensive that Rashi's *beit midrash*, the seat of Torah study in northern France at the time, can be referred to as 'the centre of interpretation'.

| | |
|---|---|
| Commentaries on the Bible | Rashi, R. Joseph Kara, R. Shemayah, Rashbam |
| Commentaries on the Mishnah and/or the Talmud | R. Shemayah, R. Meir ben Samuel (in Tosafot), R. Jacob ben Samson, R. Judah ben Nathan, Rashbam |
| Commentaries on the liturgical poems | R. Joseph Kara, R. Shemayah, R. Jacob ben Samson Also to be mentioned is R. Azriel ben Nathan, for many of their commentaries are cited by others |
| Responsa | R. Shemayah, Rashbam, R. Azriel ben Nathan, R. Jacob ben Samson |
| Halakhic monographs | R. Shemayah, R. Simhah of Vitry, R. Jacob ben Samson, R. Judah ben Abraham These booklets for the most part include Rashi's teachings, collected and edited by the named authors. Some are identical to their prayer books |
| Prayer books | R. Shemayah, R. Simhah of Vitry, R. Jacob ben Samson, R. Samuel ben Parigoros |
| Midrashic literature | R. Joseph Kara as exegete, and R. Shemayah and R. Azriel in the course of their explication of liturgical poetry |
| Liturgical poetry | Rashi, R. Jacob ben Samson |
| Grammar | Rashbam |
| History (talmudic sages) | R. Jacob ben Samson |
| Astronomy and astrology | R. Jacob ben Samson |

It is hard to imagine that interpretative literature would have flourished to such an extent and attracted such concentrated involvement as early as the eleventh century without Rashi's explicit encouragement and direction. In Germany, too, we know of students producing works even while still studying with their teachers, and it appears Rabbenu Gershom taught them to do so, but the process there was not as intensive as it became in France, nor did it encompass new areas. Rashi—'the great teacher'—did not see his task in the yeshiva as limited to his own creative work; rather, it extended to training students to follow his path. The special atmosphere that prevailed among Rashi's group of students, as evident in a variety of sources (including MS Leipzig 1, the importance of which in this context has only recently been recognized), attests to the manner in which Rashi organized his *beit midrash*. Within this group, marked by close relationships between teacher and students and among the students themselves, study proceeded in absolute freedom. Students were taught to be critical thinkers, to use numerous and diverse sources, and especially to be creative in new areas. The diversity of activity produced a community of scholars in which each member benefited from the work of his colleagues and embodied, to a degree, the mishnaic statement regarding a student 'who makes his teacher wise'.[8] It is often reported that Rashi accepted the critical remarks of Rabbi Joseph Kara, Rashbam, and Rabbi Shemayah, and it is fair to assume that he treated other students in the same way. Rabbi Shemayah recounted that Rashi had encouraged him to seek new sources, and he told of their shared joy when he succeeded in his quest. This resembled Rashi's own experience as a student, for he spoke of how he had pleased his teachers when he told them he had found new texts. In general, the search for new sources was a prominent characteristic of Rashi's literary oeuvre and that of his students.

An additional area to which Rashi's students devoted considerable effort was the writing of prayer books. These were arranged around the yearly cycle of festivals and seasons and included other material of practical import, primarily laws regarding what is ritually prohibited and permitted. They also contained quotations from the talmudic sages and the Babylonian geonim, to which are added excerpts from Rashi's teachings and descriptions of his actions and practices. On rare occasions, teachings of other scholars were included, among them the early Ashkenazi sages. Some of the prayer books do not include the actual liturgical texts, indicating only the sequence in which the prayers are recited and setting forth the laws and customs related to the various festivals. As a practical matter, they served as first-rate guidebooks to worship in the various communities. Arranging these prayer books around the annual cycle of festivals was meant to make them easier to use.

Why did many of the early French sages consider it insufficient simply to copy existing prayer books, as was the practice of their German counterparts? Why did nearly all the sages known to us in Rashi's *beit midrash* compile their own prayer

[8] Mishnah *Avot* 6: 6.

books? It appears they did so because various customs were practised within the community, and it was therefore necessary to clarify their nature and authority. In addition, it was necessary to consider the impact of newly arrived sources, whether produced by the Babylonian geonim or by the sages of Germany and France. As noted, this phenomenon had no parallel in Germany except for the book by the sons of Makhir called *Ma'aseh hamakhiri*, which can be considered a prayer book only in some respects. It is hard to imagine that either the sons of Makhir in Germany or the sages who wrote prayer books in Rashi's *beit midrash* in France would have disregarded other prayer books circulating in Germany had there been any in their possession. Since we are speaking here of a first-rate tool for organizing the religious life of a community, it is fair to assume that the German sages hesitated to compile new prayer books and were content simply to copy the existing ones. Similarly, they treated ancestral customs as sanctified, even though some of them had no roots in the Babylonian Talmud and some even conflicted with it.

The halakhic monographs written during this period in Rashi's *beit midrash* are connected to the writing of prayer books, and one finds considerable similarity between the former and the *halakhot* that appear in the latter. In my view, all of them were vitally needed resources for small, dispersed communities striving to organize their religious lives. It is possible, however, that the writing of halakhic monographs preserves an ancient practice from the Land of Israel—assuming that Mordecai Margaliot is right in suggesting that this literary genre was characteristic of halakhic writing in the Land of Israel during the early Middle Ages.[9]

Similar activities were going on in Christian society, and there too considerable attention was directed to the explication of earlier texts. I do not mean to imply direct influence by one group on the other, but it is known that these sorts of parallels frequently occur between different populations sharing a cultural climate.

The characteristics of the centre in France—enthusiastic literary creativity, a willingness to probe the nature of customs, and the rationalism of Rashi's *beit midrash*—cannot be discussed apart from the European renaissance of the late eleventh and twelfth centuries. All elements of the renaissance identified by scholars had clear parallels in the French Jewish centre. Like the effect of the Jewish–Christian polemics discussed earlier, the renaissance had a profound impact on Jewish intellectual creativity in general and on biblical interpretation in particular. It is nevertheless important to emphasize that the rationalist strain came to the fore not only in Rashbam's interpretations, where it has long been recognized, but also, and with great force, in those of the slightly older Rabbi Joseph Kara. It appears even in the 'conservative' Rabbi Shemayah, though to a lesser degree than in Rashbam and Kara. Rabbi Jacob ben Samson's involvement with astronomy and history likewise is an unmistakable expression of his contact with the twelfth-

[9] Margaliot, *Halakhot of the Land of Israel* (Heb.), 40.

century renaissance. The phenomenon appears clearly in Rashi's own activities, attesting even more to its influence.

As noted, several phenomena evince the great degree of openness in Rashi's *beit midrash*. His guiding principle was the pursuit of truth, and any method that could promote it was proper and desirable. This openness underlay Rashi's encouragement of his students to investigate things—even customs and written prayer books—and not accept them as settled.

This abundant, multifaceted openness in the literary output of Rashi's yeshiva can also be seen in the numerous literary works on many subjects brought to France from distant parts, including Babylonia and other centres in the Islamic world, Spain, Italy, and Byzantium. Use was made not only of halakhic literature but also of Midrash. Only now, with the availability (albeit only in manuscript) of the numerous commentaries on liturgical poems written by Rabbi Joseph Kara and Rabbi Shemayah, can we see the full extent to which this literature was employed. These two scholars, in their pursuit of the sources employed by the poets, demonstrate a breathtaking command of rabbinic Midrash. Rabbi Shemayah recounted his labours in searching through midrashic texts until he managed to find what he was looking for, and his account demonstrates the large number of *midrashim* available to him. He even relied on apocalyptic *midrashim*, such as *Nistarot derabi shimon bar yoḥai* and *Otot milḥemet melekh hamashiaḥ*, and on *Josippon*.

In his survey of the texts mentioned in Rashi's works, Zunz mentioned *Josippon* only a few times, thereby obscuring the special value that Rashi and his students ascribed to it. The manuscript commentaries on the liturgical poems show extensive use of it. In effect, they regarded it as part of the ancient, sanctified literature, and they manifested that view in various ways. The content of *Josippon* reinforced the sense that the work was related to sacred Scripture. Josephus' *The Jewish War*, on which *Josippon* was based, is described in it as approaching the books of the Bible in its value:

And of all this it is fitting for a man producing books to write words of truth, for it was so commanded by Joseph ben Gorion Hakohen, who was the leading writer of all the books that have been written other than the twenty-four holy [biblical] books and the books of wisdom produced by Solomon, King of Israel, and by the sages of Israel.[10]

The commentaries of Rabbi Joseph Kara and Rabbi Shemayah on the liturgical poems, which include quotations from *Josippon*, reinforce this finding. Rabbi Joseph Kara studied with the early sages of Germany, and Rabbi Shemayah with Rashi. *Josippon* was an important source for their interpretation of the liturgical poems, and they considered it to be authoritative. This is conclusively shown by Rashi's comment on Daniel 11: 2. The verse reads: 'Behold, there shall stand up yet three kings in Persia; and the fourth shall be far richer than them all.' Rashi

[10] *Josippon*, i. 143–4.

comments: 'Our rabbis of blessed memory said in *Seder olam* that this refers to Cyrus, Ahasuerus, and Darius, who built the Temple, but what is the meaning of "the fourth"? The fourth [is the king] of Media', but in the book of Joseph ben Gorion [*Josippon*] it is written that Cyrus had a son who reigned in his stead before Ahasuerus, and his name was Cambyses.' Rashi thus cites the tradition in *Josippon* side by side with that in *Seder olam rabah* without saying which seems to him to be more authoritative. It therefore is hardly surprising that Rabbi Joseph Kara and Rabbi Shemayah regarded it as an authoritative source when they set out to interpret the liturgical poems.

Various *midrashim* that appear in the writings of the sages of Provence (especially Rabbi Moses Hadarshan) were also familiar to the early sages of northern France. Of special interest are the treatises on the Hebrew calendar and astronomy that were available to Rabbi Jacob ben Samson, including some that originated in Babylonia, the Land of Israel, and Spain.

This openness may also be connected to text criticism, one of the more surprising activities of the early French sages. They would emend the received versions of sacred texts (Talmud, *midrashim*, liturgical poetry) on the basis of their own judgement, without relying on other early sources. This differed from the practice in Spain, where texts were emended on the basis of geonic literature. Rashi freely engaged in the practice, though he generally set forth his emendations only in his marginal comments: an exception is the talmudic tractate *Zevaḥim*, which he emended in the body of the text. This was noted by his grandson, Rabbenu Tam, who harshly criticized the practice overall.[11]

Although Rabbi Shemayah likewise emended sources, the practice should not be seen as unique to the sages of northern France. It was accepted in Germany too, albeit to a lesser degree. The ban pronounced by Rabbenu Gershom on those who emend books demonstrates—as Rabbenu Tam notes in his remarks—the seriousness of the problem within Ashkenazi Jewry overall. The issue is perplexing: how can we explain this sort of attitude towards the sacred texts that serve as the basis for halakhic decisions?[12]

The phenomenon may well be associated with the tendency, widespread then and later in France and Germany, to exercise great freedom when copying works by earlier sages. Copyists did not hesitate to delete, shorten, add, or change parts of the text being copied in conformance to later works or on the basis of oral traditions, and they typically did so without drawing attention to it. A blatant example is provided by Rabbi Shemayah himself, who deleted Rashi's own opinion from his esteemed teacher's commentary on the Torah and replaced it with a different

[11] Rabbenu Tam, *Sefer hayashar*, i, *Novellae*, introduction, p. 9.
[12] According to Ta-Shma, the Ashkenazi position on this issue is tied to their tradition that the Talmud was not committed to writing until after the talmudic period (see Grossman, *The Early Sages of France* (Heb.), 583–4).

interpretation that he had heard from a Jewish sage from Byzantium.[13] His underlying premise seems to have been that if Rashi in his declining days had instructed him to edit his commentary, there was nothing to keep him from doing it with other works as well. It was, after all, the pursuit of truth that guided Rashi in all his actions.

This willingness to emend may also be explained on the grounds that altering texts was considered part of the search for truth as they understood it. In taking the liberty of correcting earlier works, sages and copyists were honouring the author and showing their high regard for his work, reasoning that a great man's writings would not contain errors. Accordingly, the emendation did not constitute disrespect for the author and his work: quite the contrary.

I have noted several factors that led to the ascendancy of Rashi's *beit midrash*: its openness, its atmosphere, the encouragement within it of student creativity, the twelfth-century renaissance, and the harm wrought by the edicts of 1096 on the yeshivas in Worms and Mainz. In the wake of Rashi's efforts, there followed great advances in all the centres of Torah study in France. He had a great influence on the development of northern France as a centre of Jewish learning in the last quarter of the eleventh century and the start of the twelfth. This development, however, should not be attributed to Rashi alone. Other sages of stature worked alongside him, most notably Rabbi Joseph Kara, Rabbi Shemayah, and Rashbam.

Clear evidence of this is provided by Kara's magnificent interpretative works on liturgical poetry and the Bible, most of which were lost or have been abbreviated by copyists. Had his biblical commentary not been overshadowed by Rashi's, Kara would surely have been regarded as one of the most important medieval biblical commentators. Remnants of his works recently discovered in manuscript—including some not yet published—clearly show his importance. He was the first in the new centre in northern France to adopt the rationalist approach, and only later did Rashbam follow him. Rabbi Shemayah, Rabbi Judah ben Nathan, and Rashbam should also be considered prominent sages in their own right. Nevertheless, notwithstanding the greatness of the other early French sages, the Jewish centre in northern France would not have developed as quickly and impressively as it did without Rashi's efforts and the foundation he laid. His modes of study and pedagogy, his rationalist approach, his humility in the broadest sense of the word, and his pursuit of truth exercised great influence in his time and left a powerful and enduring legacy.

Rashi played a decisive role in the enthusiasm, openness, intellectual curiosity, and development of new ways of study that characterized his *beit midrash*. He attracted students from far and wide and encouraged them to exercise free and critical creativity and to engage in new areas of study. Above all, he trained them to collect interpretative traditions from the full range of the Jewish cultural heritage,

[13] See Grossman, *The Early Sages of France* (Heb.), 364 n. 55.

including those of Spain and Provence, and to show a degree of openness to their non-Jewish surroundings. The openness and critical approach contributed much to the development and shaping of intellectual creativity in France. Rashi's strong sense of mission also played a part, and I will consider it in Chapter II.

## Rashi's Students

Rashi's work in France was carried on by his students, who played an important part in the intellectual life of the communities in northern France at the start of the twelfth century. Only scattered fragments of their output have survived, so it is not always possible to provide a full and precise account of their work.[14] Four of them are among the most prominent northern French sages of the early twelfth century: Rabbi Joseph Kara, Rabbi Shemayah, Rabbi Jacob ben Samson, and Rashbam, Rashi's grandson. In what follows, I briefly consider the work of Rashi's most prominent students.

**Rabbi Meir ben Samuel** was Rashi's son-in-law, the husband of his daughter Jochebed 'the pious', and father of Rashbam, Rabbi Isaac, Rabbi Solomon, and Rabbenu Tam. Although his place of birth is not known with certainty, there is a general consensus that he was born in France and, like his father-in-law, went to Germany to study, but the possibility that he was born in Germany cannot be ruled out. Most of his studies were at the yeshiva in Worms, and there is evidence that he was already there in the time of Rabbi Isaac Halevi, who died in 1085. He remained at the yeshiva quite a few years, until about 1090, and by the time he completed his studies he was already a renowned scholar. Rabbi Meir provided accounts of Rabbi Isaac Halevi's actions and teachings and transmitted many of his interpretations. While in Worms, he also studied with Rabbi Solomon ben Samson and Rabbi Kalonymus ben Shabbetai of Rome.

Several of Rabbi Meir's children were born in Worms. One of Rashi's letters to him concludes with a blessing: 'May my son-in-law live long, with my daughter and the children; let them be fruitful in old age and peace.'[15] We cannot be certain, however, whether the letter was sent to him in Worms or in Ramerupt, where he settled after his return to France.

To this day we have no explicit evidence that Rabbi Meir learned Torah directly from Rashi. It seems reasonable to assume, however, that he studied with him for some time before settling in Ramerupt. Aptowitzer and Urbach believe that Rabbi Meir assisted Rashi in his literary work and that they collaborated on a halakhic responsum. I disagree with their conclusion, for the source it is based on is corrupt.[16]

---

[14] For a detailed discussion of the activities and writings of Rashi's students, especially those of R. Joseph Kara, R. Shemayah, and R. Jacob b. Samson, and for support for what follows, see Grossman, *The Early Sages of France* (Heb.), 168–74.    [15] Rashi, *Responsa* (Heb.), ed. Elfenbein, §58.
[16] For detailed discussion of this, see Grossman, *The Early Sages of France* (Heb.), 169–70 n. 166.

Rabbi Meir was known as *hayashish*, 'the old', attesting to his longevity. He seems to have lived from around 1060 to around 1140. His son Rabbi Isaac (Ribam), Rashi's grandson, died during his lifetime. His literary output was important in two ways: he preserved the halakhic and exegetical traditions of the early Ashkenazi sages, especially those of Worms, and he wrote commentaries on the Talmud and, perhaps, on the liturgical poems. While he was still studying in Germany he transmitted the teachings of its sages to Rashi, and when he returned to France he delivered to Rashi copies of commentaries he had written while studying with Rabbi Isaac Halevi and others—commentaries that Rashi went on to use extensively. Overall, Rabbi Meir served as the principal pipeline for transmitting the teachings of the German sages of the last quarter of the eleventh century to Rashi. Rabbi Meir's sons, Rashbam and Rabbenu Tam, also cited these important traditions in their writings. Rabbi Meir was one of the first sages to write Tosafot, and he and Rabbi Isaac ben Asher Halevi appear to be the originators of that genre. He may also have engaged in interpreting liturgical poetry. Various comments on those poems are cited in the name of 'Rabbi Meir', most often in the writings of Rabbi Joseph Kara. Urbach generally attributes them to Rabbi Meir ben Samuel, but most of them are by Rabbi Meir ben Isaac, the prayer leader in Worms.

**Rabbi Judah ben Nathan (Rivan)** was another of Rashi's sons-in-law, having married his daughter Miriam. For an extended time he lived with Rashi in Troyes and assisted him in his literary work. He himself wrote commentaries on the Talmud, but only scattered fragments survive.[17]

**Rabbi Joseph Kara** should be seen as Rashi's colleague as well as his student. When he came to Rashi's yeshiva, he was already a renowned scholar in his own right, having studied Torah with his uncle, Rabbi Menahem ben Helbo, and the great sages of Worms, especially Rabbi Kalonymus ben Shabbetai. He wrote commentaries on the Bible and the liturgical poems, often disagreeing with Rashi, and he can be considered a student who taught his teacher. Rashi accepted most of his criticisms and even incorporated some of them into his own commentary. In addition, Rabbi Joseph transmitted to Rashi important interpretative traditions that he had received from various scholars, especially Rabbi Menahem. These diverse traditions and the wide range of his writings make Kara's literary oeuvre particularly important.[18]

**Rabbi Shemayah** did more than any other of Rashi's students to support his teacher's work and preserve his literary legacy. One of Rashi's first students, he was also particularly close to him. The sources show clearly that he joined Rashi soon

[17] On his literary activity, see Epstein, 'Rivan's Commentaries' (Heb.); Urbach, *The Tosafists* (Heb.), i. 38–41.

[18] For a detailed discussion of the man and his work, see Grossman, *The Early Sages of France* (Heb.), 254–346.

after Rashi's return from Germany. He helped Rashi edit his commentaries, he documented his customs, and he played a crucial role in collecting his literary output. Much of this information about him has long been known, but recently discovered material, still in manuscript, has confirmed it and given us a broader picture of his own varied literary output.[19] His most important work is his commentary on the liturgical poems, which includes some of Rashi's comments that were transmitted to him orally.

The relationship between Rashi and Rabbi Shemayah was one of intimate friendship, and there are few other instances in medieval Jewish society of such close ties between teacher and student. That they were related by marriage does not account for their closeness: they were friends even before one of Rashi's grandsons married Rabbi Shemayah's daughter. Rabbi Shemayah left Troyes, at least for a while, but they maintained their ties through correspondence. Several factors account for this closeness: similar character traits, Rashi's cordial personality, and Rabbi Shemayah's humility and great esteem for Rashi, which made him willing to offer him extensive help in his literary work—to the point that even as cautious a scholar as Abraham Epstein could refer to him as Rashi's 'secretary'. Statements by Rabbi Shemayah show that he lived in Rashi's house as virtually a member of the family for many years.

According to the sources that have come down to us, no student was closer to Rashi than Rabbi Shemayah. Rashi's debt to him was great, for he helped Rashi assemble his oeuvre during his lifetime and finished the task after Rashi had died. Much of Rashi's responsa and halakhic correspondence was preserved for the ages thanks to Rabbi Shemayah's devoted efforts. The few remnants of their correspondence that have survived show the bond between them. Rashi referred to him as 'my brother' or 'our brother'; Rabbi Shemayah usually referred to Rashi as 'rabbi', 'the holy one', or 'our holy rabbi'.

It has been suggested that Rabbi Shemayah came from Byzantium, an idea that is supported by the interpretative traditions he received from 'Michael the Greek' and by his explanations of the Greek words quoted by the tosafists. But while his place of origin is an important question, the available sources do not allow for a definite answer.

Late in Rashi's life, Rabbi Shemayah moved to another community. His place as Rashi's close student and assistant in his literary work was filled by Rabbi Jacob ben Samson. Several accounts of this have come down to us, the most important being Rabbi Jacob's response to Rabbi Shemayah's request for clarification of a ruling by Rashi on the subject of purification of utensils:

That is what our rabbi, may his rest be honoured, pronounced with his mouth, and I wrote them with ink in the book—I, Jacob ben Rabbi Samson . . .—Many times I saw our rabbi

---

[19] For a detailed discussion of the man and his work, see ibid. 347–426.

do so, and I did so before him many times. And I will now tell you the reason for this, as I heard it from our rabbi.[20]

Here Rabbi Jacob uses the words of Baruch ben Neriyah, Jeremiah's servant, in describing how he had written down Jeremiah's prophecies: 'Then Baruch answered them: "He pronounced all these words unto me with his mouth, and I wrote them with ink in the book"' (Jer. 36: 18). This is no mere happenstance, for he regarded his studies with Rashi as a great privilege.

**Rabbi Judah ben Abraham**, another of Rashi's earliest students, studied under him with Rabbi Shemayah: 'I, Shemayah, and Rabbi Judah ben Rabbi Abraham heard these [words] from the mouth of the holy one, may he be remembered for good and may his rest be honoured. And our holy rabbi, may the memory of the righteous be for a blessing, found among the responsa of the geonim . . .'.[21] MS Leipzig 1 preserves a responsum written to him by Rashi that incorporates an explication of a biblical passage. The recurring us of the soubriquet 'the holy one' in reference to Rashi provides further evidence of the esteem in which he was held.

**Rashbam**, Rashi's grandson, was one of the most important interpreters of the Bible and Talmud in northern France. Spending his youth in proximity to Rashi left a powerful mark on him.[22]

**Rabbi Simhah ben Samuel of Vitry** was related to Rashi by marriage. His son Samuel was married to Rashi's granddaughter, the daughter of Rabbi Meir and Jochebed. Samuel's son (and thus Rashi's great-grandson) was Rabbi Isaac of Dampierre, a leading tosafist. Rabbi Simhah composed a prayer book that included not only liturgical matters but also laws and customs in various areas. In preparing it, he made extensive use of the prayer book composed not long before by Rabbi Shemayah, taking from it many of Rashi's teachings along with the teachings of the Babylonian geonim and the early Ashkenazi sages and adding what he himself had learned from Rashi. The book was widely distributed and extensively supplemented, particularly the version printed on the basis of the British Museum manuscript, the most extensive one to survive. Earlier surviving manuscripts include Sassoon–Klagsbald (second half of the twelfth century) and Jewish Theological Seminary of America MS Mic. 8092 (1204). Rabbenu Tam commented on the importance of Rabbi Simhah's composition and the extensive use that was made of it: 'One will find it written in the prayer book prepared by the noble Rabbi

---

[20] MS Paris 326, 41*b* (80*b* in the old pagination). The material in this manuscript was published by Neubauer ('Collectaneen', 503), but his transcription contains several minor errors. The version quoted in the text is taken from the manuscript itself.    [21] Rabbinovicz, *Dikdukei soferim*, 195*b*.

[22] For a discussion of Rashbam's oeuvre, see Urbach, *The Tosafists* (Heb.), i. 45–59, and the bibliographical notes.

Simhah, which sets forth many things from *Seder rav amram*, and *Halakhot gedolot*, and our rabbi Solomon, and other great Torah scholars, and it can be found in most places.'[23]

**Rabbi Samuel ben Parigoros** came to Troyes towards the end of Rashi's life. Excerpts from his book of *halakhot* appear in MS Vatican 318 and provide important accounts of Rashi's actions and modes of conduct.

**Rabbi Azriel ben Nathan** was an important sage active in France (and perhaps also in Germany) at the beginning of the twelfth century. His literary output was diverse; halakhic rulings and commentaries on the liturgical poems survive. MS Montefiore 98 includes three questions he and Rabbi Joseph ben Judah jointly addressed to Rashi. In his response, Rashi refers to him as 'my relation, Rabbi Azriel'. Some scholars have suggested he may have been the brother of Rabbi Judah ben Nathan, Rashi's son-in-law (hence 'my relation'), but there is no unambiguous proof for it. The fragments of his works that have survived attest to his wideranging activity and his important standing among his contemporaries.

**Rabbi Joseph ben Judah** seems to have studied with Rashi, though there is no decisive evidence for it. As noted, he joined with Rabbi Azriel in posing questions to Rashi: the questions address Rashi as 'our teacher and our rabbi', using plural pronouns. In his response, Rashi refers to Rabbi Joseph as 'my beloved and my friend, Rabbi Joseph'. When they looked to Rashi for guidance, Rabbi Azriel and Rabbi Joseph were already recognized sages and halakhic authorities. Some accounts report that Rabbi Joseph came to Rashi from Germany, having previously studied, it seems, with Rabbi Isaac ben Judah, one of Rashi's teachers.

**Rabbi Samson ben Menahem and Rabbi Matthias ben Moses** are both said to have received words of Torah from Rashi. It may be assumed that they were his students.[24]

**Rabbi Judah (Juda).** MS Vatican 422 (a prayer book that also includes a commentary on the liturgical poems) contains the following statements: 'In 'Yishtabaḥ',[a] one says *ushevaḥah*, not *shevaḥ*.[b] It is so written in *Sefer sodot* by the sage Rabbi Juda . . . may the memory of the righteous be for a blessing, a student of Rashi.' If the source is reliable, it preserves a reference to a student of Rashi not known from other sources, unless he is to be identified with Rabbi Judah ben Abraham,

---

[23] Rabbenu Tam, *Sefer hayashar*, ii, *Responsa*, §45/5, p. 82.
[24] R. Samson wrote *Seder pesaḥ* in Rashi's name, as stated in MS Cambridge 791.

[a] The blessing recited following the psalms preliminary to the morning service.
[b] Alternative forms of a noun meaning 'praise'.

previously discussed. The manuscript is a collection of prayer texts and customs, which does not bear the mark of a single author. It is dated to about the fourteenth century.

**Rabbi Hillel.** In his commentary on the Torah, Rabbi Hayim Paltiel cites a chain of tradition originating with Rabbi Hillel, 'a student of Rashi'.[25] If the tradition is accurate, we have here another of Rashi's students.

What most characterizes these students is the diversity of their output. Many of them continued to produce a rich and varied literature within the *beit midrash* even after Rashi's death.

## Library and Sources

The collection of sources Rashi used in his responsa, as in all his writings, was richer and more diverse than that of his teachers and colleagues in Germany. Their number overall was relatively large, particularly given that manuscripts at the time were costly and rare. Zunz listed seventy-five such sources, including complete major works, portions of works, and individual responsa by particular sages. In addition to these texts, which he cited by name, Rashi relied on works of uncertain character, which he referred to as 'the explainers' (*hapoterim*), 'foreign languages' (*lo'azim*), or 'aggadic Midrash'. At times, he would simply say 'I heard', without identifying his source.

Rashi did not regard the Babylonian geonic halakhic sources as invariably binding. We have already seen how he disagreed with the author of *Halakhot gedolot* regarding the disqualification of all questionable meat and held that, even in his time, slaughtered animals could be examined and held to be kosher if appropriate rather than being automatically disqualified in any case of doubt. Nevertheless, he also used geonic sources in interpreting the Talmud.

It should be noted that there were no Jewish public libraries at the time. Most of the books mentioned in Rashi's works seem to have been in his personal library or his *beit midrash*. A few were not, and in those cases he relied on notes he had taken in his youth, while studying at the German yeshivas. He also used sources sent to him by sages in Germany in response to his requests. For example, although he occasionally cited the Jerusalem Talmud, he did not have the complete work in his library in Troyes. In one of his letters, he asked that his correspondents check

---

[25]  R. Hayim Paltiel b. Jacob, *Peirush hatorah*, 191. Some scholars believe that R. Yakar b. Makhir, who was active in Mainz at the end of the eleventh century, also studied with Rashi, but that view seems to be fundamentally in error. That is true also of another student, R. Asher. According to Lipschuetz, the existence of that student may be inferred from an account in MS Montefiore 98 ('Rashi', 28). On this entire matter, see Grossman, *The Early Sages of France* (Heb.), 174 and notes.

the text of tractate *Megilah* in the Jerusalem Talmud and report to him on what they find.[26]

The sources Rashi most often used include the Babylonian Talmud, the halakhic and aggadic *midrashim*, popular stories, the Aramaic translations of the Bible, geonic responsa and halakhic works, and liturgical poetry—both classical and that composed more recently in Ashkenaz. As mentioned, he also referred on rare occasions to the Jerusalem Talmud: he appears to have only had selections that had been copied while he was in Germany. He had the works of the early Spanish Jewish grammarians and made extensive use of the writings of Menahem ben Saruk and Dunash ben Labrat. In addition, he used *Sefer yetsirah* and Shabbetai Donnolo's *Sefer ḥakhmoni*, as well as many other works. The sources on which Rashi relied have been examined by Zunz, Weiss, Lipschuetz, Maarsen, Elfenbein, and most recently Ta-Shma, who surveyed not only the list of sources used by Rashi and his colleagues but also the way they used them and how they treated them. New sources found in recently discovered manuscripts expand the list a bit. I will not consider here Rashi's connections to Rabbenu Hananel's commentary on the Talmud or to the *Arukh* of Rabbi Nathan ben Jehiel (completed in 1101), which have been extensively studied: the scholarly consensus is that Rashi did not have complete versions of those texts. He nowhere expressly cites either of them, but it is possible that he heard, late in life, some of their ideas and used them to a limited extent in his comments without mentioning them by name.

In considering Rashi's sources, it is important to take note of his great curiosity. He never ceased to be interested in the heritage and writings of Jewish cultures outside his own Ashkenazi centre, especially those of Provence, Spain, and Byzantium. He learned of traditions orally and in writing from various friends and students, especially Rabbi Joseph Kara and Rabbi Shemayah. Kara informed him of other Ashkenazi traditions and Provençal traditions, and Rabbi Shemayah conveyed to him the traditions of the Jews of Byzantium. Rashi had copies of the sermons of Rabbi Moses Hadarshan, who had been active a generation before his own, and he made more extensive use of them than did any other medieval Jewish sage. Through his students from Bohemia ('the Land of Canaan'), he learned of the customs of that Jewish community. He met with people 'who had come from the Land of Israel' and heard from them about how they read the Torah there (Rashi on *Ber.* 62*a*, *ta'amei torah*). These traditions acquainted him somewhat with other languages, such as Greek and Arabic, with different customs, and with different halakhic traditions. Rashi's ties to the diverse Jewish cultural heritage—Ashkenazi,

---

[26]  Rashi asked R. Nathan b. Makhir to check R. Isaac b. Judah's version of the talmudic order *Kodashim* for him, noting that he had annotated a tractate in his possession in accord with that version (Rashi, *Responsa* (Heb.), ed. Elfenbein, §24; see also Rashi on *Zev.* 56*a*, *dekadishi*). At that time, Christian scholars often bequeathed their libraries to the Church or to the monasteries to which they belonged (see Riché, *Écoles et enseignement*, 216).

Babylonian, Spanish, and Italian—extended his sources and his intellectual world. It has recently been discovered, moreover, that in his editorial comments on the text of the Talmud, he relied on manuscripts that reached him from Jewish communities in the Muslim East.[27] This reliance on a wide range of sources is one of the most important characteristics of his *beit midrash* in Troyes, and it shows not only his inquisitiveness but also his great degree of openness.

We have no detailed information about what became of Rashi's library. Some sages in the succeeding generations claimed that they possessed works he had written or used, but they say nothing of how they came into their hands. It may be assumed that Rashi's own works and his books passed to members of his family, who then loaned them to others. Among the sages who claimed to possess some of Rashi's own writings or books from his library were Rabbenu Tam (his grandson) and Rabbi Isaac ben Moses of Vienna, author of *Or zarua*, who wrote at the beginning of the thirteenth century.

---

[27] Noam, 'Early Textual Traditions in Rashi's Editorial Comments on the Talmud' (Heb).

## PART II

# THE WRITINGS
# OF RASHI

# CHAPTER FOUR

# Commentary on the Torah

UNIVERSALLY REGARDED AS one of the most creative figures in medieval Jewish society, Rashi produced an oeuvre encompassing nearly every literary genre used by Jewish sages in Germany and France at the time. He wrote commentaries on the Bible and the Talmud, responsa, liturgical poetry, and, perhaps, legal documents related to community affairs.[1] His students wrote, in his name, collections of halakhic rulings and commentaries on the liturgical poems. Few indeed are the literary works that influenced Jewish national culture as much as Rashi's commentaries on the Bible and the Talmud. For hundreds of years in parts of the Jewish world, knowledge of the Pentateuch with Rashi's commentary was regarded as the basic obligation of every Jewish boy, and from the time the Talmud was first printed Rashi's commentary has been printed alongside it, becoming in effect an inseparable part of talmudic study. It is, moreover, more than just a commentary, for it preserves much valuable information about Rashi's world and on occasion about his personality. It is unlikely that any other work—with the exceptions of the Bible and Talmud themselves and the *midrashim*—had as great an effect on the intellectual heritage of the Jewish people as did Rashi's commentaries. In our own time, when the poet Samson Meltzer wanted to convey his distress over the alienation of a sizable portion of the Jewish nation from its traditional cultural heritage, he referred to ignorance of Rashi's commentary on the Torah as one of the clear indicators of that alienation.[2]

Rashi gained his enduring reputation by dint of his commentaries on the Bible and the Talmud, and those commentaries have been examined broadly and in great detail. Leading scholars have dealt with these vast works, and I will not examine them in detail here. Instead, I will address myself to the principal issues in each area.

Writing a commentary on the Talmud was not a revolutionary step, for the

---

[1] I could not find enough information to reconstruct the chronology of Rashi's works, and I do not consider the matter here. Benjamin Gelles attempts such a chronology in *Peshat and Derash in the Exegesis of Rashi*, 136–43. R. Shemayah's commentary on the liturgical poems includes some material that casts light on when Rashi wrote some of his commentaries on the Prophets and Writings, but not enough to provide a full account. See Ch. 8 for discussion of Rashi's commentary on the Psalms.

[2] Meltzer, 'Ashirah lerashi', in id., *Poems and Ballads* (Heb.), 24.

precedent had been set by Rabbenu Gershom and his students. But writing biblical commentary in the Ashkenazi periphery of the Jewish world was a new departure: no one before Rashi had done so in Christian Europe.

As far as we can tell, Rashi interpreted the entire Bible, but the comments that appear in his name on the books of Ezra, Nehemiah, Chronicles, and the final chapters of Job (beginning at 40: 25) are not, in fact, his. They differ from the other commentaries in style and interpretative characteristics and include references to sages who were active after Rashi's time. Some of Rashi's comments on the end of Job survive in manuscript (though not as a continuous commentary), allowing us to conclude that he interpreted the entire book and that his comments on its final chapters have been lost.[3] The comments on Ezra and Nehemiah attributed to him may be based on interpretations that he wrote, but they were edited and expanded by his students. Rashi's comments on other books were also supplemented by his students and others, which contributed to one of the main problems in examining his biblical commentary: that of determining the correct text.

Rashi's commentaries on the Bible—both those in print and those extant only in manuscript—incorporate comments by his students, especially Rabbi Shemayah, Rabbi Joseph Kara, and Rashbam. Some of these were inserted by Rashi himself, as a supplement or alternative to his own comments, and some were written by his students as marginal notes and inserted into the body of the commentary by later copyists.

The complex textual questions of Rashi's commentaries are important in the study of his literary output. The additions introduced by copyists and the wide dissemination of the commentaries resulted in multiple versions of the text. An important attempt to produce a critical edition of Rashi's commentary on the Torah was that of Abraham Berliner, but his edition is incomplete. As he recounts in his introduction, Berliner examined more than one hundred manuscripts and numerous printed versions and added references to Rashi's sources and other important annotations.[4] Editions of Rashi's commentaries on the Prophets and the Writings that make use of manuscript versions of the text include those of Mordecai L. Katzenellenbogen (Joshua and Judges), I. Maarsen (Isaiah, the Twelve Prophets, Psalms), Abraham J. Levy (excerpts from Ezekiel), Y. Rosenthal (Song of Songs), and Abraham Shoshana (Job). An important contemporary edition is that in the rabbinic Bible *Mikra'ot gedolot haketer*, edited by Menahem

<hr/>

[3] See Rashi on Job; Penkower, 'The End of Rashi's Commentary on Job'; Shoshana, introduction to Rashi, 'On Job' (Heb.), 64–6.

[4] His edition was first published in Berlin in 1867; a second edition, with important supplements, was published in Frankfurt in 1905 and reissued in photo-offset in Jerusalem in 1962. The first edition nevertheless remains important, for it contains notes that were omitted from the second. Another important edition in which Rashi's sources in rabbinic literature are noted, sometimes more fully, is *Ḥumash meḥokekei yehudah* (see also Zahari, *Rashi's Sources* (Heb.); Rashi, *Complete Works* (Heb.); *Torat ḥayim*).

Cohen, but it is an eclectic version subject to all the associated problems. As of this writing, it is about one-third complete.[5]

## The Text of Rashi's Commentary on the Torah

Of particular importance—and of great complexity—are the textual problems associated with Rashi's commentary on the Torah. The issue requires wide-ranging analysis, for any account of Rashi's interpretative method must be based on these texts. It is evident that the manuscript versions contain numerous additions, some bearing the names of their authors—particularly Rabbi Joseph Kara. Over time the names of those sages were omitted and their annotations absorbed into the body of the commentary. No other work by a Jewish sage of the Middle Ages is subject to so much uncertainty and dispute over its proper version. Three principal factors are responsible for this confusion: multiple editions of the commentary were written even during Rashi's lifetime, the commentary enjoyed wide dissemination, and the commentary is closely tied to the midrashic literature. The commentary gained a wide distribution as early as the twelfth and thirteenth centuries. Sages who worked with it and teachers who taught it made marginal notes of various sorts on their copies, some of which were incorporated into the body of the commentary by later copyists. The nature of the commentary, largely taken from rabbinic Midrash, also contributed to the diversity of the versions, as sages and copyists altered the *midrashim*. They variously copied them in full, abbreviated them, or deleted familiar *midrashim* and added others. These alterations, too, were incorporated into the commentary itself over time.

The text of Rashi's commentary has occupied the attention of scholars since the early days of *jüdische Wissenschaft* and continues to do so today. But medieval Jewish scholars, including some of the most prominent interpreters of Rashi, were also aware of the issue and grappled with it. At times, they sought to explain his words and resolve contradictions within his interpretations by arguing that one or another comment was not, in fact, his but had been added by others. Recent years have seen the publication of several new editions of Rashi's commentary on the Torah. They are important works and contribute to the resolution of some textual uncertainties, but they are not preferable to the Berliner edition previously mentioned.

The existence of many dozens of manuscripts and early printed copies of Rashi's commentary on the Torah[6] does not make the task of identifying Rashi's

[5] See also Sokolow, 'The Text of Rashi's Commentary on Job' (Heb.); Schneerson, *Principles of Rashi's Torah Commentary* (Heb.).

[6] As noted, Berliner attested to his use of more than one hundred manuscripts, but he did not enumerate or detail them: 'It would have been appropriate to refer here to the printed books and manuscripts that I used in my work, but the project would be a lengthy one, and if I set out to list all of them, mentioning them one by one, they would fill an entire book' (Berliner, introduction to Rashi, *Commentary on the Torah* (Heb.), p. xiv). On the issue overall, see also Sonne, 'On the Textual Criticism

original version any easier.[7] Elazar Touitou discussed the point in his important
study of the textual history of Rashi's commentary on the Torah:

One who examines the manuscripts of Rashi's commentary on the Torah will find that
there is not extant a single manuscript written by Rashi himself or copied around the time
that Rashi wrote his commentary. The earliest manuscripts that have come down to us
are from the second quarter of the thirteenth century, about one hundred thirty years after
Rashi's death, and there are only a few of those (for example, MS Munich, dated to 1233).
Of the other manuscripts, a few are from the end of the thirteenth century and most are
from the fourteenth and fifteenth centuries ... Teachers of Bible during the twelfth century, whether 'scripture-masters' [*kara'im*] or 'vocalization masters' [*nakdanim*], felt free
... to make various additions on their personal copies of Rashi's commentary, and those
additions altered the original text. In general, these additions made their way into the
manuscripts that have come down to us.[8]

Touitou suggested that the matter be resolved by regarding only the narrowest,
most basic kernel—that found in the earliest manuscripts and printed copies and
marked by certain linguistic and exegetical characteristics—as the original commentary written by Rashi himself:

From a text-critical perspective, it is wholly illogical to assume that the full version is the
original one and that, over time, passages were deleted from it in stages ... What we know
of medieval copying practices suggests that a copyist plying his trade would not dare to
alter knowingly what was written in the copy from which he was working, other than to
delete marker letters and source indicators or to make small, insignificant changes.

If that is correct, substantial portions of the commentary—at least a quarter of it—
must be regarded as not written by Rashi. That, in turn, would render moot many
discussions of Rashi's commentary on various passages in the Torah, especially
those that use close reading of his formulations as the basis for drawing conclusions
about his method and world-view.

   Although Touitou's suggestion is of great interest, the medieval manuscripts
fail to confirm it. It is hard to accept his fundamental premise that a medieval copyist—whether Jewish or not—would not dare to knowingly alter what appeared in
the copy from which he was working. There can be no doubt that Jewish copyists

---

of Rashi's Torah Commentary' (Heb.), 42–56; Avinery, *Rashi's Palace* (Heb.), i. 68–77; Touitou,
'Evolution of the Text of Rashi's Commentary on the Torah' (Heb.); Heide, 'The Longer Variants'.
Recently Dahan has suggested using the Latin glosses of difficult words in Rashi written following
the polemic on the Talmud in 1240 to ascertain the original text of Rashi's commentary (see 'Un dossier
latin').

   [7] 'The popularity of Rashi's commentary is matched in magnitude by the vast range of alternative
readings and later interpolations that can be found in it' (Cohen, introduction to the Pentateuch,
*Mikra'ot gedolot haketer*, i. 12).

   [8] Touitou, 'Evolution of the Text of Rashi's Commentary on the Torah' (Heb.), 216; see also id.,
*Exegesis in Perpetual Motion* (Heb.), 229–37.

in Germany and France during the Middle Ages did not shrink from changing their sources. What remains of the oeuvre of the medieval Jewish sages, be it biblical commentary or halakhic literature, does not support the notion that the 'narrow kernel' is the best text, even if that supposed kernel is intelligible. Numerous examples of this phenomenon survive from all branches of medieval Jewish literature, and it appears in Latin literature too.[9] In my assessment, some 90 per cent of what is conventionally regarded as Rashi's commentary on the Torah is original.

## MS Leipzig 1 and Rashi's Commentary on the Torah

An important source for investigating the original version of Rashi's commentary on the Torah and how it was written and supplemented is MS Leipzig 1. Although it contains some later additions and textual corruptions, this version is very close to the original. Its margins contain important annotations by Rabbi Shemayah.

The manuscript was written by the scribe and copyist Makhir during the thirteenth century. Makhir states frequently that he possessed the manuscript of Rashi's commentary on the Torah on which Rabbi Shemayah himself had written his annotations. There is no reason not to believe him, and his statement is consistent with how he treated Rashi's commentary—that is, the copy in Rabbi Makhir's possession had been written by Rabbi Shemayah, and from it Rabbi Makhir copied both Rashi's commentary on the Torah and Rabbi Shemayah's annotations. There is abundant proof for this premise, including Rabbi Makhir's apologetic account at one point of his need to stop working from Rabbi Shemayah's book, because of a tear in its margin, and use a different source instead. This manuscript must be regarded as one of the most important documents for the study of the textual history of Rashi's commentary on the Torah, both for its early date and for the version of Rashi's commentary that it contains.[10]

Certainly not everything included in the body of Rashi's commentary in MS Leipzig 1 was actually Rashi's work. Rabbi Shemayah himself reported that he made additions and deletions. At one point, he took the liberty of deleting Rashi's interpretation and replacing it with one he had heard from a Jew from Byzantium. In that instance, evidence of the change survived, but there may well be others in which Rabbi Shemayah's alterations left no traces. There also are additions to the material in the body of Rashi's commentary. At numerous points, Rabbi Shemayah states that he inserted corrections or supplements at Rashi's explicit request ('my master directed me to annotate'); elsewhere he based changes on his own judgement. Rabbi

---

[9]  Many examples are cited in West's classic work, *Textual Criticism*. Among the texts subject to change (including deletions), he included interpretative works (p. 16). Evidence of deletions in Jewish writings is provided in Grossman, *The Early Sages of France* (Heb.), 186–7, 311–15.

[10]  On MS Leipzig 1 and its importance, including evidence for the arguments I am advancing here, see Grossman, *The Early Sages of France* (Heb.), 187–92. On R. Shemayah and his affinity to Rashi, see ibid. 347–427 and the discussion of Rashi's students above.

Shemayah's basic operational premise was that if Rashi never ceased to make changes in his commentary in order to improve it, there was no reason why he should not continue that sacred work after Rashi's death, given that the truth was Rashi's guide in all his literary efforts. It also is possible that Rabbi Makhir himself made alterations to the text, as was the practice of many medieval copyists.[11]

All these many supplements, introduced during Rashi's life and after his death, make it doubtful that the original text of the commentary can ever be reconstructed. Rashi himself kept revisiting and supplementing it, and Rabbi Shemayah continued to do so in accordance with his instructions. What, then, is to be considered the 'original version' of this commentary—the first version written by Rashi himself and including all his own supplements or the version that included Rabbi Shemayah's alterations, written at Rashi's direction and in his spirit?

Two principal conclusions follow from this discussion. First, it very difficult to speak of a single ur-text of Rashi's commentary, for multiple versions already existed during his lifetime. Second, notwithstanding the great importance of MS Leipzig 1, its version can in no sense be regarded as the original version of Rashi's commentary.

## Rashi's Interpretative Method

### The Basis: Pursuit of Significance and Message

According to Rashi, every biblical verse—and, in particular, every verse in the Torah—bears a significance and a message that go beyond merely conveying information. Accordingly, one must do more than interpret the literal meanings of the words. For example, Genesis 38: 5 tells us that Judah was in Chezib (Heb.: כזיב) when his wife gave birth to their son, Shelah. Rashi comments: '*He was at Chezib*— [Chezib] is a place name. But I say that because she then ceased to bear children, it was called Chezib[a] [as in *naḥal akhzav*[b]] . . . for if that were not so, what would the text be telling us?' Let us consider Rashi's thought process here. According to his interpretation, the place came to be called Chezib only later, after it became clear that Judah's wife was no longer fertile and that Shelah, her third son, would be her last. The disappointment was so great that Judah, or someone else, found it appropriate to depict it by changing the name of the place where Shelah was born. Rashi based this original *midrash* of his on the literal meaning of the root *kaf-zayin-beit* (כזב).[12] The first interpretation of the name Chezib is Rashi's own; the second has its origins in the *midrash*.

---

[11] On the liberties taken by Ashkenazi writers and copyists with the texts available to them, see Sussman, 'The Study Tradition and Textual Tradition of the Jerusalem Talmud' (Heb.), 41–2 n. 130.

[12] He later cites a *midrash* from *Genesis Rabbah*, but it pertains to the name 'Shelah', not to 'Chezib'.

[a] Assonant with the word for 'a disappointment'.

[b] A stream that flows only during the rainy season.

Another example: Exodus 18: 5 recounts that Jethro came to Moses 'in the wilderness'. Rashi comments: 'We [already] knew that they were in the wilderness; rather, Scripture is praising Jethro, for he dwelled amidst all earthly honour, yet his heart moved him to go out to the wilderness, a place of disorder, to hear words of Torah.'

Rashi's basic premise in both of these interpretations is that the names of people or places would not be mentioned unless they implicitly contained some additional message. The account of the blasphemer in Leviticus 24: 10 reports his mother's name—Shelomit, daughter of Dibri—but his own name goes unmentioned. Rashi takes the mother's name to have been mentioned because of its symbolic value: Shelomit, related to *shalom*, alludes to her practice of greeting everyone she met; Dibri, from *dibur* (speech), alludes to her tendency to chat with everyone rather than behaving modestly. As a result, her son blasphemed. In other words, the name, which is not her original name, is mentioned as a call to modest behaviour. The exegetical move here is identical to that used in connection with Chezib, though here Rashi relied on an existing *midrash*. And so, too, regarding the mention of Cozbi daughter of Zur, who was killed by Phineas: '*The name of the . . . woman who was killed* [Num. 25: 15]—This is to inform you of the extent of the Midianites' hatred, for they consigned a king's daughter to harlotry in order to cause Israel to sin.' The interpretation is not far removed from the plain meaning. Rashi used this approach not only with respect to personal and place names but also with respect to events. The book of Numbers, for example, recounts the conquests of Sihon against the Moabites (Num. 21: 26), and Rashi asks: 'Why did this need to be written?'

These illustrations, and countless others, lead to the conclusion that Rashi saw significance and purpose in every name, time, place, and event—indeed, in every detail—mentioned in the Torah. Neither the simple factual account nor the desire to enhance literary quality can provide a full explanation for something having been written.

The essence of Rashi's commentary on the Bible—especially on the Torah—and his extensive use of rabbinic Midrash cannot be understood without appreciating the full significance of this idea, which effectively serves as the basis for the entire commentary. As he sees it, the Torah is not merely a historical or literary work. It is, rather, a holy text conferred on human beings by God to guide them in the way of truth, and it must be read and interpreted in that light. Every detail, large or small, has its own unique value. It is therefore hardly surprising that in seeking out its meaning, Rashi would have frequent recourse to rabbinic Midrash or that he would often suggest more than one meaning. This perspective also accounts for his occasional remark that 'I do not know what this teaches us': it results from his expectation to find a message in every scriptural detail, combined with his extraordinary forthrightness and great humility. His student Rabbi Shemayah learned well from him, also acknowledging, in his supplements, that sometimes he did not know the reason for some detail. In one case, Rabbi Shemayah's comment made its way into Rashi's own commentary, inserted by copyists who were used to finding it there.[13]

## Interpreting the Verse in Isolation

Medieval Jewish biblical exegetes followed, as a rule, one of two approaches to the text. One considered only the specific words; the other looked at the broader unit and concentrated on the problems that it raised. Rashi fell within the first category. He interpreted individual verses or phrases, only rarely examining the structure and characteristics of the unit as a whole.

In treating the isolated verse, Rashi directed his attention to its linguistic, content-related, and conceptual aspects; on rare occasions he also commented on literary matters. He frequently dealt with the meaning of difficult words, often considering their roots, both grammatical and etymological, and their parallels in Scripture and in the language of the sages. He also dedicated considerable space to rabbinic Midrash and legends.

Rashi did not see himself as an objective interpreter working at arm's length from his material or dealing with an ancient historical text. He believed, rather, that the material was relevant and highly significant to the daily life of every Jew, wherever he might be, and he manifested intense emotional involvement with it. He therefore directed considerable attention—sometimes explicitly, though more often indirectly—to the pedagogical messages conveyed by the text.

Who were the intended audience of Rashi's commentary? Who was the student he envisioned as he wrote? I share the view that Rashi wrote his commentaries on the Bible and the Talmud on many levels, allowing readers to learn from them in accordance with their own education and intellectual skills. That his commentaries include conceptual and pedagogical messages—explicit as well as implicit—is the best evidence for that. At the same time, the nature of the *midrashim* he cited, the express pedagogical teachings, and the avoidance of any detailed, organized treatment of overall theoretical issues all suggest that he devoted considerable attention to 'the average person', 'the educated reader' who was not a professional scholar. He saw a need to reach this group in order to fortify their resistance to Christian religious propaganda meant to promote the conversion of Jews. I will return to the issue of Rashi's intended audience in Chapter 6, in the context of his commentary on the Talmud.

---

[13] The commentary on 'mother of Jacob and Esau' (Gen. 28: 5) states 'I do not know what this is meant to teach us'. Although the statement was inserted into the text of Rashi's commentary, in MS Leipzig 1 it appears as a supplementary note by R. Shemayah.

## Why Did Rashi Avoid the Broader Issues?

Only on rare occasions did Rashi pay attention to the broad theoretical issues raised by the biblical text, and even then he did not comment explicitly on the principal questions. He noted, for example, that the purpose of the binding of Isaac was to demonstrate to the nations of the world the magnitude of Abraham's faith, but he did so almost as an aside in the course of commenting on the verse '*For now I know that you fear God* [Gen. 22: 12]—Henceforth, I have something with which I can reply to the Satan and to the nations of the world who wonder why I have affection for you.' Rashi does not comment explicitly on the oddity of the verse. Did God not know Abraham's thoughts, and the profundity of his faith, even without the test? What need was there for a test? We wait in vain for Rashi to take the opportunity, as Nahmanides did in commenting on this episode, to deal generally with the question of testing in the Bible. Rashi was content to consider the local problem.

Another example appears in Rashi's treatment of the episode in which Jacob took advantage of his father Isaac's blindness to acquire the blessing Isaac had meant to bestow on Esau (Gen 27: 1–40). Here, too, Rashi does not explicitly discuss the pedagogical issues posed by Jacob's conduct. Instead, he treats it indirectly, at four distinct points. He begins his comments on the passage by citing a *midrash* from *Genesis Rabbah* 68: 8, according to which Isaac became blind 'so that Jacob might acquire the blessings' (Rashi on Gen. 27: 1). In other words, it was a heavenly decree, meant to demonstrate that Rebecca and Jacob, though acting deceitfully, were in fact carrying out God's will. When Esau finally appears to claim the blessing already bestowed on Jacob, Isaac says to him: 'Your brother came with guile.' Rashi, following Onkelos's translation, glosses 'with guile' as 'with wisdom'. In addressing his father, Jacob had used ambiguous wording in order to avoid, as far as possible, any outright lie (Rashi on Gen. 27: 19, 24). Moreover, by the end of the episode Isaac was reconciled to the outcome: '*Now he must remain blessed* [Gen. 27: 33]—[This is] to preclude one's saying that had Jacob not deceived his father, he would not have acquired the blessing. To avoid that, he agreed and blessed him of his own mind.'

Here, too, Rashi was a product of his time and place. Philosophy and rationalistic enquiry in general were common in Muslim lands and heavily influenced Jewish sages in Babylonia, North Africa, Muslim Spain, and even Provence. But they were not as common in Christian Europe at the time. The questions raised by contemplation of the environment, of the fate of mankind, of the biblical texts themselves—questions related to the creation of the universe, the relationship between nature and miracle, or divine justice—did not occupy people then the way they occupy contemporary men and women who expect rational solutions to problems. With the onset of the twelfth-century renaissance, discussed in the Introduction, Jewish biblical interpreters in France also began to deal with these questions and with questions regarding the reasons for the commandments. Two of the leading writers on these issues were Rabbi Joseph Kara and Rashbam, whose careers had begun by the end of the eleventh century.[14] Nevertheless, Rashi's treatment of theological questions, albeit in a localized way—as in the case of the binding of Isaac—shows that he was aware of the issues. Given his intellectual curiosity and his acquaintance with the teachings of Jewish sages in Muslim lands, it is hard to imagine he was unaware of the problematic nature of various passages in the Bible. It also is quite possible that he refrained from treating these issues in a comprehensive and systematic manner because he sensed that his generation was not ready for that sort of treatment. The problems raised by rationalistic enquiry were of no concern to most of the Jews of Germany and France. Some of them were probably exposed to these issues when they visited Muslim lands for commercial reasons, but in Rashi's time, there were very few people who might do so. In reading the commentaries of Rabbi Joseph Kara and Rashbam, one gets the sense that their new teachings, for all their great importance, are not of the sort that generate emotional attachment—a premise supported as well by the historical fate of their works and the small number of surviving manuscripts.[15]

## Rashi's Profound Affection for Midrash

Rashi's commentary on the Torah is largely taken from rabbinic Midrash. Only some 25 per cent of it, dealing primarily with linguistic matters, is original. The textual uncertainties discussed earlier preclude any precise determination of that percentage, and it is among the supplements, especially those by Rabbi Shemayah, that Midrash occupies a particularly prominent place. On occasion, Rashi cites his source; most often, he does not.

Rashi made use of aggadic Midrash in five ways: to resolve a difficulty in the wording of a passage, to explain the purpose of seemingly superfluous words, to identify anonymous people or places, to broaden the narrative background for the actions and motives of the protagonists, and to make a point for pedagogical purposes. Let me illustrate.

Exodus 15: 27 reports that during the Israelites' stay in the wilderness, they camped at Elim, 'where there were twelve springs of water and seventy palm trees'. From Rashi's perspective, that detail requires explanation—why do we need to know the number of springs and palm trees? He cites a *midrash* which explains that the numbers allude to the twelve Israelite tribes and the seventy elders who led them.[16] The biblical narrative goes on to say that 'on the fifteenth day of the second

[14] See Grossman, *The Early Sages of France* (Heb.), 302–23, 473–92, and the literature cited there.

[15] See esp. R. Joseph Kara on 1 Sam. 1: 17: 'And I know that all students of aggadah and Talmud will condemn this explanation, for they will not give up the interpretation offered by our sages in *Rosh hashanah*, and they will follow that interpretation. But the wise will know to follow the [plain] reading and interpret the matter truthfully.'     [16] *Mekhilta* on Exod. 15: 27.

month after their departure from the land of Egypt' they demanded food and were given manna. For Rashi, specification of a date is a red flag—why mention it? He replies, following a rabbinic *midrash*, that 'the date of this encampment was specified to teach that they ate the left-over dough [from the matzot baked when they left Egypt] for sixty-one meals, and the manna came down for them on the sixteenth day of Iyar' (*Shab.* 87*b*–88*a*).

Rashi often used aggadic Midrash to identify anonymous figures. The two Hebrews whom Moses found fighting (Exod. 2: 13), who go unnamed in the Torah, are identified as Dathan and Abiram, and it is they who try to save some excess manna for the next day, contrary to Moses' directive (Exod. 16: 20). 'As one of them was opening his sack' (Gen. 42: 27) refers to Levi, 'who was left alone, without his partner Simeon'. Jacob's 'granddaughters' (Gen. 46: 7) are Asher's daughter Serah and Levi's daughter Jochebed. 'Saul the son of a Canaanite woman' (Gen. 46: 10) was the son of Dinah, who had been taken by a Canaanite man.

The Torah offers only spare accounts of the lives of the patriarchs and national heroes. The midrashic literature greatly expands on those accounts, but Rashi took the middle ground. He interwove some of the *midrashim* into his commentary, making the biblical characters, through their ways of life, into more vital and fascinating bearers of enduring pedagogical messages. For example, the Torah says nothing about what Abraham and Isaac may have felt en route to and from Isaac's binding on Mount Moriah. Rashi describes the powerful emotional tension experienced by the protagonists—Abraham's misgivings and Isaac's feelings—as well as Sarah's calamitous reaction to learning what had happened. For the most part, Rashi did not explicate the meaning of the *midrashim*, leaving that to the reader. And so, for example, he begins his interpretation of the story of Isaac's binding with two opposing *midrashim*:

*And it came to pass after these things* [Gen 22: 1, OJPS]—Some of our rabbis say it was after Satan's words,[c] for he accused [Abraham], saying that 'From every feast prepared by Abraham, he did not sacrifice before You even one bullock or one ram.' [God] replied, 'He did everything for his son, but if I were to say sacrifice him before Me, he would not withhold him.' But others say it was after Ishmael's words, who exalted himself above Isaac.

As a practical matter, these *midrashim* deal with the question of who faced the greater test—Abraham, who bound his son, or Isaac, who submitted to it. Rashi does not explain the meaning of the two *midrashim*, but his selection of specifically these, in preference to many others dealing with the phrase 'after these things', makes his intent clear. In any case, Rashi's explication of the binding of Isaac is directed primarily to emphasizing Abraham's great love for God, God's affection for him, and the enduring significance of the episode. The pedagogical aspect of

---

[c] The Hebrew translated 'things' in the biblical verse is *devarim*, which can also mean 'words'.

the story and its meaning for the Jewish people guided Rashi's choice of these two *midrashim*. Rashi saw his primary contribution as situated in the pedagogical sphere, not in that of literary expansion of the story or analysis of its theological significance.

Despite his strong attachment to the midrashic literature, Rashi did not hesitate on occasion to comment that a *midrash* does not suit the wording of the biblical text. For example, he noted that the rabbinic *midrash* associating the words *leshad hashamen* ('baked with oil' [Num. 11: 8, OJPS]) with *shadayim* (breasts) was in error, for 'breasts have nothing to do with oil'. But he was not consistent in his language-based criticism and sometimes selected *midrashim* that clashed with the wording or the subject of the biblical text.

### *Peshat* and *Derash* in Rashi's Commentaries

Scholars have struggled mightily with the relationship between *peshat* and *derash* in Rashi's commentary on the Torah,[d] and opinion remains divided.[17] Let me begin with Moshe Ahrend's summation of the development of the terms:

And so we must undertake a diachronic study of the term *peshuto shel mikra* [the plain meaning of the scriptural text] and attempt to understand its various incarnations and the stages of its development. At first, it represented only the written text in context. For Rashi, it became a criterion that allowed an exegete to distinguish three sorts of interpretations: those that the verse 'incorporates' and requires; those that the verse 'tolerates', because they are consistent with it; and those that are contrary to the verse's plain meaning and cannot be tolerated by it at all. Rashi did not forswear any sort of interpretation and chose among them on the basis of theological and methodological principles that are clearly reflected in his writings. One of the most important of them is that the plain meaning of the text should never be uprooted, inasmuch as 'a verse never loses its plain meaning'.[18]

All agree that Rashi devoted much care to selecting the *midrashim* that he incorporated into his commentary. He referred to his method at several points, and though his description is not as lucid as it might be, and he is not fully consistent

---

[17] There is an extensive literature on the subject, and I will refer here only to six writers: Lipschuetz, 'Rashi' (Heb.); Halivni, *Peshat and Derash*; Kamin, *Rashi* (Heb.); Gelles, *Peshat and Derash in the Exegesis of Rashi*; Touitou, 'Rashi's Use of Rabbinic Midrash' (Heb.); Ahrend, 'Clarifying the Concept of "Plain Meaning of the Text"' (Heb.). According to Halivni, *peshat* connotes primarily the textual context of the verse. Kamin, in contrast, takes it to mean the literal meaning of the verse. Ahrend believes *peshat* refers to 'the place where the river flows' and that it likewise connotes the flow of the scriptural passage: 'This place is simply the text placed before the reader, spread out before him like a letter' ('Clarifying the Concept' (Heb.), 241). On the term's development through the ages and its meaning in Rashi's *beit midrash*, see Halivni, *Peshat and Derash*; Ahrend, 'Clarifying the Concept' (Heb.). Touitou lists seven conclusions regarding Rashi's method of using rabbinic Midrash ('Rashi's Use of Rabbinic Midrash' (Heb.), 77).

[18] Ahrend, 'Clarifying the Concept of "Plain Meaning of the Text"' (Heb.), 259.

[d] *Peshat* is the plain meaning of the text; *derash* is its midrashic explication.

in applying the method, he clearly imposed certain standards in selecting the *midrashim*. Were those standards solely exegetical, or were they also aesthetic and conceptual? Did Rashi ever cite a *midrash* for which there was no exegetical need, doing so solely for literary or pedagogical purposes? Why did he usually consider one *midrash* sufficient but sometimes cite two or more? Is there a deliberate order in his citation of these *midrashim*?

Rashi's gathering of the *midrashim* was itself a process of interpretation. He selected only a small number of the many available, and his own comments show that he did so only after close examination and careful assessment. His statements at various points regarding the criteria that guided him suggest he tried to choose the *midrashim* best suited to the wording of the verse and best integrated into its context, as well as those that could resolve difficulties in the text. In his comments on Genesis 3: 8, for example, he says: 'There are many aggadic *midrashim*, and our rabbis have already arranged them properly in *Genesis Rabbah* and other midrashic works, but I come only [to deal with] the plain meaning of the text and with aggadah that resolves the words of scripture as "a word fitly spoken" [*davar davur al ofnav* (Prov. 25: 11, OJPS)].' Even if the full meaning of what he says here is not absolutely clear, and even if Rashi did not always stick to those principles consistently, this methodological rule suggests that he set himself certain standards for the selection of *midrashim*. Nehama Leibowitz has already noted in that regard:

This bibliographic note—'our rabbis have already arranged them properly in *Genesis Rabbah* and other midrashic works'—shows that Rashi did not intend his commentary to be 'a collection of *midrashim*' or an anthology of rabbinic sayings. It is as if he is saying: one who is interested in studying *midrashim* for their own sake should not look for them in my commentary; rather, he should refer to the collections of *midrashim* and take them from there. 'But I come only [to deal with] the plain meaning of the text and with aggadah that resolves . . .'. That is, I come to explain repetitions, to resolve difficulties, but not to decorate or beautify or add to Scripture.[19]

Other statements made by Rashi suggest that the term 'a word fitly spoken' encompasses two principal components: an interpretation that adheres to the rules of grammar and that corresponds to the subject and the compositional context. This can be seen, for example, in his comment on Isaiah 26: 11: 'I have seen many aggadic *midrashim* on the verses in this passage, above and below, but they are irreconcilable either with the *grammar* or with the *sequence of verses*, so I was required to explain it in a fit manner' (emphasis added). The basic linguistic meaning of 'a word fitly spoken' is something well grounded, supported, and integrated in all respects. Rashi so interpreted the expression in his comments on Proverbs as well as in a responsum to Rabbi Shemayah, surviving in manuscript, in which he interpreted a verse from a liturgical poem:

---

[19] Leibowitz, 'Rashi's Use of Midrash' (Heb.), 503.

*Her speech is fitly engraved* [*diburah al ofan ḥakukah*]—It is spoken on a sound foundation, with a fit aspect [*ofanah*] and on a solid base; it is properly established. And that is the quality connoted by 'a word fitly spoken' [*davar davur al ofnav*], that is, the statement is *integrated and well grounded and based*. Of the same form is *nasati emeikha afunah* [Ps. 88: 16],[e] referring to it as settled within me on its base ... Thus he interpreted it in a responsum to me.[20]

Why, then, have scholars struggled so with the relationship between *peshat* and *derash* in Rashi's commentaries? The primary reason is his lack of consistency. A close examination of his commentaries shows that he uses rabbinic *midrashim* that fail to meet his two criteria of linguistic and substantive compatibility. If we judge on the basis of what appears in the sources, we find that Rashi did not always insist on those criteria. On occasion, he cites *midrashim* that are far removed from the plain meaning, linguistically or substantively, without comment, and such cases are not limited to halakhic *midrashim*. He himself sometimes alludes to the great divide between the *midrashim* he cites and the plain meaning of the verses. Some have attempted to account for Rashi's use of these *midrashim* by arguing that they satisfy one or the other of the foregoing criteria, but their somewhat contrived efforts are unpersuasive. Because the issue is central to an understanding of Rashi's method, let me offer four illustrations of my point.

**1.** The injunction against eating forbidden foods begins as follows: 'These are the living things [*haḥayah*] which ye may eat among all the beasts [*habehemah*] that are on the earth' (Lev. ɪɪ: 2, OJPS). The difficulty is obvious: why are 'beasts' referred to initially as 'living things'?[f] Rashi offers a plain-meaning interpretation, mentioned also in *Ḥulin* 70b, according to which '"beasts" are included within the category of "living things"', that is, *ḥayah* is a general noun that includes *behemah*. But Rashi is not content solely with the plain-meaning interpretation and first offers a rather remote *midrash*: '*These are the living things*—it refers to life, for Israel is bonded to God and ought to be alive. He therefore separated them from impurity.' In other words, the statement 'These are the living things which ye may eat' means that the commandment instils life into the Israelites. This interpretation is far removed from the plain meaning of the biblical text and from the 'fitness' that Rashi repeatedly emphasizes.

Is it conceivable that Rashi did not sense the magnitude of the divide between this *midrash* and the plain meaning of the verse? It is evident that he—like the

---

[20] MS Parma 655, fo. 33, emphasis added.

[e] The English versions do not reflect Rashi's understanding of this verse: OJPS: 'I have borne thy terrors, I am distracted'; NJPS: 'I suffer your terrors wherever I turn', with a note that the meaning of the Hebrew is uncertain.

[f] The two Hebrew terms often indicate different sorts of creatures.

author of the *midrash*—was motivated by pedagogical considerations whose purpose was to energize the Jews to avoid forbidden foods and to emphasize the advantage they enjoyed over the non-Jews who ate them. That, rather than any linguistic or substantive factor, is what led him to make use of this *midrash*.

**2.** In describing the animals that boarded Noah's ark, the text refers to 'all that lives' (Gen. 6: 19). Rashi interprets: 'even demons'. Could he have had any linguistic or contextual rationale for citing that *midrash*?

**3.** Replying to her family's question, Rebecca says she is willing to go with Abraham's servant: '"Will you go with this man?" And she said, "I will go"' (Gen. 24: 58). Rashi comments: 'I will go of my own will, even if you do not wish it.' Rashi may have selected this *midrash* because Rebecca used the verb 'I will go' instead of simply replying 'Yes', but he was familiar enough with biblical style to know that there was no real problem here requiring explanation. In any case, there is no linguistic or substantive basis for the interpretation. He evidently cited the *midrash* because he wanted to portray Rebecca in a positive light, as one who rejected her father's house, a place of idolatry and deceit.

**4.** Joseph, looking for his brothers, was told by the man he met in the field that he had heard them saying 'Let us go to Dothan [*dotainah*]' (Gen. 37: 17). Rashi interprets, in accordance with the plain meaning, that the reference is to a place called Dothan, but he adds a midrashic interpretation that he also mentions in his comment on *Sotah* 13*b*, *misham genavuhu*: '*Dotainah*—to seek contrivances based on religion [*datot*] that can be used to kill you'. In other words, the brothers were seeking excuses based on halakhah for killing Joseph. The word *dotainah*, which clearly means 'to Dothan', presents no difficulties that would warrant reference to that *midrash*, which is removed, linguistically and substantively, from the simple meaning. What criterion, then, did Rashi use in selecting *midrashim* to be incorporated into his commentary?

Rashi's statement that he considered only the plain meaning of the text should be taken as merely a declaration of intent, one that guided him with respect to most of the *midrashim* he selected. It has been suggested that the declaration pertains only to the individual verse in which it appears and not to his commentary overall, but that strikes me as unreasonable. In general, one can identify the linguistic or substantive link between the wording of the verse and the *midrash* Rashi cites, and Rashi himself sometimes comments on the link. Nevertheless, one cannot take the declaration as an unambiguous and universally binding principle, and there are two factors that led Rashi to stray from it. In writing his commentary on the Bible, Rashi set himself two goals, whose value, he believed, exceeded that of linguistic and substantive exegesis: to educate Jews and to fortify them and equip them for the difficult confrontation with Christian supersessionist propaganda. He attributed overriding importance to these goals and invested great effort in their achievement. When he found a rabbinic *midrash* that promoted one of these goals, he did not hesitate to cite it, even if it was far removed from the plain meaning of the verse. But even these two goals cannot fully explain Rashi's use of aggadic Midrash. It is evident that he felt deep affection for these *midrashim*, and he sometimes found it hard to refrain from citing one even if it clashed with his declaration of intent. Nor should we forget that Rashi took literally the sages' 'historical' legends, seeing them as an accurate reflection of historical reality.

Evidence for that can be found in Rashi's choosing 'divided *midrashim*', that is, *midrashim* that contradict each other. The problem posed by this practice, which I will consider further below, has troubled many interpreters of Rashi, and their failure to take adequate account of the considerations just discussed has led them to offer various far-fetched solutions. It seems to me that the reason for the practice was Rashi's deep affection for rabbinic *midrashim*, which led him to cite them in cases where he thought they could make an important literary or conceptual contribution. And he did so even where they stood in conflict with another citation from the midrashic literature, which he likewise cited where it was appropriate.

## Midrash as Dough to be Kneaded

That so large a part of Rashi's commentary on the Torah is taken from the midrashic and talmudic literature raises a basic question: in what sense can Rashi be considered a great exegete, and how did a book that was largely a collection of excerpts become, not long after it was written, a signal work that would have a decisive influence on Jewish culture through the ages?

It would be a great mistake to see Rashi's commentaries as nothing more than anthologies. It was only after careful consideration that he selected the rabbinic *midrashim* that he regarded as best suited to his purpose, and after selecting a *midrash* he had to decide how to formulate it. He often reworked the rabbis' wording, deleting parts of the rabbinic give-and-take, adding or removing words, and generally altering the text. He strove to conform the *midrash* to the wording of the verse and to present it clearly and understandably. On occasion, his reworking seems to have been intended to conform the *midrash* to his own pedagogical agenda. All this reworking of the *midrashim* produced stylistic consistency, and his commentaries thus appear as unified compositions rather than a patchwork. At the same time, the variety, the linguistic wealth, the repetitions, the consolidation, the integration, and the turns of phrase were frequently subordinated to the author's exegetical purposes.

Rashi's comments on the legal portions of the Torah are nearly identical to the halakhic *midrashim*, though here, too, he tried to follow the rules he had set for his commentary overall with respect to the choice of *midrashim* and their style and wording. In the legal portions, as in the narrative, he saw his primary task as exegetical. He carefully chose a few of the *halakhot* related to each subject and sometimes noted that he would not deal with the halakhic *midrashim* because they did not align with the plain meaning. And, as noted, in a few instances he interpreted the verse in a manner contrary to the halakhic ruling based on it.

On the face of it, Rashi's commentary was an easy one to write, but a closer look discloses the hard work he put into it and the way he transformed the collected *midrashim* into a work bearing the mark of one creative personality. To illustrate, let me compare two of his comments on Exodus 1 with their underlying midrashic sources in *Sotah*. This sort of comparison offers two benefits: one can identity the version of the *midrash* that Rashi used—namely, the version in the Talmud—and one can compare his biblical commentary with his commentary on the Talmud.

On the verse 'a new king arose' (Exod. 1: 8), Rashi wrote: 'Rav and Samuel [disagree as to the meaning]. One says [a] genuinely new [king]; the other says his decrees were renewed.' The version of the *midrash* in its source in *Sotah* (11a) contains an explanation of the second opinion, according to which the Bible is speaking of a king who became estranged from Israel rather than a different king: 'for it is not written that the king of Egypt died and another reigned in his place'. Rashi omitted the explanation not only for the sake of brevity but also because he did not consider it a serious explanation. Another instance pertains to Rashi's comment on Pharaoh's statement 'Let us deal shrewdly with them' (Exod. 1: 10). The Talmud records Rabbi Hama bar Hanina's *midrash*, which explains why the Egyptians decided to drown the Israelite children rather than afflicting them in some other way. True to his form in other places, Rashi omits Rabbi Hama bar Hanina's name, shortens the dialectic give-and-take, and deletes part of the *midrash*.

In most instances, Rashi was content to cite the rabbinic statements after reworking them to make them fit his personal style. Only rarely did he deal with the significance of the *midrashim* and examine their conceptual messages. I am speaking here not only of 'historical' *midrashim*, which he accepted literally, but also of 'remote' *midrashim* bearing conceptual or symbolic messages; they too were cited without consideration of their meaning. For example, on the verse 'So Moses took his wife and sons, mounted them on the [NJPS: an] ass, and went back to the land of Egypt' (Exod. 4: 20, OJPS), Rashi cites the *midrash* in *Pirkei derabi eli'ezer* (ch. 31): '[It was] the special ass, the ass that Abraham saddled to go to the binding of Isaac and on which the King Messiah is destined to be revealed, as it is said, "humble, riding on an ass" [Zech. 9: 9].' The author of the *midrash*, and Rashi after him, was dealing with two questions: why was it necessary to recount that Moses mounted his wife and sons on an ass, and why does the Torah speak of 'the ass' (*haḥamor*, with the definite article), implying that it was a specific, well-known ass. The author of the *midrash* associated the ass with two others—the one that transported Abraham to the binding of Isaac and the one on which the Redeemer is destined to ride in accordance with Zechariah's prophecy. What idea is embodied in this *midrash*? Clearly, its writer did not think the Bible was referring to a certain ass endowed with extreme longevity. Rashi avoided that question and simply cited the *midrash* itself.[21]

Only in a handful of cases did Rashi grapple with the message implicit in the *midrash*. One instance pertains to the treatment in *Genesis Rabbah* 76:14 of the precision with which the Torah recounts the number of male and female animals sent by Jacob to Esau as an appeasement gift. After citing the *midrash*, Rashi wrote: 'I do not know the precise intention of this *midrash*. But it seems to me that we learn from it that the frequency of conjugal relations is not the same for everyone; rather, it depends on the extent of his other obligations' (Rashi on Gen. 32:15). He goes on to consider in detail the message of the *midrash* regarding the obligatory frequency of conjugal relations.

## Allusions to *Midrashim*

At dozens of points in his commentary on the Torah, Rashi alludes to rabbinic *midrashim* without actually citing or discussing them. He does not even mention what the *midrashim* say, with the result that only a scholar learned in Midrash will realize what he is hinting at. Rashi refers to these *midrashim* in terms such as the following: 'there are aggadic *midrashim*, but they cannot be reconciled with its plain meaning' (on Gen. 3:22), 'and there are many aggadic *midrashim*' (on Gen. 5:1), 'there are many aggadic *midrashim* on "shall not abide", but this is its bright plain meaning' (on Gen. 6:3), 'there are many aggadic *midrashim*, but this is its plain meaning' (on Gen. 12:3); 'and there are aggadic *midrashim*, but I have explained the wording of the verse' (on Gen. 20:16); 'and there are many aggadic *midrashim* on this passage' (on Gen. 33:14); 'and there are aggadic *midrashim* on many aspects' (on Gen. 27:28). Many other examples can be found.

Why did Rashi want to note the existence of these *midrashim*? Of what use is a general allusion to *midrashim* without any hint of their content or even, in most cases, of where they are located? The practice is even more surprising in light of the scarcity of books at the time. Manuscripts were extremely costly, and most people had no access to them.

Two possible explanations may be offered. First, Rashi felt a need to make excuses for his disregard of *midrashim* that dealt with the verses he was interpreting.

[21] Most likely, the midrashist wanted to make the point that Israel was redeemed from Egypt by virtue of Abraham's meritorious actions, represented by his saddling his ass early in the morning, and that they are destined to enjoy the future, final redemption by virtue of the binding of Isaac. In other words, the purpose of the *midrash* was to teach the great importance of Abraham's binding of Isaac, which earned an eternally enduring reward for Israel. Another possibility is that the ass (*ḥamor*) represents, by assonance, materiality (*ḥomriyut*). The midrashist in that case means to teach that the redemption will come by virtue of overcoming one's sensual (materialistic) impulses.

He is saying, in effect, that he knows about those *midrashim*, but he cannot use them because they are ill-suited to the nature of his commentary and therefore his disregard of them should not be cause for wonder. The other possibility is that by alluding to those *midrashim*, he meant to encourage people to consult them on their own. It seems to me that in most instances, Rashi was accounting for his disregard of the *midrashim*, and only rarely did he mean to promote their being read independently. If the latter had been his primary purpose, he would have mentioned their content and source. A general reference to the existence of *midrashim*, without any reference to what they say and where they can be found, can hardly be seen as an encouragement to study them.

It is no wonder that Rashi felt the need to apologize for ignoring some *midrashim*. At the time, there were sages who did not take a favourable view of dealing with the plain meaning of the text and disregarding the *midrashim* that presented a different way of understanding it. I have already mentioned Rabbi Joseph Kara's comments about sages who objected to disregarding *midrashim* in favour of the plain meaning of the text.

## Dual Interpretations

In many cases, Rashi did not rest content with a single interpretation of a text and offered two or occasionally more. For example, on the verse 'Wisdom is more of a stronghold to a wise man than ten magnates' (Eccles. 7: 19) he offered, following the *midrash*, six alternative interpretations and concluded: 'All of these aspects are in the *midrash*, and I cannot reconcile them with the underlying verse.' In most cases, the first of the interpretations follows the plain meaning, while the second is derived from the *midrash*, though sometimes both are based on rabbinic *midrashim*. In any case, even when Rashi offers two interpretations, he routinely avoids evaluating them and expressing a preference for one or the other. Interpreters and scholars of Rashi have struggled with the question of whether there is any consistency here or whether it is a matter of chance. Some have argued that when Rashi saw flaws in each interpretation, he preferred to cite both.[22] This view was quite popular and can explain many of the dual interpretations, but it does not suit every case. Anyone guided by the search for truth and wanting to avoid far-fetched explanations will have to acknowledge that we lack an adequate explanation for all the many instances that appear in the commentary, and that in at least some cases, it was Rashi's affection for Midrash that led him to cite more than one.

The question of Rashi's dual interpretations has recently been considered by Amnon Shapira. In his view, 'Rashi's dual interpretations are not dual in the sense that they include a plain-meaning interpretation and a midrashic interpretation in

---

[22] R. Elijah Mizrahi and several other classical explicators of Rashi took that view, as did Nehama Leibowitz (*The Study of Biblical Commentators* (Heb.), 62).

and of themselves, rather their duality reflects a fundamentally dualistic position.'[23] Among his conclusions are the following:

In his dual interpretations of the narrative portion of the Torah (75 instances in the commentary on Genesis; 157 in the commentary on the entire Torah), not once does Rashi decide, even indirectly, between the two interpretations. This differs from his practice outside the context of dual interpretations and from the accepted practice of other medieval commentators when they cite two interpretations for a narrative passage in the Torah . . . Within the context of dual interpretation, Rashi took the two interpretations not as competing alternatives but as coexisting side by side, consistent with an organic understanding. Not only do they not contradict each other; they complement each other. If Rashi had thought that both explanations were somehow 'flawed', there would have been room to decide, at least in some instances, in favour of the interpretation that he regarded as less 'flawed'.[24]

As I have said, I believe it was Rashi's affection for Midrash that frequently led him to cite more than one. For example, on the verse 'Hear, O Lord the voice of Judah . . . Though his own hands strive for him, help him against his foes' (Deut. 33: 7), Rashi first cites a *midrash* from *Sifrei*, which explains that Moses here blessed the kings of Judah—including David, Solomon, Asa, and Jehoshaphat—with divine assistance in the warfare they would encounter. He then cites another *midrash*, also from *Sifrei*: 'Another interpretation: *Hear, O Lord the voice of Judah*—He alluded here to a blessing for Simeon within the blessings for Judah.' The author of this *midrash* played on the similarity between the verb translated 'hear' (*shema*) and the name Simeon (*shimon*). The first interpretation presents no problem that would warrant citing the second had Rashi not found it a pleasing and interesting *midrash* that brought another tribe into the circle of those blessed. Rashi was motivated simply by his affection for Midrash. In many instances, he valued the ideas embodied in both *midrashim* and therefore cited both. It is not always possible to discern the grounds for that affection. It encompasses many diverse pedagogical purposes and sometimes purposes growing out of the sad historical experiences undergone by Rashi and evidently by the authors of the *midrashim* themselves. A notable example is his interpretation of the verse 'A new king arose over Egypt who did not know Joseph' (Exod. 1: 8). As already mentioned, Rashi cited the dispute between the *amora'im* Rav and Samuel over the meaning of the word 'new': literally a new king or the same king 'whose decrees were renewed and who pretended not to know him'. It is unlikely that Rashi was unaware of the meaning of the word 'new' and assumed that Joseph 'and all his brothers and all that generation' died—as the verse states—leaving only Pharaoh still alive, the beneficiary of extraordinary longevity. The historical experience of the Jews—who had devoted all their strength and energy to the economic benefit of the lands in which they lived and those lands'

[23] Shapira, 'Rashi's Twofold Interpretation' (Heb.), 290.      [24] Ibid. 294.

rulers, only to see those rulers turn away from them and from Jews in general—was what moved Rashi to cite this interpretation too.[25]

On occasion, Rashi took several alternative *midrashim* (which he introduced with the phrase 'something else') and combined them as complements. For example, for the verse 'Sow your seed in the morning and don't hold back your hand in the evening' (Eccles. 11: 6), *Ecclesiastes Rabbah* 11: 10 offers four interpretations in the names of four different sages. Rashi cites them side by side as complements, treating them as if they had been written by a single sage.

## Repeated Interpretations

In dozens of instances, Rashi repeats the interpretation of words and subjects that appear in the Torah more than once. Frequently, these repetitions include variations, some minor and some significant. The phenomenon has been studied by Nehama Leibowitz and Moshe Ahrend and by David Zafrani.[26] Zafrani listed sixty-seven instances of such repetitions. Let me offer one example to clarify what I am referring to. In the context of the commandment to appear at the sanctuary for the pilgrimage festivals, the Torah three times uses the words 'all your males shall appear'—twice in Exodus (23: 17; 34: 23) and once in Deuteronomy (16: 16). Rashi interprets both verses in Exodus but does not comment on the verse in Deuteronomy, and there is a subtle difference between the two interpretations in Exodus. In 23: 17, he interprets 'all your males' as 'the males among you'; in 34: 23, he interprets it as 'all the males among you'. Why does he add the word 'all'? Zafrani showed that Rashi was referring to the halakhic rulings on the issue. On the one hand, the halakhah exempts women from the commandment (hence 'all your males'); on the other hand, it obligates certain groups of males who, according to some opinions, are also exempt. Adding the word 'all' emphasizes that point.

Leibowitz and Ahrend and Zafrani identified six reasons for Rashi's repeated interpretations: (1) to highlight the difference between two similar (but not identical) words, (2) to explain a word appearing with a meaning different from its usual one, (3) to explain a word that appears several times with different meanings, (4) to explain a verse in accord with the halakhah, (5) to reject a rabbinic interpretation that cannot be reconciled with the plain meaning of the text, and (6) to reject some other interpretation that was widespread at the time.

---

[25] *Sot.* 11a accounts for the view that Scripture is speaking of the same king on the grounds that the text does not say that the former king died and was succeeded by a new king, but it seems unlikely that Rashi—or, for that matter, the sage advancing the view—was impressed by that argument. In my view, it is the tendentiousness pointed out above that underlies this *midrash*.

[26] Leibowitz and Ahrend, *Rashi's Commentary on the Torah* (Heb.), 56–61; Zafrani, 'On "Repeated Commentary" in Rashi' (Heb.).

## Contradictory *Midrashim*

Rashi's commentary includes mutually contradictory *midrashim* and interpretations. They are usually called 'divided *midrashim*' and have been broadly considered by Rashi's interpreters. Among them is Rabbi Judah ben Elazar, one of the 'tosafists on the Torah', whose comprehensive work *Minhat yehudah* (1313) is largely devoted to Rashi's commentary. (Rabbi Judah says his work is devoted entirely to consideration of Rashi's writings; in fact, the figure is more like 80 per cent.) At the beginning of the work, he writes: 'At times, Rabbi Solomon's words will appear mutually contradictory to my wondering eyes, as in his commentary on the portion *Yitro*, where he says "Jethro was called by seven names" [Rashi on Exod. 18: 1], though elsewhere he says, "he was called by two names" [Rashi on Num. 10: 29], in the portion *Beha'alotekha*.' He goes on to list other contradictions.

Some of the divided *midrashim* can be satisfactory resolved, but others cannot. Let me illustrate.

1.  In the account of Jacob's reunion with Esau, Rashi writes: 'And Dinah, where was she? He placed her in a box and locked her in, so Esau would not cast his eye on her. And Jacob was punished for that, for he denied her to his brother, though she might have brought him back to virtue: she [therefore] fell into Shechem's hands' (on Gen. 32: 23). On the face of it, Rashi seems to share the view of the midrashist who believed not only that Esau would fail to be a bad influence on Dinah but that she might have been a good influence on him. But Rashi frequently cites *midrashim* whose authors thought it better to stay far from the company of bad people, among them Esau, lest one be subject to harmful influence. For example, when the Israelites in the wilderness encounter the Edomites (Esau's descendants), Rashi writes: 'It is telling us that because they here joined with Esau the wicked, they too transgressed, and they lost that righteous one [that is, Aaron, whose death is there described]' (on Num. 20: 23).

2.  After the Exodus from Egypt, Israel was commanded to camp 'before Baal-zephon' (Exod. 14: 2). Rashi writes: 'He alone remained of all the gods of Egypt, so they would be misled and say their [that is, Israel's] God is having a hard time. On this, Job said "He exalts nations, then destroys them" [Job 12: 23].' In other words, though the Bible reports God's statement, 'I will mete out punishments to all the gods of Egypt', Baal-zephon was not harmed in the course of the Exodus so that the Egyptians would be misled into thinking that the God of Israel was not equipped to do battle with him. Rashi relies on a verse from Job—'He exalts nations, then destroys them'—but reads the word *masgi* ('exalts') with a right-dotted letter *shin* rather than a left-dotted *sin*, making it *mashgi* ('deceives'). The sense is that God deceived the Egyptians into thinking they were triumphant, thereby making their eventual defeat even more impres-

sive. In his comments on Job, however, Rashi adheres to the standard Masoretic Text, interpreting the word as *masgi*, from a root meaning to flourish and grow, as in Psalm 92: 13—'they thrive [*yisgeh*] like a cedar in Lebanon'. It is hard to imagine that Rashi was unaware of the contradiction between his two interpretations. In Job, however, he was interpreting in accord with the plain meaning, while in Exodus he was quoting a contradictory *midrash* taken from *Mekhilta*. He did so out of his affection for the *midrash*, even though it diverged from the wording of the text. It goes without saying that both interpretations, though especially the second, had contemporary significance for him. The triumph of the non-Jewish nations is only temporary, and the higher they rise, the harder they will fall.

3. The sages disagreed over the manner in which the Tabernacle was transported in the wilderness. Some say it was carried in column formation, 'as a sort of plank'; others say it was carried in the formation it took on at an encampment, 'as a sort of box'. Rashi referred to the dispute and cited both opinions (on Num. 10: 25). He himself interpreted once in accord with the second opinion—that they marched 'as a sort of box' (on Num. 2: 9)—and once in accord with the first opinion, saying they marched 'as a sort of plank' (on Num. 10: 21).

4. The fourth example pertains to the status of the tribe of Gad. At one point, Rashi describes it as one 'of the weakest of the tribes' (on Deut. 33: 18); elsewhere, he describes it as one of the strongest tribes, relying on its portrayal as a lion (Deut. 33: 20). The two interpretations are in close proximity, and it is clear that Rashi well knew what he had written on the earlier verse when he commented on the later one. The difference grows out of his reliance on two different *midrashim* taken from the *Sifrei* on Deuteronomy: each one seemed to him to suit the verse he was dealing with at the time.

The conclusion to be drawn is that Rashi usually selected *midrashim* that suited the wording and context of the verses he was commenting on, but that he sometimes strayed from that course. On occasion, he even cited *midrashim* that contradicted each other. In many cases, he was motivated in doing so by his affection for Midrash.

## General Characteristics of the Commentary

### Increased Commitment to *Peshat* in Rashi's Later Years

Rashi's inclination to interpret in accordance with the plain meaning of the text goes back to his years of study in Germany. This is evident from some of his teachers' interpretations that have survived, especially those of Rabbi Isaac Halevi. For example, Rabbi Isaac interpreted the verse 'The lazy man buries his hand in the bowl [*batsalaḥat*]' (Prov. 19: 24) in a way that departed from the conventional understanding and evinced a highly developed linguistic sense along with devotion to the plain meaning: 'In the name of Rabbi Isaac, I heard that *batsalaḥat* . . . is used because of the cold and frost that crack and cross [*tsoleḥin*] the hands.'[27] This is not the only such example.[28]

Even if Rashi did not receive this example and others directly from Rabbi Isaac Halevi, it is clear that the latter had an affinity for plain meaning. When he returned to France, Rashi was exposed to the work of the Spanish Hebrew grammarians, another important impetus to the tendency of his commentary to follow the plain meaning. That tendency grew stronger later in Rashi's life, as is evident from his grandson Rashbam's account of his grandfather telling him that he would compose new commentaries if he had the strength to do so. From the context of that account, it is clear that those new commentaries would be more directed towards the plain meaning. The discussion shows that the relationship between *peshat* and *derash* was a subject that continued to engage Rashi and his students even towards the end of his life and remained central to their discussions:

And our Rabbi Solomon, my mother's father, who illuminates the eyes of the diaspora and who interpreted the Torah, Prophets, and Writings, set his heart to interpreting the plain meaning of Scripture. And I, too, Samuel son of Rabbi Meir his son-in-law, may the memory of the righteous be for a blessing, debated it with him and before him, and he acknowledged to me that if he had the opportunity, he would have to write different commentaries, in accord with the plain meanings that newly emerge each day.[29]

All three factors that led Rashi to interpret in accordance with the plain meaning grew stronger towards the end of the eleventh century. That is particularly true of the close affinity to the Hebrew grammarians at work in Spain.

## Interpretations at Odds with Halakhah

On rare occasions, Rashi interpreted a verse in a manner inconsistent with halakhah. He did so where it appeared to him that the plain meaning of the verse corresponded more to the view that was not accepted as halakhah. Let me offer two illustrations.

1.  **Deuteronomy 23: 19 states:** You shall not bring the fee of a whore or the pay of a dog into the house of the Lord your God in fulfilment of any vow, for both are abhorrent to the Lord your God.' 'Both' (*gam sheneihem*, more literally: 'also both') calls for interpretation, for the word *gam*, which usually indicates emphasis, seems superfluous. Rashi interprets: '[*Also*] *both*—to include their transformations, such as wheat that has been made into flour.' In other words, the additional word extends the prohibition beyond the tainted fee itself, to

---

[27] Rashi continues: 'And I heard that *batsalaḥat* means a smooth cut.' He may be referring to a comment by R. Jacob b. Yakar.

[28] See Grossman, *The Early Sages of Ashkenaz* (Heb.), 288–9.        [29] Rashbam on Gen. 37: 1.

include things that are produced from it. That is the view of the House of Shammai (*BK* 65*b*; *Tem.* 30*b*), but it is the contrary view of the House of Hillel that was accepted as halakhah. Rashi may have interpreted the word as he did because the Talmud itself recognizes that the word *gam* remains problematic on the House of Hillel's interpretation.

2. **Exodus 23:19 states:** 'The choice first fruits of your soil you shall bring to the house of the Lord your God.' Rashi says: 'Even the [fruits of] the sabbatical year are subject to the law of first fruits; that is why it is said here, too, "first fruits of your soil".' This interpretation is contrary to halakhah, which exempts fruits of the sabbatical (*shemitah*) year from the law of first fruits. Rashi's interpreters, both early and late—including Rabbi Elijah Mizrahi and Abraham Berliner—sought in various ways to account for Rashi's interpretation. Some, again including Rabbi Elijah Mizrahi, even suggest removing the words 'even the [fruits of] the sabbatical year are subject to the law of first fruits'. They appear, however, in the reliable manuscripts of Rashi's commentary on the Torah, including MS Leipzig 1, and should not be removed simply because the interpretation is contrary to halakhah.

Further support for the premise that the words are, in fact, Rashi's own can be found in the literary structure of the entire unit of text as he saw it. In his opinion, the entire passage (Exod. 23:10–19) is connected to the commandment of the sabbatical year with which it begins. Rashi tied even the sabbath and pilgrimage festival commandments as there set forth to the sabbatical year: 'Even during the sabbatical year, you are not to displace the sabbath of creation' (Exod. 23:12); 'because the subject is the sabbatical year, there was a need to mention that the three pilgrimage festivals are not displaced' (Exod. 23:17). This literary structure led Rashi to favour an interpretation that does not accord with the halakhah. As noted, this phenomenon appears elsewhere in Rashi's commentary as well as in the commentaries of his students, including his grandson Rashbam.

### The Aramaic Translations and the Cantillation Marks

The Aramaic translations (*targumim*) were important sources for Rashi. In his commentary on the Torah, he made extensive use of Targum Onkelos, reading it closely, interpreting it, offering proofs for its conclusions, and establishing rules for its study. He even describes it as something originally 'given at Sinai' (Rashi on *Kid.* 49*a*, *harei zeh meharef*). Nevertheless, he did not hesitate to disagree with the translation at many points. In his commentary on the Prophets and the Writings, Rashi made extensive use of Targum Jonathan.[30]

---

[30] For detailed consideration of Rashi's use of the *targumim*, see Melammed, 'Rashi's Commentary on the Bible' (Heb.), 378–95; Pozen, *Targum from Sinai* (Heb.).

In addition, Rashi gave extensive consideration to the cantillation markings, which he valued highly and often relied on: 'Had I not seen the *zakef gadol* on the word *ufeneihem* [their faces], I would not have known how to interpret it' (on Ezek. 1: 11). Yet he did not hesitate to offer interpretations that ran contrary to the markings.

## Pedagogical Tendencies

A central question in the study of Rashi's commentary on the Torah is whether his purpose was exclusively exegetical or whether he also set himself pedagogical goals. Scholars past and present have struggled with the question and taken diverse views. Some believe Rashi dealt solely with interpretative questions, and some have gone so far as to introduce their consideration of Rashi's interpretations by trying to identify the textual crux to which the interpretation was meant to respond.[31] Among the recent proponents of that view is Nehama Leibowitz, who deserves much credit for bringing into today's world the wealth of traditional Jewish biblical interpretation from the Middle Ages. Leibowitz took an extreme view on the issue at hand, maintaining that Rashi was an exegete, not an educator, and that his exclusive motivation was to deal with textual cruxes in the biblical books. The classic question that she posed to students of Rashi was 'What did Rashi find difficult here?' Her basic premise was that, but for the difficulties in the texts themselves, Rashi would have offered no interpretations. Her position has greatly influenced the study of Rashi during the past two generations.

At first glance, Rashi's own words seem to lend credence to this position. As mentioned, he described his approach to aggadic Midrash and wrote that his sole purpose was to consider the plain meaning of the text along with aggadah 'that resolves the words of Scripture as a word fitly spoken'. He reiterated this declaration several times in his commentary on the Torah. It follows that he meant to deal with two matters only: the plain meaning of the text and rabbinic aggadah that suits the wording of the biblical text. Had he also had pedagogical goals, he would not have described his method by saying 'I did not probe anything except . . .'. The word 'except' indicates that he was guided solely by the exegetical motive. We have already examined what he meant by this declaration, and even one who is disinclined to accept that explanation must acknowledge the basic fact, made evident by an examination of the commentary on the Torah, that Rashi was not moved solely by a drive towards exegesis. Exegesis clearly was his primary purpose; but along with it, he felt obligated to take advantage of the biblical text and rabbinic

---

[31] The commentator who epitomized this view was R. Shabbetai Meshorer Bass, author of the supercommentary on Rashi known as *Siftei ḥakhamim*. Other prominent interpreters of Rashi—R. Elijah Mizrahi, R. Abraham Bukarat (author of *Sefer hazikaron*) and R. Judah Loew b. Bezazel (Maharal of Prague)—also treated the question extensively, and in most instances it is indeed a response to a textual crux that underlies Rashi's comments.

Midrash as an important tool for teaching people and for bolstering resistance to Christian propaganda.

In my view, Rashi's commentary on the Torah evinces a clear pedagogical inclination alongside the exegetical and overshadowing the historical. He took advantage of opportunities to comment on issues of morality or values that he found particularly important. He indirectly linked many of them to the wording of the verses, but for others he offered only contrived support that made no exegetical contribution and had only a pedagogical purpose.

Many examples could be cited in support of my view. Because of the great importance of the issue and the variety of views regarding it, let me offer five illustrations.

**1.** Clear evidence of a pedagogical purpose is preserved in Rashi's explanation of the place name Rithmah, one of the Israelites' encampments. The Torah portion *Masei* mentions forty-two stations on the Israelites' trek through the wilderness, and Rithmah is the only one whose name Rashi explains. The Torah states: 'They set out from Hazeroth and encamped at Rithmah (Num. 33: 18), and Rashi comments: 'It is so called on account of the spies' slander, as it is said "What can you profit, what can you gain, O deceitful tongue? A warrior's sharp arrows, with hot coals of broom-wood [*gaḥalei retamim*]" [Ps. 120: 3].' The harm caused by a 'deceitful tongue' is as intense as the heat of broom-wood coals, which burn at a very high temperature, and Rashi associates the name Rithmah with the word for broom-wood by assonance. His pedagogical purpose here is clear: he means to explain the great harm caused by slander and the concrete impression it leaves. The place where the slanderous words were uttered was tainted by the negative atmosphere caused by those words, to the point that it was named for them.

Did Rashi have an exegetical motive for this interpretation? It is hard to imagine one. The account in Numbers 12: 16 reports that 'after that the people set out from Hazeroth and encamped in the wilderness of Paran', seeming to contradict the verse just discussed, which recounts that they journeyed from Hazeroth to Rithmah. But, in fact, the contradiction is illusory, for the 'wilderness of Paran' refers to the entire region, and Rithmah is a site within the region. All the other place names used in the account of the Israelites' journeys and encampments likewise refer to specific sites, and it is not surprising that the general term 'wilderness of Paran' is not mentioned among them. It is clear that they spent time in that wilderness, as explicitly stated in Numbers 10: 12. Ibn Ezra dealt with the matter in his commentary on Numbers 10: 31.

Something so obvious would not have been missed by Rashi, just as it would not have been missed by the midrashist who gave the place name Rithmah so far-fetched an interpretation. The link is entirely an associative one, based on the word 'broom-wood' (*retamim*), but that word in itself—as distinct from the combined form 'coals of broom-wood'—has no negative connotation whatsoever. The prophet Elijah, en route to Mount Horeb, sat 'under a broom bush' and an angel of the Lord appeared to him there (1 Kgs 19: 4–5). Why not link the place name to that episode and generate a positive *midrash* about the study of Torah and closeness to God that took place at Rithmah? Clearly, the midrashist chose the far-fetched negative association for pedagogical reasons. Moreover, the place name could have been interpreted simply by reference to a stand of broom-wood bushes growing there. Rashi, too, who selected this *midrash* and incorporated it into his commentary while disregarding the *midrashim* on some of the other place names mentioned in the passage, intended to educate his readers and impress on them the severity of the prohibition on slander. This is a notable example of Rashi citing a *midrash* with no substantial connection to the plain meaning of the verse being interpreted.

2.  In interpreting the word 'galbanum' (*ḥelbenah*—Exod. 30: 34), Rashi writes: 'A spice of foul odour, called galbena. Scripture included it among the spices making up the incense to teach us that we should not disdain the inclusion in our fasts and prayers of the sinners in Israel; rather, they should be counted among us.' The source for this *midrash* is *Keritot 6b*. Why did Rashi so interpret the word? He made his interpretation into a moral lesson regarding the unity of the Jewish people and the inclusion of 'the sinners of Israel' within it. Additional evidence for the tendentious nature of the interpretation can be found in its formulation, especially its concluding with the exhortation that 'they should be counted among us'. The talmudic source is not worded so forcefully and does not have the exhortative qualities of Rashi's interpretation.

3.  After explaining the sin that had been committed by Miriam (Num. 12: 1), Rashi adds: 'And if Miriam, who did not intend to defame him [Moses] was so punished, a fortiori, one who [wittingly] defames his fellow [will be punished].' The verse presents no linguistic or substantive difficulty that might impel Rashi to add this *midrash*, taken from *Sifrei*. He was moved to cite it by a clear pedagogical purpose.

4.  Rashi associated various *midrashim* in praise of humility with biblical verses. In most of those instances, there was no direct connection between the *midrash* and the linguistic or contextual interpretation of the verse, and it is evident that Rashi's purpose was to emphasize the importance of humility. One example appears in the passage dealing with the ritual of the red heifer, in which the priest is directed to cast into the heifer's ashes 'cedar wood, hyssop, and crimson stuff' (Num. 19: 6). The ashes are to be used in purifying those who have become impure. Nevertheless, Rashi cites the *midrash* of Rabbi Moses Hadarshan: 'The cedar is the highest of all trees and the hyssop is the lowest, a sign that the highest person, who sinned in his pride, must lower himself like the hyssop and the [crimson-dye-yielding] worm, and he will then secure atonement' (Rashi on Num. 19: 22). Unlike his usual practice, Rashi here suggested a rationale for the commandment.

**5.** Another example appears in the following interpretation: '*Then he became king in Jeshurun, when the heads of the people assembled* [Deut. 33: 5]—The yoke of his sovereignty is always upon them; whenever they assemble ... Another interpretation: *assembled*—when they are assembled together in unison and there is peace among them, he is their king, but not when there is dissension among them.' The alternative explanation of 'not when there is dissension'—which also appears in the manuscripts—lacks any linguistic basis. The verb 'assembled' itself does not connote peace and brotherhood; in fact, some assemblies are marked by harsh differences of opinion and by conflict. It was his pedagogical goal that led Rashi to cite this *midrash*.

I will consider the nature of some of the pedagogical values implicit in Rashi's commentaries separately, in Chapters 8–10.

## Religious Polemics

Jewish–Christian polemic reached one of its climactic points at the end of the eleventh century. There can be no doubt that Rashi was profoundly affected by it, and his commentary on the Torah clearly shows as much. I noted this in the Introduction, and I will consider it again in Chapter 8 in connection with his outlook on the nations of the world. It is generally agreed that there are clear references to that polemic in Rashi's comments on the Song of Songs, Psalms, Isaiah, and the Twelve Prophets. As for the commentary on the Torah, some believe it contains no such references, but I cannot agree with them. For while it is true that the commentary on the Torah does not give as extensive a voice to the polemic as do the commentaries on the other books and that its references to the polemic must be sought between the lines, there is no doubt that they are present.

Thus, for example, Rashi's intense hostility to Esau, which pervades his commentary on the Torah, can be understood only against the background of his hostility to Christianity, of which Esau is the pre-eminent symbol. From the wealth of rabbinic *midrashim*, Rashi selected those that accuse Esau of all the acts regarded by the Jewish tradition as cardinal sins, including idolatry, illicit sexual relations, and bloodshed. Rashi's inclination here is made even more evident by his not recognizing any distinction between *peshat* and *derash* in considering the figure of Esau. When he cites aggadic *midrashim* on the subject, he does not identify them as such, and he departs from his usual practice of offering plain-meaning interpretations alongside them.[32]

---

[32] The story of Esau is told in Genesis 25–33. The only time in this lengthy passage that Rashi mentions the distinction between *peshat* and *derash* is in his comment on 'until I come to my lord in Seir' (Gen. 33: 14), and even there he does not do so to mitigate the accusations against Esau. For particularly harsh allegations against Esau, see Rashi on Gen. 25: 27–8, 34; 27: 5, 30; 28: 9; 29: 11; 32: 7; 33: 7, 11; 36: 2, 5, 24. See also Cohen, 'Esau as Symbol'.

Many examples could be offered; I will mention only three.

1.  On the verse 'Esau came in from the field, and he was faint' (Gen. 25: 29, OJPS), Rashi comments that Esau was tired on account of committing 'murder'. He does not even mention that this is a *midrash*, and that Esau's faintness, according to the plain meaning of the text, has a quite different cause.

2.  According to Rashi, it was not Jacob who misled his father, by contriving to acquire the blessing, but Esau, by hypocritically feigning righteousness.

3.  The account of Jacob's reunion with Esau concludes with the statement: 'So Esau started back that day on his way to Seir' (Gen. 33: 16). In its plain meaning, the verse is referring not only to Esau but also to the 400 men he had brought with him to his meeting with Jacob and who returned with him. Rashi does not refer at all to the plain meaning, citing only the *midrash* in *Genesis Rabbah* 78: 16 according to which the 400 men had already abandoned Esau. In other words, Esau gave up his plan to attack Jacob not because he was merciful but because he had no choice, having been abandoned by his forces.[33]

This tendency to seek out negative elements in Esau's character and actions even when there is no linguistic or contextual basis for them is even more pronounced at other points in his commentary on the Torah. He cites, for example, the *midrash* explaining that Abraham did not bless Isaac before dying 'because he anticipated that Esau would be his descendant' (Rashi on Gen. 25: 11). And while he says that Ishmael, before his death, recognized Isaac's supremacy (on Gen. 25: 9), he says nothing analogous about Esau. The Torah relates that Timna was Esau's concubine. Rashi cites the *midrash* noting that she was of a distinguished family ('the daughter of nobles') but nevertheless agreed to be Esau's concubine 'to declare the greatness of Abraham and the extent to which people craved joining with his progeny . . . she said: "If I am not privileged to marry him, let me at least be his concubine"' (on Gen. 36: 12). He takes no account whatever of the possibility that she wanted to become Esau's concubine simply because he himself had favourably impressed her.

In his blessing of Joseph, Jacob says he is granting him 'one portion more than to your brothers, which I wrested from the Amorites with my sword and bow' (Gen. 48: 22). Rashi says 'the Amorites' refers to Esau, and he offers two possible reasons for the designation: 'From Esau, who acted like an Amorite. Another view: He ensnared his father with the words of his mouth.'[g] Both suggestions, which originate in *Genesis Rabbah* 97: 9, are far removed from the plain meaning of the verse. Associating 'Amorite' with 'words of his mouth' by mere assonance, without

---

[33]  Yet at the beginning of that passage Rashi cites the words of R. Simeon bar Yohai: 'It is a well-known rule that Esau is the enemy of Jacob; nevertheless, his mercy was aroused at that moment and he kissed him wholeheartedly' (on Gen. 33: 4).

[g]  *Imrei fiv* ('words of his mouth') is assonant with *amori* ('Amorite').

any comment on the plain meaning of the verse, is clear evidence of Rashi's polemical tendentiousness here. He does something similar in interpreting a verse in Jacob's blessing to Simeon and Levi: '*Their weapons are tools of lawlessness* [Gen 49: 5]—Their craft of murder is a possession that they gained by robbery: it was part of Esau's blessing. This is his craft, and you robbed him of it.'

Rashi interprets the verse 'I will rouse them to jealousy with a no-people' (Deut. 32: 21, OJPS) to mean that God will punish Israel 'by a nation having no name . . . Of Esau he says: "You shall be most despised" [Obad. v. 2].' In its plain meaning, the verse neither mentions nor even alludes to Esau, yet Rashi introduces him to advance his polemic. Esau, who symbolizes Christianity, is the despised nation (a 'no-people') destined to harm the Jews. He represents evil and provides refuge for other sinners. Rashi follows the *midrash* in explaining why Jacob put off, until he was on his deathbed, his condemnation of Reuben for having 'confused' Jacob's bed: he feared that Reuben, angered by the condemnation, might react by abandoning the traditions of the House of Jacob and joining up with Esau ('lest you abandon me and join with Esau my brother' (Rashi on Deut. 1: 3)). Even being close to Esau is wrong and highly dangerous. The Torah recounts Aaron's death at Mount Hor, 'on the boundary of the land of Edom' (Num. 20: 23). Rashi, following *Midrash tanḥuma* ('Bemidbar Ḥukat', 14), says the name is specified for pedagogical reasons rather than to convey geographic information: 'It tells us that because they here drew near to evil Esau, their actions violated norms and they caused that righteous one [Aaron] to be lost.' It is certainly no surprise that Rashi associated Amalek—the pre-eminent symbol of hatred for Israel and God—with Esau.

What is most striking in these examples is that they associate biblical verses with Esau even when the plain meaning of the verse has nothing at all to do with him. Moreover, Rashi often takes a similar tack in his treatment of Lot and Ishmael, portraying them in negative terms through the tendentious use of *midrashim*. For example: Lot was wicked and, because of his presence in Abraham's household, '[God's] word departed from him [Abraham]' (Rashi on Gen. 13: 14); Lot's shepherds were as wicked as their master, and Abraham's shepherds rebuked them (on Gen. 13: 7); Lot was ready to dwell among the wicked (on Gen. 13: 13); he did not take pains to preclude the introduction of idolatry into his household (on Gen. 18: 4); he was hospitable not because hospitality came naturally to him but because he had learned it from Abraham (on Gen. 19: 1); he tarried in Sodom to save his wealth (on Gen. 19: 16); he joined with the Sodomites in committing evil acts and was saved only through Abraham's merit (on Gen. 19: 17); he did not decline to drink wine on the second night, after learning what his eldest daughter had done to him the night before (on Gen. 19: 33); Lot's bad reputation led Abraham to distance himself from him (on Gen. 20: 1); and so on. As for Ishmael, he was a brigand 'hated by all and the object of their anger' (on Gen. 16: 12); he lived a life of idolatry, illicit sexual relations, and murder (on Gen. 21: 9); he was hated by

Abraham because he lived a corrupt life (on Gen. 21: 14); he was saved from dying of thirst only by the merit of his present actions (on Gen. 21: 17). The denigration of Ishmael is meant to deny that his descendants have any claims on the Jews or on the Land of Israel, but the denigration of Lot is more surprising; it may be meant to suggest that only the descendants of Isaac are chosen and that the Moabites and Ammonites have no claim to the Land of Israel.[h]

The polemical tendencies in Rashi's commentary on the Torah are also expressed in his avoidance of any criticism of the patriarchs and his habit of justifying all their actions. This contrasts sharply with the inclination to find flaws in the non-Israelite biblical figures, such as Noah, Nimrod, Lot, Esau, Ishmael, Pharaoh, Balak, and Balaam, while emphasizing Israel's high standing and closeness to God—something I consider further below. This dual motif of glorifying Israel and denigrating the other nations is pervasive, and it is evident that Rashi used various *midrashim* in an attempt to engage in polemic with Christianity and Islam, the dominant religions of the time. Rashi repeatedly presents the idea, originating in Midrash, that God first offered the Torah to the other nations, who rejected it, and that only Israel agreed to accept it, thereby forging a powerful bond of love between Israel and God. Not only did the other nations reject the Torah, they also despise yet envy Israel for agreeing to accept it.[34]

Consistent with this strain of thought, Rashi also emphasized God's oath never to replace Israel as the chosen nation, an oath that made the covenant between God and Israel an eternal one. Even if Israel sins, it will be impossible to replace it: 'Because he spoke to you and swore to your ancestors that he would not replace their progeny by some other nation, he prohibits you, by these oaths, from provoking him, for he cannot withdraw from you' (Rashi on Deut. 29: 12). This interpretation and others like it defiantly reject Christian supersessionism; that is, the claim that Israel sinned and was displaced by God and that the Church is the true Israel (*verus Israel*), the 'spiritual Israel' that has taken its place. Rashi emphasized not only that no nation of the world had taken Israel's place but also that God's presence had not dwelled on any other nation. Indeed, even Balaam's prophecy was not the result of God's presence alighting upon him (on Exod. 33: 17). The overall conclusion is that anyone who opposes Israel attacks God too, becoming 'an enemy of the divine' (on Exod. 15: 7).

In sum, Rashi's extreme positions on this subject, his heavy emphasis on Esau's sins, the frequent reiteration of these motifs, and the recurring use of *midrashim* having no basis in the biblical text all demonstrate a clear polemic against Christianity and Christological interpretation of the Bible.

[34]   For detailed discussion of this topic, see Ch. 8, which considers Rashi's view of the nations of the world.

[h]   According to the Bible, the Moabites and Ammonites were the offspring of Lot's incestuous unions with his daughters (Gen. 19: 30–8).

## Defending the Actions of the Patriarchs

A prominent feature of Rashi's commentary on the Torah is its defence of all of the patriarchs' actions, seemingly as part of a religious polemic against Christianity. The Spanish sages, Nahmanides among them, took the liberty of criticizing some of the patriarchs' actions, but Rashi avoided any criticism of them or their ideas. According to Rashi, all their deeds and thoughts were justified and meant for the sake of Heaven. He even avoided citing *midrashim* that might imply criticism, albeit only indirectly, of the patriarchs or their wives. We search in vain, for example, for any criticism of Sarah's oppressive treatment of Hagar; on the contrary, Rashi cites only *midrashim* that sing Sarah's praises and denigrate Ishmael. As he presents it, Sarah was an even greater prophet than Abraham, and everything she did was directed by the holy spirit. Similarly, when Abraham sets out to sacrifice Isaac, he acts promptly, lovingly, and for the sake of God's will. At no point does he wonder whether what he is about to do may be improper or contrary to the principles of his faith. The only possible reservation appears in the comment on 'The boy and I will go up there' (Gen. 22: 5): '*Up there* [*ad koh*]—that is, a short distance to the place that is before us. An aggadic *midrash*: I will see what has become of God's statement to me that "So [*koh*] shall your offspring be".'

Rashi neither cited nor even alluded to the *midrashim* that portray Abraham's indecision. The episode is depicted as replete with love and understanding between Abraham and Isaac and between the two of them and God. Jacob's actions likewise are described in a positive light, with not the least bit of criticism—not even of his obtaining the blessing through deceit.

Reuben, too, is defended by Rashi, at least in part, following the midrashic understanding of his actions. The verse 'Reuben went and lay with Bilhah, his father's concubine' (Gen. 35: 22) is taken to mean he changed ('confused') his father's couch, removing Jacob's bed from the tent of Bilhah, Rachel's handmaiden, out of concern for his mother's honour. According to the *midrash*, 'he said: If my mother's sister was my mother's rival, should the handmaiden of my mother's sister be my mother's rival?'

Jacob's rigorous criticism of Simeon and Levi for having killed the men of Shechem is very much moderated in Rashi's interpretation. Following Targum Onkelos, he interprets 'with guile' (*bemirmah*) in the verse 'Jacob's sons answered Shechem and his father Hamor—speaking with guile' (Gen. 34: 13) to mean 'with wisdom' or 'wisely'. He then continues: 'Scripture says there was no deceit, for he had defiled Dinah their sister.' The severity of their action is thus diminished. Following the *midrash*, Rashi likewise moderates the curse Jacob invokes on them—'cursed be their anger so fierce' (Gen. 49: 7)—by noting that 'even when delivering rebuke, he cursed only their anger, not them'.

Miriam and Aaron spoke against Moses, for which Miriam was punished by being subjected to a skin affliction (Num. 12: 10). Nevertheless, according to Rashi, they meant well, intending only to remedy the wrong Moses had committed against his wife Zipporah by declining to engage in conjugal relations. Many similar examples could be cited.

What moved Rashi to portray the patriarchs and matriarchs as perfect people whose actions were entirely for the sake of Heaven? Two principal factors were at play. First, it was the patriarchs with whom God had entered into a covenant that included the pledge of enduring progeny and possession of the Land. Any complaint, however minor, against the propriety of the patriarchs' actions could be taken to impair the covenant, which Rashi saw as the guarantee of the Jewish people's existence even in his own time. The second factor was Jewish–Christian polemic. The Christians sought to identify flaws in the patriarchs' conduct, especially that of Jacob and his sons. Fully justifying everything they did thus served an important goal in that harsh polemic.

## Enduring Influence of the Commentary

Rashi's commentary on the Torah attained very wide circulation. For hundreds of years, Jews read the weekly Torah portion in its light, and through it they absorbed rabbinic *midrashim* and the pedagogical values embodied in them. Thanks to Rashi's commentary, these *midrashim* became enduring assets of Jewish culture. In many places, study of the weekly Torah portion with Rashi's commentary became an accepted assignment for every Jewish schoolchild. Rabbi Judah Kalatz, who moved from Spain to North Africa during the second half of the fifteenth century, recounted that during his wanderings in the Kingdom of Granada, he was asked to teach the Pentateuch with Rashi. He noted that 'the practice already exists among all Jews to teach beginners to read Rashi'. The commentary thus achieved great influence not only in the various Ashkenazi communities but also in Spain and many other centres of Jewish life. Few works have exerted so great an influence over Jewish life through the ages as Rashi's commentary on the Bible, something already noted in our discussion of Rashi's standing.

Rashi's commentary on the Torah was the first book printed in Hebrew, published in 1470 or 1475. Numerous supercommentaries were written on it: among the most important are those of Rabbi Elijah Mizrahi, Rabbi Abraham Bukarat, and Rabbi Judah Loew ben Bezalel (Maharal of Prague).[35] *Arba'ah turim* and *Shulḥan arukh* both rule that one may fulfil the obligation to read the weekly Torah portion 'twice in the original and once in translation' by reading Rashi's commentary

---

[35] On Rashi's interpreters in general, see Schapiro, 'Interpreters of Rashi on the Torah' (Heb.); Ovadia, 'Rashi on the Torah and his Interpreters' (Heb.); Freimann, 'Manuscript Supercommentaries' (listing 134 of them). On these commentaries and others, see Grossman, *The Early Sages of France* (Heb.), 213 n. 270.

instead of Targum Onkelos.[36] Of particular importance is Rashi's great influence on the development of the plain-meaning school of interpretation in France, a school at whose centre stood Rabbi Joseph Kara, Rashbam, Rabbi Joseph Bekhor Shor, and Rabbi Eliezer of Beaugency. The tosafists' commentaries on the Torah, written in France during the thirteenth and fourteenth centuries, were generally constructed around what Rashi had said; for example, Rabbi Judah ben Elazar began his book *Minḥat yehudah* with a declaration that his primary purpose was to explain Rashi:

This is a book that teaches one to understand the words of Rabbi Solomon regarding explanations of the written Torah whose ways are not evident to many and to understand elliptical verses whose explanation cannot be found in Rabbi Solomon's words, which are sometimes obscure . . . I therefore took it upon myself to compose this book so as to illuminate my eyes and my heart with the words of Rabbi Solomon, which are elliptical.[37]

Beginning in the thirteenth century, Christian scholars also showed interest in Rashi's commentaries, and some were influenced by him following the polemic over the Talmud in 1240. Particularly noteworthy is Nicholas of Lyra, an important medieval Christian biblical interpreter. He knew Hebrew well and was quite familiar with other Hebrew commentaries on the Hebrew Bible. Some believe he had Jewish ancestry. He frequently relied on Rashi and mentioned him by name.[38]

In the seventeenth century Rashi's commentary began to be translated into other languages, including German, Yiddish, English, and French. Dozens of later commentaries on the Torah routinely used Rashi's commentary, and they, in turn, served as the starting point for further commentaries. Publishers hesitated to publish a commentary on the Torah without including Rashi: he became, in effect, the accompaniment to the Torah.

What brought about the wide dissemination and far-reaching influence of Rashi's commentary? Why did other excellent commentaries, such as those of Ibn Ezra and Nahmanides, take a back seat to Rashi's? Some have attributed it to Rashi's clear style, dear to students' hearts. Two facts, however, call that explanation

---

[36] *Arba'ah turim*, 'Oraḥ ḥayim', §285: 2; *SA*, 'Oraḥ ḥayim', §285: 2; see, further, Gross, 'Rashi and the Spanish Tradition' (Heb.), 37–9. According to Gross, this development began as early as the thirteenth century under the influence of Nahmanides and later R. Asher b. Jehiel (Rosh), 'the Ashkenazi sage who arrived from Ashkenaz and was appointed rabbi of Toledo, a leading centre of Spanish Jewry, at the start of the fourteenth century. And, indeed, Rosh writes, while already in Spain, that "it appears that one who reads the commentary on the Torah discharges thereby his obligation regarding translation, for each and every word is there explained"' (Gross, 'Rashi and the Spanish Tradition' (Heb.), 39; see also Grossman, *The Early Sages of France* (Heb.), 213 n. 271).

[37] Judah b. Elazar, *Minḥat yehudah*, 223.

[38] On the interest in Rashi shown by Christian scholars following the disputation of 1240, see Hailperin, *Rashi and the Christian Scholars*. For additional sources, see Grossman, *The Early Sages of France* (Heb.), 214 n. 273.

into question: Rashi's commentaries on the Prophets and Writings, written in that same clear style, did not attain the renown of his commentary on the Torah; and, however endearing his style, it is hard to imagine that it alone could have so forcefully attracted scholars and common folk alike throughout the Jewish world. It is hard to provide a clear and unambiguous answer to the question, but it seems that several factors came together to produce the result.

**1.  The commentary's close affinity to Midrash combined with its emphasis on plain meaning.**  Two characteristic qualities of Rashi's commentary constitute one of the factors that account for its wide dissemination. The first is its use of rabbinic interpretation to flesh out the terse biblical narrative, thereby producing a pleasing integration of *peshat* and *derash*. The commentary did more than offer students an important collection of rabbinic *midrashim* frequently tied to the biblical text, something of value in itself, it also expanded the narrative and added depth and colour to the biblical stories. It identified anonymous characters, sought out the protagonists' motives, added gripping conversation between the characters, and provided details omitted by the biblical text—all in a way that captured readers' hearts and fired their imaginations. These interpretations can also be found in the classical midrashic works, but the narrative there is too broad, the text harder to read, and the links to the biblical verses more tenuous. Moreover, copies of the midrashic works were rare and costly during the Middle Ages. But the second characteristic accounting for the commentary's wide circulation is its pursuit of plain-meaning interpretations. The plain-meaning interpretations of Ibn Ezra and Rashbam were addressed to scholars and experts in Hebrew grammar, and their readership was drawn largely from the social and intellectual elite. The mass of people wanted a commentary that would simply supplement the picture provided by the biblical text, provide added depth and meaning, and enrich their intellectual and emotional world. Did Ibn Ezra's important grammatical analyses and mysteries speak to the heart of the rank-and-file Jew? Could Rashbam's plain-meaning interpretations attract many readers? Could their commentaries invigorate their readers and fortify Jews seeking to understand their suffering in exile? Indeed, Nahmanides, in the introduction to his commentary on Genesis, described his own method as follows:

I shall conduct myself in accordance with the custom of the early scholars to bring peace of mind to the students, tired of the exile and the afflictions, who read in the *seder* [the assigned Torah portion] on the sabbaths and festivals, and to attract them with the plain meanings of Scripture and with some things that are pleasant to the listeners.[39]

Notwithstanding Nahmanides' rhetorical flourishes here, one can certainly understand the plain meaning of students 'weary of exile and woes' who are in need of 'pleasant words' to invigorate them.

---

[39] Nahmanides, *Commentary on the Torah*, i. 15.

2. **The commentary's suitability for students with diverse levels of learning.** This factor was of considerable importance. Everyone who studied the commentary, simple folk and scholars alike, could understand it in a manner consistent with his own intellectual level, identify with it, and sense that the commentary was speaking to him.

3. **The historical situation of Jewish communities from the beginning of the thirteenth century until the end of the Middle Ages.** The gradual decline in the status of Jews—the deterioration and decline of Spanish Jewry during the fourteenth and fifteenth centuries and their expulsion from various cities in Germany during the fifteenth—generated a great need to revive flagging spirits. The plain-meaning interpretations, centred on linguistic analysis, were seen as dry and lifeless. The selected *midrashim* that Rashi incorporated into his commentary and which he set forth in clear language were by their very nature better able to capture the hearts of the common folk, to increase their interest in studying the Bible, and sometimes even to fortify those whose faith had been weakened. Moreover, Rashi's commentary on the Torah had a prominent pedagogical component. The student's sense that Rashi's commentary on the holiest books of the Bible was leading him along the path of truth likewise contributed to the esteem in which it was held.

Yitzhak Baer overstates the case when he says that all of Rashi's commentary was written primarily to contend with the surrounding Christian world.[40] Nevertheless, the commentary frequently served that purpose, whether by direct polemic against Christological interpretations or by accounting for Israel's suffering in the diaspora. Moreover, the Spanish kabbalists saw Rashi's commentary as an important weapon in their struggle against philosophy and the elite Jewish circles in which it was pursued. It is no coincidence that Nahmanides, a prominent leader of the kabbalists in that struggle, described Rashi's commentary on the Torah as 'the lamps of the pure candelabrum' and as worthy of the 'rights of the firstborn'. The matter was considered earlier, in the discussion of Rashi's standing.

4. **Rashi's authoritativeness as the pre-eminent interpreter of the Babylonian Talmud.** Rashi's standing and fame contributed greatly to the wide circulation of his commentary on the Bible. It is difficult to separate the great popularity of his commentary on the Torah from the wide recognition of his worth as an interpreter of the Talmud. It can fairly be assumed that the opponents of philosophy in Provence and Spain, which were at the centre of the controversy over Maimonides' writings during the thirteenth century, took advantage of the situation by presenting Rashi's commentary as a faithful expression of the original Jewish tradition.

5. **His laconic, bright, heart-warming style.** Some scholars have attributed people's profound affinity for Rashi's commentary to its lucidity and accessibility.

---

[40] Baer, 'Rashi and the Historical Reality of his Time' (Heb.), 325.

Even if this is only one factor among many, it is an important one. It is no coincidence that the poet Samson Meltzer, in his ballad already referred to ('Ashirah lerashi'), described his great affection for Rashi as flowing both from the integration of expansive *midrashim* into his commentary and from his lucid style. He depicts the commentary as a song that could ignite the hearts of young students. His words are quoted as the epigraph to this book.

In the next chapter, on Rashi's commentaries on the Prophets and the Writings, I will consider linguistic and literary aspects of the commentary as well as Rashi's ties to mysticism, the elements of day-to-day life, and historical background.

CHAPTER FIVE

# Commentaries on the Later Books of the Hebrew Bible

I N HIS COMMENTARIES on the later books of the Hebrew Bible (the Prophets and the Writings, collectively referred to by the Hebrew acronym *Nakh*), Rashi made extensive use of rabbinic material, though to a lesser degree than in his commentary on the Torah.[1] About a quarter of the commentary on the Torah is original material; in the commentaries on *Nakh*, the figure is about two-thirds, the amount varying with the nature of each book and its commentary. He makes less use of midrashic language, and the commentaries differ somewhat in character too. He gives more consideration to historical background, to literary devices, and, especially, to anti-Christian polemic. In this chapter, I consider these phenomena and others. In some instances, the discussion will encompass matters that appear in the commentary on the Torah but were not considered in the preceding chapter.

## Language, Grammar, and References to Daily Life

### Questions of Language and Grammar

Questions of language and grammar receive considerable attention in Rashi's commentaries. With regard to lexicography, he was substantially influenced by the tenth-century Spanish grammarians, most notably Menahem ben Saruk and Dunash ben Labrat. But his grammatical method differed from theirs, and even in lexicography he did not always follow their lead and sometimes differed from them outright. In some respects, his work was superior to theirs.[2]

---

[1] As noted at the beginning of Ch. 4, the commentaries on Ezra, Nehemiah, Chronicles, and the end of Job attributed to Rashi in the printed editions are not in fact his.

[2] Melammed noted Rashi's ties to the Spanish Hebrew grammarians (see 'Rashi's Commentary on the Bible' (Heb.), 398–402). He writes: 'Rashi refers to Menahem by name some 170 times, about 60 of them in Psalms. But the large majority of the references in Psalms do not appear in any manuscript: they are copyists' additions which were then included in the early printed editions. It must be noted that Rashi does not quote Menahem and Dunash verbatim. Instead, he rephrases their comments in his own style, thereby making them more readily understandable than they are in their authors' rather difficult style . . . Dunash himself is mentioned very rarely in Rashi's commentaries, only about twenty times . . . He cites them together about thirty times, usually referring first to

Rashi's achievements as a grammarian were many, and he greatly influenced the biblical commentators who succeeded him in France. Gradually, however, the Spanish grammarians came to prevail in France, and Rashi's grammatical understandings yielded to theirs. In his commentaries, he established numerous important rules of usage and dealt with the different nuances of synonyms. In doing so, he made extensive use of rabbinic language, sometimes distinguishing between biblical and rabbinic Hebrew but also explaining some 120 biblical words according to rabbinic Hebrew. Ninety of these words were not to be found in the works of earlier sages. On occasion he did so even if he found no parallel or support in the Bible itself, and Rashbam criticized him on that account.[3] Rashi interpreted about 1,000 words through the use of French terms (*lo'azim*).[a] These terms are of considerable importance for the study of the French of Rashi's time, as some of them were not preserved in medieval French literature and appear only in Rashi's writings. On occasion Rashi also used German and Slavic *lo'azim*, though some of those are later additions. Many of the *lo'azim* have been corrupted by copyists' and printers' errors.[4]

Rashi's guidelines were that Scripture can be interpreted from within. He sought linguistic parallels elsewhere in the Bible for difficult words and relied on them extensively. His commentaries contain hundreds of examples, and they attest, among other things, to his breathtaking biblical erudition. In the absence of parallels, he looked to rabbinic usage and the Aramaic translations, without explicitly mentioning that biblical Hebrew and rabbinic Hebrew are distinct.

There are several studies of Rashi's grammatical and lexicographical methods, and some of his approach to interpreting words. First and foremost is the comprehensive dictionary of Rashi's biblical and rabbinic language, *Rashi's Palace* by Isaac Avinery. The dictionary includes the innovative interpretations of language and

Menaḥem's comments' (ibid. 400). In addition to the explicit references, Rashi used Menaḥem's dictionary (the *Maḥberet*) without mentioning him by name, as Mirsky has shown (see 'Rashi and Menaḥem's *Maḥberet*' (Heb.)).

[3] In interpreting the word 'lintel' (*mashkof*) in Exod. 12: 7, Rashbam comments: 'And one who interprets it as referring to the door striking it [as Rashi does, citing examples in rabbinic Hebrew] must find parallels in the Hebrew language of the Torah and the Prophets.'

[4] Arsène Darmesteter's important study clarifies many of these foreign terms. He examined the various *lo'azim* that appear in the manuscripts, established the preferred readings, and transcribed them into French. In all, he dealt with more than 3,000 *lo'azim* preserved in Rashi's biblical and talmudic commentaries. His work was continued by David. S. Blondheim, who examined many more manuscripts (see Darmesteter and Blondheim, *Les Glosses françaises*). Menahem Banitt (*Rashi, Interpreter of the Biblical Letter*) and Mochè Catane (*Foreign Words in Rashi's Writings* (Heb.); id., *Life in Rashi's Time* (Heb.); id., 'Le Monde intellectuel de Rashi') made important contributions to our understanding of these terms. For additional studies, see Grossman, *The Early Sages of France* (Heb.), 203 and notes.

[a] *Lo'azim* is the plural form of a biblical word meaning 'strange speech' and traditionally taken as an acronym for the Hebrew *leshon am zar*, 'language of a foreign nation'.

grammar scattered throughout his works and praises Rashi's style as a model worthy of emulation. Ezra Zion Melammed likewise directed considerable attention to matters of language in Rashi's commentaries but did not analyse his linguistic approach. Of considerable importance is Moshe Ahrend's study, which dedicated five of ten Open University of Israel units (in a book on Rashi's commentary on the Torah) to matters of language.[5] In his view, Rashi was an exegete, not a grammarian. Chanoch Gamliel disagrees, and his principal findings will be cited below: his primary contention is that Rashi had an original grammatical concept.[6] According to Menahem Banitt, Rashi was influenced also by *reshimot poterim* ('interpreters' lists' which included translations of biblical words into French). He believed that Rashi possessed a translation of the entire Bible in French and relied on it for the explanations of words in his commentaries. Ahrend, however, questions this: 'Rashi makes only a few explicit references to interpreters, and, as a practical matter, no books of interpretation that precede Rashi have survived. The documentation we possess for *la'az ha'olam* dates mostly from the thirteenth century.'[7]

Rashi often went beyond the meaning of a word and discussed its etymology and formation. He dealt with syntax infrequently, but did so most often when one word could have multiple meanings depending on the preposition it was combined with. Rashi noted the evolving meanings of words, and his great biblical erudition stood him in good stead. Modern scholarship has paid considerable attention to grammatical matters in his commentaries. Melammed and Avinery have dealt with many such questions.[8]

Of considerable importance is Chanoch Gamliel's recent study, *Linguistics in Rashi's Commentary*. The central question it poses is whether Rashi had a comprehensive and systematic concept of grammar that served as a key factor in his interpretations. After an in-depth examination, Gamliel offers a positive answer. This finding is of considerable value with respect to Rashi's attitude to linguistic matters.

Some of Gamliel's findings demonstrate Rashi's daring in this area and show that he carried the study of syntax further than his predecessors, including those in Muslim lands. But they also show the gradual displacement, even in France, of Rashi's grammatical concepts in favour of those of the Spanish grammarians. He sums up Rashi's achievements in this area as follows:

The picture of Rashi's grammatical approach that emerges here is an impressive one. When we examine the grammatical subjects treated by Rashi in his commentaries, we find key syntactic issues, and their combination makes for a singularly impressive array of subjects. Of particular interest are the cases in which Rashi takes an idea that appears in rabbinic sources and makes it into a grammatical rule . . . Also of interest is a comparison

---

[5]  Leibowitz and Ahrend, *Rashi's Commentary on the Torah* (Heb.).

[6]  Ahrend, 'Rashi's Method of Explaining Words' (Heb.), 21.        [7]  Banitt, *Rashi*, 68–9.

[8]  Avinery, *Rashi's Palace* (Heb.), 70–142; Melammed, 'Rashi's Commentary on the Bible' (Heb.), 398–414.

of this sort between what we find in Rashi and in Rabbi Sa'adiah Gaon. Sa'adiah Gaon was a pioneer in linguistic theory and practice, and such a comparison is of considerable interest. If we make that comparison, it becomes clear that, in the area of syntax, the concept as found in Rashi is much more comprehensive and more profound than that found in Sa'adiah Gaon . . . With respect to the system of tenses, Rashi's treatment again is no less comprehensive and intensive than that of Sa'adiah Gaon. Rashi directed attention to the various questions [related to tense], and his commentaries reflect a complete system of tenses, a system that does not fall short of Sa'adiah Gaon's . . . The influence [of Menahem ben Saruk and Dunash ben Labrat] within Rashi's *beit midrash* was particularly strong . . . That seems to be the case in the lexical area, but with respect to Rashi's grammatical conception and its reflection in his commentary on the Torah, as we have presented them in this thesis, the matter is not proven. It is entirely possible to agree with Rabin that the penetration of the Spanish grammatical literature into France was among the factors that obstructed the development of Rashi's system . . . The more deeply one probes his various linguistic comments, the better one sees his various grammatical conceptions; and when one considers them, it becomes clear that Rashi had a clear mode of linguistic thought, which he regarded as a significant interpretative factor. Without doubt, Rashi's accomplishment in the area of grammar was concealed, and its extent was hidden, by his humility and by the reality that 'Rashi the exegete with all his might held back his profound knowledge, which becomes evident only after detailed examination.'[9]

As already discussed in Chapter 4, Rashi also ascribed great importance to the cantillation marks in the biblical text, relying on them extensively, and made wide use of Targum Onkelos in his commentary on the Torah and Targum Jonathan in his commentary on the Prophets and the Writings.

## References to Daily Life

Rashi's involvement with all aspects of daily life is remarkable, exceeding that of any other medieval Jewish commentator. He dealt abundantly with them in his commentaries on both the Bible and the Talmud, and his students Rabbi Shemayah and Rabbi Joseph Kara pursued a similar path. It is difficult to determine whether Rabbi Joseph Kara was influenced by Rashi in this regard, but it is nearly certain that Rabbi Shemayah was following in his teacher's footsteps. An examination of Rashi's comments on the construction of the Tabernacle and the Temple shows the considerable attention he devoted to the subject and that his expertise in its details surpassed that of all other exegetes. I will cite only one of many examples with reference to the priestly garments:

*On the two shoulder-pieces of the ephod underneath* [Exod. 28: 27, OJPS]—The settings are placed at the ends of the upper shoulder-pieces of the ephod, which go on his shoulders, opposite his throat, and they are folded over and descend in front of him. The rings he

---

[9] Gamliel, 'Syntactical Issues' (Heb.), 350–5. The concluding quotation is from Fraenkel, *Rashi's Methodology* (Heb.), 210.

commanded to be placed at their other end, which is connected to the ephod, as is said, 'close by the coupling thereof', near the place where they are attached to the ephod, slightly above the sash, so that the coupling is opposite the sash; and they are placed at the height of the straightened shoulders. That is as it is written, 'above the skilfully woven band of the ephod', and they are opposite the end of the breastplate. And he places a thread of blue through those rings and the rings of the breastplate and buttons them to that thread to the right and the left, so that the bottom of the breastplate does not move back and forth and knock against his belly; rather, it is nicely set on the robe.

Rashi used drawings to clarify difficult subjects. Dozens of his drawings appear in his commentary on the Talmud; some were added by copyists. Among them is a map of the Land of Israel, preserved in various manuscripts. It is evident that in drawing the map he followed the practices of Christian mapmakers of the time.[10]

Rashi also looked to common contemporary items in order to make things clear to his readers. For example, he explained the priestly ephod as something similar to the apron worn by feudal noblewomen of his time:

*And an ephod* [Exod. 28: 4]—I neither heard nor found in any *baraita* an explanation of its structure. I imagine it was tied behind him, its width was that of a man's back, as a sort of apron . . . that noblewomen wear while horseback riding, that is how it is made beneath. I imagine too that there is proof that it is a type of garment.

Rashi was very conscious of his readers' reactions, and, as a first-class pedagogue, it was important to him that his writings be easy to read. This is evident in his description of the making of the ephod, where, in addition to interpreting the details of the garment, he sees the need to present a summary so that the reader will have a full picture:

Were I to interpret the making of the ephod and the breastplate following the sequence in the biblical verses, the interpretations would be set out item by distinct item and the reader might err in putting them together. Accordingly, I am writing about the overall way in which they are made, so that the reader may read through it quickly [and I will then interpret in accord with the order of the verses]. (Rashi on Exod. 28: 6)

He then goes on to describe all the details of the ephod and the purpose of each. This is clear proof of his pedagogical skill, as he envisions the reader struggling to understand the passage.

In his commentaries, Rashi considers various aspects of everyday life, including military tactics, nature, coinage, glassmaking, engraving on stone, bird hunting, agriculture, and animal husbandry. This aspect of his work was broadly studied by Esra Shereshevsky, who assembled a remarkably long list of passages that deal with

[10] The map is preserved in several early, reliable, manuscripts (see Grossman, *The Early Sages of France* (Heb.), 207–8; Grossman and Kedar, 'Rashi's Maps of the Land of Israel' (Heb.)). Kedar noted the similarity between Rashi's maps and maps of the Land of Israel drawn by his Christian contemporaries. See also Gruber, 'Light on Rashi's Diagrams'.

such matters. Noah Shapira, who examined Rashi's writings on various technical matters and arranged them by topic, concluded: 'Rashi was amazingly multi-faceted, and there is almost no branch of the technology of his day that he did not touch on, showing profound knowledge of some and lesser knowledge of others.'[11] The important information he provided has facilitated the study of day-to-day life in his time.[12] Of particular value is Mochè Catane's book *Life in Rashi's Time*, which examines life in eleventh-century France on the basis of the writings of Rashi and his students. Because Rashi often compared biblical artefacts and technology to those of France in his own time, his commentaries are a rich source of information about medieval France. Catane studied thirty-two areas of daily life, divided into categories such as 'interior design', 'raw materials', 'decorative arts', 'cosmetics', 'spices', 'coiffure', 'kitchen utensils', 'hunting', 'roasting', 'cheeses', and 'pastries'.

In his commentaries, Rashi identified geographical sites mentioned in the Bible. The considerable effort he invested in doing so is evident in his comments on Joshua 15. Lacking reliable tools, he was compelled to infer the implicit from the explicit. He relied on various biblical verses in drawing the map of the Land of Israel mentioned above, using them to construct an approximate representation of its regions.

## Historical Background and Introductions to the Commentaries

In his commentaries on *Nakh*, Rashi sometimes referred to the historical background of the prophecies and based his interpretations on it. A notable example is provided by his comments on Isaiah. Although he lacked modern historical resources, he was able to explain most of the prophecies in chapters 1–39 against the background of the rise of the Assyrian empire, its wide conquests, and Sennacherib's fall at the gates of Jerusalem. Consistent with that, he even associated with those events prophecies that, on the face of it, do not pertain to them. His vision here was superior to that of some other medieval commentators and, on occasion, even to that of some moderns. Nevertheless, most of these references to historical background come from the midrashic literature, and they do not always correspond to the conclusions reached by modern research.

Rashi generally did not write introductions to his commentaries. The sole exception is his introduction to the Song of Songs, where he emphasizes his intention to interpret the book as a love song between God and Israel and as a promise to protect Israel in exile and redeem it in the future.[13] The sages of Spain and

---

[11] N. Shapira, 'On Rashi's Technical and Technological Knowledge' (Heb.); see also Shereshevsky, *Rashi: The Man and his World*, 155–239.

[12] For examples of these studies, see Grossman, *The Early Sages of France* (Heb.), 207 n. 256.

[13] The introduction is suffused with longing. I consider its distinctive style at two points in the present book. See below in this chapter, in the discussion of polemics with Christianity. A brief

Provence, in contrast, often wrote introductions to their biblical commentaries, in accordance with their rationalist approach and under the influence of the surrounding Muslim culture.

## Style of the Commentaries

### Literary Devices

In contemporary biblical scholarship, much attention is devoted to literary devices, and dozens of such devices have been identified. Some of them are purely aesthetic, meant to serve as rhetorical enhancements; some are meant to impress readers and arouse their emotions and help them identify with the values expressed in the Bible; still others convey a substantive message in such ways as forging connections between seemingly unrelated events. The subject is a broad one, and this is not the place for even partial consideration of the full array of such devices.

The talmudic sages and the medieval biblical interpreters—Jews and Christians alike—were well aware of the importance of these literary devices and referred to some of them. But they lacked modern scholarly tools, and we cannot expect to find in their commentaries any systematic analysis of the matter. The subject was considered in Rashi's *beit midrash*, and his friend and student Rabbi Joseph Kara and his grandson Rashbam devoted considerable attention to it, even more than Rashi himself did.

Modern study of literary devices focuses on three subjects: individual words (or word groupings), individual verses, and the overall unit of text. Rashi, too, considered these three areas, devoting more attention to individual words, less to individual verses, and still less to overall units.

My purpose here is not to survey this broad area but only to deal with Rashi's treatment of it. As mentioned, on rare occasions Rashi examined the literary structure and arrangement of an entire unit of text and how they contributed to the messages it conveyed. For example, in his comments on Isaiah, he considered the close connections among three units of text in Isaiah's prophecies in chapters 1–14: (1) Sennacherib's conquests in Judah, (2) the fall of Sennacherib and his forces and the wondrous rescue of Jerusalem, and (3) the fall of Babylon to Cyrus. The first two events, described in chapters 1–12, took place in 701 BCE. The third, described in chapters 13–14, took place in 539 BCE, some 160 years later, but it is juxtaposed in the book with the two earlier events. Rashi was alert to this deliberate confusion. In his view, the blows inflicted on Judah by Sennacherib and his sudden sharp demise are a model for the similar events to take place in the future, especially in the days of the messiah. The fall of Sennacherib and the fall of Babylon attest to the mirac-

introduction to Zechariah also exists in one of the manuscripts (see Marcus, 'Rashi's Historiosophy in the Introductions to his Bible Commentaries'). But it does not appear in the reliable manuscripts and lacks Rashi's characteristic literary devices. It is therefore difficult to regard it as authentic.

ulous rescue of the Jewish nation following severe tragedies and loss of hope, and the precedent for all of them is the fall of the Egyptians at the Sea of Reeds (Rashi on Isa. 10: 26). In the controversy with Christianity, Rashi thought it proper to emphasize that the prophecies of consolation pertained not only to the past redemptions and the return to Zion but also to the days of the messiah (on Isa. 11: 11). For that reason, he interpreted the words of consolation at the beginning of chapter 14 as pertaining to the future, full, redemption: '*For the Lord will have compassion on Jacob* [Isa. 14: 1, OJPS]—to preserve the promise of their redemption from Babylon; *and will yet choose Israel*—in the future, He will redeem them with full redemption.' Rashi thus bound together the fall of Sennacherib, which took place in Isaiah's time, the fall of Babylon some 160 years later, and the future redemption that will take place in the days of the messiah; he did so through taking account of how the passages in this unit are juxtaposed.

Rashi also considered the literary symbols that closely link the fall of Assyria to the fall of Pharaoh and his army at the Sea of Reeds (on Isa. 10: 26–7). He was not seduced into seeing the prophecies of consolation in Isaiah 1–39 as referring to some abstract event that will take place at the end of days. Instead, he tied them (except for chapters 25–6) to historical events associated with the conquests by the Assyrian army (during the years 732–701 BCE). Not many early commentators considered the close literary connection among these diverse units.

**Editorial tendencies: juxtaposition of passages.** Rashi frequently dealt with the juxtaposition of passages, almost always following the *midrash* in interpreting it. Most of his explanations have a pedagogical quality. For example, the Torah juxtaposes the procedure for the wife suspected of adultery with the rules regarding the priestly gifts in order to teach that 'if you delay bringing the priestly gifts, by your life, you will have to come to him to bring a suspected wife'. 'Why is the passage about the nazirite juxtaposed with the passage about the suspected wife? To tell you that one who sees a suspected wife shown to have strayed should withdraw from wine like a nazirite, for it brings about adultery' (Rashi on Num. 6: 2, following *Sot.* 2a). 'Why was the passage concerning the spies juxtaposed with the passage about Miriam? Because she was afflicted on account of the slander she had spoken about her brother, and these evil men saw that and did not learn a lesson' (on Num. 13: 2, following *Midrash tanḥuma*, 'Shelaḥ lekha', 5). And why was the passage about Zelophehad's daughters juxtaposed with the passage about the spies? To teach that women were not subject to the decree of death imposed on those in the wilderness following the spies' sin (on Num. 26: 64). There are other examples, grounded in rabbinic Midrash.

**Quid pro quo.** On this device as well, Rashi generally followed the lead of the *midrash*. He even took advantage of words having the same meaning in order to emphasize the link between sin and punishment. A few examples: the serpent that enticed Eve is said to have been 'the shrewdest of all [*mikol*] the wild beasts' (Gen. 3: 1); at his downfall, it is said 'more cursed shall you be than all [*mikol*] cattle and all the wild beasts' (Gen. 3: 14). According to Rashi, following the *midrash*, this antithesis, expressed through use of the same linguistic structure, teaches that because he was shrewd, he ended up falling: 'in accord with his shrewdness and greatness, so was his fall—"shrewdest of all [*mikol*]"; "more cursed than all [*mikol*]"'. The word *mikol* (identical in the Hebrew, despite its slightly different translations) is what links the two. So, too, with respect to the Flood: 'On that day, all the fountains of the great deep burst apart—it was quid pro quo; they sinned in that "great [*rabah*] was man's wickedness" [Gen. 6: 5] and were struck by "the great [*rabah*] deep" [Gen. 7: 11].' When they sin, the generation of the dispersion say 'Come, let us build us a city, and a tower'; when they are punished, God says 'Come, let Us go down, and there confound their language.' Rashi comments '[This is] quid pro quo: they said "Come, let us build", and He, in meting out to them, said "Come, let Us go down"' (on Gen. 11: 7, following *Midrash tanḥuma*, 'Noaḥ', 18). 'Because Judah had deceived his father by means of a kid, in whose blood he dipped Joseph's tunic, he, too, was deceived through a kid (on Gen. 38: 23, following *Genesis Rabbah*, 35: 20). Finally, Isaiah says to Hezekiah 'everything in your palace ... will be carried off ... *nothing* will be left behind' (Isa. 39: 6), Rashi comments: '[This is] quid pro quo, corresponding to "there was *nothing* in his palace [that Hezekiah did not show the Assyrians]" [Isa. 39: 2].'

**Use of the same word to highlight the contrast between two events.** This device was a favourite of Rashi's; he usually noted it with the words 'corresponding to what was said'. For example, in reaction to the spies' report, the Israelites said: 'Let us head back [***nitenah rosh venashuvah***] for Egypt.' In contrast, Zelophehad's daughters said to Moses, 'Give us [***tenah lanu***] a holding' in the Land. Because the women showed a positive attitude to the Land, in contrast to the negative attitude of the spies, they were not subject to the decree of dying in the wilderness (Rashi on Num. 26: 64). Another instance: '*Depart, go up hence* [Exod. 33: 1, OJPS]—Corresponding to what He said to him when angry, "*Go*, get thee down" [Exod. 32: 7 OJPS], He said to him when pleased, "Depart, *go* up hence."'

In the account of the people returning to Zion from the exile, it is said that 'I will make all My mountains a road' (Isa. 49: 11). Rashi writes: 'Corresponding to what was said about the time of the destruction, that "highways are desolate" [Isa. 33: 8]; now they will return and travellers will traverse it.'

Isaiah described the practices of a nation that casts aside the flock—it is to shepherd and instead attends only to its personal interests: '[His] watchmen are blind, all of them' (Isa. 56: 10). Rashi interprets: 'Having said "Seek the Lord while He can be found" [Isa. 55: 6], and so forth, to which they do not listen, he reiterates and says "they are shouting at them, declaring [the availability of] penance and the ensuing good, but their leaders are as if blind".'

**Allusion.** This device resembles the preceding one, as both are based on the use of identical wording to draw a connection, of identity or contrast, between two different events. Rebecca told Jacob to flee to Laban and remain in his household 'a few days' (Gen. 28: 43–4, OJPS). The same wording is used in describing Jacob's feelings while working for Laban in order to obtain Rachel's hand: 'they seemed unto him but a few days' (Gen. 29: 20, OJPS). According to Rashi, the latter statement is deliberately meant to teach that 'these are the "few days" of which his mother spoke to him' (on Gen. 29: 18, following *Genesis Rabbah*, 70: 19). Apparently, Rashi uses this *midrash* because the locution 'a few days' is rare: in the entire Bible it appears only in these two instances.

He finds a nice allusion in Isaiah's words 'O House of Jacob! Come let us walk [*venelekhah*] by the light of the Lord' (Isa. 2: 5) to the beginning of the vision: 'And the many peoples shall go [*vehalekhu*] and say "Come, let us go [*lekhu*] up to the Mount of the Lord" [Isa. 2: 3]'.[b] Isaiah's prophecies of destruction with respect to the nations of the world include a special term reserved for Egypt (Isa. 19: 1), and this is no coincidence. Rashi writes: 'That the prophet spoke of Egypt's troubles in these terms, not used for any other nation, is because they are accustomed to being afflicted in this way ... and it is the way of the world to frighten a person [by threatening] an injury with which he has previously been afflicted.' The prophecy 'Oh, let your dead revive! Let corpses arise!' (Isa. 26: 19) employed this wording deliberately to emphasize the contrast between this prophecy and the prophecy on the same subject, recorded earlier, with respect to the nations of the world ('it is the replacement for what is written above, "They are ... shades, they can never rise" [Isa. 26: 14]'). And the wording 'the weight it supports shall be destroyed' (spoken against Shebna, Isa. 22: 25) is likewise deliberate and precise: 'Because he compared him to a peg, he compared those who glorify him and depend on him to a weight hanging from a peg.'

**Redundancy and repetition.** An example of a different sort is the mention of Joseph's name by Zelophehad's daughters: 'of the families of Manasseh the son of Joseph' (Num. 27: 1, OJPS). Everyone is aware that Manasseh was Joseph's son, so why the reference? Scripture, Rashi answers following *Sifrei* on Numbers, meant to allude to the affection for the Land felt both by Joseph and by Zelophehad's daughters.

Allusion of another sort appears in God's telling Moses that he should 'read ... aloud to Joshua' the obligation to destroy the descendants of Amalek

---

[b] The allusion is lost in translation but is evident in the repeated use in the Hebrew of verbs from the root *heh-lamed-kaf*.

(Exod. 17: 14). According to Rashi, following *Mekhilta*, 'here it was hinted to Moses that Joshua would bring Israel into the Land'. Were that not the case, why would he have to direct Joshua to do so?

One device employed by Rashi was gradual intensification, as in '*Happy is the man that hath not walked [in the counsel of the wicked]* [Ps. 1: 1, OJPS]—for inasmuch as he has not walked, neither has he *stood*; and inasmuch as he has not stood, neither has he *sat*.' But though the device is widespread in the Bible, Rashi did not make extensive use of it.

**Word association.**   At times, Rashi used word association to construct comparisons and connections between diverse areas. It is told that when Noah became drunk after the Flood, 'he uncovered himself within his tent' (Gen. 9: 21). Rashi interprets: '"His tent" [*oholo*] is written with a final *heh* [*oholoh*] to allude to the ten tribes, who are named for Samaria, which is called *oholoh*, and who were exiled because of dealings with wine, as it is said, "They drink [straight] from the wine bowls" [Amos 6: 6].' The comparison between Noah's inebriation and the drinking parties of the people of Samaria is far removed from the plain meaning and has a pedagogical purpose. In *Genesis Rabbah* 36: 21, however, a connection had already been established between Noah's drunkenness and the exile of the ten tribes, though not on the basis of the associative link suggested by Rashi.

**Lexical ambiguity.**   This device has recently enjoyed a revival in biblical studies. It refers to the use of a word or phrase that simultaneously conveys two different meanings, both of which are intended by the speaker. Rashi used this device on several occasions. He interprets the text 'they shall rule [*veyirdu*] the fish of the sea' (Gen. 1: 26) as follows: 'This wording connotes subjugation [*ridui*] and descent [*yeridah*]. If man is worthy, he will subjugate the wild and domestic animals; if he is not worthy, he will descend and be diminished before them and they will rule him.' In the account of the fabrication of the golden calf, it is said 'This . . . he cast [*vayatsar*] in a mould' (Exod. 32: 4). Rashi comments: 'This should be translated in two ways. In one, *vayatsar* refers to tying; in the second, *vayatsar* refers to forming.' Rashi also interpreted the phrase 'the strains of your [the Babylonians'] lutes [*hemyat nevaleikha*]' (Isa. 14: 11) as ambiguous: it refers to musical instruments played by the Babylonian soldiers (from the noun *nevel*, lute) but also to soldiers whose actions are vile (*nevalah*) (according to the reliable manuscripts).

On the verse 'an unhappy business [*inyan ra*] that, which God gave men to be concerned with [*la'anot bo*]' (Eccles. 1: 13), Rashi writes: '*Inyan* can be interpreted to mean a dwelling [*ma'on*] and residence, or it can be interpreted to mean enquiry [*iyun*] and thought. And that is true also of *la'anot bo*.' In interpreting the word 'flood' (*mabul*), Rashi offers three different meanings, all intended by Scripture (on Gen. 6: 17). And in interpreting the phrase 'Is not he thy father that hath gotten thee?

[*halo hu avikha kanekha*]' (Deut. 32: 6, OJPS), he likewise offers three meanings for
the final word: 'acquired you [*kena'akha*]; set you in a nest in the mountains
[*kinenekha*]; improved you [*tikenekha*] with every sort of improvement'.

Elsewhere, too, I believe, Rashi uses the expression 'and one may also interpret
... [*ve'od yesh lefaresh*...]' to offer an interpretation in addition to, not instead of,
the one first proposed. I can offer no unambiguous proof for this, but it seems quite
reasonable. Rashi chose his words carefully. When he offered an alternative explanation—that is, one that would displace the explanation initially offered—he introduced it with the words 'something else' (*davar aher*), a phrase he used dozens of
times.[14] 'And one may also interpret' occurs much less frequently, and it appears to
signify an additional explanation that coexists with the initial one. The very words
'something else' suggest negation of the initial interpretation and its replacement
by the second, but 'one may *also* interpret' implies something in addition to the initial interpretation. Let me offer two examples from the poem in the Torah portion
'Ha'azinu'. The first pertains to the verse 'He set him atop the highlands' (Deut. 32:
13). Rashi first interprets it as an economic blessing, describing the fertility of the
Land and the abundance of cattle and other wealth. But he then adds: 'One *may
also interpret* the verse in accordance with Onkelos's translation "I will place them
over the mighty ones of the Land"', that is, as a symbol of the Jews' dominion over
the Land of Israel, which they took from the mighty nations that had been there
before Joshua's conquest.

Another example appears later in the poem. Rashi interprets the verse 'who
stirred not your fathers' fears [*lo se'arum avoteikhem*]' (Deut. 32: 17) to mean 'they
were not afraid of them; their hair [*sa'aratam*] did not rise on their account. It is the
way of human hair to stand on account of fear; it is so interpreted in *Sifrei* on
Deuteronomy. But one *may also interpret* that *se'arum* is related to "And there shall
satyrs [*se'irim*] dance" [Isa. 13: 21]; *se'irim* are demons, and your fathers did not make
such satyrs.'

At times, Rashi made use of the ambiguity of a word without expressly commenting on it. For example, in explaining the verse 'they camped [*nafal*] alongside
all their kinsmen', describing the spread of Ishmael's descendants' settlements
(Gen. 25: 18), Rashi writes '*nafal* [means] dwelled'. But after citing another verse
where the word has this meaning, he goes on to present a *midrash* from *Genesis
Rabbah* 62: 18 without noting that he is citing a rabbinic *midrash*: 'Here he speaks
of "falling" [the more usual meaning of *nafal*], but elsewhere he says "he shall dwell
[*yishkon*] alongside all his kinsman" [Gen. 16: 12]. Until Abraham died, "he shall
dwell"; after Abraham's death, "he fell" [that is, attacked].' Rashi simultaneously
used two different senses of the verb *nafal*.

---

[14] As noted in Ch. 4, Amnon Shapira takes the view that all of Rashi's dual interpretations represent
alternatives and that the second is not meant to displace the first. The issue remains disputed, however,
and it is difficult to regard Shapira's position as a universally applicable rule.

**Individual words.** Rashi paid much attention to the nature of individual words—their etymologies, grammatical forms, and meanings. According to Avinery in *Rashi's Palace*, in looking into meanings, Rashi occasionally considered literary aspects as well.

Two examples will suffice. The first is evidently original to Rashi. In connection with Joseph's interpretation of Pharaoh's dream, he wrote: 'With respect to the seven good years, it is said "[God] has told Pharaoh", because it is near [in time], but with respect to the seven years of famine, it is said "God has revealed to Pharaoh"; because the matter was far off, wording related to a vision is appropriate to it' (on Gen. 41: 26). In other words, something distant from a person, whether in space or time, is not so powerfully perceived by his senses as something nearer, and it is necessary to use an imagined vision to make him aware of it.

The second example pertains to the description in Isaiah 43: 6 of the return to Zion: 'I will say to the North, "Give back!" and to the South, "Do not withhold!"' Rashi interprets:

*I will say*—to the north wind; *give back*—the exiles in the north; *and to the South*—a strong wind; *do not withhold*—from blowing mightily, to return my exiles. It similar to 'Awake, O north wind, come, O south wind!' [S. of S. 4: 16]. Because the north wind is weak, it must be strengthened; it therefore is written 'Awake'. But of the south wind, which need not be strengthened, it is written 'Come'—as it is. So, too, 'Do not withhold'.

In sum, despite the great interest in Rashi's use of literary devices, it is hard to see him as a pathbreaker in this area. He dealt with them even less than his friend Rabbi Joseph Kara, who devoted much attention to literary devices in the Bible. Rashi was greatly influenced by Midrash in this regard, and a very important point to recall is that he almost never mentioned literary devices in and of themselves. He noted them when they encompassed some conceptual message or when they contributed to the interpretation. It follows that the list cited in his interpretations does not reflect his understanding of the Bible's literary devices in themselves.

## Writing Style

In Chapter 2, while discussing Rashi's personality, I noted the close connection between his way of writing and his character traits and enumerated several notable features of his writing style. Let me here point out a few more. Rashi was a master of Hebrew—biblical and rabbinic alike—and many of his innovative words and phrases have made their way into modern Hebrew. These linguistic riches gave him a rare and impressive ability to write with great precision and to describe, with clarity and grace, all manner of phenomena in all their details. According to Yonah Fraenkel, Rashi began to contemplate natural phenomena and daily life and to attempt to understand their detailed workings when he was preparing for the monumental interpretative task he had undertaken. He was continually conscious of what was needed to discharge that task, and it was those needs that moved him to in-depth contemplation of the world around him:

Rashi could not have successfully provided such detailed descriptions of the active life—domestic and commercial, industrial and agricultural—had he not circulated in those spheres with eyes open to see and understand what was going on there. Rashi's commentary on the Talmud was certainly conceived primarily in the room in which he studied and the *beit midrash* in which he taught, but his interpretative aspiration was all-encompassing and certainly bore interpretative fruit even when he was engaged in secular activity. For Rashi, preparing the commentary was not a labour; it was a way of life.[15]

The discussion that follows pertains to Rashi's biblical commentary as well as to his talmudic commentary. He attempted to integrate the source he was interpreting into the commentary itself, and so the head word (*dibur hamathil*) from the source must usually be read together with the interpretation. For example, Rashi interprets the clause 'Will You slay people even though innocent?' (Gen. 20: 4) as 'Even if he is innocent, will You slay him?', integrating two words from the verse itself into his comment. Another example can be found in the verse 'But as the heavens are high above the earth, so are My ways high above your ways and My plans above your plans' (Isa. 55: 9). Rashi interprets: 'There is a difference and a distinction. The virtues and glory of My ways exceed your ways and [those of] of My plans exceed your plans as the height of heaven over earth.' The words of the source are integrated into Rashi's comment as if an inseparable part of it.

Fraenkel also considered the diversity in Rashi's writing:

Variation is the characteristic most frequently encountered in Rashi's writing; one may say that he never repeats anything with precisely the same wording. And because the structure of talmudic passages and the methods by which the Talmud cites sources and moves from subject to subject create a need to explain the same matter more than once, it becomes possible to trace the variation in Rashi's language in almost every passage.[16]

Another notable and enriching feature of Rashi's writing is his use of word pairs. He would use two words identical or similar in meaning to emphasize the idea he meant to express, and he therefore integrated many synonyms, verbs as well as nouns, into his commentaries. As already noted, in his explanation of the verse 'But as the heavens are high above the earth' (Isa. 55: 9), Rashi uses 'difference and distinction' and 'virtues and glory' though it would have been enough to use only one word of each pair. The doubling is meant not only to enrich the language but also to emphasize the point. The phenomenon is especially prominent in his comments on the Song of Songs, in both the introduction and the commentary itself. Rashi may have been influenced by that book's rhetorical style, or he may have

---

[15] Fraenkel, *Rashi's Methodology* (Heb.), 123.        [16] Ibid.

meant the doubling to add emphasis as he sought to persuade his readers to reject Christian propaganda and resist the pressures to convert.

The use of word pairs ('the dual explanation') is a regular feature of Rashi's commentary on the Talmud too, especially where he explicates difficult words. Isaac Avinery and Yonah Fraenkel have already considered the point.[17] At times, Rashi even offered a threefold explanation, as in 'when they [the eggs] are pressed, ensconced, and fixed in the egg-canal' (Rashi on *Bets. 7a, min ha-shalal shel beitsim*); 'the soil is scant', which Rashi interprets as 'it is thin, scant, and slight' (on *Sot. 34b, dikelisha ar'a*); 'withdrew', which Rashi interprets as 'a term connoting separation, withdrawal, and distancing from something' (on *BM 77a, ve'imeru*); 'flowing [fire]', which Rashi interprets as 'a fire that flows, ascends, and rises' (on *BK 61a, ela beko-laḥat*).

Why did Rashi favour this style? The dual explanation (and the threefold even more so) makes it possible to provide an exact explanation of the word being interpreted, one that fits the context and allows for an interpretation that is concrete and precise.

Avinery lists some additional characteristics of Rashi's style.[18] I will note three of them. First, Rashi frequently explains, as an aside, a word that is not even mentioned in the text being interpreted. These include, for example, many Aramaic and other words that appear in the Talmud but are nowhere mentioned in the Bible. Rashi cites them, as synonyms or antonyms, to clarify the meaning of the biblical expression he is examining. He does the same thing with respect to many biblical words, explaining them somewhere other than where they appear, usually in another text dealing with the same subject.

Second, Rashi tends to use synonymous pairs of nouns in construct form; for example, he writes *sof gemar hayofi*—'the end of, the conclusion of, beauty'; *itei yemei ha'adam*—'the times of, the days of, man'; *naharei naḥalei devash*—'rivers of, streams of, honey'.

Finally, Rashi coined many new words. Avinery writes:

The dictionary of Rashi's neologisms comprises more than 1,300 words. Most are entirely new, though some are existing words given novel meanings. Many will be surprised by the idea of Rashi as a lexical innovator, something they had not even suspected. But so it is—Rashi is to be counted among the innovators who expanded the Hebrew language. And if it is difficult to sense that innovativeness, if even a perceptive and experienced eye cannot always discern those innovations, it is because most are so simple and natural that they appear to have been part of the language since Creation ... Who could imagine that words as simple and routine as *hatslaḥah* [success], *haskamah* [approval], *she'ifah* [aspiration], *temikhah* [support], *ma'asar* [imprisonment], *shekidah* [diligence], *re'idah* [quaking], *yahadut* [Judaism], *hafukh* [reversed], *be'ur* [explanation], *takhuf* [frequent], *mitakesh*

---

[17]  Yonah Fraenkel offers numerous examples (ibid. 96–8).
[18]  Avinery, *Rashi's Palace* (Heb.), i. 17–20.

[acting stubbornly], *tamu'ah* [surprising], *peridah* [departure], *badḥan* [jester], *parshan* [interpreter], *shatkan* [silent one], *kitsur* [abbreviated version], *gimgum* [hesitant or incoherent speech], *geviyah* [collection], *taḥboshet* [bandage] and many others are not attested in Hebrew prior to Rashi?[19]

Avinery did not make use of the manuscript versions of Rashi, so his conclusions are not always entirely persuasive. Nevertheless, his work is of great importance.

## General Characteristics of the Commentaries

### Mysticism

Rashi's ties to Jewish mysticism have not been extensively considered in the literature, and views on the matter diverge. According to the traditions of the Ashkenazi pietists (*ḥasidei ashkenaz*), some of the pre-eminent early French sages dealt with mystical doctrines. Although Rashi knew of those teachings, his commentaries show no direct evidence of ties to Ashkenazi mysticism. Nevertheless, various later sages linked him to it strongly. For example, Rabbi Hayim Joseph David Azulai (Hida, 1724–1806), in the name of mystical masters, wrote that 'Rashi fasted 613 fasts before writing his commentary on the Torah . . . and it generally appears that Rashi wrote his commentary in accord with mystical teachings and his words contain supernal secrets.'[20] Evidently, Rashi's great fame led the mystics to claim him as one of their own.[21] In examining the question, scholars have not taken account of the books that were available to Rabbi Shemayah as revealed by his commentaries on the liturgical poems. Some of those commentaries were written while Rashi was still alive, meaning that Rashi had access to them as well. The same may be said of Rashi's use of the *merkavah* literature (the literature of early Jewish mysticism), some of which was known in his time in various Jewish centres, and Rashi may have used it. The question is unresolved and remains the subject of scholarly dispute.[22] What is clear, nevertheless, is that Rashi used *Sefer yetsirah*, knew of *Sefer ḥakhmoni*, and may have known of the *midrash Otiyot derabi akiva*. For example, in his comment on Job 28: 27, Rashi writes:

He [God] looked into [the Torah] and created the world with its letters. In accord with their order and frequency He created all creatures, as is written in the mystery of *Sefer yetsirah* . . . He counted the letters, doubled and plain, first, medial and final . . . and all is explained in the mystery of *Sefer yetsirah*.

[19] Avinery, *Rashi's Palace* (Heb.), i. 102 (glosses by J.L.).

[20] Azulai, *Shem hagedolim*, s.v. 'Rashi'.

[21] For the literature on the issue, see Grossman, *The Early Sages of France* (Heb.), 205 nn. 248–9; see also Mondschein, 'Rashi and Mysticism' (Heb.), 108–9; Gross, 'Spanish Jewry and Rashi's Commentary on the Pentateuch' (Heb.), 50–3; Kanarfogel, *Peering through the Lattices*, index, s.v. 'Rashi'.

[22] On Rashi's ties to the *merkavah* literature, see Dan, 'Rashi and the Merkabah', which argues that Rashi was not familiar with it. For a different view, see Halperin, *The Faces of the Chariot*, 184, 210, 219–20, 243. See also Wolfson, 'Mysticism of the Ashkenazi Pietists' (Heb.), esp. 138–9.

## Pedagogical Tendencies in the Commentaries on *Nakh*

In discussing Rashi's commentary on the Torah (Chapter 4), I gave extensive consideration to his pedagogical tendencies. Similar tendencies appear also in his commentaries on *Nakh*, especially on Psalms, Proverbs, and Ecclesiastes, and they led him to interpret many verses allegorically. I will cite numerous examples when I consider Rashi's world-view (Chapters 8–10) and will here offer only one additional illustration.

Ecclesiastes 8: 15 is an extremely problematic verse, preaching physical pleasure and seeing it as man's highest goal: 'I therefore praised enjoyment. For the only good a man can have under the sun is to eat and drink and enjoy himself.' Rashi takes 'enjoyment' (*simḥah*) to refer to the study of Torah and cautions against a literal understanding of the verse:

> *Enjoyment*—he should rejoice in his lot and pursue [God's] righteous commands, which gladden the heart, and should not pursue great wealth through interest, usury, and theft. One who does not rejoice in his lot and pursues mammon is destined to sin with respect to theft, price gouging, and interest. And one who does not rejoice in his lot with respect to his wife is led to pursue women and crave another man's wife.

He interprets Ecclesiastes 9: 9 in a similar vein. The verse states: 'Enjoy happiness with a woman you love'; Rashi interprets, 'Have the understanding to learn a trade so you may earn a living from it while studying Torah.'[c]

Rashi treated the entire book of Ecclesiastes in the same way. According to his interpretation, the rabbinic dispute over its canonization was unnecessary. His clear departure from the plain meaning of the verses, and his reliance on *midrashim* in explaining them, offer the most conclusive evidence of his interpretative agenda.

## Bible Interpretations in the Commentary on the Talmud

Hundreds of biblical verses are interpreted in Rashi's commentary on the Talmud, and various talmudic passages are interpreted in his biblical commentaries. The relationship between the commentaries raises questions, for there are differences between their interpretations of many biblical verses and talmudic passages. Resolving these issues is made more difficult by the uncertainty over which was written first (something considered in the next chapter).

According to Isaac Hirsch Weiss, Rashi's biblical commentaries offer interpretations reflecting the verse's context in the Bible while the talmudic commentary interprets in accordance with the talmudic passage, that is, with how the verse is used in the talmudic give-and-take. Weiss senses, however, that while this explanation can account for most of the contradictions, it cannot account for all:

---

[c] The phrase translated 'enjoy happiness' is *re'eh ḥayim*: literally 'see life'. Rashi's words translated 'have the understanding' are *re'eh vehaven*: literally 'see and understand'. His comment is thus more closely tied to the text than is evident in translation.

But something else of importance must be noted here. We find in countless places that he interprets [biblical] words and statements in his commentary on the Talmud and contradicts what he wrote in his commentary on the Bible, and we do not know whether one or the other is correct in his eyes or whether both may be right, depending on situation, context, and place ... For in his commentary on the Bible, he explains [a verse] in accordance with his view [of its meaning], without concern about how the sages of the Talmud interpreted the same verse ... But this rule is worthy of being maintained, for it is the only way to explain most of the contradictions between his commentary on the Talmud and his commentary on the Bible.[23]

Yo'el Florsheim published a three-volume study of Rashi's interpretations of biblical verses in his commentary on the Talmud.[24] In the introduction to the first volume (comments on verses from the Torah) he noted the importance of these sources for the study of Rashi's commentary overall and that Weiss's explanation cannot successfully account for all the differences between the commentaries. He even showed that in some cases, Rashi interpreted entire biblical verses in his commentary on the Talmud, even though only a portion of the verse is cited in the talmudic discussion. Florsheim's work is of great importance, but he, too, has not offered an adequate explanation for the differences and contradictions between Rashi's two interpretations.

## Anti-Christian Polemic

In discussing Rashi's commentary on the Torah, I already considered the important role of religious polemic. The polemic is even more frequent, forceful, and clear in the commentaries on *Nakh*, especially on the Song of Songs, Psalms, Isaiah, and the Twelve Prophets. In her article 'Rashi's Commentary on the Song of Songs', Sarah Kamin gave extensive consideration to the polemic in that commentary, traces of which are evident at dozens of points. In principle, Rashi did not break new ground here, for the midrashists offered similar interpretations; but he gave added force to their comments and presented them as firmly anchored in the words of the biblical text themselves. Moreover, he prefaced his comments to the Song of Songs with an introduction clearly meant to bolster those whose faith might be failing. He did so primarily by forging a close connection between the meaning of the text, as he interpreted it, and Israel's state of exile in his time. For example:

And I say that Solomon saw, through the holy spirit, that Israel was destined to suffer exile after exile, destruction after destruction, and, during that exile, to mourn [the loss of] its earlier glory. And he established this book through the holy spirit, using the language of a rejected woman, a living widow longing for her husband, yearning for her beloved, recalling her youthful love for him and mentioning the kindnesses of her youth,

[23] Weiss, 'Life of Rabbi Solomon bar Isaac' (Heb.), 165.
[24] Florsheim, *Rashi on the Bible in his Commentary on the Talmud* (Heb.).

the pleasantness of her beauty, and the skilful actions through which she was bound up with him in a powerful love.

The emphatic repetitions attest not only to the intensity of Rashi's feelings but also to his interest in stressing the profound ties between God and Israel.

Rashi interpreted many passages in the book in this light, linking verses to the exile in his time. For example, on the verse 'savouring [*nazkirah*] [Your love] more than wine' (S. of S. 1: 4), Rashi comments: 'Even today, in living widowhood, I recall [*azkir*, the more frequent meaning of the word translated 'savour'] Your earlier expressions of love . . . even today, they still delight and rejoice in it.' On 'tell me, You Whom [my soul] loves so well; where do You pasture Your sheep? Where do You rest them at noon?' (S. of S. 1: 7), he offers: 'The community of Israel say before Him, as a woman to her husband: Tell me, You Whom my soul loves, how You can pasture Your sheep amidst these wolves . . . and how do You rest them at noon in this exile, a time of trouble . . . how will they pasture and be saved from their oppressors . . . so Your children are not destroyed?'

In his comments on the Psalms, Rashi similarly found ample place for polemic with Christianity, linking many of the psalms to it. The links are often artificial, for the psalms in question speak neither of polemic with Christianity nor of the persecution of Israel. Nevertheless, this is a very important aspect of Rashi's comments on the Psalms, for he interpreted about half of its chapters as pertaining to the nations' hatred of Israel, the great suffering of the Jews in exile, and the future redemption. In many cases, he stressed that the psalmist was referring to 'Esau' or to 'Edom', that is, to the Christian world. I have elsewhere treated this subject extensively[25] and will limit myself here to only three examples.

*Why do nations assemble?* [Ps. 2: 1]—Our rabbis interpreted this with reference to the King Messiah, but by its meaning, and to respond to the heretics, it is proper to interpret it with reference to David himself, as it is said, 'When the Philistines heard that Israel had anointed David as king over them, the Philistines assembled in their military encampments' [paraphrase of 2 Sam. 5: 17] and fell in his hands; and of this he said, 'Why do the nations assemble and all gather together?'

There can be no doubt that Rashi used 'heretics' to refer to Christian exegetes who used these verses, taken as referring to Jesus, in their propaganda. Rashi objected to interpreting them to refer to the King Messiah because he believed that doing so could lend support to the Christian interpretation: if all concur that the verses refer to the King Messiah, it becomes easier for Christians to interpret them as referring to their messiah, Jesus. That is especially so in the context of Psalm 2, which states 'The Lord said to me, "You are My son, I have fathered you this day."' But if the texts are speaking of King David, a specific personality who lived and was

---

[25] See Grossman, 'Rashi's Commentary on Psalms' (Heb.).

active in days past, it becomes harder for Christians to press their interpretation in polemics with Jews and draw support from Jewish exegesis itself.

A second example appears in Psalm 5, which is attributed to David. On its plain meaning, it appears to be a continuation of Psalms 3 and 4, which speak of David's personal enemies. It was so interpreted by the medieval Jewish sages and in *Midrash tehilim*. But Rashi interprets the psalm as speaking of 'the enemy forces advancing on Israel' and, on that basis, understands the words 'murderous, deceitful men the Lord abhors' (Ps. 5: 7) to refer to Esau and his progeny, that is, the Christians.

The third example is found in Psalm 39. The psalm appears to be the personal plea of a man in distress, praying for salvation and rescue, and it was so interpreted by Rabbi David Kimhi (Radak, *c.*1160–*c.*1235), Ibn Ezra, and others. Rashi, however, interprets it as a polemic against Christianity. The circumstances he describes are typical of those experienced by Jews in Christian Europe at the time, especially with respect to the Jewish–Christian polemic:

> We wanted to maintain ourselves in the face of all the troubles that came upon us, avoiding any harsh thoughts or statements against the attribute of judgement, despite the evil ones who face us and torment us. We remained quietly silent for many days, and also kept our silence with respect to the good, even with respect to words of Torah, on account of our fear of them. As a result, we were pained, crestfallen, and frightened, and in our silence, our hearts burn within us and our inner thoughts burn within us like fire, causing us to speak out before You, and this is what we say: Tell us, O Lord, our term, how long we will suffer, so we may know when we will be done with it (on Ps. 39: 2).
>
> *The butt of the benighted* [Ps. 39: 9]—do not make me the butt of the wicked [MSS: Esau]; make him also suffer injury and pain so he will be unable to say to me that you are struck but we are not struck.

It seems to me that the great hatred for Christianity expressed in Rashi's comments on the Psalms can be linked to the time in which they were written. Rabbi Shemayah's commentary on one of the liturgical poems implies that the comments on the Psalms were written late in Rashi's life, evidently following the edicts of 1096.[26] Those edicts brought about the death of thousands of Jews in Germany, among them some of Rashi's closest friends, who had studied with him in the German yeshivas.

I will have more to say about many of the verses in *Nakh* that Rashi interpreted polemically when I consider, in Chapter 8, the place of the nations of the world in Rashi's teachings.

### Addenda and Corrigenda

Rashi did not consider his commentary on the Bible to be a completed, closed book. He inserted addenda and corrigenda on the basis of his own study, his exchanges with his friends and students, and the new sources that he acquired. In

[26] See Grossman, 'Rashi's Commentary on Psalms' (Heb.), 72–4.

that, we see one of his prominent character traits, which I have already noted: his commitment to truth and his unceasing effort to obtain it.

Evidence of his addenda and corrigenda is preserved in various places. The most impressive example appears in the version of his commentary on the Torah as set forth in MS Leipzig 1, which was preserved together with Rabbi Shemayah's annotations. (See Chapter 4 for a discussion of the nature and importance of this document.) Rashi's own annotations are introduced by Rabbi Shemayah with the words 'my rabbi interprets', 'from the mouth of my rabbi', or, most often, simply 'my rabbi'. At one point, the manuscript's copyist, Rabbi Makhir, even notes that the reference is to Rashi. At two points, Rabbi Shemayah mentions that the annotations were made at Rashi's express request ('my rabbi ordered an annotation'; 'my rabbi ordered me to annotate').[27]

The number of annotations in MS Leipzig 1 that originated with Rashi comes close to fifty. More than thirty conclude with the attribution 'my rabbi'. In cases where the marking is the letter *resh* as an abbreviation, it is impossible to tell for certain whether Rashi expressly requested Rabbi Shemayah to make the annotation or whether the reference is to interpretations and thoughts that arose in discussions between Rashi and Rabbi Shemayah and that were inserted by the latter on his own, as an annotation to Rashi's original interpretation.

Rashi's annotations are of various sorts. They include interpretations, linguistic points, discussions of real-world matters (such as the borders of the Land of Israel), and brief quotations from rabbinic *midrashim*. In his own annotations, Rabbi Shemayah even comments on Rashi's thoughts and actions.

Rashi also annotated his comments on the Prophets with addenda and corrigenda. In his letter to the sages of Auxerre, he expressly mentioned the annotations he had introduced in his comments on Ezekiel: 'In any case, I erred in that interpretation . . . and so I [re]interpreted at the end of the matter and my words contradicted each other, and I now dealt with the matter with our brother Shemayah and I annotated it.'[28]

The comments on the Psalms were similarly corrected and supplemented, as is evident from Rabbi Shemayah's account, and the tendency is one that that pervades all of Rashi's commentaries on the Bible. From his words and those of Rabbi Shemayah, it is evident that Rashi invested considerable effort in clarifying the text of his commentaries, ensuring their precision. It follows that when the elderly Rashi told his grandson Rashbam that, given the opportunity, he would write new commentaries on the Torah 'in accord with the plain meanings that newly emerge each day', he was not engaging in a mere rhetorical flourish; he was accurately characterizing his method.

[27] R. Shemayah, marginalia to Rashi on Num. 32: 17, MS Leipzig 1, fos. 157*b*–158*a*.

[28] Rashi, *Responsa* (Heb.), ed. Elfenbein, §10; the passage pertains to Ezek. 40: 17. He uses 'our brother' to refer affectionately to his student, R. Shemayah.

Did Rashi produce multiple editions of his commentaries on the Bible or did he rest content with a single edition and its addenda and corrigenda? As far as we can tell, it was the latter. There is no reliable evidence of multiple editions in the modern sense of the word, that is, various layers of interpretation. Moreover, Rashi's commentaries gained wide distribution primarily after some of these addenda and corrigenda had already been introduced. This is attested to by the fact that some of the annotations that Rabbi Shemayah attributes to Rashi's express direction (and are so recorded in MS Leipzig 1) also appear in the versions of the commentary preserved in various other manuscripts, such as MS Munich 5, MS Vienna 23, and MS St Petersburg Evr. I: 11—all of them early and reliable versions. Early sages, to be sure, spoke of 'editions' of Rashi, but it appears they used the term 'edition' to refer only to annotations and variant readings.

# CHAPTER SIX

# Commentary on the Talmud

RASHI'S MOST IMPORTANT literary creation, the work that gained him his greatest fame through the ages, is his commentary on the Babylonian Talmud, one of the finest Hebrew works ever written. Other sages preceded him in writing commentaries on various talmudic tractates or even on the entire Talmud, but none of them matched Rashi's interpretative achievements, and their ongoing influence on the study of Talmud was relatively minor. Rashi's commentary displaced nearly all those written in Ashkenaz before his time, and many of those other commentaries were simply forgotten.

Research into Rashi's commentary on the Talmud is centred on six principal questions, which will be considered over the course of this chapter:

1.  What is the scope of the commentary? On which tractates did Rashi himself comment? Are all the printed commentaries attributed to him in fact his own work? In what order were they written?

2.  What qualities made Rashi's commentary the preferred one?

3.  To what degree is Rashi linked to other interpretative traditions, especially to earlier commentaries written in Ashkenaz?

4.  Is the version of the commentary that has come down to us authentic?

5.  Are there multiple editions of the commentary?

6.  What accounts for the changes and internal contradictions in the commentary?

Before turning to these questions, let me first consider the commentary's target audience.

## For Whom Did Rashi Write his Commentary on the Talmud?

Scholars disagree on the identity of Rashi's intended audience. Most believe that the talmudic commentary—and, to a certain degree, the biblical commentary—was meant for advanced students, not beginners. As Lipschuetz puts it, '[Rashi] did not write his commentary to be an open book for the masses and the common people; rather, [he meant it] for the educated people of his time, those versed in

Torah.'[1] Yonah Fraenkel offered proof of this: he examined Rashi's interpretation
of one hundred terms in the Babylonian Talmud and found that rare terms—that
is, those appearing no more than five times in the entire Talmud—were explained
every time they appeared. Other terms were treated in inverse proportion to their
frequency of appearance; very common terms were not explained at all unless they
were used in an unusual manner. It follows, according to Fraenkel, that Rashi did
not write his commentaries for beginners.[2]

Other scholars early and late have taken what I regard as the highly reasonable
view that Rashi's commentaries on the Talmud and the Bible were written, in the
first instance, for a community of students having varied levels of knowledge.
Everyone could benefit from them in a way consistent with his own background.
Israel Ta-Shma recently re-emphasized the point:

> One of the wonders is the degree to which Rashi's commentary suits any reasonable level
> of study that may be encountered ... The benefit to be realized from the commentary
> varies directly with the level of the student: the higher the student's level, the greater the
> benefit he can derive from the commentary, for he will be able to discern—or, at least,
> imagine that he discerns—Rashi's deliberate allusions and linguistic layers, appreciate
> what is said and what goes unsaid, and penetrate his 'deepest' meanings ... It is enough
> to consider the simple fact that numerous and diverse scholarly modes have arisen during
> the 900 years since Rashi's commentary was written, each with its own distinctive style
> of studying Talmud, yet all of them, without exception, have used Rashi's commentary to
> provide support for their own interpretations, and all have seen him as a faithful repre-
> sentative of their thought process ... However high a rank a student attains, he will
> encounter Rashi's commentary at his right hand, helping him—to the extent the student
> has the capacity—to rise still higher and higher. At the same time, the student will come
> to recognize ever more profoundly the commentary's value and its author's greatness,
> which are without limit.[3]

The comments of Rabbi Isaac Lattes, Rabbi Isaac ben Jacob Canpanton, and
Rabbi Hayim Joseph David Azulai, cited below in the discussion of the qualities
of Rashi's commentaries, show that they, too, noticed the existence of varied
degrees of depth in Rashi's commentaries.

This observation also pertains in part to Rashi's biblical commentary. The
beginner can certainly make good use of it, as attested by the myriads of children
studying Torah with Rashi throughout the Jewish world. Only an advanced student, however, can plumb the depths of Rashi's words and derive their full benefit.
Chanoch Gamliel has shown that many of Rashi's linguistic comments and his
grammatical system overall were intended in the first instance for the 'erudite and
probing' student.[4]

[1] Lipschuetz, 'Rashi' (Heb.), 174.          [2] Fraenkel, *Rashi's Methodology* (Heb.), 199.
[3] Ta-Shma, *Talmudic Commentary in Europe and North Africa* (Heb.), i. 49.
[4] Gamliel, *Linguistics in Rashi's Commentary* (Heb.), 228–30.

# Extent of the Commentary

Rashi interpreted most tractates of the Babylonian Talmud and possibly all of them. Some printed commentaries attributed to him are not, in fact, his, however, and others remain of uncertain authorship. The latter were attributed to Rashi by printers of the Talmud at the end of the fifteenth century, but we do not know whether these attributions were based on a reliable tradition (written or oral) or on an erroneous one. Doubts about the authorship of some commentaries attributed to Rashi were raised by early scholars, and Azulai devoted detailed attention to the question.[5]

Rashi's commentaries on tractates *Ta'anit*, *Nedarim*, *Nazir*, *Bava batra* (from fo. 29*b*), and *Makot* (from fo. 20*a*) have not been preserved. The commentaries on tractates *Ta'anit*, *Nedarim*, *Nazir*, and *Horayot* printed and attributed to him in the standard Vilna edition of the Talmud are not his work; they are among the commentaries written in Mainz. Nor is the commentary on *Mo'ed katan* his. Rashi's commentary on that tractate was first published in 1961 by Ephraim Kopper. Doubts likewise have been raised about the commentary on portions of tractates *Zevaḥim*, *Menaḥot*, *Bekhorot*, *Temurah*, and *Me'ilah*, and Rashi's authorship of the commentary on *Sanhedrin* 10 (the chapter known as *Ḥelek*) likewise is a matter of debate. The Venice edition (1521) of the commentary on *Bava batra* includes the following statement at folio 29*a*: 'Thus far the commentary of Rashi, may the memory of the righteous be for a blessing; from here on, the commentary of Rabbi Samuel ben Rabbi Meir.' The version of this commentary appearing in the Pizarro edition states 'here died Rashi, may his memory be for a blessing'. The Venice edition (1520) of the commentary on *Makot* states, at folio 19*b*, 'Our rabbi, whose body was pure and whose soul departed in purity, interpreted no further. From here on, the words of the student, Rabbi Judah ben Rabbi Nathan.'

Although various scholars have suggested that Rashi never wrote commentaries on these tractates or portions of tractates, I favour the hypothesis that those commentaries were lost. That hypothesis, I recognize, appears problematic at first, for it stands at odds with the facts that Rashi had gained wide renown and that his commentaries were widely and quickly disseminated in Jewish communities in Europe and elsewhere. But the commentary on *Mo'ed katan* published by Kupfer— a unique manuscript, containing what seems to be Rashi's original commentary on the tractate—and findings noted above with reference to other tractates demonstrate that commentaries may have been lost and that the possibility should not be rejected on the basis of prima facie rational considerations. We therefore may conclude that the commentary on *Ta'anit* likewise was lost, for the tractate is part of

---

[5] For a comprehensive and detailed bibliography regarding the tractates or portions thereof of which Rashi's authorship of the commentary is in doubt, see Grossman, *The Early Sages of France* (Heb.), 216–18 nn. 275–9.

the much-studied talmudic order *Mo'ed* and it is hard to imagine that Rashi never wrote a commentary on it. Nor should the notes cited above from tractates *Bava batra* and *Makot* mislead us into thinking that Rashi died before completing his commentaries on these tractates. It is entirely possible that the manuscript used by the scribe or copyist working on *Bava batra* lacked the rest of the commentary and that he therefore assumed that Rashi had been unable to complete it before dying. Indeed, it is hard to imagine that Rashi would have moved on to another tractate before completing his work on the previous one, and there is no basis for assuming that this was the last tractate to be interpreted. Moreover, it is unreasonable to think that Rashi began to interpret two tractates (*Bava batra* and *Makot*) late in his life and that he would start work on the second even though he was still at the beginning of the first. This hypothesis is further supported by the version of the note appearing in the manuscript of Rashi's comments on *Makot*: 'thus far the words of the teacher; from here on, the words of the student'. Moreover, Jacob Nahum Epstein has shown that the commentary on *Makot* by Rabbi Judah ben Nathan, Rashi's son-in-law, encompasses the entire tractate and not only the portion beginning at folio 19*a*; that, too, supports the premise that Rashi completed his commentary on the tractate. It thus seems that we are dealing here with nothing more than the vagaries of manuscript transmission.

The sequence in which Rashi wrote his commentary remains a mystery. In writing his commentary on the Torah, he followed the order of its books, as suggested by allusions to earlier books in later ones. The inter-tractate allusions in the talmudic commentary are too few to cast light on which tractates were interpreted earlier and which later, but they suffice to demonstrate that Rashi did not follow the talmudic sequence. Yonah Fraenkel made an interesting attempt to determine the order in which Rashi wrote on the basis of the nature and characteristics of the commentaries, setting forth his conclusions very cautiously:

We assume that the interpretative methods became more sophisticated as the work was conducted; that is, a tractate interpreted more elegantly was a later work. Examining the tractates with an eye to the level of the interpretative method can lead us not only to an approximation of the chronological sequence—which is solely of bibliographic importance—but, more importantly for our purposes, to an assessment of the interpretative methods we have suggested ... It appears that we may distinguish between the tractates Rashi worked on earlier (*Berakhot, Sanhedrin, Menahot, Bekhorot, Arakhin,* and *Keritot*) and those he worked on later, in a more mature manner (*Sotah, Gitin, Bava kama, Bava metsia, Bava batra, Shevuot,* and *Hulin*). The remaining tractates show no characteristics pointing in one direction or the other, and they may be said to constitute a third group, that is, an intermediate stage in the history of Rashi's Talmud commentary.[6]

In my opinion, the commentary on tractate *Shabat* also should be assigned to the early period of Rashi's work. But it goes without saying that this sort of enquiry does not necessarily establish the sequence in which the commentaries were written.

## Interpretative Characteristics

Rashi's commentary on the Talmud runs continuously, explaining the talmudic text rather than only selected passages.[7] For the most part, it deals with the plain meaning of the text, and it avoids raising and resolving difficulties. Still, Rashi does not interpret every word or every subject, skipping over whatever he considered to be straightforward and clear—including, at times, matters that would not be clear to a beginner. It follows that he addressed his commentary to advanced talmudic students. Fraenkel has suggested that Rashi's premise was that beginners would have a teacher who could guide them through the basics and that he, Rashi, would complement the teacher with greater depth. Ta-Shma wrote to similar effect:

Rashi's commentary was meant to be laboured over, like the Talmud itself, to direct study rather than lighten its yoke, and certainly not to replace it. The commentary is laconic and its precise meaning deliberately somewhat concealed, requiring close examination. Anyone familiar with Rashi knows that he is of greatest value to one reviewing a passage, not necessarily to one studying it for the first time. For a youngster lacking adequate experience in Talmud study, Rashi's commentary cannot replace the efforts of a teacher and cannot by itself prepare the student for independent study.[8]

Some of the commentary's linguistic qualities have been discussed in Chapter 5. It is written in rabbinic style and closely bound to the talmudic text. The comments are terse, often comprising only a few words and sometimes only one or two. Rashi's succinct language is clear, deliberate, and precise; its purpose is to resolve doubts, reject erroneous opinions, and, on rare occasions, to allude to parallel passages. Various sages have considered the mysteries of his succinctness and the need to probe deeply into the commentary and consider each word carefully. For example, the thirteenth-century Provençal sage Rabbi Isaac Lattes wrote that 'the leading treatises written in the form of a commentary are the commentaries of our rabbi Solomon ben Isaac . . . Its virtues are evident only to individuals, for with one word it sometimes resolves a bundle of difficulties.'[9] Rabbi Isaac ben Jacob Canpanton, a leading Spanish sage of the second half of the fifteenth century, wrote similarly:

The practice and method of Rashi, may his memory be for a blessing, was to say nothing unnecessary, not even a single word; that is, when he spoke, he spoke of the Talmud's

---

[7] The most important study of Rashi's commentary on the Talmud is Fraenkel, *Rashi's Methodology* (Heb.); see also Ta-Shma, *Talmudic Commentary in Europe and North Africa* (Heb.), i. 40–56, and the literature cited there.

[8] Ta-Shma, *Talmudic Commentary in Europe and North Africa* (Heb.), i. 42.

[9] Lattes, *Sha'arei tsiyon*, 174.

wording, to explain it because it was vague; to preclude some other, erroneous explanation; to object or raise some difficulty; or to correct the wording.[10]

Azulai observed that the very letters used by Rashi were worthy of careful examination: 'He was extremely precise in his wording, hinting at some novellae by changing a letter.'[11]

A central characteristic of Rashi's commentary, and one sharply differentiating it from the talmudic exegesis of the generation that followed him in Germany and France, is its localized nature; that is, it does not reach beyond the bounds of the passage being interpreted. At times, to be sure, he refers to parallel passages, but he does not regularly compare and contrast passages in the way that is so characteristic of the tosafists. Only rarely does he refer to some other passage to raise a question regarding the text being interpreted. Central to his interpretation was the inner logic of each passage, as Yonah Fraenkel has discussed in detail. As in his commentary on the Torah, Rashi selected the interpretation that he regarded as best suited to a passage only after first examining the alternative exegetical suggestions that appeared in the sources that were available to him or that he himself thought of.

A notable feature of Rashi's method is his use of one or more words from the talmudic passage to link his interpretation to the text. The quotation of the Talmud's wording is a guidepost not only for the course of the talmudic passage but also for Rashi's interpretation. At times, the two are integrated. In that way, the commentary accompanies the student through the passage by focusing on the difficult words that require explanation. Later, these head words were termed *dibur hamathil*, 'the introductory word'. Most commentaries that preceded Rashi's, especially those of the Babylonian geonim, did not use this technique; instead they paraphrased the talmudic passage.

Other characteristics of Rashi's commentary include the use of a question-and-answer format (sometimes only implicitly); integration of the interpretation with the talmudic text; presentation of several interpretative alternatives, sometimes pointing out their respective advantages and shortcomings; considerable attention to variant readings and reasoned textual emendations; the use of precisely chosen words; and the offering of guidance to the student (sometimes only allusively) with respect to matters not explicitly stated. By providing guidance in this way, Rashi simultaneously operated on two levels in his commentary, one directed to the ordinary student and one to the student who probes more deeply and analytically. Rashi devoted greater attention to textual variants than did any previous Ashkenazi talmudic commentator. Such matters, to be sure, were treated by the Mainz exegetical school in general and Rabbenu Gershom in particular, but that treatment was not as intensive as Rashi's.

It is a commonplace that Rashi exerted great influence on the text of the Talmud

---

[10] Isaac b. Jacob Canpanton, *Darkhei hatalmud*, 59.      [11] Azulai, *Shem hagedolim*, s.v. 'Rashi'.

as it appeared in its printed editions. Printers often favoured his emendations, and Ta-Shma has noted how the printing of Rashi's commentary side by side with the talmudic text in all editions furthered that process. Rashi's extensive treatment of textual matters and alternative readings is consistent with the intellectual climate of his period in general. A notable feature of the late eleventh- and twelfth-century European renaissance was that scholars insisted on working with accurate texts.

A common didactic element in Rashi's commentary, described extensively by Fraenkel, is his way of directing students to material appearing later in the passage or in ensuing passages. Fraenkel sees this technique as an effort to allow for independent study. When the student locates the subsequent material that Rashi points to, he will be able to understand it on his own, because of what he has already learned. Fraenkel believes this and other methods adopted by Rashi betoken the profound, consistent, and ongoing didactic thinking that marks Rashi's commentary on the Talmud. At the same time, we should recognize that making the subsequent material easier comes at the price of making the earlier material more difficult, for it requires the student to consider difficulties in future passages along with those he is already grappling with. The measure is deliberate, however, as Rashi encourages the student to devote greater effort now and reap its benefits in the future.

Fraenkel noted two additional characteristics of Rashi's commentary on the Talmud, describing the first as follows:

Rashi thought more deeply about terminological rules than any other commentator before or since . . . It therefore seems surprising at first that he enumerates terminological rules only rarely. We have found ten terminological rules dispersed throughout the entire Talmud; what they share is their association with some exegetical crux. Rashi, the devoted exegete, suppressed his profound knowledge, revealing it only after a precise examination. He interprets every difficult passage from a terminological aspect, but he forces himself to do no more than interpret.[12]

As for the second characteristic:

Rashi interpreted the entire Talmud as a single book; that is, the Talmud stood before him in its entirety and he applied his exegetical standards uniformly, throughout his commentary. We can determine clear rules regarding Rashi's method, and we find almost no instances that are inconsistent with his one system for interpreting talmudic terms.[13]

The finding of uniformity is persuasive in principle, but it cannot be extended to the entire work. Rashi's commentary is longer on some tractates and shorter on others. This can be attributed, I believe, not only to objective differences among the tractates in the difficulty of the questions they pose, but also to subject matter and, perhaps, to the time at which the commentary was written. A subject that was current and widely dealt with in Rashi's time—especially the existence of divergent

---

[12] Fraenkel, *Rashi's Methodology* (Heb.), 200.     [13] Ibid.

customs—merited a longer commentary. A clear example is the commentary on tractate *Ḥulin*, which is more detailed than most and in which Rashi devoted more effort than in any other tractate to halakhic rulings. This appears to stem from the practical importance of the tractate with regard to *kashrut*, an area that was then subject to many uncertainties arising out of the varied traditions and customs that reached Germany and France during the tenth and eleventh centuries.

## Connections with Other Interpretative Traditions

The partial talmudic commentaries of Rabbi Sherira ben Hanina Gaon (tenth century) and his son, Rabbi Hai Gaon (939–1038) were not available to Rashi, and it is also doubtful that he knew of the commentary by Rabbi Hananel ben Hushiel (Rabbenu Hananel, 990–1053). Nevertheless, he made use of the interpretative traditions of the Babylonian geonim and other Jewish sages in Islamic lands, which had reached him through European Jewish merchants who had travelled to the East, as well as the interpretative traditions passed on to him by various sages in France and Germany. His explanations of stories alluded to in the Talmud but not set forth there in full attest to the interpretative traditions he had in his possession, for without those traditions, transmitted from generation to generation or preserved in writing, he could not have explained those stories. At the same time, Rashi had a strong affinity with the commentaries written in Germany during the eleventh century by Rabbenu Gershom and his students. In their day, these commentaries gained wide renown and made an important contribution to the reputation of the German yeshivas and to their ability to attract students.

As mentioned, most of these earlier commentaries were displaced by Rashi's and therefore did not leave the mark they deserved to on later halakhic literature. Scribes and copyists had little interest in them; their reputations therefore dwindled, and only a few survived. Not surprisingly, they are preserved in relatively good shape on those talmudic tractates that Rashi did not interpret or for which his interpretations were lost. Some of them (the Mainz commentaries) were preserved together with Rashi's comments on several tractates in the order *Kodashim*[14] and were printed in the standard Vilna edition. But even though the booklets survive for only a few tractates, there can be no doubt that they originally encompassed others, perhaps all of them. The remnants preserved in various sources—especially *Sefer ha'arukh*—demonstrate as much.

Similar interpretative booklets were written in Worms, especially during the efflorescence of the Torah centre there during the last third of the eleventh century. These booklets, from both Mainz and Worms, were not considered to be the final versions of the commentaries they contained, and they were subject to correction

[14] *Bekhorot, Arakhin, Temurah, Keritot, Me'ilah, Tamid, Menaḥot,* and *Ḥulin.* These commentaries are also printed in tractates *Ta'anit, Nedarim, Nazir,* and *Mo'ed katan,* and in *Bava batra,* where Rashi's commentary is preserved only to fo. 29*a*.

and supplementation on the basis of comparisons between the notes of the students and the various teachers.[15] Rashi attended both of these yeshivas and knew their interpretative traditions at first hand. Some of the commentaries that were written after his return to France came to him via his son-in-law, Rabbi Meir ben Samuel, who studied at the yeshiva in Worms.

What is the relationship between Rashi's commentary and these earlier ones, and did he use them systematically and continually? His commentaries do not offer an unambiguous and exhaustive answer, but there can be no doubt that the interpretative tradition of the German yeshivas strongly influenced his own commentaries and underlies many of them, as they attest in various ways. At times, Rashi expressly cites his teachers' interpretations, and in most of the cases where he does so, he adds a different interpretative tradition (usually introduced with *lashon aḥer*, 'another comment'). This suggests that where Rashi refers only to his teachers' interpretation, he does so without noting the source.

At many points in his talmudic commentary, Rashi refers to 'things he has heard'. Examination of those 'things heard' clearly shows that at least some of them came from the German sages. Moreover, we have clear evidence that Rashi relied on written commentaries by early German sages that were available to him, even if he did not refer to them explicitly.

A comparison between Rashi's commentaries and those written earlier in Germany, including those written by his friend and contemporary Rabbi Eliakim ben Meshullam, shows numerous similarities in both content and form and confirms the presence of an identical interpretative tradition. It thus appears that there is a close connection between Rashi's commentaries and those of the German sages who preceded him. In many ways, Rashi was the epitome of the Ashkenazi tradition of talmudic interpretation, bringing it to its highest point. That said, it is clear that he often strayed from that tradition, whether because of his independent examination of the sources or of his reference to other traditions—primarily those of the Babylonian geonim, brought to Rashi's yeshiva in Troyes by Rabbi Elijah ben Menahem the Elder, Rabbi Joseph Tov Elem, and others.[16]

## Versions and Editions of the Commentary

In recent times, extensive analysis of manuscripts has led to a re-examination of questions about the versions of Rashi's commentary on the Talmud. Scholars engaged in this work have sought to uncover the lines of transmission of the manu-

---

[15] For a good discussion of the *kuntresim* (the 'booklets' of commentaries[a]), see Lipschuetz, 'Rashi' (Heb.), 55–67.

[16] On the writings of these two sages, their dissemination within and beyond France, and their close ties to the teachings of the Babylonian geonim, see Grossman, *The Early Sages of France* (Heb.), chs. 2–3.

[a] The term *kuntres* is sometimes applied to Rashi himself.

scripts and examine the relationships among the manuscripts and between the manuscripts and the printed version. These and other studies have shown that the manuscripts of Rashi's talmudic commentary differ from one another even more than do those of his biblical commentary. The wide dissemination of the talmudic commentary hastened the introduction of numerous annotations and editorial changes, and differing versions of the commentary were in the hands even of early sages. For example, Rabbi Isaac ben Moses of Vienna, the author of *Or zarua* (early thirteenth century), cited rulings included in Rashi's commentary on *Ḥulin* in the name of Rabbi Solomon ben Samson of Worms and sometimes noted that they appeared, for reasons unknown, only in some of the texts in his possession.

How did these differing versions come to be? Several scholars have considered the question and different conclusions have been reached. Many believe that the variants originate with Rashi himself. They reason that he included the rulings by Rabbi Solomon ben Samson in the first edition, written in Worms, but omitted them from the final edition. Others, including J. N. Epstein, believe that we are dealing with later additions, written as marginal notes and then inserted into the commentary itself. I lean in the latter direction.[17] Rashi went back and edited his commentaries on the Talmud, as is evident from many sources. A striking piece of evidence is the comment by Rabbi Isaac of Vienna:

I have seen in the commentaries that he wrote with his own holy hand that he first wrote thus . . . but he then deleted *she'uvin* and wrote above *she'uvin* . . . And he made this sort of mark on the word *leita* and wrote on the page . . . And some word was written near *shi'ur* but deleted, and I could not see what it was, but I believe *mikveh* was written there.[18]

Are we dealing here with Rashi's corrigenda to his commentaries or with actual editions, that is, with recognizable differences between the commentaries as originally written and those written at a later stage? The question is among the most interesting raised in the study of Rashi's literary output. Those who believe Rashi wrote 'varied editions of his commentary' draw support from references by early sages to a 'first edition' (*mahadura kama*) and a 'later edition' (*mahadura batra*) of the commentary, but the matter is one on which scholars have been divided since the early days of *jüdische Wissenschaft*, and I cannot here present all the many opinions.[19] Lipschuetz examined the commentaries on the various talmudic tractates one by one, and he, too, reached the conclusion that there were multiple editions. The first edition, he believed, was written by Rashi while he was still studying in the German yeshivas:

Rashi composed the first edition on the basis of his teachers' traditions and their booklets [the commentaries on the Talmud] . . . and when he had gathered a large amount of new

[17] See Grossman, *The Early Sages of France* (Heb.), 225–6.
[18] Isaac of Vienna, *Or zarua*, pt. 1, §61. The discussion pertains to the proper reading of Rashi's comment on *Ḥulin* 107a, *ein notelin mimenu leyadayim*.
[19] They are listed in Grossman, *The Early Sages of France* (Heb.), 327–8.

material on the pages of his booklet, he edited the second edition by recopying the booklet, correcting the language, deleting what needed to be deleted, and inserting all the new material into the commentary . . . Rashi composed the third edition as he taught Torah to his students; accordingly, it was only there that he reached the height of his development. The booklet was formed and grew through his living and teaching at the yeshivas, and through teaching, it attained the heights. It is self-evident that novellae came into being as he taught.[20]

In contrast, J. N. Epstein believed that the 'later edition' was not a different work but simply the first edition as edited by Rashi. Most of the foregoing scholars relied on the printed editions of the commentary, however, and recent study of the manuscripts has cast great doubt on some of their conclusions.

Yonah Fraenkel and Shamma Friedman have lately considered the issue, and their opinions diverge. Fraenkel examined Rashi's commentary on *Bava kama* by comparing the printed version to the manuscripts and concluded that we are not dealing with an 'edition' as the term is commonly used today but with addenda and corrigenda:

The manuscript evidence proves that when the Tosafot were edited, 'second and first edition' began to be used to refer to different versions in the manuscripts of Rashi that were available to them . . . These changes have nothing to do with varied levels of interpretation . . . 'Edition' [*mahadurah*] is a technical term for variants in the manuscripts to which the tosafists had access, and Rashi never prepared [multiple] editions of his commentary . . . Our enquiry into the problem of editions and emendations has shown that there is no basis in the sources for the premise that Rashi's commentary on the Talmud, as we now have it, is anything other than a unitary work.[21]

Friedman, in contrast, maintains that a greater number of changes originated with Rashi. In his view, the additions to Rashi's commentary in the manuscripts are not necessarily supplements introduced by later scribes and copyists, as many have thought. Some of them preserve supplements introduced by Rashi into his commentary late in his life, and these additions were not included in manuscripts that were copied from the earlier version. Some of the supplements were the result of renewed examination of the passage, and many others derive from writings and traditions of the Babylonian geonim and other sages that reached Rashi's *beit midrash* only after the earlier version had been written.

Friedman finds support for his position in various turns of phrase preserved in the printed editions and manuscripts, including stylistic variants among Rashi's commentaries on various tractates. 'At times these variations in style can indicate developments in the level of interpretation and the sequence in which tractates were commented on.'[22]

One gets the impression that some of the scholarly disputes are a matter of

---

[20]  Lipschuetz, 'Rashi' (Heb.), 77, 79.      [21]  Fraenkel, *Rashi's Methodology* (Heb.), 12, 15.
[22]  Friedman, 'Rashi's Talmud Commentary: Annotations and Editions' (Heb.), 173.

semantics. All agree that Rashi edited his commentaries, adding to them and making deletions from them, and the dispute is over the scope of the changes. To date,
there is no unambiguous proof that Rashi wrote multiple editions of his commentary on the Talmud, that is, that he reworked it anew on different interpretative
planes. At the same time, it is clear that he went back and revised the commentary—
some tractates more extensively and others less so. It is hard to imagine that he did
not compile, while studying in Germany, booklets of interpretations for those tractates he studied with his teachers there, as that was the common practice of students.
Moreover, it is fair to assume that even at that early time, Rashi thought about writing a commentary on the Talmud, and it is hard to imagine that he would not have
seen fit to use those commentaries, modifying and supplementing them in accordance with his own understanding and analysis, when he came to write his own. As
already noted, he followed that course in writing his commentary on the Bible—of
that, we have explicit evidence—and there is no reason for him not to have done the
same when he commented on the Talmud. He would then go back and re-examine
the commentary while studying the various passages with his students. All that said,
however, there are no accounts of actual editions of the commentary. It is probable
that the supplements originated in these addenda and corrigenda by Rashi himself,
though they are sometimes the later additions of copyists.

A related question involves the nature of Rashi's commentaries printed with the
halakhic treatise *Hilkhot harif* by Rabbi Isaac ben Jacob Alfasi (Rif, 1013–1103), with
the book *Ein ya'akov* by Rabbi Jacob ben Solomon ibn Habib (*c.*1445–1515/16),
and with the *Seridei bavli*, pages of the Babylonian Talmud that were written in Spain
between 1482 and 1497 and recently published by H. Z. Dimitrovsky. Major differences exist between these texts and the standard version of Rashi's commentary on
the Talmud. The matter has long been the subject of enquiry, and Zunz believed that
the commentary attributed to Rashi printed with *Hilkhot harif* is not, in fact, Rashi's
work. Some scholars have attempted to identify the author.

Ta-Shma believes that Rashi's commentary on Rif was not written by one individual. It represents, rather, a tradition of scribes and copyists that first took shape
within the *beit midrash* and is linked to the rising interest in and extensive study of
Rif's works during the fourteenth century. Ta-Shma assigns considerable importance to the Provençal tradition regarding the wording of this commentary. Rabbi
Jonathan ben David Hakohen of Lunel (*c.*1135–*c.*1210) provided a major impetus to
the study of Rashi's commentaries, and he exercised considerable influence over all
interpreters of Rif and the Talmud who came after him in Provence. The basis for
the text of Rashi's commentary on Rif, therefore, is the Provençal version. The
process continued thereafter in the yeshiva of Rabbi Asher ben Jehiel's sons and
students in Toledo during the first half of the fourteenth century. When *Hilkhot
harosh* began to be studied intensively, the pages of Rashi's commentary were transferred to that treatise too.

Even more complex is the question of Rashi's commentary printed with *Ein ya'akov*. Some scholars thought it reflected an early Sephardi version of Rashi's commentary, and they relied on it heavily in their attempts to find the original version of Rashi's commentary on the Talmud. Others thought it was dependent upon the early printed versions—Soncino or Pizarro—rather than the Sephardi printings and that it had no substantial value for the study of Rashi's original version.[23]

## Changes and Contradictions

Rashi's comments on parallel talmudic passages sometimes exhibit differences of style and, on occasion, even of substance. The differences appear not only between tractates but sometimes even within the same tractate, and they were noticed by early writers: 'And so it is in an old commentary of Rashi … and know that the text of Rashi here is the reverse of what it is there; but there is no need for concern about that, since it is his way to interpret here in one manner but elsewhere to interpret differently.'[24] 'And one should not be surprised if Rashi in his commentaries disagrees with himself, for he, may his memory be for a blessing, prepared many editions [*mahadurot*].'[25]

Some investigators have linked this issue to the question of multiple editions just discussed. According to Weiss, the phenomenon reflects instances in which Rashi changed his mind about earlier interpretations:

His commentaries include contradictions that cannot be explained, and we must conclude that Rashi changed his mind about his earlier interpretation and offered a different one. The tosafists have already noted some of the contradictions, mostly in instances where the change in interpretation pertains to halakhah.[26]

According to Abraham Berliner, the cause was Rashi's having studied with several teachers:

As a rule, Rashi set as the foundation of [his commentary on] each tractate the interpretation he had heard from his master and teacher when he studied it. And so he considered, while working, the interpretations of his teachers, which he had received orally, as well as written notes.[27]

Victor Aptowitzer devoted special attention to the subject, and his work is of considerable importance. Some of his conclusions follow:

In Rashi's commentaries on the Talmud, we see a remarkable sight unparalleled in all the

[23] For a more expansive discussion of these issues, including bibliography, see Grossman, *The Early Sages of France* (Heb.), 230–1.

[24] R. Samuel Eliezer Halevi Edels (Maharsha), *Novellae*, on BT *Kid.* 44*a*, *kelal eino*.

[25] R. Joseph Kurkus, cited in Malachi b. Jacob Hakohen, *Yad malakhi*, 185*b*.

[26] Weiss, 'Life of Rabbi Solomon bar Isaac' (Heb.), 166.

[27] Berliner, 'On the History of Rashi's Commentaries' (Heb.), 185.

interpretative literature, namely, differences in the interpretation of matters common to several tractates. The differences are of two sorts: (1) differences in the essence of the interpretation; and (2) differences in the length, style, order, and location of the wording . . . These differences appear not only between one tractate and another but even between two places in a single tractate, sometimes between places that are in close proximity . . . I am not aware of anyone having commented on changes of the second sort, but they are of great importance to the study of Rashi's commentary.[28]

After citing numerous examples of these differences and contradictions, Aptowitzer offered his innovative explanation:

I here suggest to investigators my solution to this remarkable riddle, namely: Rashi's interpretations were born through his oral teaching of his students, and one who teaches orally does not usually preserve his words and has no fixed forms of expression. The interpretative language used today may differ from that used for the same matter yesterday. Moreover, the students differed in their ages, their intellectual abilities, and their degrees of prior knowledge, and the teacher suited his interpretations to his students. At times, he would be moved to interpret something simple only by a question from a student to whom it was not so simple.[29]

Aptowitzer's explanation is original but hard to accept. One obvious weakness in his analysis is that he considered the various examples on the basis of the printed versions of Rashi's commentaries, without referring to the manuscripts. And Rashi's commentary, with all it encompasses, is not something that would be created through a teacher's oral presentations to his students.

Yonah Fraenkel maintains the contradictions are entirely illusory. Rashi's interpretations at various places refer to and complement one another, 'and it seems clear that the commentator was aware of the parallels':

Rashi's practice was to create unity within every section, to interpret identical passages differently, each in a manner well suited to the section in which it appears. Accordingly, they contradict each other despite the literal identity of the passages being interpreted. These are the seeming 'contradictions' that are the most prominent and surprising; but we must accept at the outset that in Rashi's view, one should not say that 'this section appears there as well'; rather, each passage is integrated into its surroundings and can be interpreted only within that framework.[30]

As long as the text of Rashi's commentary on the Talmud has not been subjected to a fundamental investigation on the basis of the manuscripts, and as long as the nature of the various manuscripts that copyists and printers worked from has not been clarified, it will remain difficult to come to a full and precise understanding of every instance of this phenomenon. Without a basic enquiry into the

---

[28] Aptowitzer, 'On the History of Rashi's Commentaries on the Talmud' (Heb.), 286–8.
[29] Ibid. 293.                          [30] Fraenkel, *Rashi's Methodology* (Heb.), 284, 290–1.

versions of the text, any consideration of the problem must remain incomplete. Still, it is possible to note some of the factors responsible for the differences:

1. **The actions of copyists.** Some of the differences and contradictions simply did not appear in the source written by Rashi: copyists introduced them.

2. **Rashi's reliance on written interpretations derived from the German sages, including the notes he took while studying with his various teachers.** Because these interpretations originated in various *batei midrash* and with various teachers, they cannot be regarded as a unitary work. It is only natural that there will be differences among them. Rashi relied on them and did not always take care to ensure their consistency with what appeared in other sources. The diverse interpretative traditions and styles left their mark on Rashi's commentaries.

3. **Rashi's addenda and corrigenda.** At times, Rashi would edit his commentary on one tractate without making corresponding corrections to parallel passages in other tractates.

4. **Contextual interpretation.** As Fraenkel suggests, Rashi would interpret identical passages in the context of the sections in which they appear. This seems to be the explanation for most of the 'contradictions'.

## Halakhic Rulings in Rashi's Commentary on the Talmud

Only on rare occasions did Rashi rule on halakhic matters in his talmudic commentary, a fact that gives rise to two questions. Why did he generally avoid halakhic rulings? What accounts for the few exceptions to that rule?

As far as we can tell, Rashi's reticence here represents a continuation of the Ashkenazi interpretative tradition going back to Rabbenu Gershom, as expressed in *Kuntres magentsa* and the commentaries written in Worms. These commentaries generally do not include halakhic rulings, and they differ in that regard from the practice of Rabbi Sherira Gaon, Rabbi Hai ben Sherira, and even Rabbenu Hananel, who often dealt with halakhic determinations. The Spanish sages did likewise, even in their interpretative works. An additional factor was one of Rashi's basic tendencies in his commentary. He saw himself first and foremost as an exegete, not as a halakhic authority, and he therefore directed all his attention to his interpretations:

The Talmud contains hundreds of units that conclude in a way that differs from the halakhah as it was practised in Rashi's time. It contains thousands of subunits and perhaps myriads of steps in the give-and-take that take positions that come to be rejected at the end of the section or on account of other parallel sections. Rashi never omitted any of these passages, explaining them with precision and applying his interpretative methods to them no less than to sections in which the Talmud deals with basic aspects of everyday halakhah . . . Rashi would never interpret a section in a way that conflicted with its content, its logic, and its unity in order to bring it into line with halakhic rulings.[31]

Why did Rashi occasionally depart from his usual practice and write halakhic rulings? It is difficult to provide a full answer, especially without a comprehensive and systematic examination of the manuscripts.

Of particular interest are Rashi's disagreements with his teachers and colleagues, as expressed in the rulings included in the commentary. An examination of his responsa, in which the same disagreements appear, shows that we are dealing with intense debates that aroused considerable emotion in Rashi. As he saw it, his teachers and colleagues relied on traditions that they possessed, but those traditions did not correspond to the conclusions that may be inferred from the Babylonian Talmud. It was natural that in interpreting these passages, Rashi would be unable to overcome his emotions and that he would express his opinion on the halakhic question presented by the section being interpreted. A notable example is whether it is permissible to eat on the second day of a festival an animal or bird captured on the first day. Rashi sharply disagreed on this with his teacher Rabbi Isaac Halevi and with Rabbi Solomon ben Samson and other sages in Worms. In interpreting the passage in *Betsah* 24*b* that is central to his give-and-take with the other sages, he recounted the dispute in detail. It is hard to imagine that he would have dealt with the halakhic ruling in the section but for the polemic in which he was engaged. In general, we find that he wrote rulings not only with respect to disputes in which he himself participated but also with respect to other issues widely debated at the time. That explains the relatively high incidence of halakhic rulings in his comments on *Ḥulin*, whose subject area—*kashrut*—was one over which customs at the time were particularly divided.

If that premise is right, we may say that many of the halakhic rulings in Rashi's commentaries were the result not of exegetical considerations raised by the passage but of contemporary reality. But while the agent was the chance one of contemporary events, it can account for many of the cases in which Rashi deals with halakhic rulings in his commentaries.[32]

---

[31] Fraenkel, *Rashi's Methodology* (Heb.), 302.

[32] Benjamin Ze'ev Benedict likewise takes the view that Rashi occasionally went beyond exegesis and incorporated into his commentary halakhic rulings motivated by practical considerations: 'It is not Rashi's nature to issue halakhic rulings in his commentaries except in instances where he disagrees with the accepted view . . . When Rashi stood opposed to the accepted opinion in his time, which appeared to him to be incorrect, he would depart from the exegetical framework and include his halakhic opinion' ('On Rashi's Rulings' (Heb.), 21, 23).

# CHAPTER SEVEN

# Rulings, Responsa, Liturgical Poems, and Commentaries on Liturgical Poems

## Rulings

RASHI'S SURVIVING OEUVRE offers no evidence that he himself wrote any comprehensive halakhic works. Lipschuetz attributes this to his extreme humility and fear of issuing halakhic rulings:

Notwithstanding all his intellectual qualities, Rashi was unprepared to be a decisor in the Sephardi mode . . . A man so grounded in modesty cannot bear the mantle of a halakhic decisor. Humility will prevent him from developing the energy and self-confidence needed by a decisor. All of Rashi's teachers were fearful of issuing rulings, and that reticence was in the air of the humble French yeshivas. In Spain, where halakhic ruling was the principal rabbinic activity, that sort of trepidation could not have emerged . . . Rashi's intellectual qualities did not draw him to decision-making, and he was never privileged to leave his mark on a major halakhic enterprise.[1]

I cannot accept this explanation. As I have already suggested, Rashi was not one who feared to issue rulings. Nor is there any basis for the conclusion that 'all of Rashi's teachers were fearful of issuing rulings'. That is not true of Rabbi Isaac Halevi and certainly not of Rabbenu Gershom (though he, too, wrote no general halakhic works). Books of halakhic rulings simply were not an accepted literary genre in eleventh-century Germany and northern France. Except for collections of customs or brief monographs, there is no evidence of any comprehensive halakhic work being written in Ashkenaz at that time—a state of affairs quite different from that among the Babylonian geonim or Spanish sages. Like the French sages who preceded him, Rashi couched his halakhic decision-making primarily in the form of responsa.

Rashi, however, can be seen as one who inspired and contributed to the development of another important branch of the tree of halakhic creativity: the writing of halakhic monographs. These monographs were not written by Rashi himself;

---

[1] Lipschuetz, 'Rashi' (Heb.), 130–1.

rather, they were collected, organized, and committed to writing by his students, some of them during his lifetime and under his direction. Some of them state explicitly that they were directly influenced by Rashi's teachings, and he may have played an active part in their writing. For example the treatment of the laws of Pesach states: 'And this long [discussion] is explained with his discourses and rationales, arranged on the basis of oral teaching by [*mipi*, literally: 'from the mouth of'] our rabbi Solomon, may his memory be for a blessing.'[2] One should not rely solely on headings of this sort, which may have been inserted by later editors; *mipi* can be used in medieval rabbinic literature to indicate the transmission of a teaching in the name of a particular sage. In some cases, however, the evidence is provided by students close to Rashi himself. For example, Rabbi Shemayah, at the end of his *Seder leil pesaḥ*, states: 'I, Shemayah, and Rabbi Judah ben Rabbi Abraham heard these [words] from the mouth of the holy one, may he be remembered for good and his resting place honoured.'[3] Some of the monographs were written soon after Rashi's death, as can be inferred from their content; his teachings and spirit are very evident in them. Rashi's students saved this work from oblivion, as Lipschuetz has noted:

With respect to the booklets [of commentaries], Rashi's students were wise copyists, but with respect to halakhic rulings, it was they who saved their teacher's work from destruction. But for them, all memory of his halakhic rulings would have been lost, and only through their efforts did a large portion of his work in that area attain literary form. Had they not written down the practices of their teacher, they would not have become jurisprudential events, rather they would have been erased like human footprints in the sands of the desert.[4]

These monographs are based primarily on Rabbi Shemayah's notes and rulings, and they include three principal sources: Rashi's teachings; extensive passages from the book *Ma'aseh hamakhiri*, written in Germany at the end of the eleventh century;[5] and the relevant responsa of the Babylonian geonim. Rashi's teachings in these works take the form of rulings, instructions, responsa, actions, and explanations of customs.

A substantial part of the work of gathering this material was done by Rabbi Shemayah, Rashi's devoted student, who personally wrote down many of his rulings. Rabbi Shemayah integrated Rashi's instructions into his own rulings, along

[2] *Sefer hapardes*, 48 and parallels.

[3] R. Shemayah, *Seder leil pesaḥ*, in Rabbinovicz, *Dikdukei soferim*, 195*b*.

[4] Lipschuetz, 'Rashi' (Heb.), 144–5.

[5] On this work, see Grossman, *The Early Sages of Ashkenaz* (Heb.), 374–86. The teachings of the Makhir school occupy a more important place in these monographs than was previously thought. One of the principal reasons for the earlier underestimation of that place was the mistaken impression that the words 'R. Solomon' always referred to Rashi. In fact, they sometimes refers to R. Solomon b. Samson of Worms. Further discussion is beyond the scope of this book.

with Rashi's actions and customs and the traditions he had received from his teachers, especially Rabbi Jacob ben Yakar. He attributed some of the material explicitly to Rashi but quoted much of it without mentioning his name. As a result, it is not possible to differentiate the various layers of the texts and uncover their precise source. Nevertheless, it is clear that Rashi's teachings occupy an important place in these works, alongside Rabbi Shemayah's own teachings. This point can be demonstrated through one example from the laws related to the blessings associated with eating a meal. These laws can be found, with only minor differences among the versions, in several books that originated in Rashi's *beit midrash*; their source is a work by Rabbi Shemayah. The version in *Sidur rashi* reads as follows:

This was established by[a] our rabbi [Rashi], may his soul rest in the bonds of life: *netilat yadayim*[b] is so called after the vessel used to pour the water, the *antal* . . . And we asked my teacher [Rashi], what of one who relieves himself and washes his hands ritually . . . and he replied to us: I, too, asked Rabbenu Jacob ben Rabbi Yakar and he said to me . . . And it is as my teacher [Rashi] said, the washing serves both purposes. And I asked my teacher, does he recite the blessing *al netilat yadayim* each and every time? And he replied . . . and my teacher so taught and his words seem right. And that is the halakhah, from my teacher. One who drinks water during a meal . . . From my teacher. One who eats a nut dipped in honey during a meal recites a blessing over it. And wine consumed during a meal . . . seems to my teacher . . . On that basis, my teacher says that one who recites a blessing after wine drunk during a meal, as long as he has not yet washed his hands following the conclusion of the meal, is to be praised . . . And several days earlier, we stood at our rabbi's table and we requested him to let us see him bless after drinking that wine during the meal so we might see the halakhah applied in practice; so it seemed to my teacher; at times I saw my teacher when there was placed on his table nuts flavoured with honey.[6]

The monographs written by Rashi's students are full of accounts of this sort, showing the important part played in them by Rashi's teachings but also the extent to which they were reworked by his students. In some cases, however—especially on the laws of menstrual impurity included in *Maḥzor vitri*—the personal comments by Rashi's students are very few, and it may be that he played an active role in writing those sections.

These monographs cover various subjects, primarily ritually forbidden and permitted activities and day-to-day religious life, but also contemporary issues. Topics include the fringes on garments, phylacteries, the sabbath, festivals in general as well as the specific observances for Passover and other holidays, prayer, the slaughter of animals for food, improperly slaughtered animals, menstrual impurity, birth, and marriage. The subjects are not divided into subdivisions, sections, or subsections in

---

[6]   *Sidur rashi*, §§102–22.

[a]   *Mipi*: literally 'from the mouth of'.       [b]   Pre-meal ritual hand-washing.

any conceptual sequence, as was the practice of the Spanish sages and, to an extent, the Babylonian geonim, as seen especially in Maimonides' *Mishneh torah*.

The foregoing should come as no surprise. The treatises written in Muslim lands were composed in an Islamic cultural context which left a clear mark on halakhic literature. But that was not the style in which Jewish sages in eleventh-century Germany and France wrote. Only in the twelfth century did the practice of the sages in Germany change, as they began to write more general halakhic works, such as the treatises by Rabbi Eliezer ben Nathan (Raban) and Rabbi Eliezer ben Joel Halevi (Ravyah). As far as we can tell, this was caused both by changes in historical conditions (the need for treatises of this sort) and by the influence of Rif's *Sefer hahalakhot*.

These short monographs in all their variety were incorporated into the works of Rashi's students, including *Mahzor vitri*, *Sidur rashi*, *Sefer hapardes*, *Sefer ha'orah*, *Sefer isur veheter*, and *Sefer hasedarim*. Large parts of them were copied into various manuscripts, including some written in Spain, demonstrating their great vitality.

## Responsa

Rashi is regarded as one of the greatest medieval writers of responsa. Hundreds of them have survived in print or manuscript, offering an abundance of halakhic, historical, and cultural material, but it is clear that many have also been lost. Although his students did not prepare comprehensive collections of them, it appears that partial collections were assembled at an early date. This is evident from the group of responsa appearing in MS Montefiore 98,[7] thought to date from the fourteenth century. The copyist selected several groups of responsa and worked them into his book, adding responsa from other sources. They were interwoven by subject into various books, particularly anthologies of material from Rashi's *beit midrash*. At the same time, some large groups of responsa survived on their own. Various medieval sages referred to 'Rashi's responsa' as if they formed a single literary collection ('Rashi wrote in his responsa'; 'I found in Rashi's responsa'), but that does not prove that those responsa were collected in a separate work. It is nearly certain that these references are to a work into which certain of Rashi's responsa, among other things, were copied. To this day, there is no proof that Rashi's responsa were assembled into a separate book by medieval sages or scribes.

The first known work in which several dozen of Rashi's responsa are collected and organized by subject is in the *mahzor* of Rabbi Shemayah.[8] Another collection is preserved in a sixteenth-century Izmir manuscript, in the library of the Jewish Theological Seminary in New York. Joel Müller prepared an important list of many of Rashi's responsa in his introduction to *Tahtsul*.[9] Menahem M. Kasher published

---

[7] *Tahtsul*, §§11–42.      [8] See Grossman, *The Early Sages of France* (Heb.), 395–403.

[9] Müller, introduction to *Tahtsul*, pp. xxvii–xxviii.

a small collection of Rashi's responsa with annotations. Israel Elfenbein published a more comprehensive collection, comprising hundreds of printed and manuscript responsa with introduction, annotations, and indexes. Along with the responsa, Elfenbein included accounts of Rashi's actions, instructions, and customs. He described the book's structure in the introduction:

> To properly organize this entire assemblage, I first divided the material into three books. Book 1 encompasses responsa to questions posed to Rashi by contemporary sages and students in the yeshiva wanting to receive Torah from him. It includes [responsa] cast into doubt by recent scholars, but that are indeed Rashi's, as I have clearly proven in my annotations ... Book 2 is a collection of directions, rulings, and decisions by Rashi's court, to which are added various items attributed to our rabbi. I have set them apart, one by one, in a special group entitled 'Responsa/Rulings of Rabbenu Solomon and Actions of His Court'. Book 3 encompasses, in addition to the foregoing, 'Responsa Attributed to Rashi'. There I have included responsa erroneously attributed to Rashi by early compilers and recent scholars but that are not, in fact, his.[10]

This was the first attempt to assemble all of Rashi's responsa, including those in manuscript. But for all the importance of this work and the great effort invested in it, it has several failings. I note only some of them:

**1.** Elfenbein included responsa that were not written by Rashi. In some cases he recognized that they had been written by others but included them anyway and marked them as pseudonymous. In others, he included them in error as Rashi's own. The first group includes responsa by Rashi's teachers, Rabbi Isaac ben Judah and Rabbi Isaac Halevi.[11] Elfenbein explains neither why he included responsa by those sages even when they had nothing to do with Rashi nor why he included some of their responsa but not others.

**2.** Other responsa that Elfenbein erred in attributing to Rashi were by Rabbi Solomon ben Samson, who lived and was active in Worms during the second half of the eleventh century. The misidentification of the author of these responsa results primarily from the appearance without a patronym of the shared name 'Solomon', which Elfenbein mistakenly took as a reference to Rashi. The responsa in sections 75–9 of Elfenbein's book are by Rabbi Solomon ben Samson. They come from a unit of MS Montefiore 98 published in Müller's book *Taḥtsul* and comprising fourteen consecutive responsa (§§43–56). In his introduction, Müller speculated that all of them had been written by Rabbi Solomon ben Samson, and there is no doubt he is correct. Elfenbein attributed the final five responsa to Rashi, but I disagree with him. In some of them—*Taḥtsul*, §§47–49—Rabbi Solomon ben Samson's name is explicitly stated, and §§43 and 45 are attributed to him in other sources.

---

[10] Elfenbein, introduction to Rashi, *Responsa*, p. ix.
[11] See e.g. Rashi, *Responsa*, ed. Elfenbein, §§52–4, 67–68, 102, 107, 122–6, 150–6.

Sections 47–56 are entirely responsa of Rabbi Solomon ben Samson to Rabbi Isaac ben Isaac: they conclude with the statement: 'Here end the responsa directed to Rabbi Isaac ben Isaac.' All fourteen of them have a unitary structure, and contain turns of phrase that appear in responsa explicitly attributed to Rabbi Solomon ben Samson. All these factors conclusively show that this entire group of responsa was written by him.

**3.** Another group of responsa, directions, and customs included in error in Elfenbein's book come from the book known as *Ma'aseh hamakhiri*, written in Germany during the last quarter of the eleventh century by the sons of Makhir. Because these sources appear in books that originated in Rashi's *beit midrash* (such as *Sefer hapardes*, *Sidur rashi*, and *Sefer ha'orah*), whose editors took them from *Ma'aseh hamakhiri*, Elfenbein thought them to be associated with Rashi. He assumed that the writer's teacher (referred to as *rabi*, with no specification) was in all cases Rashi. As noted, however, the writings originated with the sons of Makhir, and their references to *rabi* are generally to Rabbi Isaac ben Judah. We are thus dealing here not with Rashi's teachings but with those of the German sages. This confusion is widespread in manuscripts that drew both on literature written by Rashi's students (in which *rabi* with nothing else refers to Rashi) and on literature prepared by the sons of Makhir (in which case *rabi* refers to a German sage).

**4.** Elfenbein included three responsa from Italian sages to 'Solomon the Isaacite' (*hayitshaki*) on the premise that the questioner was Rashi. Various sages, including Rabbi Hayim Joseph David Azulai, held that opinion, and it appears also in academic studies, including some recent ones; but it is almost certainly grounded in error. The three responsa appear in *Or zarua*. The first one concludes: 'and thus they replied to me, I, Solomon ben Rabbi Isaac, may the memory of the righteous[c] be for a blessing, Rabbi Nathan, Rabbi Daniel, and Rabbi Abraham, sons of Rabbi Jehiel, may the memory of the righteous be for a blessing'.[12] In the second and third responsa, he is referred to as 'Solomon the Isaacite'. There is, to be sure, no unambiguous proof that this is not referring to Rashi; however, it is quite likely that the reference is not to him but to a different sage of the same name, known from other sources to have lived and been active in Italy at the time. That sage posed another question to the authors of the responsum, who were the sons of Rabbi Jehiel of Rome, and there it is clear that the reference is to an Italian questioner, not to Rashi. Two further considerations tilt the balance towards identifying this 'Solomon ben Isaac' as the Italian sage of that name. First, there is no evidence linking Rashi to any Italian sages. Any questions he raised were posed to his teachers in Germany, Rabbi Isaac Halevi and Rabbi Isaac ben Judah, who continued to be active during

---

[12] Isaac of Vienna, *Or zarua*, pt. 2, §52.

[c] That is, R. Isaac, the writer's father.

the 1080s. It was Germany in which he had studied and from which he drew his Torah, and it is illogical to think he would pose questions to Italian sages. After the death of his two teachers, Rashi had already become a great and renowned sage in his own right, and it is unlikely he would still need to be instructed by others. In addition, the second of the three questions speaks more of custom than of express halakhah: 'If an infant dies before the age of eight days, is it necessary to remove his foreskin after his death?'[13] Infant mortality was very high during the Middle Ages and this was, accordingly, a recurring question, as suggested by the comments of the respondents. To some extent, the same may be said of the third question: when should circumcision be performed on Rosh Hashanah—before or after the Torah reading and the sounding of the shofar? It is unlikely that Rashi would have meant to reject local French custom in these matters and adopt the customs of distant parts. And were he to seek different customs, it is reasonable to assume he would have looked to Germany, where his teachers were active.

Aptowitzer, aware of some of these objections, assumed that Rashi had addressed questions to the Italian sages when he was still a young halakhic decisor in Troyes, before going off to study in the German yeshivas. This idea squared with his theory that Rashi was born some ten years earlier than the generally accepted date. But this entire structure is a house of cards, as I explained earlier, in the discussion of Rashi's life history.

**5.** As well as including responsa not written by Rashi, Elfenbein omitted several responsa that Rashi did write and that have appeared in print, as well as others that remain only in manuscript.

**6.** Elfenbein did not always select the best text to use in his compilation.

**7.** Elfenbein's listing of parallel printed sources is important but incomplete—though, in fairness, we should recognize that the wide dispersion of the material makes the task difficult. Despite these failings, Elfenbein's book serves as an important point of departure for any study—halakhic, literary, historical, or linguistic—of Rashi's responsa and for any future collection of those responsa.

### Topics Considered in the Responsa and their Importance

Rashi's responsa treat a wide and varied range of subjects: interpretations of the Bible, Midrash, and Talmud; laws related to prayer, food, the sabbath, and festivals; proper and improper slaughter of animals for food; *kashrut*; immersion of utensils; wine produced by non-Jews; circumcision; mourning; sexuality and marriage, divorce, and levirate marriage; oaths and excommunications; sales and gifts; partnership; interest; bailment; and communal affairs.

---

[13]  Ibid.; Rashi, *Responsa* (Heb.), ed. Elfenbein, §40.

These responsa are important not only for the light they shed on Rashi himself but also for the information they provide about the conditions of the Jewish communities in France at the time and the difficulties they faced in maintaining authority over their members. In addition, the responsa provide important accounts of the Jews' activities overall, of their relationships with the non-Jewish authorities, and of the improved status of Jewish women brought about by the important part they played in supporting their families. In my earlier discussion of Rashi's image, I considered the difficulties faced by these Jewish communities, as evidenced in his responsa.

Few of Rashi's responsa deal with questions of civil law: most pertain to ritual prohibitions and daily religious life. That imbalance becomes even more pronounced in comparison to the extensive treatment of civil law in the responsa of Rabbenu Gershom and Rabbi Judah Hakohen, who were active in Germany during the first half of the eleventh century. The question was first raised, albeit in a different context, by Joel Müller, who considered it in his treatment of the halakhic rulings that appear in Rashi's commentary on the Talmud:

> We should no longer be surprised to see that most of the responsa we have found scattered throughout Rashi's commentary on the Talmud deal with matters ritually prohibited and permitted, and practices related to sabbath and festivals. For we have seen that most of the responsa that have survived in our possession, found in [*Sefer*] *ha-pardes*, likewise deal with these matters . . . It may be that not many questions were addressed to him with respect to civil law matters.[14]

Müller's suggestion—that few civil law questions were directed to Rashi—seems unlikely, and there is simply no apparent reason for his limited treatment of these issues. The responsa of Rabbenu Gershom and Rabbi Judah Hakohen contain ample evidence of the role played by Jews in international trade. Although that role was diminished somewhat during the second half of the eleventh century, Jews continued to engage in trade, internationally as well as locally, and conducted business through partnerships. It is only natural that many disputes would arise and be brought before sages for resolution. Evidence for that can be seen in the extensive treatment of civil law matters by Rabbi Eliezer ben Nathan some two generations after Rashi. Just as historical reality did not change, neither did human nature. That Rashi received only a few questions related to civil law would be at odds with what we know of his historical circumstances and his great fame.

Elfenbein attributes the failure to deal much with civil law issues to Rashi's extreme humility, which led him to avoid involvement in his responsa with interpersonal disputes and with cases arising outside his community.[15]

But this likewise seems unlikely. As already noted, Rashi did not fear to issue halakhic rulings. He certainly was a man of great humility, but that is a far cry from

---

[14] Müller, introduction to *Taḥtsul*, pp. xxvi–xxvii.
[15] Elfenbein, introduction to Rashi, *Responsa* (Heb.), pp. xxiv–xxv.

being unwilling to become involved in monetary disputes. Rashi did not hesitate to disagree with his teachers 'as a lion' when he saw a need to do so, and there is no reason to assume he was unwilling to take up interpersonal disputes and decide who was in the right. It is the obligation of a spiritual leader to foster peace in the community, as Rashi himself noted forcefully, and a leader who hesitates to resolve disputes between people cannot do so. Rashi's expressions of humility—such as his surprise at being asked a question—should not be taken literally but only as a way of showing deference to the questioner. Moreover, how can Elfenbein explain the 'approximately thirty-five instances' in which Rashi in fact agreed to respond to civil law questions even though a large majority of them took place 'away from his dwelling place'?[16] In these cases, Rashi did not write hesitantly or diffidently; rather, he responded decisively, writing as one confident of his power and knowledge.

I would attribute the paucity of surviving civil law responsa by Rashi to something entirely different, namely, the ways in which his responsa were collected and preserved. As already noted, they were not collected in an orderly manner in a dedicated anthology. His students dispersed them in various books on specific subjects. These were intended from the outset to deal with laws related to day-to-day religious life and ritual prohibitions, and many of Rashi's responsa on those subjects were preserved. That is especially so with respect to the *maḥzor* written by Rashi's foremost student, Rabbi Shemayah. He collected Rashi's responsa and arranged them by subject, and they were thus preserved for the ages. Most of the responsa included in Elfenbein's book are derived from collections based on Rabbi Shemayah's *maḥzor*, which included responsa dealing with 'the prohibited and the permitted' and with festivals and the like—as is the nature of a *maḥzor*—but not responsa on matters of civil law. An examination of the early manuscripts of *Maḥzor vitri* (as distinct from the later, printed version) shows that it, too, contains numerous responsa by Rashi placed with the responsa of the Babylonian geonim on the same subject. Those texts were gathered from the monograph by Rabbi Shemayah. Support for this premise can be found in MS Montefiore 98, which collected responsa by Rashi not only from Rabbi Shemayah's *maḥzor* but also from other sources. The scribe and copyist assembled within it the responsa of German and French sages along with those of the Babylonian geonim on various subjects that interested him, and that manuscript preserves many responsa by Rashi on civil law matters.

We can safely say, then, that Rashi was in fact extensively engaged in resolving interpersonal disputes, but that many of his responsa in this area have been lost.

---

[16] Ibid.

### Rashi's Method in Writing Responsa

Rashi's responsa suffered a similar fate to that of responsa by other Jewish sages of the high Middle Ages: many of them, though preserved in printed books and in manuscript, did not survive in their original or full versions. Frequently, the questions Rashi was responding to were omitted or abbreviated, and many of the responsa themselves were likewise truncated. Later writers of responsa, and sometimes even copyists, were content to cite only highlights. This is a well-known phenomenon, by no means limited to Rashi. It was brought about by the high cost of the parchment on which documents were written and by the specific needs of the later writer, who would select from the earlier responsum only the portions related to his subject or simply paraphrase the ruling. In many cases, Rashi's students did the same, including in their works only portions or summaries of their teacher's responsa and often omitting the question altogether. The responsa preserved in MS Montefiore 98 and included in Müller's *Taḥtsul* are in better shape. The scribe usually copied the source in its entirety or in large part, though he too paraphrased many questions. These circumstances make it difficult to characterize the method used by Rashi in writing his responsa, but the following brief account is based primarily on MS Montefiore 98.

In many instances, Rashi begins with extended praise for the questioner and expressions of concern for his welfare. In replying to prominent sages, he voices surprise at their having directed their questions to him, and in replying to students, he conveys warm greetings. Occasionally, he refers to the questioner affectionately as 'my dear friend' or 'my brother'. He sometimes begins the response with 'as I have been shown from the Heavens', a turn of phrase frequently used in responsa by the Babylonian geonim (where it is worded in the plural, 'as we have been shown . . .') and by Rabbenu Gershom. On rare occasions, he says 'in my humble opinion'. At times he writes expansively, examining the question from all sides to a greater extent than usual among his Ashkenazi predecessors; at other times, he is succinct and issues a summary ruling. He often considers questions related to the correct reading of the sources and examines the various versions; here, too, he is much more expansive than is common among the sages who preceded him in Germany and France. On many occasions, he cites rules of halakhic decision-making and incorporates them into his responsum.

Rashi's responsa, like all his works, are written clearly, simply, and precisely. He makes use of biblical idioms and midrashic, talmudic, and geonic linguistic coinages, integrating all of them into his own presentation in a natural way. His responsa are marked by characteristic turns of phrase, many of which are listed in Elfenbein and not in need of reiteration.[17]

---

[17] Elfenbein, introduction to Rashi, *Responsa* (Heb.), pp. xxxv–xlv.

# Liturgical Poems[d]

Like most of his contemporary sages in Germany and France, Rashi composed liturgical poems. Seven survive, all of them *seliḥot*; other *seliḥot* are attributed to him but the attribution remains uncertain. We know nothing of other liturgical poems he may have written. He may have chosen to write *seliḥot* rather than compositions in other genres because they allow the poet more freedom to express his feelings, especially about the sufferings of his people and their yearning for redemption.[18] Rashi's poems are not marked by any particular poetic attributes. As a rule, their language is simple and flowing, but it sometimes poses great difficulties. He cannot be counted among the greatest of the liturgical poets active in Germany and France during the eleventh century, but his poems are important for what they say about his personality and about the feelings of his contemporaries. In them, Rashi describes the persecution and suffering of the Jews, their yearning for redemption, their degradation and humiliation, the economic decrees issued against them ('they impede and crush us with their taxes'), and their devotion to the study of Torah. His poems reveal him to be a person of sensitivity, feeling the pain of his persecuted people and sharing their anticipation of redemption. Although it cannot be clearly proven, some of his descriptions may also pertain to the pogroms associated with the First Crusade in 1096. In one poem he writes:

> Demand [O Torah] an accounting for the degradation of those devoted to you,
> For the shedding of the blood of your learned ones,
> [An accounting] from the hand of the sons of harlotry, they who destroy
>     those who study you.
> They who rend your parchment panels and trample your letters
> And in an instant of anger [cf. Isa. 54: 8] destroyed your dwelling places.[19]

The reality reflected in these lines is consistent with the accounts of the edicts of 1096 that appear in various chronicles, with respect both to the rending of Torah scrolls and the murder of sages and students in the yeshivas of Worms and Mainz.

[18] On the Italo-German school's treatment of the *seliḥah* as a distinctive type of poetic work, see Fleischer, *Hebrew Liturgical Poetry* (Heb.), 468–71.

[19] Rashi, *Liturgical Poems* (Heb.), 23. Early writers maintained a tradition that Rashi had written the poem 'Tenot tsarot' (Luria, *Responsa* (Heb.), §29, and several MSS). Poems such as these were already being written in the classical age of liturgical poetry, before Rashi's time. For further discussion see Ch. 2, on Rashi's character, and Grossman, *The Early Sages of France* (Heb.), 144–5, and the literature cited there.

[d] Liturgical poems (*piyutim*) were written to be inserted at various points in the standard liturgy. There are various genres of *piyutim*, nearly all of them formally intricate. They are often written as alphabetical acrostics, and they allude extensively to midrashic literature. An important category of liturgical poem are the *seliḥot*, penitential poems, recited on fast days, other commemorative occasions, and during the high holiday season.

It is nearly certain that the lines were composed against this background, though they might also be seen as a general description of how diaspora Jews felt during the Middle Ages.

Rashi's liturgical poems also convey a sense of the atmosphere of Torah study within the *batei midrash* of his time, a subject considered further in the discussion of scholars in Chapter 10. His comments are influenced by the accounts in midrashic literature of love for Torah study, but they can also be seen as an expression his contemporary experience. His *seliḥot* have been collected by Abraham M. Haberman.[20]

## Commentaries on Liturgical Poems

Interpretations of liturgical poems also occupy an important place in Rashi's oeuvre. None of the scholarly literature undertakes an examination of his work in this area, for most of it remains in manuscript only, and it was not known until recently that Rashi was its source. The sages of France and Germany had begun to work in this genre somewhat before Rashi's time, but the writing of these commentaries flourished within his *beit midrash*, where poetry and early poets were highly esteemed.

To this day, we do not know of any commentaries on liturgical poems that Rashi wrote himself. His many surviving interpretations were included in the commentaries by his student, Rabbi Shemayah. On rare occasions, Rabbi Shemayah noted them explicitly, most often by use of the term 'I heard'; more typically, however, he cited them without attribution. Only in some cases, such as where Rashi disagreed with other interpreters or where Rabbi Shemayah was not persuaded by Rashi's suggested interpretation, did he see a need to identify Rashi as the source. It is easy enough to prove that many of Rabbi Shemayah's interpretations were written while Rashi was still alive and Rabbi Shemayah was still within his sphere of influence. Here, too, as in the halakhic monographs, the surviving works were not written by Rashi but much of his material is contained within them.

That most of Rashi's interpretations of the liturgical poems are assimilated into Rabbi Shemayah's commentaries and are difficult to locate precludes any full description of his interpretative method. Nevertheless, the passages that can be identified as Rashi's allow us to ascertain some of his characteristic interpretative techniques. His interpretations are marked by such features as close adherence to the plain meaning, devotion to matters of language, opposition to deriving meanings from acronyms and to other interpretations that stray far from the plain meaning, and attention to the editing of the poetic texts.

---

[20] See Rashi, *Liturgical Poems* (Heb.). Rashi signed one of his poems 'Solomon, son of Rabbi Isaac—the lesser; may he grow in Torah and good deeds' (ibid. 11–12). On Rashi's use of liturgical poems in his biblical commentaries, see Fraenkel, 'Liturgical Poems and Commentary' (Heb.).

Interpretation of liturgical poems—a subject that occupied an important place in the oeuvres of Jewish sages in France and Germany—thus formed a part of Rashi's literary efforts. Together with his students, he dealt with it extensively at his yeshiva in Troyes, and he encouraged his students to do work in the area, thereby making a major contribution to its growth and development. Rashi made use of liturgical poems in his biblical commentary as well.

## PART III

# RASHI'S
# WORLD-VIEW

# CHAPTER EIGHT

# The Uniqueness of the Jewish People

## Methodological Introduction

In his book *Rashi: His Jewish World-View*, published in 1995, Dov Rappel wrote that 'thousands of studies have been devoted to Rashi, but not one of them attempts to present his view of the world'.[1] Though perhaps somewhat overstated, the observation is essentially accurate. This odd situation may be attributed to the fact that Rashi left no detailed, explicit ideological legacy. Like other sages in eleventh-century Germany and France, he never offered his readers a statement of his beliefs and opinions. In Spain, Provence, and the Muslim lands, the study of philosophy had a powerful impact on Jewish culture and led Jewish sages to formulate their beliefs and world-views in ordered and explicit terms. That was not so in eleventh-century Germany and France, where the study of philosophy was widespread neither among the Jews nor among their Christian neighbours. Rashi instead integrated his thoughts and perspectives into his responsa, his liturgical poems, and his biblical commentary. On rare occasions he did so in his talmudic commentary. Using measured words and gentle allusions, he conveyed his ideas and his polemic against the Christian surroundings.

Not surprisingly, therefore, many scholars have maintained that Rashi's commentaries shed no light on his world-view. Nehama Leibowitz took a particularly strong stand on this, and her position exercised considerable sway. In her view, Rashi set out to do one thing and one thing only in his commentary on the Torah— to interpret the text:

Rashi made use of *midrashim* only when they respond to a question raised by the written text, resolve some difficulty, cut through a knot, or fill in a gap. Which is to say: when they help the reader understand the verse. He does not cite *midrashim* to 'adorn words of Torah with rabbinic pearls', to engage in 'mere homiletics', to preach morality, or for other similar purposes.

Rashi was not guided in his exegetical work by his broad perspective, his beliefs and

---

[1] Rappel, *Rashi's Jewish World-View* (Heb.), 11.

opinions, or his personal experiences. The biblical text itself, the wording of Scripture, provided his context.[2]

In recent years, several scholars have called Leibowitz's basic premise into question. They maintain that Rashi's commentaries, including the rabbinic legends he often incorporated into them, were influenced not only by exegetical considerations but also by his perspective on the world and by current needs. Some of these scholars offered their suggestions cautiously, arguing that only a few of Rashi's interpretations reflected his inner world; others took a more radical stance, maintaining that most interpretations were of that sort. Their understanding was based principally on the premise that Rashi's selection of certain *midrashim* from among the many available to him, and the changes he made to them, tell us much about his view of the world.

Dov Rappel, whose brief but valuable study was mentioned earlier, is noteworthy among those who take a broad view and see the ideological motive as the principal factor guiding Rashi's choice of *midrashim*. Rappel's basic premise is that the lion's share of Rashi's interpretations reflect his ideological world:

From our perspective, if it is clear that the idea does not flow from the verse itself, that proves the idea to be part of Rashi's intellectual world. For if the idea is not the correct interpretation of the verse, why would Rashi have cited it at all were it not correct in its own right?[3]

Consistent with that understanding, Rappel used Rashi's Midrash-based interpretations to describe his 'Jewish world-view'. I doubt, however, that so broad a view is warranted. In my opinion, some of Rashi's interpretations do not reflect his world-view and were offered either because of his great admiration for Midrash or to satisfy contemporary needs.

According to Elazar Touitou, 'from among the many opinions expressed by our rabbis, Rashi drew the one that best explained the verse in all respects, both exegetically and ideologically. When Rashi selected a particular opinion and cited it in his commentary, it became his personal possession.'[4] Touitou went on to suggest as follows:

As a rule, a dual interpretation indicates that one interpretation fits well with Rashi's overall understanding but is weaker as an explanation of the wording of the verse, while the second interpretation is better exegetically but does not blend with the work's overall theoretical approach.[5]

---

[2] Leibowitz and Ahrend, *Rashi's Commentary on the Torah* (Heb.), 363–4, 460.
[3] Rappel, *Rashi's Jewish World-View* (Heb.), 7.
[4] Touitou, 'From Exegesis to Ethics' (Heb.), 316.
[5] Ibid.; for a similar view, see Rachaman, *Rashi's Aggadah* (Heb.); Ahrend, 'Rashi's Torah Commentary' (Heb.).

In other words, according to Touitou, some of the interpretations offered by Rashi are driven not by exegetical considerations but by his broader concept of the world.

In principle, I share the view that Rashi was guided by more than purely exegetical purposes. That notwithstanding, I am far from certain that the *midrashim* cited in his commentaries always reflect his own world-view. One way or another, this enquiry entails serious methodological difficulties. A decisive majority of Rashi's biblical interpretations were taken from the midrashic and talmudic literature, and it was his exegetical inclinations that guided him, as a rule, in selecting these *midrashim*. Less frequently, he chose them, or reformulated them, for pedagogical or ideological reasons. The question to be answered, then, is whether his world-view and his positions on issues can be described when the entire analytical structure rests on fine distinctions and sometimes seems to hang by a thread.

While this methodological difficulty requires the investigator to redouble his caution, it does not warrant abandoning the effort to uncover the world-view of a sage whose literary heritage has exercised a powerful influence on Jewish culture over the course of hundreds of years. I believe we can identify non-exegetical motivations in Rashi's commentary, and draw inferences about his world-view, by examining five principal items:

1. *Midrashim* **selected and cited by Rashi even when they are not exegetically preferable to other available *midrashim* (that is, better suited to the wording and context of the verse) and, even more so, when they are far removed from the plain meaning of the text and have a clear pedagogical inclination.** An example is Rashi's explanation of the place name Rithmah, one of the Israelites' wilderness encampments, discussed in Chapter 4. As explained there, his pedagogical purpose is clear: he means to explain the great harm caused by slander and the impression it leaves. This is a prominent example of the *midrashim* included by Rashi even though they lack any real connection to the plain meaning of Scripture.

2. *Midrashim* **that Rashi included more than once, even though they are set forth only once in their original source and associated with a specific verse.** For example, in the passage dealing with the ritual of the red heifer, the priest is directed to cast into the heifer's ashes 'cedar wood, hyssop, and crimson stuff' (Num. 19: 6). The ashes are to be used in purifying those who have become impure through contact with a corpse. Nevertheless, Rashi cites the *midrash* of Rabbi Moses Hadarshan: 'The cedar is the highest of all trees and the hyssop is the lowest, a sign that the highest person, who sinned in his pride, must lower himself like the hyssop and the [crimson-dye-producing] worm, and he will then secure atonement' (on Num. 19: 22). In its source text, this *midrash* is presented in the context of purification of a leper (*Midrash tanḥuma*, 'Vayikra', 3),

and Rashi also cites it there (on Lev. 14: 4).[a] He had no reason to cite it again in the context of one defiled by contact with a corpse, a form of impurity unconnected with slander, and it is likely that he cited it a second time because of the great pedagogical importance he ascribed to it.

3.  **Changes made by Rashi in the wording of a *midrash*, when there is no exegetical reason for the change and when the rewording betokens a pedagogical purpose or an anti-Christian polemic.** For example, in commenting on the opening of the book of Leviticus, Rashi says:

> *The Lord called to Moses [and spoke to him]* [Lev. 1: 1]—All [divine] sayings, all statements, and all commandments are preceded by a call. It is affectionate wording, wording used by the ministering angels . . . To the prophets of the nations of the world, however, [God] revealed himself in casual and impure wording, as it is said, 'God manifested himself to Balaam' [Num. 23: 4].

Rashi here blended interpretations from *Sifra* and *Leviticus Rabbah*, with the clear purpose of acclaiming the revelation to Moses and distinguishing between it and the revelations to non-Jewish prophets. He disregarded other *midrashim* in *Leviticus Rabbah* that preceded the *midrash* acclaiming Moses and disparaging Balaam even though those other *midrashim* treated the same question: why did God 'call' to Moses before speaking to him? *Leviticus Rabbah* offers six interpretations of the distinction between Israelite prophets and prophets of the nations of the world, and the interpretation of Rabbi Issachar of Kefar Mandu (other versions: Magdu) is the harshest of them, depicting the revelation to the prophets of other nations as using 'impure wording'. It is that *midrash* that Rashi selected for use.

4.  **Allusions to *midrashim* and the manner in which they are cited.** For example, at the beginning of the book of Deuteronomy, Rashi explains that Moses followed Jacob's example and rebuked the Israelites only on his deathbed. He adds that one should act that way as rule: 'There are four reasons to avoid rebuking a person until one is close to death, namely, so that one does not repeatedly rebuke, and so that the person being rebuked does not [later] see the one who rebuked him and feel ashamed, etc., as is said in *Sifrei* [on Deut. 2].' The factors cited by Rashi are meant to protect the dignity of the person being rebuked: one close to death will not be able to rebuke a person a second time, nor will the receiver of the rebuke have occasion to be shamed by meeting the person who rebuked him. Rashi attributes these factors to *Sifrei* on Deuteronomy, but does not mention the remaining two reasons that make up the four listed in *Sifrei*—to avoid provoking controversy and enmity over the matter of the

---

[a]  In the Bible, the illness usually translated 'leprosy'—a condition differing from that which modern medical science calls leprosy—is sometimes regarded as punishment for slander.

rebuke, for one does not argue with a man about to die—and simply alludes to them with 'as is said in *Sifrei*'. Why mention two factors and disregard the other two? I believe he did so because of the importance he ascribed to the message taught by the factors he cited—avoiding impairment of another person's dignity even if the person is one who deserves rebuke.

5. **Explicit pedagogical preaching added to the commentary.** I considered this in detail earlier, in the discussion of the pedagogical tendencies in Rashi's commentary on the Torah.

For the sake of brevity, I consider in this chapter and the next two only fifteen topics from among Rashi's teachings, listing only the highlights of each.

# The Election of Israel

In Rashi's view, Israel was chosen as God's cherished possession for three reasons: (1) the merit of the patriarchs, especially Abraham's recognition of God, the covenant between the pieces, the binding of Isaac, and God's promise to the patriarchs to give the Land to their progeny; (2) Israel's agreement, in contrast to the position taken by the other nations, to accept the Torah and fulfil its commandments; (3) the mutual love between God and his people, flowing from the progression of history, especially the Exodus from Egypt, the acceptance of the Torah, the erection of the Tabernacle, Israel's devotion to God even in exile and persecution, and the willingness to give one's life for the sanctification of God's name.

Israel's agreement to accept the Torah and observe its commandments had a powerful effect on all of human history. The world was created for one purpose only, namely, acceptance of the Torah, 'the delight of the Holy One, Blessed Be He' (Rashi on Exod. 32: 16). Inasmuch as Israel agreed to accept the Torah, it is by Israel's merit that the entire world exists. In interpreting 'the sixth day', Rashi wrote:

The Lord added 'the' to 'sixth day'[b] at the conclusion of the act of Creation to state that He conditioned them [all that had been created] on Israel's acceptance of the five books of the Torah.[c] Another interpretation: *The sixth day*—all were contingent on and waiting for the sixth day, namely, the sixth of the month of Sivan, the day set for the giving of the Torah. (Rashi on Gen. 1: 31)

Only after Israel accepted the Torah did the world attain stability. Both of these interpretations, based on Midrash and Talmud, make the point that the world would not have had the right to exist had Israel not accepted the Torah. That Rashi

---

[b] That is, he used the definite article, in contrast to the other days of Creation, which are mentioned without the definite article.

[c] The definite article is represented by the Hebrew letter *heh*, which has a numerical value of five.

cited both of them, even though they express the same idea, shows his twofold didactic intention: to emphasize the importance of Israel and the importance of the Torah. It comes as no surprise, therefore, that he interprets a verse in Psalms in a similar vein: '*The wonders You have devised for us* [Ps. 40: 6]—For us you created your world.'

Humanity as a whole continued to benefit from this arrangement. God spared the generation of the Tower of Babel from annihilation for the sake of the Israelites, 'who would be the future descendants of the sons of Shem'. Rashi there goes on to explain that God took pity on them because of Jacob, who had three sorts of merit: 'the merit of his grandfather, the merit of his father, and his own merit . . . he and his descendants would be [God's] portion, but not Ishmael son of Abraham and not Esau, Isaac's son . . . for it was [Israel] that accepted His Torah, His sovereignty, and His yoke' (on Deut. 32: 8–9).

Substantively, there is nothing new in the three reasons given for the election of Israel; they are referred to in Midrash and the liturgy. Rashi's innovation is in tying them to biblical verses, emphasizing them, and reiterating them. What is surprising is his devoting more attention to the third cause—God's love for Israel—than to the others (merit of the patriarchs and acceptance of the Torah). He evidently did so because he thought it would fortify and lift the spirits of his contemporaries. Let me provide a few more examples of references to these factors.

'*Tell the Israelites to go forward* [Exod. 14: 15]—The merit of their fathers and their faith in Me in leaving [Egypt] are capable of splitting the sea for them.' '*Till Your people cross whom You have ransomed* [OJPS: *gotten*] [Exod. 15: 16]—You cherish them more than other nations, as a possession acquired for a high price, which a person cherishes.' '*You shall be My treasured possession* [Exod. 19: 5]—A cherished treasure . . . a precious vessel with priceless jewels that kings hide away; so you shall be for Me more treasured than other nations.' '*The Lord came from Sinai* [Deut. 33: 2]—He set out to greet them when they came to stand at the bottom of the mountain, like a bridegroom coming to greet his bride.' '*He shone upon them from Seir* [Deut. 33: 2]—He first asked the children of Esau [the Christians] if they would accept the Torah, but they did not want to.' '*He appeared from Mount Paran* [Deut. 33: 2]—He went there and asked the children of Ishmael [the Muslims] if they would accept it, and they did not want to.' 'God's presence went forth to greet them like a bridegroom going forth to greet his bride' (on Exod. 19: 17). 'The betrothed of the Holy One, Blessed Be He, is Israel' (on Exod. 34: 1). 'The assembly of Israel, who are betrothed to Me' (on Lev. 20: 3).[6]

Rashi had great affection for this motif of the giving of the Torah as a ceremony celebrating the marriage of God and Israel, and he referred to it several times. Another recurring motif is the description of the Jewish nation as God's children.

---

[6] It is clear that biblical texts (such as Jer. 2: 1–3) and rabbinic teachings provided a foundation for these interpretations.

At one point he even refers to it as God's twin brother—'they resembled one another' (on Deut. 21: 23).

Just as one who harms a man's beloved effectively harms the man himself, those who harm Israel are as if they have harmed God: 'One who stands against Israel is as if he is standing against the Holy One, Blessed Be He' (Rashi on Exod. 31: 3). Rashi returns to this idea at several points in his biblical commentary. As mentioned, he devoted considerable space to the love between God and Israel, and the idea dominates the whole body of his work—his commentaries on the Torah, the Prophets, the Writings, and the Talmud, his liturgical poems, and, especially, his comments on the Song of Songs. Contrary to his usual practice, he wrote an introduction to that commentary, in which he emphasized the mutual longing between God and his people after the people were exiled and left the Land of Israel, the home of the 'beloved'. This motif, whose source is midrashic, recurs throughout the comments on the Song of Songs, and Rashi cites it even when there is no exegetical need for it. For example, in interpreting 'the crown that his mother gave him' (S. of S. 3: 11), Rashi offers the parable of Rabbi Elazar ben Yosi:

[It is compared] to a king who had an only daughter, whom he loved greatly. He cherished her to the point of calling her 'my daughter', as it says, 'Hearken, O daughter and consider' [Ps. 45: 11, OJPS]; he cherished her to the point of calling her 'my sister', as it says, 'Open to me, my sister, my love' [S. of S. 5: 2, OJPS]; and he cherished her to the point of calling her 'my mother' . . . Rabbi Simeon bar Yohai stood up and kissed him on his head.

As Dov Rappel has already noted, for exegetical purposes, Rashi needed only the final clause, the metaphor of the mother, but he quoted the entire *midrash* because of its terms of endearment for the people of Israel.[7]

God's affection for Israel is a recurring motif, as in '*One bull* [Num. 29: 36]—corresponding to Israel, and it is affectionate language'; '*their king's acclaim is in their midst* [Num. 23: 21]—language of affection and fondness'; 'And He loved you' (Rashi on Deut. 1: 27); 'His compassion and affection are still with you' (on Deut. 10: 12). God sent the manna down to Israel 'affectionately' (on Exod. 16: 7).

The affection is sensed too in the interpretation of the verse 'love covers up all faults' (Prov. 10: 12); lovers tend to disregard the failings of their partners. A preeminent proof of Israel's election is prophecy, given exclusively to Israel because of its intimacy with God. Moses explicitly requested that the divine presence alight only on Israel and not on the nations of the world. God granted his request, and no prophets arose among the nations. Baalam is not an exception to this rule, as his level of prophecy was extremely low. 'We will be distinguished in this manner from all nations . . . My presence will not alight ever again on the nations of the world; and Balaam's words were not [uttered] by means of God's presence alighting but he was "fallen down yet with opened eyes" [Num. 24: 16, OJPS]' (Rashi on Exod.

7  Rappel, *Rashi's Jewish World-View* (Heb.), 58.

33: 16). As a general rule, in Rashi's scheme of things, 'the divine presence alights on prophets only on account of Israel' (on Deut. 2: 17). Even Moses, the master of all prophets, was affected by this, 'for throughout the thirty-eight years that Israel was castigated [on account of the sin of the spies], [God's] word did not join with him in affectionate language, face to face, and calmly' (on Deut. 2: 17).

According to this view of things, derived from midrashic sources, God's love for Israel is expressed in various arenas, both legal and moral. The ruling that concern for human life supersedes nearly all the Torah's commandments is grounded in this love: 'for the souls of Israel are more beloved before God than are the commandments' (Rashi on *Yoma* 82*b*, *mai ḥazeit*). The Talmud itself does not refer in that passage to this explanation for the ruling. God does not deal with Israel in accord with justice in all its rigour; rather, he goes beyond the letter of the law and diverts his gaze from their sins without being overly punctilious:

The Holy One, Blessed Be He, *did not see the iniquity in Jacob*—When they transgress His words, He does not follow up punctiliously . . . There will yet be a time when their love will be revealed to all who sit before Him and learn Torah from Him, and their place will be ahead of the ministering angels. (Rashi on Num. 23: 21–3)

The torments visited by God on the Israelites after their transgressions exceeded all bounds are themselves acts of kindness, administered for Israel's good (Rashi on Deut. 3: 29; 29: 12; 32: 23; etc.). They do not detract from God's love: 'Although you did all this, His mercy and love are still directed towards you' (on Deut. 10: 12).

A high point of Rashi's Midrash-based doctrine of divine love for Israel is his argument that even if God wanted to sever relations with Israel on account of its sinful behaviour, he would now be powerless to do so. His promise to the patriarchs and his love for the people bind his hands, as it were, and he therefore pleads with Israel not to sin: 'Because he spoke with you and swore to your ancestors not to displace their progeny in favour of another nation, He forbids you, by these oaths, to scorn him, for he cannot separate himself from you' (Rashi on Deut. 29: 12).

Every Jew must be conscious at all times of his closeness to God, expressed through the covenant with him, but that alone does not suffice. Like any loving relationship, the relationship with God must be nurtured: 'Think of every day as the one on which you entered into the covenant with Him' (Rashi on Deut. 27: 1).[8] The important place occupied by this idea in Rashi's thought is demonstrated by his selection and frequent use of *midrashim* that deal with the merit of the Jewish people, the reiteration of the foregoing motifs, and the widespread use of the word *ḥibah*, meaning 'love' or 'affection'. Rashi's thinking here, in my opinion, cannot be separated from the reality he faced, marked by Jewish–Christian disputations

[8] Rashi made similar observations about studying Torah, fulfilling the commandments, and dwelling in the Land of Israel.

centred on Christian supersessionist claims that the Jews had been displaced and the Church had emerged as the 'true Israel'. It is understandable that Rashi interpreted Scripture as saying not only that God had entered into a covenant with Abraham, pledging that his line would never end, but also that God would never exchange Israel for another nation (on Gen. 15: 10).

Rashi did much to play down the significance of the sin of the golden calf and to emphasize that God's love for Israel remained fully in place even after that event. This, too, I believe, is tied to the religious polemic with Christianity, which took advantage of that sin to disparage the Jews and show their recklessness and ingratitude. One of the classic polemical texts—*Nitsaḥon yashan* (An Ancient Victory)—cites the Christian arguments and recommends ways to confront them. Christian biblical interpretation likewise contains echoes of the polemic.[9] Rashi adopted three strategies for diminishing the impression left by the sin of the golden calf: he blamed Satan, he blamed the 'mixed multitude' (Egyptians who joined the Israelites in leaving Egypt), and he spoke extensively about the love that had not been impaired. With respect to the first, he wrote: 'Satan came and confounded the world. He displayed an image of darkness and confusion, saying that Moses had certainly died' (on Exod. 32: 1). He later expanded on Satan's actions: '*These are your gods, O Israel* [Exod. 32: 4]—It does not say "these are our gods". [We learn] from this that it was the mixed multitude that went up from Egypt that gathered against Aaron, made [the calf], and later caused Israel to stray after it.'

God rebuked Moses for having converted the mixed multitude: 'At that moment, Moses was subjected to a ban by the heavenly court . . . The mixed multitude that you accepted on your own and converted without consulting Me, and of whom you said "it is good that proselytes bond with the divine presence"—it is they who acted corruptly and corrupted [others]' (Rashi on Exod. 32: 7). Israel was forgiven 'joyfully and wholeheartedly' (on Exod. 33: 11). The love remained in place: 'Although you did all this, His compassion and affection are still with you' (on Deut. 10: 12). 'You are desired more than all other nations as of this day' (on Deut. 33: 11, 15).

Did Rashi add anything new to the concept of Israel's election and merit? I do not believe he did. Some of the ideas mentioned appear in the Bible itself, others in the midrashic and liturgical literature. Nevertheless, anyone who reads carefully what Rashi has to say on the subject, especially what he repeats and emphasizes, cannot but sense his intense personal involvement in the subject. He worked energetically to persuade his readers of the force of the divine promises of continued national existence and to instil those promises in their hearts. His commentaries contain consolation and encouragement no less than they contain exegesis. 'The heart knows its own sorrow', and Rashi knew the relevance of this subject well, perhaps more than any other that he dealt with, for diaspora Jews in general and those

---

[9] See Berger, *The Jewish–Christian Debate*.

of his time in particular. Moreover, the distinctive, emotion-laden style he used in some of his writings on this subject, especially the comments on the Song of Songs, shows how the matter touched his own soul. His introduction to the commentary on the Song of Songs reads almost as poetry in its own right, attesting to its writer's great emotional involvement in the subject.

## The Land of Israel

Rashi had a profound attachment to the Land of Israel, something he shared with most of the medieval Jewish sages.[10] In some ways, however, his position was novel and unique. I refer principally to his belief that there was distinctive value to fulfilling the commandments in the Land of Israel.

### The Advantage of Fulfilling the Commandments in the Land of Israel

In interpreting the words 'bind them as a sign on your hand' (Deut. 11: 18), Rashi wrote: 'Even after you are exiled, you are to be marked [*metsuyanim*] by commandments. Don phylacteries and make *mezuzot* [for your doorposts] so they are not new [that is, unfamiliar] to you when you return. And so it is said "Erect markers [*tsiyunim*]" [Jer. 31: 20].' In other words, fulfilling the commandments related to phylacteries and *mezuzot* in the diaspora does not have the same value as fulfilling them in the Land of Israel.

  This surprising interpretation implies that fulfilling the commandments outside the Land of Israel after the Jews have been exiled from it lacks independent value. One does so solely to ensure that the commandments will not have been forgotten when they again become relevant, upon the return of Israel to its land. This understanding of Rashi's position is supported by the quotation from Jeremiah cited by Rashi as a proof text: 'Erect markers'. The sages elsewhere interpreted that verse as referring to actions whose entire purpose is to recall the Land of Israel even when the people of Israel are in exile. Had Rashi rested content with saying 'even after you are exiled, you are to be marked [*metsuyanim*] by commandments', he might have been understood to mean that one should go beyond the letter of the law and perform, while in exile, even the commandments dependent on the Land, lest they be forgotten. But his express reference to phylacteries and *mezuzot* precludes that interpretation. As discussed below, Rashi certainly did not dissent from the talmudic texts and halakhic *midrashim*, among them *Sifrei* on Deuteronomy, that expressly characterized phylacteries as 'a bodily obligation', not dependent on the Land. Why, then, did he describe its performance while in exile as nothing

---

[10] On this issue, see esp. Halamish and Ravitzky (eds.), *The Land of Israel in Medieval Jewish Thought* (Heb.). On Rashi's view of the matter, see Grossman, 'Erets Yisra'el in the Thought of Rashi' (Heb.). The enquiry there is more comprehensive, but the present discussion includes some material discovered since I wrote that article.

more than a memento of the Land? The implication is that fulfilment of the commandments outside the Land of Israel—including those halakhically defined as 'bodily obligations', not dependant on the Land—has a lesser value than fulfilment of those commandments in the Land of Israel. Rashi diminishes the value of religious acts done on foreign soil and of religious life in the diaspora in general. This is the position expressly taken by Nahmanides, who believed the entire Torah to be fundamentally the Torah of the Land of Israel and assigned special value to the performance there of all the commandments, maintaining that only in the Land of Israel could one live an authentic Jewish religious life.

Rashi preceded Nahmanides by five generations. If the inference we have drawn from his words is accurate, he may be regarded as the first of the medieval Jewish sages to take the view that performance of the commandments—including 'bodily obligations'—in the Land of Israel is preferable to performing them in the diaspora.

Later Jewish sages were quite surprised by Rashi's interpretation of 'bind them as a sign on your hand', but their efforts to explain it away are unpersuasive. Close examination of his statement and of the sources in *Sifrei* on Deuteronomy on which it is based shows his words to be direct and precise and to reflect the significance of the Land of Israel in his teachings. *Sifrei* offers two interpretations of the verse at issue. The first is the one that Rashi obviously used. The second explains that phylacteries and Torah study are 'bodily commandments not dependent on the Land, applying both in the Land and outside the Land'.[11]

Rashi disregarded the second interpretation and selected the first, adding the reference to phylacteries, which are not alluded to in the original source. This is obviously noteworthy. It is quite likely that he favoured the first interpretation because of its implied message that performance of the commandments in the Land of Israel is of especially great value.

Further support for this understanding is provided by Nahmanides' treatment of Rashi's position as close to his own, grounded on the premise that the Land of Israel enjoys a special spiritual advantage and is the place for the 'principal' fulfilment of all the commandments:

Now the honoured God is God of gods, and Lord of lords over the whole world. But the Land of Israel, the centre of the settled world, is God's portion, dedicated to His name ... Outside the Land of Israel, though all belongs to the honoured God, its purity is not perfect ... Now, the passage that says 'you will soon perish [from the good land (that is, be exiled from it)] ... impress these my words' [Deut. 11: 17–18] makes only the commandments bearing on individual action, [such as] phylacteries and *mezuzot*, binding in the diaspora. And [Rashi] interpreted this to mean that that this should be done so they are not new [that is, unfamiliar] to us when we return to the Land, for the *principal* [*fulfilment*] *of all the commandments is by those who dwell in the Land of the Lord*.[12]

---

[11] *Sifrei* on Deut. 11: 18.
[12] Nahmanides on Lev. 18: 25, emphasis added by A.G.; trans. J.L.

Nahmanides concludes that Rashi made a distinction between the value of commandments—including 'bodily commandments' such as phylacteries and *mezuzot*—performed in the Land of Israel and those performed in the diaspora. His statement that 'the principal [fulfilment] of all the commandments is by those who dwell in the Land of the Lord' clearly shows that in his opinion, Rashi, too, maintained that all commandments, including 'bodily commandments', had special, greater value if performed in the Land of Israel. It may be that his interpretation of Rashi influenced his own position, for he held Rashi and his commentaries in great esteem, as is evident throughout his oeuvre and as he explicitly declared in the introduction to his commentary on the Torah.

## The Dream and the Exile: Dwelling Outside the Land of Israel as a Sin

In the discussion of dream interpretation in *Berakhot*, the case of a man who dreams he is naked is recorded. The interpretation draws a distinction: 'One who stands naked in a dream: if in Babylonia, he stands without sin; if in the Land of Israel, he is naked without [the merit of] commandments' (*Ber.* 57a). Rashi there interprets: 'In Babylonia, he stands without sin, for outside the Land, it has no merits [Guadalajara printing: 'for outside the Land, they have no merits]; rather, it is a sin to dwell there, and this [man] stands naked without those sins. In the Land of Israel—many commandments are dependent on it, and this [man] stands naked, as a sign that he is naked of its commandments.'

Rashi compared the Land of Israel with Babylonia (and other lands) and noted two drawbacks to being in the diaspora. First, according to the Guadalajara version, these lands, or the Jews living in them, have no merits. Second, the very act of dwelling there entails a transgression. In the Land of Israel, the many commandments that are dependent on the Land envelop a person. They are symbolized by one's clothing, so a dream that one is naked means he is divested of them. Foreign lands, in contrast, including Babylonia, lack all merit, and dwelling in them is a sort of sin. The clothing that enwraps a person living in the diaspora and symbolizes his existence has a negative quality. Being divested of it in a dream, therefore, symbolizes something positive for the person, even though a Jew in the diaspora still fulfils many commandments. This approach can be understood if Rashi in fact believed that the performance of commandments in the diaspora, even those considered 'bodily obligations', has value only insofar as it prevents their being forgotten until the return to the Land, and that commandments in the diaspora lack the independent value they possess in the Land of Israel.

Particularly deserving of attention is that Rashi saw fit to mention two factors contributing to negative characterization of living in the diaspora. He could easily have limited himself to the second—the sin of living in the diaspora—and the meaning of the dream would have remained unchanged. Adding the first factor—that the diaspora or the Jews dwelling in it lack merit—has considerable significance, as does the idea that dwelling in the diaspora itself partakes of sin.

## Circumcision and the Land of Israel

According to Rashi, circumcision was given as a sign not only of the special connection between God and the nation of Israel but also of their inheritance of the Land of Israel: '*I will establish my covenant between Me and you* [Gen. 17: 2]—A covenant of love and a covenant of the Land, to bestow it on you through this commandment.' This idea that circumcision is also a sign of the inheritance of the Land lacks any basis in Scripture. The promise of the Land, to be sure, is reiterated in the Torah in close proximity to the commandment of circumcision (Gen. 17: 8–10), but not as part of the covenant of circumcision itself, and the other medieval commentators drew no such connection between circumcision and the promise of the Land. They saw circumcision as a special covenant attesting to the profound link between God and the nation of Israel, and they associated it with the verse 'Walk in My ways and be blameless [or perfect]' (Gen. 17: 1).[13]

Rashi applied this notion consistently. In his comments on the talmudic passage discussing the blessings ('grace') following a meal, he wrote to similar effect: '*He must mention the covenant* [*of circumcision*] [*Ber.* 48*b*]—In the blessing about the Land,[d] for it was through the covenant that [the Land] was given to Abraham in the biblical passage on circumcision.'

Rashi's linking of circumcision and the Land of Israel is particularly important. Circumcision is evident on the body of every Jewish man, and it is generally seen as a sign that distinguishes a Jew from members of other nations and attests that he belongs to the nation that God chose as his treasured possession. This follows from the verse 'You shall circumcise the flesh of your foreskin, and that shall be the sign of the covenant between Me and you' (Gen. 17: 11). According to Rashi, the body of each male Jew bears a sign of his covenant not only with God but also with the Land of Israel. It goes without saying that this interpretation bears heavy emotional baggage and that it considers the merit of the Land of Israel great enough to be comparable to the exalted station of the covenant between God and the nation of Israel.

The ensuing portion of the commentary offers additional support for the premise that Rashi carefully chose his words to convey the meaning I have

---

[13] The only medieval commentator other than Rashi who seems to connect the covenant of circumcision with the Land of Israel is Radak, but his understanding of the matter is, in fact, different. In his view, the Torah and the Land of Israel are given to the people of Israel on condition that they observe the covenant of circumcision, but he does not share Rashi's opinion that circumcision serves as a covenant by virtue of which Israel acquires the Land, for that is not its purpose (see Radak on Gen. 17: 8, 11).

[d] One of the blessings making up the grace after meals.

suggested: '*To be God to you ... as an everlasting holding* [Gen 17: 7–8]—There, I will be God to you, but one who dwells outside the Land is as one for whom I am not his God.'[14] Rashi took a rabbinic *midrash* that appears at the end of *Ketubot* (110*b*), referring to a verse in Leviticus, and transferred it here because he saw a connection between the two parts of the verse, thereby forming a complete and comprehensive literary structure to emphasize the virtue of the Land of Israel. On the one hand, the covenant of circumcision attests to the profound link between the nation and the Land; on the other hand, one who does not dwell in the Land of Israel is as one whose god is not the Lord. Rashi even changed the wording of the *midrash*, for the Talmud states: 'one who dwells outside the Land is as one who has no god'. Rashi reformulates it as 'one for whom I am not his God', thereby greatly reinforcing the connection among the Land of Israel, the nation of Israel, and the God of Israel.

## Awareness of the Land's Virtue: 'As if it were given to you today'

In interpreting the verse 'And when the Lord has brought you into the land of the Canaanites ... and has given it to you' (Exod. 13: 11), Rashi writes as follows, on the basis of the *Mekhilta*: '*And has given it to you*—you should regard it as if it were given to you that very day; you should not regard it as an ancestral legacy.' That is, Rashi believes everyone who dwells in the Land of Israel must each day sense excitement over its sanctity and virtue. He writes to similar effect about the covenant with God—'You should regard each day as the day on which you entered into a covenant with Him' (on Deut. 27: 9)—and about the Torah: 'Each day you should regard them as new, as if that day you were commanded with respect to them' (on Deut. 26: 16). All three of these positions—regarding the nation of Israel, the Torah of Israel, and the Land of Israel—have midrashic bases, but their selection shows that in Rashi's mind, they were bound up with each other.

## Israel's Right to the Land

The eleventh century witnessed an intensified struggle between Christianity and Islam over the Holy Land, especially Jerusalem, and the Jews were drawn into the struggle. Early in the century, during the reign of the Fatimid Caliph al-Hakkam, the Church of the Holy Sepulchre was destroyed. The event brought about an attack on the Jews of Christian Europe, who were alleged to have encouraged the Muslims in their destructive act. The struggle reached its peak in the First Crusade, with Christians conquering the Land of Israel and Jerusalem in 1099. The Jews were perplexed by that development, but they also saw in it glimmers of hope for the messianic redemption. They were amazed to see other nations fighting over their inheritance, pressing their claims to it, and later even dividing it between them. Rashi carried on a polemic against Christianity in his commentaries on the

---

[14] According to MS Leipzig 1 and other reliable manuscripts.

Prophets and the Writings, especially the commentary on Psalms, which seems to have been written after the edicts of 1096. Among the points he emphasized was the right of the Jewish people to the Land of Israel. That represents the divine will, he argued, and the Jews, therefore, may not be criticized for having expelled the Canaanite nations and having taken possession of their land. Rashi made this point at the very beginning of his commentary on the Torah, citing *Midrash tanḥuma*, 'Bereshit', 11: 'If the nations should say to Israel, "You are brigands, for you conquered the lands of the seven [Canaanite] nations", [Israel] may reply to them, "The entire earth belongs to the Holy One, Blessed Be He; He created it and He gave it to whom he saw fit."' That Rashi began his explanation of the Torah by discussing the nation of Israel's right to the Land is highly significant, of course, and it conveyed a message to the Jews of Europe and their neighbours in his time.

Rashi interpreted other verses in Genesis and elsewhere in a similar vein. Some examples: '*Creator of heaven and earth* [Gen. 14: 19]—by making them He acquired them to be His',[e] and it follows that he can distribute the earth as he wills. Although Abraham did not request a sign to confirm the promise of progeny, he did request a sign for the promise of the Land, which was dear to him: 'how shall I know that I am to possess it?' (Gen. 15: 8). At the covenant between the pieces (Gen. 15: 12–14), God already hinted to Abraham about the torments his progeny would endure in all their exiles until their return to their Land and about the punishment that would be imposed on their oppressors.

In Rashi's opinion, based on midrashic sources, Esau expressly waived his rights to the Land of Israel by leaving it and going to Seir. The right to the Land of Israel was conditional on the willingness to endure exile until the time of the redemption, as Abraham was told at the covenant between the pieces, and Esau waived his right because he was unwilling to accept that condition: 'He said: I will depart from here. I have no share in either the gift you gave him or in the redemption of the debt' (Rashi on Gen. 36: 7). Esau was the pre-eminent symbol of Christianity for Jews in the Middle Ages and even earlier, and the implications of this interpretation for Rashi's time and anti-Christian polemic are obvious.

Jacob also bought Esau's share in the cave of Machpelah, paying with the best of his silver and gold. He had earned that wealth while residing with Laban, and he considered it undesirable because it had been acquired in exile. Wealth amassed by a Jew in the Land of Israel has greater worth: '*The wealth that they had amassed in the land of Canaan* [Gen. 46: 6]—But what they had amassed in Padan Aram was given in its entirety to Esau for his share in the cave of Machpelah. He [Jacob] said: Assets from outside the Land are not worth having.' The source of this interpretation is *Midrash tanḥuma* ('Vayeḥi', 6), but Rashi's selection and incorporation of

---

[e] The word translated 'creator' (*koneh*) means both 'maker' and 'acquirer'. The former meaning is more common in biblical Hebrew; the latter in rabbinic Hebrew. The comment reflects that dual meaning, which is not evident in the English.

this *midrash* and his emphatic statement that Esau received both silver and gold in exchange for his share support the premise that he saw this as an opportunity to express an aspect of his world-view.[15] Not only does the interpretation emphasize the Jews' right to the Land of Israel, it also refutes the charge, repeatedly levelled by Christians against Jews in the medieval polemical literature, that Jacob, the father of the Jewish nation, acquired the Land of Israel through fraud, when he deceived Esau and misappropriated from him the blessing and the right of the first-born.

The Jewish nation's right to the Land of Israel and the future realization of the divine promise in that regard are also emphasized in Rashi's comment on Exodus 6: 4. The verse refers to the divine covenant with the three patriarchs, in which God promised the Land of Israel to their progeny. Rashi thought it appropriate to quote all three of those promises, even though he could easily have simply listed them without setting forth their specific wording. Moreover, he quoted the verse again only a few chapters later, in explaining 'which he swore to your fathers to give you' (Exod. 13: 5).

Rashi likewise accepted the midrashic interpretation in *Sifra* that the phrase *am ha'arets*,[f] which appears frequently in Scripture, refers to the nation of Israel in its entirety and reflects its rights to the Land of Israel (hence the definite article before 'land'): 'a nation on account of which the Land was created . . . a nation destined to possess the Land' (on Lev. 20: 2).

## Praise and Love for the Land of Israel

Rashi's biblical commentaries contain dozens of statements in praise of the Land of Israel, referring to its material and its spiritual qualities alike. Most of these comments are taken from rabbinic *midrashim*, but they nevertheless tell us much about Rashi's own world-view. His choice of certain *midrashim* from among the many that were available to him is significant in that regard, for many of those he selected were not literarily superior to those he disregarded nor were they more closely linked to the texts being interpreted. The matters he emphasized or repeated are likewise instructive. It is evident that Rashi was aiming to increase his readers' love and affection for the Land of Israel and that he selected and repeated *midrashim* with that purpose in mind. Some examples follow.

In commenting on Genesis 24: 53, Rashi wrote that because the fruits of the

---

[15] This interpretation also appears in other places (see *Sot.* 13*a*). At first glance, Rashi seems to have inferred this from the reference in the verse to 'the wealth they had amassed in the land of Canaan', which appears to be unnecessary, unless it implies that they brought only that wealth and not wealth they had amassed elsewhere. But the beginning of the verse—'they took along their livestock'—can easily be interpreted as referring to the livestock they had brought with them from Aram, and the verse therefore provides no unambiguous proof for the interpretation.

[f] People of the land, i.e. the local populace.

Land of Israel are of particularly high quality, Abraham's servant brought some of those excellent fruits with him when he went to Haran to find a wife for Isaac, hoping thereby to impress the girl's family. He offered a similar interpretation for Moses' blessing in Deuteronomy 33: 25. Isaac was able to achieve a rich harvest in the land of the Philistines ('a hundredfold', Gen. 26: 12) even though it was not as fertile as the Land of Israel; one may infer a fortiori that the Land of Israel itself is exceptionally blessed. Azikah is 'the name of a city in the Land of Israel whose fruits are of high quality'; that is why a non-Jew outside the Land of Israel who wants to sing the praises of his wares says 'they are from Azikah' (*Yev.* 122*a*). The Talmud itself contains no hint of any such interpretation; it says that the non-Jew 'sold fruit in the market and said, "these fruits are *orlah*, these fruits are from Azikah, these fruits are *neta reva'i*"'.[g] Only one who believed the fruits of the Land of Israel to be superior would say that a merchant in the diaspora who wanted to tout his merchandise would say they had come from the Land of Israel. It is not surprising that Rashi hinted that his interpretation lacks much support and was the product of his own thinking. He introduces the comment by saying 'it seems to me', and other commentators on the Talmud do not accept his view.

The Land of Israel also has its own angels, who differ from those for outside the Land; the former may not leave the Land, and the latter may not enter it (Rashi on Gen. 28: 12; 32: 2–3). God commanded Jacob to return from Laban's home to the Land of Israel, 'and there *I will be with you,* but while you remain caught up in the impure, it is impossible for My presence to alight on you' (Rashi on Gen. 31: 3). The verse 'Now Hebron was founded seven years before Zoan of Egypt' (Num. 13: 22) is meant 'to recount the praises of the Land of Israel', for Hebron is the least of places in the Land of Israel, yet it is better sevenfold than the best of places in Egypt. Rashi cited this *midrash*, derived from *Midrash tanḥuma* ('Shelaḥ lekha', 8) in great detail. The references to the various names of Mount Hermon likewise are meant 'to proclaim the praise of the Land of Israel, for four kingdoms were boasting over it, this one saying "let it be named for me" and that one saying "let it be named for me" [Deut. 3: 9]' (*Ḥul.* 60*b*). He interpreted 'the ends of the earth one and all' (Deut. 33: 17) in a similar vein: 'There is no king or ruler who did not acquire a palace and a holding in the Land of Israel, for it is important to all of them.' 'The Galilee of the Nations' (Isa. 8: 23) is the entire Land of Israel, 'which had all the nations roll [*golel*] towards it, for all craved it'. Israel's virtues are so well known among the nations that the Ravshakeh, the emissary of King Sennacherib of Assyria, in attempting to convince the men of Jerusalem to submit to him, suggested that they move to another land as good as their own (2 Kgs 18: 32). One might have expected him to entice them into accepting his offer by telling them he would move them to a better land than their own, but he knew that doing so would have revealed him as a fraud and caused his offer to be rejected, for there is no land

---

[g] The first and third terms refer to young fruit trees subject to certain restrictions on their use.

better than the Land of Israel. Rashi emphasized the merit and sanctity of the entire Land of Israel, not only parts of it (on Deut. 3: 27 (God showed Moses the entire Land, even though Moses had asked, as he reports in v. 25, to see 'the good land'; it follows that the entire Land is 'good'); 2 Kgs 5: 17). He did not interpret the verse 'for he was cut off from the land of the living' (Isa. 53: 8) in accordance with its plain meaning, as referring to one who had died, but took it to refer to one compelled to leave the Land of Israel and go into exile. 'The land of the living' is the Land of Israel, and he likewise interpreted Ezekiel 32: 32. When David sought 'to walk before God in the light of life' (Ps. 56: 14), he meant 'to return to the Land of Israel'; when he spoke of 'a thirsty land', he was referring to the lands of the diaspora, not to the Judean wilderness or similar terrain.

Rashi drew a distinction between the Land of Israel and all other places in the world. Because they are not comparable to it, the Land is mentioned separately, in the midrashic understanding of the verses, even when the whole universe is referred to. Rashi quoted these *midrashim* because they are useful in emphasizing the merit of the Land of Israel, as in his commentary on 'The earth is the Lord's and all that it holds, the world and all its inhabitants' (Ps. 24: 1). He writes: '*the earth*—the Land of Israel; *the world*—all other lands'. He does likewise in commenting on 'Who gives rain to the earth, and sends water over the fields' (Job 5: 10): '*the earth*—the Land of Israel; *the fields*—by messenger to the other lands'. And again, '*He had not yet made earth and fields* (Prov. 8: 26)—the Land of Israel and the other lands.' It goes without saying all of these verses are simply using synonymous parallelism and that there is no linguistic or syntactic support for these midrashic interpretations.

Rashi gave particularly extensive attention to the beauty of the Land of Israel: 'The Land of Israel, which is the height and loveliness of the world' (on Ezek. 36: 2); the 'beautiful land' (Dan. 8: 9) is the Land of Israel, known for its beauty. It is 'higher than all lands'. Rashi here followed the talmudic exegesis (*San.* 87*a*), relying on the biblical use of *la'alot* ('to go up', 'to arise', 'to ascend') in the context of travelling to the Land of Israel ('Go up there into the Negeb' (Num. 13: 17); 'then shalt thou arise and get thee up' (Deut. 17: 8, OJPS), etc.) and inferring from that that the Land of Israel is situated at the highest point of the world. Rashi returns to this idea frequently, mentioning it wherever the biblical wording provides an opportunity to do so. Jerusalem is particularly exalted, higher than the rest of the Land of Israel.

Many other examples could be cited. Their large number, the frequency with which they are reiterated, and the emphasis that is placed on them attest clearly to Rashi's ascription of great merit to the Land of Israel and to his intention to influence his readers. In most instances, as noted, no exegetical need drove the interpretation. It follows that the very choice of these *midrashim* is instructive as to Rashi's world-view.

## The Boundaries of the Land of Israel

Rashi's great affection for the Land of Israel found expression too in his frequent discussions of its boundaries and settled areas, in which he made extensive use of passages in the Torah and the Former Prophets. No medieval Jewish biblical commentator devoted as much attention to the boundaries of the Land of Israel. Rashi attempted to identify the location of each nation that bordered the Land and described, at length and in great detail, the journey of the Israelites through the wilderness and the lands they passed through. He ultimately drafted a map—one of two in his commentary on the Torah. It is preserved in a few early manuscripts (including Leipzig 1 and Munich 5), but most copyists omitted it. It appears from the texts in our possession that Rashi was the first person in the Jewish world to draw a map of the Land of Israel, and he executed the map on the basis of the models then common in the Christian world.[16]

Rashi tried to identify not only international boundaries but also other sites mentioned in Scripture. He considered the general area in which they were to be found, the places to which they were adjacent, and, in particular, whether they were included within the boundaries of the Land of Israel. He did so on the understanding that the detailed listing of boundaries in Numbers ('this is the land that shall fall to you', Num. 34: 2) was meant to clarify whether the residents of the various locations were obligated to observe the commandments dependent on the Land. He did the same in his interpretation of the detailed list in Joshua 15.

As mentioned, the reliable manuscript versions of his commentary on the Torah show that Rashi drew two maps of the Land of Israel. One was focused on its boundaries and the other on its settled areas. There is no doubt that the maps are Rashi's work, for his grandson, Rashbam, stated in his commentary (on Num. 34:2) that Rashi had drawn the boundaries of the Land of Israel. Rashi's extensive treatment of real-world details throughout his commentaries on the Bible and the Talmud is one of their defining features, but the attention he devoted to the boundaries and settled areas of the Land of Israel far exceeds even that. This intensive treatment of the Land's geography cannot be easily explained except as a result of the special affection he felt for the Land of Israel. And it supports the idea I suggested earlier that Rashi's view was close to that of Nahmanides, according to which 'the principal [fulfilment] of all the commandments is in the Land of Israel'.[17]

# Miracles

Throughout his biblical commentary, and especially in commenting on the Torah, Rashi often spoke of the miracles encountered by the Israelites, some explicitly

[16] See Grossman and Kedar, 'Rashi's Maps of the Land of Israel' (Heb.), 26–9.
[17] Nahmanides on Lev. 18: 25; on Gen. 26: 5.

described in the Bible and others not. He may have referred to some of them for exegetical reasons, but that certainly cannot be said of all of them, and their inclusion represents a characteristic pattern, not an occasional event. Rashi described miracles that are mentioned in the midrashic literature, even if they are not mentioned or even alluded to in the Bible itself,[18] and he differed in this regard from Rashbam, Ibn Ezra, Bekhor Shor, Radak, and Nahmanides. The other commentators discussed the miracles expressly mentioned in the Bible but rarely mentioned those only included in Midrash; and that was true even of the commentators who were immersed in the world of the talmudic sages and often cited their *midrashim*. Rashi followed his practice in describing the patriarchs (especially Jacob), Moses and his acts and battles, the generation of the wilderness, Joshua, some of the judges, the Israelite prophets, and others. Some examples follow.

**1.** In depicting the generation of the wilderness, Rashi often speaks of the miracles that the midrashists say were encountered daily by the Israelites—miracles that transformed their stay in the harsh, dusty, and sun-swept wilderness into a secure, stress-free, and pleasant experience. He twice emphasizes how the clouds of glory did not merely guide the Israelites but also protected them and made their stay in the wilderness more comfortable:

*And the Lord's cloud kept above them by day* [Num. 10: 34]—Seven clouds are mentioned in the course of their journeys, four from the four winds, one above them, one below them and one before them, lowering the high places and raising the low and killing serpents and scorpions.[19] *The clothes upon you did not wear out* [Deut. 8: 4]—The clouds of glory would brush their clothes and press them, making them like pressed clothes. And the clothing of their young would grow as the young grew, like the skin that clothes a lizard, which grows with it.

Scripture says their clothes did not wear out and their legs were not injured, but it says nothing of the clouds ironing the clothes or of the clothes growing with the children who wore them.

**2.** In describing the giving of the Torah, Scripture says: 'All the people witnessed the thunder' (Exod. 20: 15). Following Midrash, Rashi interprets the verse as implying that none of the Israelites was blind, deaf, or dumb. What he clearly means is that the Israelites who left Egypt included people with such disabilities, but all of them were cured and made whole—in precisely what manner Rashi does not say— by the merit of the encounter at Sinai. In all three cases, he relies on the word 'all'.

---

[18]   Dov Rappel has already noted this (*Rashi's Jewish World-View* (Heb.), 26–9). I have provided additional examples and broadened the discussion.

[19]   *Mekhilta* on Exod. 13: 21 ('the Lord went before them in a pillar of cloud by day') cites several opinions regarding the number of clouds. Rashi chose the number seven, apparently because the cloud is mentioned in Scripture a total of seven times.

It goes without saying that the interpretation does not follow from the plain meaning of the text.

**3.** Rashi provides extended accounts of the miracles, alluded to in *midrashim*, that the Israelites encountered as they wandered among the streams adjacent to the Dead Sea. Scripture recounts that they there sang a song, and the plain meaning is that they sang of the abundant water that came their way ('Spring up, O well—sing to it', Num. 21: 17). In Rashi's opinion, this refers to the miraculous rescue of the Israelites in the plains of Moab. The foes stood on two adjacent mountains and planned to throw stones and rocks at the Israelites passing through the valley below. Miraculously, the mountains came together and crushed the enemies setting the ambush.

**4.** The prophet Elisha is described in the Bible as 'one who poured water on the hands of Elijah' (2 Kgs 3: 11). Understood plainly, this is a figurative way of saying that Elisha served as Elijah's personal attendant. Rashi used the opportunity to emphasize the miracles encountered by Elisha even in his youth: '*Who poured water on the hands of Elijah*—At Mount Carmel, and when he poured, his fingers became as water fountains, until the trench was filled.' He likewise interpreted Elisha's request that Elijah 'let a double portion of your spirit pass on to me' (2 Kgs 2: 9; see also 3: 1) as referring to the miracles performed by Elisha, which numbered twice as many as those performed by Elijah (sixteen compared to eight). He based all of these interpretations on rabbinic *midrashim*.

**5.** Rashi stressed that miracles would continue to be performed for Israel in the future, culminating in the building of the Third Temple by God himself (on Jer. 31: 3). Even more, all of creation will be renewed, according to Rashi's interpretation of 'For behold! I am creating a new heaven and a new earth' (Isa. 65: 17). Other commentators took the verse in its plain sense, as an allegory. Radak, for example, wrote: 'all the good things that will happen will make the world seem as new'. He even cited the interpretation offered by Ibn Ezra, who took the same approach. Rashi, in contrast, wrote: '*A new heaven*—The angels on high will be renewed, and Israel's angels will be above and the angels of the nations will be below. And some say it means literally a new heaven, and *that is the primary sense of it*' (emphasis added). In support of this view, he cites the verse 'For as the new heaven and the new earth which I will make shall endure by my will' (Isa. 66: 22). Of course, the latter verse proves nothing; its meaning depends on the meaning of the earlier verse and both can easily be taken allegorically.[20] Rashi's interpretation departs from his

---

[20] Traditional biblical interpreters likewise understood the verse to refer to the eternity of creation rather than its renewal. Radak, for example, writes: 'He called them "new" because they retain their freshness and do not wither. As they were on the day they were created so they are today and so they will remain' (on Isa. 66: 22).

general treatment of miracles and may imply that he saw the redemption as an era of important change in the universe overall, including fundamental renewal of creation. I have already discussed the subject in considering Rashi's teachings on the redemption.

**6.** Rashi's tendency to emphasize the importance of miracles, their regular occurrence, and the obligation to contemplate, recognize, and be grateful for them, appears in his comments on *Shabat*. A *baraita* there states:

Our rabbis taught: Who wrote *Megilat ta'anit* [the Scroll of Fasts]? They said: Hananiah ben Hezekiah and his circle, for they cherished [the recollection of] troubles. Rabban Simeon ben Gamaliel said: We, too, cherish [the recollection of] troubles, but what can we do? If we tried to write [a listing of them], we could not complete it (*Shab.* 13*b*).

Rashi interpreted as follows: '*They cherished [the recollection of] troubles*—From which they are redeemed, and they recall the miracle with affection, praising the Holy One, Blessed Be He, and noting in writing the days on which the miracles took place, to make them festivals . . . And thus some miracles come our way and we do not recognize them.' He was no doubt influenced by *Megilat ta'anit*, which lists the days on which fasting is forbidden (in recognition of redemptive miracles that took place on those days), but the statements of the Talmud and of Rabban Simeon ben Gamaliel could still be understood in accordance with their plain meaning: 'we could not complete it' because of the great number of troubles. Moreover, a similar rabbinic expression—'they cherish torments'—certainly cannot be connected, on the basis of talmudic context, with miracles (see *Ber.* 5*a–b*; *San.* 101*a*). Compare *Kidushin* 40*b*: 'The Holy One, Blessed Be He, subjects the righteous to torments in this world, so they may possess the world-to-come.'

Rashi followed this course consistently. The Talmud relates Rabbi Yohanan's practice of rising and honouring non-Jewish elders ('elders of the Arameans') as well as Jewish elders, saying 'how many adventures have they gone through' (*Kid.* 33*a*). Rashi explained: '*Adventures*—Events and troubles; they saw many miracles and signs.' The Talmud speaks not of miracles but of 'adventures', which Rashi interpreted as 'events and troubles', yet he added the reference to miracles.

Many other examples could be cited, arising in diverse contexts. Most pertain to Israel's past, especially the Exodus from Egypt, the wanderings in the wilderness, the giving of the Torah, and the conquest of the Land; some pertain to the nation's future destiny. The large number of examples, and their wide variety, show them to be central to Rashi's commentaries.

Miracles occupy an important place in Rashi's teachings as a means for strengthening faith in God. They express his greatness and providential concern and love for Israel. For example: '*I am the Lord your God Who brought you out from the land of the Egyptians* [Lev. 26: 13]—You ought to believe that I can do all this, for I have taken you out of the land of Egypt and performed great miracles for you.' This purpose likewise is served by miracles performed for non-Jews. The miracle wrought for the king of Sodom is meant to teach the nations of the world about the miraculous rescue of Abraham in Ur of the Chaldeans: 'For they were caught up in the mud, and a miracle was done for the king of Sodom so he might escape from there. There were some among the nations who did not believe that Abraham had been rescued from Ur of the Chaldeans, but when this one [the king of Sodom] emerged from the mud, they believed in Abraham retroactively' (Rashi on Gen. 14: 10). Another example involves Hagar, Sarah's maidservant: '*An Egyptian maid-servant* [Gen. 16: 1]—She was Pharaoh's daughter, and when he saw the miracles done for Sarah, he said: better that my daughter be a maidservant in this house than a mistress in another house.' The source of this *midrash* is *Genesis Rabbah* 45: 1, but there is no linguistic or exegetical crux in the verse that would warrant its being cited.

Clear evidence of Rashi's tendentiousness here is provided not only by the frequency with which he treats miracles but also by his attitude towards them. As a rule, when Rashi made use of a *midrash* far removed from the plain meaning, he would preface a plain-meaning interpretation and then add the midrashic understanding. When it came to miracles, however, he departed from that practice, citing only the *midrash* referring to the miracle and treating it as the plain meaning of the verse. And, as we saw in his comment on 'a new heaven', he would sometimes state that the miraculous interpretation is the primary one.

Rashi's extensive consideration of miracles, even in the absence of exegetical need or textual basis, also shows that his purpose went beyond exegesis. At times, the *midrash* and the miracle it discusses are so far removed from the plain meaning of the text that they can only be explained as part of some agenda of Rashi's. For example, in interpreting the account of Jacob's journey from Beersheba to Haran, Rashi relies on the talmudic statement that after Jacob's quick arrival at Haran as a result of 'jumping of the way',[h] he said: 'Might I have passed by a place where my fathers worshipped [that is, Mount Moriah] and not worshipped there?' (*Ḥul.* 91*b*). On Rashi's interpretation, a great miracle was performed for Jacob in that Mount Moriah came to meet him at Beth-El: 'I say Mount Moriah was uprooted and came to here [to Beth-El].' This, of course, represented a dramatic change in the natural order. Nahmanides disagreed with Rashi and, after a long and detailed examination, rejected what he had written: 'None of this seems at all reasonable to me . . . neither that he returned to Beth-El nor that Mount Moriah jumped and went there. And not one of the *midrashim* says what Rashi says.'[21] Rashi's supercommentators devoted considerable attention to the issue, but this is not the place

---

[21] Nahmanides on Gen. 28: 17, trans. J.L.

[h] *Kefitsat derekh*, a midrashic concept analogous to seven-league boots.

for detailed consideration. In any case, Nahmanides seems to have been using a version of Rashi's comments that differed from what appears in the reliable manuscripts.

Further evidence of Rashi's inclination to find numerous miracles and to broaden the definition of 'miracle' appears in his interpretation of the thanksgiving offering: '*If he offers it [the sacrifice] for thanksgiving* [Lev. 7: 12]—If it is in thanks for a miracle that was performed for him, such as those who journey over sea or through the deserts, those freed from prison, and an ill person who is cured.' Rashi bases his comment on the talmudic discussion in which it is related, in the name of the *amora* Rav, that the four categories of people mentioned by Rashi are obligated to give thanks. Not once, however, is the word 'miracle' mentioned in that talmudic discussion: the people identified are obligated to give thanks simply because they safely emerged from the dangerous situations they had been in. Indeed, Rashi himself so interprets: 'They must give thanks when they emerge from danger' (on *Ber.* 54b, *arba'ah tserikhin lehodot*). In his biblical commentary, however, Rashi defines these people as ones for whom a miracle has been wrought, thereby suggesting that personal providence and divine assistance should be seen as miracles. Rashi thus broadened the concept of miracles for which one must give thanks to encompass any escape from danger.

Why did Rashi follow a course so different from that taken by other commentators? He certainly knew that the rabbis characterized various biblical and rabbinic expressions as parables or exaggerations. Of course, his great esteem for rabbinic legends and *midrashim*, which he saw as reflecting historical reality, provided the underpinnings for his approach. In some instances, he was moved by exegetical factors, but that is far from universally true. It appears that something else was at work here: his desire to emphasize God's great love for the nation of Israel. Because of that love, God was concerned about the nation's welfare even with respect to minor matters (such as 'pressing their clothes' in the dusty wilderness, so they would be as new), and because of that love, he will, in the future, lead and rescue them in non-natural ways. By emphasizing these ideas, Rashi hoped to enhance the faith of the Jews of his time, who were experiencing the harsh conditions of exile, and to strengthen their hopes for miraculous redemption. As already discussed, the effort to fortify the Jews in their struggles in those difficult days is prominent at many points in Rashi's oeuvre. It also is possible that we see here a defiant stand towards the Christians, who claimed to be 'the true Israel'. Emphasizing the miracles performed for the nation in the past, at all stages of its entry into its land, and that will be performed for it in the future demonstrates that God's love for Israel has never waned. Finally, it may be that the miracles are cited as a counterweight to the miracles attributed to Jesus in the Gospels.

# Exile and Redemption

The harsh and lengthy exile was particularly oppressive to Rashi and his contemporaries. Their distress resulted not only from persecutions and economic discrimination but also from the intense polemic with Christians, who treated the lowly state of the Jews in exile as clear evidence that God had rejected them in favour of the Church. The doctrine of the 'Jewish witness' (the humiliation of the Jews as evidence for the truth of Christianity) had been formulated by Augustine as early as the fifth century, but in the eleventh and twelfth centuries it occupied a central place in religious disputations and strongly influenced Jewish–Christian relations.[22] It is no wonder, then, that the subject is often considered and analysed from various perspectives in the writings of Rashi and his circle.

## The Place of Exile in Rashi's Teachings

The centrality of the exile in Rashi's teachings and consciousness can be inferred from four characteristics of his commentaries:

1.  **The relationship he draws between prophecies of consolation or of doom and his own time.** The clearest evidence appears in his comments on the Song of Songs, which, as he says in the introduction, he relates to the exile of his own time ('this exile').

2.  **The abundant use of *midrashim* that deal with exile and redemption and the preference for them even when others are more closely tied to the text.** The phenomenon is very widespread in his commentaries.

3.  **The integration in the commentaries of express pleas for redemption from the sorrows of exile.** In effect, exegesis becomes transformed into pleading and supplication. For example, '*The companions hearken for Thy voice* [S. of S. 8: 13, OJPS]—They come to the synagogue to hear Your voice . . . *Make haste, my beloved* [S. of S. 8: 14, OJPS]—From this exile, and redeem me from among them. *And be Thou like to a gazelle*—to hasten the redemption, and cause your presence to alight *upon the mountains of spices*, that is, Moriah, and the Temple, may it be built speedily in our day, Amen.'

4.  **The association with exile and its travails of verses that deal with other subjects, even when there is no basis in the text for the association that is drawn.** For example, Rashi takes a verse from the Psalms that speaks in dramatic terms of the poet's closeness to God—'You have held my eyelids [*shemurot*] open; I am overwrought, I cannot speak' (Ps. 77: 5)—and connects it to the exile: '*Shemurot* refers to the watches of the night [*ashmurot lailah*], the time when a

---

[22] For a broad discussion of this doctrine in Augustine's teachings, see Cohen, *Living Letters of the Law*, 67–146.

man awakens from his sleep and feels calm and at ease, but I am not like that during this night of exile. My eyes are always stuck open, like a man falling asleep with a troubled heart; the troubles I see take my breath away and leave me speechless.'

Although he offered some novel and original interpretations of verses dealing with redemption, Rashi introduced no substantively new ideas into the discussions of exile and redemption. He did not consider the question that greatly occupied Jewish sages in eleventh- and twelfth-century France and Germany: should one passively await the miraculous coming of the messiah or should one actively promote it by emigrating to the Land of Israel, following which the messiah would be revealed? Three generations after Rashi, great French sages—especially those in the *beit midrash* of Rabbi Isaac ben Abraham (Ritsba) and his brother, Rabbi Samson, in Sens—adopted the second view:

It should not occur to anyone that the King Messiah will reveal himself in an impure land, nor should anyone err and think that He will come to the Land of Israel among the non-Jews.[23] One who errs in that regard is not sensitive to the honour of the King Messiah . . . And now, many are rousing themselves and volunteering to go up to the Land of Israel. And many think that we are nearing the coming of the Redeemer, when they see that the nations have increased the weight of their yoke on Israel in most places . . . And let it not occur to anyone to say that in Egypt, our fathers were redeemed with great glory and a mighty hand and an outstretched arm and great signs. Our sins brought about [the absence of] all that.[24]

In contrast, sages from the circles of *ḥasidei ashkenaz* (the medieval Ashkenazi pietists) firmly opposed group emigration to the Land of Israel before the time of the redemption, seeing it as a serious sin. Saladin's great victory in the Battle of Hattin in 1187 and the later defeat of the crusaders in the Land of Israel gave rise to messianic hopes among the Jews and inspired them to action. In contrast, the crusaders' conquest of the Land in 1099 had greatly increased the Jews' discomfort, for the Christians saw the victory as fulfilment of the biblical promise of *their* redemption. Messianic expectations were not aroused in Rashi's time, and that is the principal reason why he did not discuss, in his commentaries, the question of contemporary immigration to the Land of Israel, even though he paid considerable attention to the Land's merit and sanctity. His main purpose was to lift his readers' spirits and help them fight back against the Christian propaganda that sought to use the exile as an argument to promote their conversion. The strengthening of the

---

[23] In other words, the messiah will not appear in the Land of Israel when it is inhabited by non-Jews and Jews are living in the diaspora. The immigration of Jews to the Land of Israel is a precondition of the appearance of the messiah.

[24] MS Firkovits 764; MS Darmstadt 25. The writer is a student of R. Isaac b. Abraham. The source has been widely considered in the scholarly literature, but this is not the place for a full discussion.

Church in eleventh- and twelfth-century Europe lent added force to its efforts against the Jews.

In Rashi's teachings, redemption was to be effected entirely through miracles. He taught that the Temple, in the age of redemption, would not be rebuilt by human hands but would miraculously descend from heaven, fully built. That motif appears in the seventh-century *Sefer zerubavel*, and Rashi adopted it from there or from one of the later works that made use of it. Human nature, too, would change in messianic times, and instincts would 'change for the better', as he says in his comment on 'And I will give you a new heart' (Ezek. 36: 26).

## Jewish Unease

The exile ensued primarily because the people of Israel had sinned, ever more gravely, over the course of generations. Particularly blameworthy were their contacts with non-Jews, who exerted a harmful cultural influence. Only four years after building the Temple, Solomon married a daughter of Pharaoh, and it was then decreed that the Temple would be destroyed. Rashi took this to be the meaning of a difficult verse in Jeremiah: 'This city has aroused My anger and My wrath from the day it was built until this day; so that it must be removed from My sight' (Jer. 32: 31). Rashi comments: 'On the day the Temple was founded, Solomon married Pharaoh's daughter.' The idea also appears in rabbinic texts, which recount that the day Solomon married Pharaoh's daughter was the day on which Rome, which destroyed the Temple, was founded (*Shab.* 56*b*).

A principal cause of Jewish suffering in the diaspora was the affront to Israel's honour brought about by the extended exile. Christians placed it at the centre of their religious polemic during the Middle Ages, for it could easily be used to score points against the Jews. It posed greater difficulties for Jewish sages than any other question: how to explain, if they were indeed the chosen people as they claimed, their extended presence in so humiliating an exile. Did the exile not support the Christian claim that God had become fed up with the Jewish people and had chosen the Church instead? Did the humiliation of the Jews in exile not attest to the truth of Christianity? It was not by happenstance that Rashi emphasized that 'is become like a widow' (Lam. 1: 1) in reference to Jerusalem does not refer to a permanent loss but only to a temporary one: 'Not an actual widow. Rather, she is like a woman whose husband has journeyed to a distant land but intends to return to her.' But could anyone think, given the comparative particle in 'like a widow', that the phrase does not mean an actual widow? Only his fear of powerful Christological propaganda can explain Rashi's offering this sort of interpretation. Later in that book, in commenting on the verse 'Your iniquity, Fair Zion, is expiated; He will exile you no longer' (Lam. 4: 22), Rashi wrote: 'From the Edomite exile; ongoing'; that is, from the exile under the Christian yoke, the final exile. Here he is also responding to the Christian argument that Israel had already returned (after the Babylonian exile) only to be exiled again, and that this prophecy of the end of exile cannot apply to it.

In support of their arguments, the Jews cited the first exile (in Babylon) and the return to Zion as irrefutable evidence that the exile of the Jewish nation does not attest to its having been cast aside or to the annulment of its selection, rather it serves the positive purpose of refining and purifying the nation. The greater the Jews' suffering in alien lands, the greater their atonement and purification. The Christians rejected this claim, arguing that the first exile had been very brief and could not be instructive with respect to the current, second exile, already in its second millennium.

It should be recalled that in the Middle Ages, Christians and Muslims alike saw a man's success as evidence of his faith in God and his righteousness. The success or failure of a community likewise was a measure of its religion's truth: the one that succeeds is the chosen and righteous one. As early as the first half of the ninth century, Al-Jahiz—one of the greatest Muslim prose writers of the Middle Ages— had written that the Muslim masses despised the Jews and their religion because they believed the Jews' lowly political status was evidence of their rejection by God and of the flaws in their religion:

When the masses considered the Jews and the Christians, it seemed to them that the standing of the Jewish religion among religions was like the standing of their trade among the ways of making a living, and that their apostasy was the worst of apostasies, for they are the lowliest of all ethnic groups.[25]

### Exploitation of the Jews and the Cruelty of their Persecutors

Another prominent motif in Rashi's account of Jewish discomfort is that of their exploitation. This, too, should be seen against the background of the harsh Jewish–Christian polemic over the identity of the 'true Israel'. The Jews' difficult economic situation provided fodder for Christian polemicists, who used it as valuable evidence of the Jews' humiliating rejection by God. Rashi and his colleague Rabbi Joseph Kara dealt with this motif not only where the biblical text alluded to it, but even where the plain meaning of the text had nothing at all to do with it. For example, in treating the verse '[He will] wreak vengeance on His foes' (Deut. 32: 43), Rashi writes: 'for the theft and the robbery'. Needless to say, the vengeance spoken of in the verse does not necessarily pertain to theft. The Jews' efforts to gather assets in the diaspora were also doomed to failure. Consistent with their experience in Europe in his time, Rashi wrote: 'We have toiled to gather money and wealth, but we have not been allowed to . . . for the enemies steal and grab everything through taxes and capitations and assessments' (on Lam. 5: 5). At the same time, the Jews in the diaspora had to avoid giving the impression that they were overly

---

[25]  Sadan, 'Polemics as Religious and Literary Writing' (Heb.), 52.

acquisitive. In Rashi's view, the Jews of Ahasuerus' kingdom refrained from taking booty even though they had the king's express permission to do so, 'showing to all that they had not acted for the sake of money' (on Esther 8: 11). That interpretation has no basis in the main rabbinic *midrashim* in *Megilah*, and it may be assumed that Rashi offered it as, among other things, a response to Christian charges that the Jews have always been, and still are, avaricious and deceitful.

If Rashi's interpretation is taken as actual guidance on how his wealthier readers should conduct themselves within Christian society, using that guidance would have required them to walk a very fine line. On the one hand, they would have to avoid actions that might cause their neighbours to see them as avaricious. On the other hand, in commenting on the verse 'Indeed, the Lord your God has blessed you in all your undertakings' (Deut. 2: 7), Rashi writes: 'Therefore, do not belittle[26] his goodness, as if to show you are poor; rather, show yourselves as wealthy.' Rashi thus calls for allowing everyone to see the Jews' success, which attests, as noted, to the truth of their religion and to God's care for them. At the same time he says they must avoid showing their power to excess, lest they arouse the envy and hatred of the Christians among whom they live.

One way in which Rashi conveys a sense of how severely the Jews of his time were persecuted and how maliciously they were treated by the authorities is by emphasizing the cruelty of Israel's persecutors in the Bible and their hatred for the people of Israel. He had three purposes in doing so: to portray the persecutors of his time as continuing the practices of antisemites through the ages, to describe the boundless intensity of their hatred for Jews, and to comfort the suffering Jews of his time, by situating them within an ancient historical process going forwards in accordance with a divine plan that includes an end to the suffering and an ultimate redemption. The suffering is worth enduring because it has a deliberate purpose, and, even during the worst of the subjugation and persecution, God watches over the nation of Israel: '*And God took notice of them* [Exod. 2: 25]—He paid attention and did not avert His gaze.' Even if God's involvement is not evident and it appears that Israel has been abandoned to its enemies, it is God who directs all that happens, and all events follow a preordained and precise plan leading to the redemption. To emphasize this, Rashi selected not only *midrashim* close to the plain meaning of the text but also some quite remote from it. In describing Moses' death, the Bible relates that God showed him 'the whole land . . . as far as the Western Sea' (Deut. 34: 2).[i] Rashi interpreted: 'The western land in [both] its serenity and its destruction. Another explanation: read not "the final sea [*yam*]" but "the final day [*yom*]". The Holy One, Blessed Be He, showed him all the events that would befall

---

[26] The Hebrew reads *tikhpu*, from *kefiyat tovah* ('ungratefulness'). Some versions read *tikhperu* ('atone for'), but *tikhpu* is the better reading and appears in MS Leipzig 1, fo. 165*b*.

[i] *Yam aharon*: literally 'final sea'.

Israel until the dead return to life.' The source for this *midrash* is *Sifrei* on Deuteronomy. God even prepares the remedy before the onset of the affliction. That principle is formulated in BT *Megilah* as 'Said Resh Lakish: The Holy One, Blessed Be He, does not afflict Israel unless He has first prepared the remedy.' Rashi changed it, referring to the remedy first: 'For the Holy One, Blessed Be He, creates a remedy for Israel's affliction [even] before He brings the affliction upon them' (on Esther 3: 1, following *Meg.* 13*b*). Even though Israel's many afflictions were planned in advance, there is no risk that the entire nation of Israel will be destroyed. One of the harshest verses in Moses' song—'I will sweep misfortunes on them [Israel]; use up My arrows on them' (Deut. 32: 23)—is transformed by Rashi, following the sages, into a source of comfort: 'This curse becomes a blessing as things get worse. My arrows are used up [that is, finished] but they [the Israelites] are not finished.' And hence the great value of describing for Israel, in advance, the exile and its rigours (Deut. 32: 35).

## The Non-Jews' Malice

Consistent with his tendency to portray non-Israelite biblical figures in negative terms, Rashi selected *midrashim* that portray Pharaoh not only as an ingrate and a persecutor of Israel but also as a man of boundless cruelty. Not satisfied with harshly enslaving the Israelites in Egypt and throwing their sons into the Nile, he adopted the practice of bathing in the blood of small Israelite children: '*The king of Egypt died* [Exod. 2: 23]—He became leprous and would slaughter Israelite infants and bathe in their blood.' This was a widespread tradition in medieval literature, and its source remains uncertain.[27] In any event, the portrayal of Pharaoh as one who actually slaughtered Israelite children himself, and did not merely command surreptitiously that they be killed, is meant to emphasize his malice even more.

Vashti, Ahasuerus' wife, mocked Jewish women and compelled them to appear naked and to violate the sabbath. For that reason, 'it was decreed that she would appear naked on the sabbath' (Rashi on Esther 1: 12, following *Meg.* 12*b*). *Megilah* emphasizes that she was punished in accord with *lex talionis*, and the implication for Rashi's contemporaries, Jews and Christians alike, is clear.

Rashi also culled from *Megilah midrashim* that disparaged Ahasuerus, even when they have no basis in the biblical text. Rashi describes Ahasuerus as a wicked king 'from start to finish' (on Esther 1: 1). Jews are endangered by fraternization with non-Jews, and their enjoyment of Ahasuerus' banquet is one of the principal factors that brought about the genocidal decree issued by Haman with the king's concurrence (on Esther 4: 1, following *Meg.* 12*b*). Even Mordecai, the leading sage of his generation, was not beyond criticism. He lost the support of many of his con-temporary sages 'because he became close to the government and took time away

[27] See Ginzberg, *Legends of the Jews*, i. 497, 499 n. 101; *Exodus Rabbah* 1: 34 and Sha'anan's notes in his edition (p. 99 n. 37).

from his study'.[28] In a similar vein, Rashi added that Mordecai rejected outright the directive to bow before Haman. He is described as the model of a Jew who would never bow to a non-Jew: 'He would *never* bow, for he is a Jew' (on Esther 3: 4; emphasis added). The word 'never' does not appear in the biblical text.

Laban, Esau, Balaam, Orpah, Delilah, Sennacherib, Nebuchadnezzar—all of these, and others, are described by Rashi in terms more negative than those used by Scripture. He frequently emphasized the ingratitude of non-Jewish rulers who exploited the Jews, disregarded the help Jews gave them, and persecuted Jews with great cruelty. He was familiar with the tendency for feudal rulers to support anti-Jewish rioters and ignore their murderous activities. Rashi's purpose was to use the experience of the past to teach his contemporaries that 'non-Jews are untrustworthy'.

## The Curse of Exile

According to Rashi, the exile is the most severe punishment to be visited on Israel (on Deut. 11: 17). Israel's very presence in the diaspora entails a spiritual decline, as we saw in examining the Land of Israel in Rashi's thought. Moreover, subservience to non-Jews in the diaspora is itself equivalent to idolatry: '*There you will serve man-made gods* [Deut. 4: 28]—In serving those who serve them, it is as if you are serving them.'

One of the harshest afflictions of exile, in Rashi's view, is the wide dispersion of the Jews: '*And you I will scatter among the nations* [Lev. 26: 33]—This is a harsh measure, for when citizens are exiled to one place, they see one another and are comforted.' The dispersion puts the very existence of the nation in jeopardy. Scripture states '[You] shall perish among the nations and the land of your enemies shall consume you' (Lev. 26: 38), and Rashi comments: 'When you are dispersed, you will be lost from one another. *Shall consume you*—they are those who die in exile.' That final point is surprising; in what sense are those who die in exile 'consumed'? Those who die in the Land of Israel are no less gone from the world. And if his point is that they will remain in exile until the day of their death, he should have said 'until you die in exile', not 'they are those who die in exile'. Rashi may be alluding here to the Talmud's statement (*Ket.* 111a–b) that those who die in the Land of Israel have an advantage over those who die in exile, in that they will be resurrected immediately and be exempt from rolling through the tunnels that will return them to the Land. The harshest condemnation of the diaspora is that of the *amora* Rabbi Elazar: 'They who die outside the Land of Israel do not return to life,

---

[28] Rashi on Esther 10: 3, based on the scriptural wording 'popular with the multitude of his brethren'. Rashi takes 'multitude' (*rov*) to mean most but not all, suggesting that some did not support Mordecai, disregarding the plain meaning of *rov* as 'multitude' or 'numerous'. See e.g. 'his great wealth and many [*rov*] sons' (Esther 5: 11) or 'the many [*rubei*] teachings I wrote for him' (Hos. 8: 12). Rashi clearly was not unaware of this meaning, but he favoured the rabbinic *midrash* because it suited his purpose of teaching the Jews to be cautious both about drawing too close to the authorities and about forgoing Torah study.

as it is said, "I will set glory in the land of the living" [Ezek. 26: 20, OJPS]—in the land that I desire, those who die will live' (*Ket.* 111a).[j] The Talmud sought to soften his words and his deprecation of those who die outside the Land of Israel, but the point remains and Rashi presumably had it in mind. Not only will the Jews be exiled from their land and wander among the nations; even their death and burial in exile will impair them, as the alien soil 'consumes' them.

The accursed nature of exile and the merit of the Land of Israel are here emphasized quite clearly. This *midrash* has no parallel in *Sifrei* or other midrashic literature, except an oblique allusion to it in Targum Jonathan. Here, too, we find evidence of Rashi's thinking on the accursedness of exile and the importance of the Land of Israel. That the Jews are situated in exile and subjected to all its associated degradations is itself an impairment of the nation's dignity and a boon to idolatry: servitude to those who worship idols is as idol-worship itself (Rashi on Deut. 4: 28).

### Anticipating Redemption

Another motif often emphasized by Rashi, following rabbinic teachings, is the importance of anticipating the redemption, believing in it, and not giving up hope even in the harshest of exilic times. This faith and the loving acceptance of tribulations are guarantors of the redemption. The tribulations atone for the nation's sins, which were responsible for the exile, and the more intense the tribulations, the greater their capacity to atone (Rashi on Lev. 26: 41). The atonement is not only for current sins but also for those of the past, including the sin of the golden calf. People who know that their suffering is atoning for the sins of their ancestors will be more at ease.

Horrific suffering also entails an element of blessing, in that it draws Israel closer to their Father in heaven: 'The curses and tribulations allow you to endure and set you before him' (Rashi on Deut. 29: 12). The destruction of the Tabernacle and the Temple have a positive aspect: 'Their destruction is an atonement for souls' (on Num. 24: 5). That is, but for the destruction, the punishment borne by people would have been harsher.

It is when the decline is at its worst that salvation will appear. When God sees that 'the enemy's hand is growing ever stronger against them' (Rashi on Deut. 32: 36), not only will the nations recognize Israel's salvation; they will even praise Israel for having survived all the hardships of exile: 'See the glory of this nation, which held fast to the Holy One, Blessed Be He, through all the hardships that befell them and did not abandon Him. They knew His goodness and glory' (on Deut. 32: 43).

Joyous acceptance of the yoke of exile, and sanctification of God's name during the persecutions, are characteristic of the nation of Israel:

---

[j] The comment reflects a play on the word *tsvi* in the biblical verse, translated 'glory'. Rashi associates it, by assonance, with *erets tsivyoni*, 'the land that I desire'.

Even at times when you favour the nations and deliver Israel into their hands. *Their hal-lowed are all in Your hand* [Deut. 33: 3]—All their righteous and good adhered to You and did not draw away from You, and You protect them. *They followed in Your step*—they accept Your decrees and rulings with joy.

In interpreting the verse 'Moses charged us with the teaching, as the heritage of the congregation of Jacob' (Deut. 33: 4), Rashi has the people making a declaration: 'The teaching [Torah] with which Moses charged us is the heritage of the congregation of Jacob; we grasped it and will not abandon it.' Following the *midrash*, he compares Israel to a dove that is faithful to its mate until death: '*Do not deliver Your dove to the wild beast* [Ps. 74: 19]—When a male dove dies, its partner does not mate with another; so, too, Israel has not exchanged you for some other god, even though you have distanced Yourself from them and she has become as a widow.' The statement is meant less as scriptural exegesis and more as encouragement against conversion, whatever the circumstances.

Additional encouragement appears in the statement, based on midrashic sources, that God went into exile with his people and 'suffers' with them in their tribulations:

*Then the Lord thy God will [re]turn thy captivity* [Deut. 30: 3, OJPS]—It should have said *veheshiv* [in the causative form, rather than *shav*, in the simple indicative form of the Hebrew verb]. Our sages learned from this that the divine presence is with Israel in the misfortune of their exile, as it were, and their redemption dictates His redemption, for He will return with them. It also may be said that the ingathering of the exiles will be a great and difficult day, as if He Himself with His own hands brings each person back from his place.

And Moses had already been promised as much: 'I will be with them in this misfortune as I will be with them in their subjugation to other sovereigns' (Exod. 3: 14).

On occasion, one can sense Rashi adopting an accusatory tone over God's failure to react to Israel's suffering and over the long duration of the exile. For example, he adds his own expression of wonderment to the prophet Habakkuk's accusations: 'So said the prophet; and why are You silent about all this?' (on Hab. 1: 3). The accusation is not expressly made in that verse, though it is invited by the entire book. On the verse 'On none but me He brings down his hand again and again, without cease' (Lam. 3: 3), Rashi writes: 'I alone am always struck, for all His repeated stripes are upon me.' In interpreting Psalm 39: 2, he explicitly asks God to inflict pain on the children of Esau (the Christians) so they will be unable to boast that 'you [Israel] are struck and we are not struck'.

One of his accusations is strikingly forceful. On the verse 'All my foes heard of my plight and exulted, for it is Your doing' (Lam. 1: 21), Rashi writes, following midrashic sources: 'You brought about their enmity for me, for You set me apart from their food, from their drink, and from intermarrying with them. If we intermarried with them, they would have mercy on me and on the children of their daughters.'

Loving acceptance of tribulations, anticipation of salvation, and heart-felt (not merely rote) penance—these are considered by Rashi to be the guarantors of emergence from exile and of hastened redemption:

God is my portion, and it is proper that I await Him . . . It is good for a man to wait in silence, anticipating God's salvation . . . a term for awaiting . . . when we lift our hands heavenwards, our hearts, too, are raised with them, to turn and return our hearts before the omnipresent One Blessed Be He. (Rashi on Lam. 3: 24, 26, 41)

## The Nations of the World

Relations with the other nations of the world occupied a central place in medieval Jewish biblical interpretation. This is hardly surprising, for the goal of the commentators was not only to explicate the biblical texts but also to serve important Jewish communal interests. This was certainly true of Jewish biblical interpreters in France from the eleventh to the thirteenth centuries, who devoted considerable attention to Jewish–Christian polemic and to the fate of the Jewish people in exile. The uniqueness of the Jewish people and its fate during the harsh years of exile experienced in the Middle Ages were central to the interreligious polemic, the pace of which was then picking up. Likewise central to the polemic were certain biblical verses, and most Jewish exegetes were therefore compelled to deal with them and sometimes to interpret them in ways departing from their plain meaning. Christological biblical interpretation was regarded as a menace to the Jewish community, given the concern that it might lead Jews to convert.

It was Rashi who opened the door to a degree of comfort, and he served as a model to those who succeeded him in France and Germany. His biblical interpretation overall cannot be separated from Jewish–Christian polemic, which reached one of its peaks in his time and left clear traces on his biblical commentary and his teachings in general. What I want to examine here are his principal ideas regarding the nations of the world in the scheme of history and the relationships between those nations and the Jews.

Rashi had close personal contacts, both social and economic, with his non-Jewish neighbours and, as already mentioned, his writings overall attest to his close familiarity with the worldly culture of his time in both Germany and France. He felt no alienation from his surroundings; on the contrary his writings evince a love for the natural scenery of his country, and those scenes play a part not only in his intellectual world but also in his spiritual and emotional worlds. Nevertheless, his writings convey a sense of animosity towards the nations of the world. In my judgement, his principal positions regarding the nations were influenced both by the polemic already mentioned and by the anti-Jewish edicts issued in his time.

## Animosity towards the Nations

In Rashi's commentaries on the Bible and the liturgical poems, the nations of the world, especially Christendom, are portrayed as beasts of prey lying in wait to attack and devour the Jewish people. Rejoicing over the Jews' misfortune, they are hypocritical, cruel, thieving, corrupt, wallowing in lust, and involved in idolatry, sexual immorality, and bloodshed. He selected *midrashim* that depict these characteristics, favouring them over others. The intensity of the nations' hatred of the Jews is expressed in their extreme cruelty: 'The wicked of the nations would punish them [the Jews] with death and with burial as asses in the bellies of dogs' (Rashi on Isa. 53: 9). Accordingly, 'The Holy One, Blessed Be He, will in the future take vengeance on Edom, and He Himself will begin by killing their prince [or angel]' (on Isa. 63: 1).

Rashi viewed the nations of his time as the heirs of Israel's great biblical enemies, carrying on in their ways. That is especially true of the Christians, whom he regarded as the descendants of Esau, pre-eminently represented by Amalek. That understanding was not new: it appears in rabbinic *midrashim* and early liturgical poetry. It was not by chance that Rashi, in his comments on Genesis, depicted Esau in an extremely negative light, as discussed above.

The same attitude appears in Rashi's depiction of Balaam, the greatest non-Jewish prophet. The midrashic literature is of two minds about his character. As a rule, he is depicted negatively, but some *midrashim* speak favourably of him and especially about the quality of his prophecy. No trace of those *midrashim* can be found in Rashi's commentary, however, and the negative ones he selected were among the harshest. They present Balaam as a lowlife: lustful, avaricious, conceited, and possessed of minimal prophetic power ('the holy spirit alights on him only at night'; '[*God*] *met* [*Balaam*] [Num. 23: 4]—the word [translated 'met', *vayikar*] evokes the impurity of a seminal emission [*keri*], that is, with difficulty and humiliation'). Balaam's hatred for Israel exceeds even that of Balak, and he therefore wilfully defied even God (see Rashi on Num. 22: 6, 8, 11, 13, 18, 21, 22, 23, 29, 34; 23: 3‒4, 28; 25: 1; 35: 8, 16).

According to Rashi, the reason for Balaam's prophecy and for the divine presence alighting on him was only 'to avoid giving the nations the opportunity to say: if we had had prophets, we would have mended our ways. He therefore established prophets for them, and they breached the world's fences [against improper conduct]. They initially were bound by the avoidance of improper sexuality, and this one advised them to give themselves over to licentiousness' (on Num. 22: 5). In vain do we try to locate in Rashi's commentary any allusions to the *midrashim* that speak in praise of Balaam or of the quality of his prophecy—including *midrashim* that describe his prophecy as greater even than that of Moses or that tell of his having been born circumcised. Rashi selected the texts that spoke most negatively of

Balaam, consistent with his overall tendency to disparage the nations of the world.[29]

At various points, Rashi emphasizes the nations' ingratitude, sometimes through the use of far-fetched *midrashim*. For example, in discussing the Bible's detailed identification of the murderers of King Jehoash of Judah, he says:

And why did Scripture provide these details? To teach that the Holy One, Blessed Be He, exacted vengeance from him [Jehoash] through people who were like him: An Ammonite and Moabite, who are ingrates—for they showed no gratitude for the good Abraham did for [their ancestor] Lot in fighting against the kings on Lot's behalf, and instead hired Balaam to curse [Abraham's] descendants—took vengeance on Jehoash, who was not grateful to Jehoiada, and killed his son Zechariah, as recounted in Chronicles. (Rashi on 2 Kgs 12: 22)

## The Nations of the World in the Messianic Era

The most impressive evidence of Rashi's powerful animosity towards the nations of the world appears in his commentaries on biblical passages that deal with the redemption and the place of non-Jews in the messianic era.[30] Rashi speaks of the conversion to Judaism of the best of the non-Jews, who will survive and not be destroyed like most of the nations. He even details the steps of the process. The Christian rulers, descendants of Esau, are held responsible for the welfare of the Jews exiled to their lands: 'O sword! Rouse yourself against My shepherd, the man in charge of My flock' (Zech. 13: 7), which Rashi interprets as 'against Esau, whom I placed in charge of My exiled sheep'. Accordingly, the nations will be punished in three stages: first, 'the king of Rome the wicked' will be smitten; then, '*I will turn My hand against* [Zech. 13: 7]— I will again strike *the shepherd boys*—the rulers who are younger than the kings; finally, *one-third of it shall survive* [Zech. 13: 8]—they will convert and live.' But that will not exhaust the pain to be borne by the enemies. The masses of the nations will be punished too, and only one-third of them will remain. But even then, '*that third I will put into the fire* [Zech. 13: 9]— . . . so that they suffer, and some of the converts share with Israel the distress of the birth pangs of the messiah and the war of Gog and Magog. On that basis, the truthfulness of their conversion will be tested, for many who become Jews in the first instance will return to their straying ways and join with Gog, as we find in the rabbinic tales [aggadah].'[31]

---

[29] See *Avot derabi natan*, version B, ch. 5 and parallels. On Jewish attitudes towards Balaam, including his identification with Jesus, see Urbach, 'Rabbinic Homilies on Non-Jewish Prophets' (Heb.), esp. 281–4; Berger, 'Three Typological Themes in Early Jewish Messianism', 162 n. 78; Yuval, *Two Nations in Your Womb*, index, s.v. 'Balaam'.

[30] On the fate of non-Jews in the messianic era, see Yuval, *Two Nations in Your Womb*, 109–15, and additional bibliography in n. 60; Grossman, '"Proselytizing Redemption"' (Heb.); Berger, 'On the Image and Destiny of Gentiles in Ashkenazic Polemical Literature' (Heb.).

[31] Cf. *AZ* 3a and see the comments of Maarsen in Rashi, *Parshandata* (Heb.), i. 104 n. 18.

Rashi stressed that even those whose repentance would be willingly accepted will not attain the high status of the Jews. That idea recurs frequently in his commentaries, and it clearly forms an important touchstone of his thinking. Let me therefore cite four examples. The first is in Isaiah, which tells of the powerful impression that will be left on Egypt by Sennacherib's fall at the gates of Jerusalem. The prophecy ends with the following statement: 'On that day, Israel shall be a third partner with Egypt and Assyria as a blessing in earth, for the Lord of Hosts will bless them, saying, "Blessed be My people Egypt, My handiwork Assyria, and My very own Israel" [Isa. 19: 24–5].' The plain meaning of the text is that 'My people' and 'My handiwork' refer to Egypt and Assyria. Rashi, however, interprets them as referring to Israel:

*Will bless them*—Israel; *Blessed be My people Egypt*—Israel, whom I chose to be My nation when they were in Egypt; *My handiwork Assyria*—I showed them My might, which I manifested against Assyria, and as a result of those miracles, they will return to Me and be as if I had made them anew, and they will be *My very own Israel*.

This interpretation is far removed from the biblical text and, while Rashi based it on Targum Jonathan, he could easily have interpreted the verse otherwise. That he offers an interpretation so clearly at odds with the plain meaning (which appears in the commentaries of Radak, Ibn Ezra, and others) shows that he was not motivated by exegetical considerations. Moreover, Rashi suggested—in accordance with the plain meaning—that the entire chapter relates to the events following Sennacherib's fall at the gates of Jerusalem. He could easily have understood the verses in question to mean that in the wake of Sennacherib's wondrous fall, Egypt was moved to recognize God.

A second example appears in Psalm 47. In accordance with the plain meaning, Rashi takes the psalm to describe the future recognition by all nations of the God of Israel: 'All you peoples, clap your hands, raise a joyous shout for God' (Ps. 47: 2). The psalm concludes with 'The great of the peoples are gathered together, the retinue of Abraham's God; for the guardians of the earth belong to God; He is greatly exalted' (Ps. 47: 10). In its plain meaning, 'the great of the peoples' refers to the nations of the world, who have joined with the Jewish people, and many medieval commentators so interpreted it. Surprisingly, Rashi declines to follow the plain meaning and interprets the words as referring to Jews who have yielded their lives for the sanctification of God's name, that is, to Jewish martyrs; at the time of the redemption, all will recognize their greatness:

*God reigns over the nations* [Ps. 47: 9]—All will say, *God is seated on His holy throne*—Now the throne is complete and His greatness is acknowledged; they will recognize that *the great of the peoples are gathered together* to His city, those who gave themselves to be slaughtered and killed for the sanctification of His name. *The retinue of Abraham's God*—[Abraham] was the first to be generous, the first convert. Now it will be known that *the guardians of the earth belong to God*, He has the ability to protect all who trust in Him.

A clear account of the selected nations joining with Israel has here been transformed into a parochial prophecy pertaining to those Jews who have died to sanctify God's name. Rashi's purpose evidently was to encourage the Jews of his time to hold fast to their faith and to be prepared to give their lives in sanctification of God's name, for their future status will be exalted.

Had Rashi interpreted 'the great of the peoples' as referring to the non-Jewish nations, who attain, in the messianic era, the high status of the Jews, he might thereby have weakened the concept of Jewish chosenness and uniqueness and the consequent willingness of his fellow Jews to suffer the harsh burdens of exile. Rashi's commentary on Psalms was written, as already noted, following the edicts of 1096, hence the meaning it had for his contemporaries.

A third example refers to the prophet Zechariah's statement that 'the many peoples and the multitude of nations shall come to seek the Lord of Hosts' (Zech. 8: 22). This is clearly an account of repentant nations coming to seek God, but Rashi added an idea not mentioned or even alluded to in the text, namely that these nations would not be privileged to attain Israel's status: 'And all the tribes of Israel are more important to God than all the ancient nations . . . all the nations will belong to the Holy One, Blessed Be He, but Israel will be as valued as all of them together.' Rashi repeated the very same idea in interpreting Zechariah 9: 1: 'For all men's eyes will turn to the Lord, like all the tribes of Israel.'

The fourth example appears in Rashi's interpretation of Zephaniah 3: 9–10. The text reads: 'For then I will make the peoples pure of speech, so that they all invoke the Lord by name and serve Him with one accord. From beyond the rivers of Cush, My suppliants shall bring offerings to Me in Fair Puzai.' Here, too, Rashi abandoned the plain meaning in order to avoid portraying the best of the non-Jewish nations as having the same status as the Jews in the messianic era. In his view, the prophet is speaking of the Jewish exiles ('the peoples') who are 'beyond the rivers of Cush', and 'Fair Puzai' are 'the assemblies of my dispersions, whom I have dispersed'.[k]

In line with this fundamental attitude, Rashi sought out negative qualities in foreign nations and found criticisms of them even in Solomon's prayer following the completion of the Temple. In that prayer, Solomon asked God to accept the prayers of foreigners too:

Or if a foreigner who is not of Your people Israel comes from a distant land for the sake of Your name—for they shall hear about Your great name and Your mighty hand and Your outstretched arm—when he comes to pray towards this House, oh, hear in Your heavenly

[k] The association of 'Fair Puzai' with 'my dispersions' reflects wordplay lost in translation. In the Hebrew, 'Puzai' is *putsai*; 'my dispersions' is *nefutsotai*. OJPS translates in a manner consistent with Rashi's interpretation: 'For then will I turn to the peoples a pure language, that they may all call upon the name of the Lord, to serve Him with one consent. From beyond the rivers of Ethiopia shall they bring My suppliants, even the daughter of My dispersed, as Mine offering.'

abode and grant all that the foreigner asks You for. Thus all the peoples of the earth will know Your name and revere You, as does Your people Israel; and they will recognize that Your name is attached to this House that I have built (1 Kgs 8: 41–3).

Even though Solomon clearly stated that the purpose of accepting the foreigner's prayer was so that 'all the peoples of the earth' would know God's name, recognize the merit of the Temple, and, most of all, 'revere You as does Your people Israel', Rashi saw a need to criticize the foreigners, emphasizing the difference between their fear of God and Israel's:

*All that the foreigner asks You for* [1 Kgs 8: 43]—but when speaking of Israel, he says 'render to each man according to his ways' [1 Kgs 8: 39]. This is because Israel recognizes the Holy One, Blessed Be He, and knows His capabilities, so if his prayer is not granted, he blames himself and his sins. But the foreigner challenges [God] and says: 'This is a house whose name is known throughout the world, and I made the effort to travel far and come to pray in it and found nothing, just as there is nothing in idolatry; accordingly, 'grant all that the foreigner asks You for'.

In other words, Rashi sees something negative even in the best of the non-Jews, who take the pains to travel long distances to the Temple to call on God. It is because of their weak belief that Solomon asks God to accept their prayers in all instances, even if they are not worthy.

This negativity towards non-Jews also is evident in Rashi's serious concerns about overly close interaction with them. Even the wisest of all men, King Solomon, sinned gravely in marrying Pharaoh's daughter. Rashi presumably accepted the sages' premise that Solomon converted all his wives, including Pharaoh's daughter, whose conversion the Talmud expressly refers to (*Yev. 76a*). Nevertheless, Rashi suggested that one of the biblical verses harshest on Israel be understood as referring to Solomon's marrying Pharaoh's daughter, a step that bears much of the blame for the destruction of Jerusalem. The verse reads: 'This city has aroused My anger and My wrath from the day it was built until this day; so that it must be removed from My sight' (Jer. 32: 31). Rashi writes: '*From the day it was built*—The day on which the Temple was established was the day on which Solomon married Pharaoh's daughter.' In commenting on 1 Kings 3: 3, he elaborates further:

*And Solomon . . . loved the Lord and followed the practices of his father David*—For four years, until he began to build the Temple, but when he began to build, 'Solomon allied himself by marriage with Pharaoh'. Hence it is said 'This city has aroused My anger and My wrath from the day it was built until this day.' So it is taught in *Seder olam*.

The quotation from *Seder olam* is not essential to an understanding of the verse. Rashi chose it because of its implicit pedagogical message.[32]

---

[32]  *Seder olam*, ch. 15; cf. Rashi on Lam. 2: 8.

## Conversion

Despite Rashi's tendency to detract from the standing even of 'good' non-Jews in messianic times, he was clearly willing to accept their future repentance. Many of them, he wrote, 'will come of their own accord to learn' from Israel (on Isa. 42: 2). He foresaw two stages in the process: vengeance against Israel's enemies, during which many non-Jews will be destroyed, followed by the final stage of redemption, in which those who remain, having seen the decisive defeat of Israel's enemies who had attacked Jerusalem, will acknowledge the God of Israel and accept the yoke of his sovereignty. The non-Jews' repentance, and their affiliation with the nation of Israel in the wake of the messianic era's events, will take place even before the prophets expressly call on them to take those steps. That is the implication, for example, of his comment on the opening verses of Isaiah 42:

> It will not be necessary to rebuke and prophesy against the peoples, for they will come of their own accord to learn from [Israel], as it is said, 'Let us go with you, for we have heard that God is with you' [Zech. 8: 23] … for the earth will be filled with knowledge, and they will heed them, as it is said, 'For then I will make the peoples pure of speech', etc. [Zeph. 3: 9], and that is [the meaning of] 'the coastlands shall await His teaching'—all will heed His Torah.

Their repentance will be lovingly accepted, even though they will not attain the high station of the Jews.

Rashi's notion of two successive stages of redemption is based primarily on Scripture itself and on rabbinic *midrashim*, which depict the harsh blows to be inflicted on the enemies of Israel who wage war against Jerusalem, followed by the survivors' recognition of God's sovereignty.[33] But the items he chooses to emphasize, and his association of the two stages even with verses that do not call for any such interpretation, show that this is his own opinion, which he wants to advance through his commentaries. Let me cite a few more examples.

In commenting on Isaiah 56: 3, Rashi places considerable emphasis on the motif of conversion: '*Let not the foreigner say*—Why shall I convert; will not the Holy One, Blessed Be He, differentiate me from His people when He rewards them?' Later, on verse 7, he writes: '*For My house shall be called a house of prayer for all peoples*—Not for Israel alone, but for converts too.' And on verse 8: '[*Thus declares the Lord God,*] *who gathers the dispersed of Israel: "I will gather still more to those already gathered"*—From among the peoples who have converted and affiliated with them.' Rashi could have interpreted the final clause as referring not to the nations of the world but to the nation of Israel and its more remote exiles who are destined to be reunited with those who have already returned to the Land. That interpretation

[33] e.g. Rashi on Ezek. 38; on Zech. 14. He interprets Isa. 41: 5 to mean that at the start of the redemption, when the non-Jews come to perceive what is happening, they will join together to wage war against the nation of Israel.

would be closer to the plain meaning and was adopted by Ibn Ezra and others. Later in the chapter, Rashi describes in detail the varied attitudes of the nations of the world towards conversion and differentiates between the 'good' and the 'bad' among them. In the messianic era the 'good' nations are those who will attack those who decline to convert: '*All you wild beasts* [Isa. 56: 9]—all the nations *come* and draw near to me and *devour all you beasts of the forest*—the mighty nations who stubbornly resisted converting.[34]

At that time, the people of the world will come to understand that Israel's lowly state was meant to atone for the sins of the nations: 'We see that it was not because of its [inherent] lowliness that these were visited upon it; rather, it was tormented so that all the nations could be atoned for through the suffering of Israel. It bore the misfortune that should properly have come on us' (Rashi on Isa. 53: 4).

There exists no orderly and systematic statement of Rashi's teachings on the fate of the nations of the world in messianic times. Nevertheless, it is clear that he recognized in principle that they would become affiliated with the Jews, though never attaining their high standing.

## Summary

Rashi's profound animosity towards the nations of the world included both rational and emotional considerations, and it is evident throughout his works. He took every opportunity that came his way to disparage them, including the use of interpretations far removed from the plain meaning of the biblical text. That most of his comments have some basis in rabbinic *midrashim* does not diminish their significance as characteristic features of his ideology, for the fact is that he favoured these *midrashim* over others, even in the absence of any exegetical justification for doing so. In Rashi's opinion, the nations are deficient in their religious beliefs and in the ways they act towards other human beings. They declined to accept the Torah but are envious of the Jews, who did accept it, and are therefore hostile to them. That hostility is deeply rooted within the nations and flows also from their hatred of God: their hatred of the Father led to their persecution of his children. Another factor contributing to their animosity towards Israel is the Jews' religiously motivated social separatism. Social isolation as a contributory factor to hatred of Jews is referred to by rabbis and medieval Jewish sages and appears in the writings of Christian and Muslim polemicists. Rashi's recognition that some non-Jews will

---

[34] Compare Rashi's interpretation of Isa. 14: 1 (which reads 'shall join them' (*venispeḥu*)) and of Zech. 2: 15 ('will attach themselves' (*venilvu*)) with his comment on Isa. 54: 15: 'And our rabbis interpreted this as pertaining to converts, to teach that converts are not to be accepted in messianic times. But the plain meaning may also support that interpretation: [only] those who became converts in the time of your misfortune will dwell with you [*alayikh yipol*], as "they camped [*nafal*] alongside their kinsmen" (Gen. 25: 18)'. Cf. *Yev.* 24*b*; *AZ* 3*b*: 'R. Yosi says: In the future, idolaters will come to convert … but they will become converts who tag along on their own [*geirim gerurim*]'; Rashi comments: 'They convert on their own but we do not accept them' (cf. Rashi on Isa. 44: 4; 45: 23).

repent in the messianic era is only a weak sweetener, for even then, they will not attain Israel's exalted status.

A notable expression of Rashi's animosity towards the nations of the world, especially Christianity, is his near total disregard of biblical and rabbinic statements that laud foreign leaders and heroes, especially Esau and Balaam. Even where the plain meaning of the biblical text is favourable to them, Rashi recasts the verse to be disparaging.

What are the roots of this profound animosity? Does it flow from some religious-ideological concept grounded in ancient sources or is it the result of Rashi's harsh personal experience of Jews being persecuted in Germany and France? The persecution reached its peak with the edicts of 1096, wreaking havoc on Jews, particularly in the Torah centres of Mainz and Worms. Even if one accepts the view of scholars who tend to diminish the historical significance of those events, it is hard to imagine that Rashi was not severely affected by the deaths of his close friends, whom he had known since they had studied together in the 1060s.

But one must be wary of attributing such decisive weight to these personal considerations. A large majority of Rashi's oeuvre was written before 1096. He died in 1105, and it is inconceivable that he produced much of his vast output in the few years that remained to him after 1096. That is all the more so because in his final years, Rashi suffered from a seriously debilitating illness that preventing him from carrying on his literary work. Moreover, it is difficult to draw conclusions in this regard from Rashi's liturgical poems. The motifs he used appear also in mournful liturgical poems written in the Land of Israel and in other centres from the early Middle Ages on, and they could be seen as merely a literary convention. Later poets followed in the paths broken by their predecessors, including Rabbi Eleazar Kallir, who was highly regarded in Ashkenaz.

In my opinion, the principal factor driving Rashi's animosity towards the nations of the world was the serious unease felt by many of his contemporary Jewish sages as they were confronted by increasing Christian pressure to convert. This pressure was both spiritual and physical, grounded in a comprehensive theological world-view, and the Jewish sense of humiliation and inferiority was intensifying. Rashi assigned this array of feelings an important place in his writings, both expressly and allusively.

Naturally, Rashi felt a personal obligation to come forward and help his fellow Jews in those difficult times. He regarded biblical interpretation as a sacred mission, not only because it brought Torah to the masses but also because it confronted the powerful Christian polemic. He studied the Christian claims that were grounded in biblical texts and sought not only to refute them but to counter-attack by portraying Christianity as the enemy of God. Rashi expressly declared the sense of mission that he felt within himself, as shown by a comment on Song of Songs 7: 9–10. The verses read, in part, 'Let your breasts be like clusters of grapes, your breath like the fragrance of apples, and your mouth like choicest wine.' Rashi comments: 'Now I confirm my words, so you do not stray after the nations; and let *your best and wisest* [emphasis added] be firm in their trust, so as to refute the words of those who would seduce your little ones into learning from them. Be cautious in your responses; let them be as good wine.' As he puts it, the 'best and wisest' are duty-bound to argue against the seducer in order to save the 'little ones', those who are weak-willed. This comment reflects not only the sense of mission that Rashi felt within him, but also the unease and pressure that led him to seek an explanation for his people's suffering in exile. In this regard, Rashi had his principles and lived up to them.

CHAPTER NINE

# Values

## Torah and Torah Study

### Love of Torah

No subject was treated by Rashi more extensively and lovingly than Torah study and its practitioners. The subject occupies a central place in the Bible itself and in rabbinic Midrash, and that no doubt had a bearing on Rashi's approach to it. But his devotion to the subject cannot be detached from his intellectual world or from the pedagogical goals he set for himself in writing his commentaries. The highest of those goals was to educate people to love the Torah and its study. Only in this light can we explain his extensive treatment of the subject even at points where the plain meaning of the biblical text has nothing to do with it. Drawing on rabbinic concepts, he emphasized that the Torah was the pre-eminent symbol of God's love for Israel and that the world could not exist without the Torah, 'a thoroughgoing delight'.[1] The Jews, unlike the other nations, accepted the Torah and thereby 'came to the domain' of God, forging a profound link between themselves and God (Rashi on Hos. 9: 1). Rashi's desire to propagate Torah within Israel flowed also from a sense that the diaspora communities were in very difficult circumstances and that Christian pressure on them to convert would only become stronger. He believed that the Torah served as surety for the preservation of Jewish existence even in those hard times and that it symbolized Jewish independence. On the verse 'we will find [nazkirah, also meaning 'we will remember'] Thy love more fragrant than wine' (S. of S. 1: 4, OJPS), Rashi wrote: 'Even today in [my; that is, Israel's] living widowhood, I will remember Your early affection . . . today, too, we delight and rejoice in it; even in their torment and sorrows they delight in Torah and there recall his affection.'

Rashi's view of the matter was not atypical. Many other sages of the time shared it, including Rabbenu Gershom, for whom Rashi had great esteem. According to Rabbenu Gershom, after the destruction of the Temple and the exile of the people, 'nothing remains for us but this Torah'.[2] It is quite clear that Rashi's

---

[1]  Rashi on 1 Kgs 20: 6. See also on Ps. 105: 8 ('the world cannot endure without Torah'); 136: 26 ('for twenty-six generations the world existed without the Torah and it survived by God's grace'), etc.

[2]  Gershom Me'or Hagolah, 'Zekhor berit' ['Remember the Covenant'], in Goldschmidt (ed.), *Order of Selihot According to the Polish Rite* (Heb.), 104.

entire intellectual world and literary activity were directed towards the goal of spreading love of Torah study among the people. These feelings seem to have played an important role in shaping his biblical commentary, as I have already discussed at length.

Anyone wanting to observe the clear orientation of Rashi's biblical commentary need look no further than the commentary on Proverbs, in which the Torah serves as a central motif. In Rashi's system, it is the key thing symbolized by the book's 'parables', as he notes at the very outset: '*Proverbs* [Prov. 1: 1]—all His words are symbols and parables;[a] the Torah is symbolized by a good woman, and idolatry is symbolized by a harlot.' Wisdom, frequently referred to in the book, is nothing but Torah: '*Wisdom cries aloud in the streets, raises her voice in the squares*—The wisdom of Torah in its streets calls to you to warn you . . . and what are "its streets"? The study halls' (Rashi on Prov. 1: 20, following *Midrash mishlei* 1). '*The Lord founded the earth by wisdom* [Prov. 3: 19]—By the Torah; Torah, understanding, and knowledge are the same.' 'He who finds a wife [literally, 'a woman'] has found happiness' refers to Torah' (on Prov. 18: 22). Such examples abound.

In commenting on 'It will save you from a forbidden woman . . . who forsakes the companion of her youth' (Prov. 2: 16–17), Rashi explains his interpretative method for this book. The verse states that wisdom can rescue a man from 'a forbidden woman'. Rashi writes: 'It makes no sense to say it is speaking of an actual adulteress, for how would it praise Torah to say "it will save you from a forbidden woman", but not from other transgressions? Rather, it is referring to apostasy, which constitutes throwing off the yoke of all the commandments.' Rashi applied this method even where the text does not speak of 'wisdom'; examples include: '*He who makes trouble for his household shall inherit the wind* [Prov. 11: 29]—a lazy man who always has wind [that is, lack of substance] as his portion and expends energy neither on Torah nor on labour.' '*He who tills his land shall have food in plenty* [Prov. 12: 11]—As its plain meaning. But its meaning as a parable refers to one who reviews what he has studied so it is not forgotten.' '*The heart alone knows its bitterness* [Prov. 14: 10]—The labour and exertion it devoted to Torah.' There are dozens of other examples. Some will be presented below, especially in the discussion of scholars.

Rashi's commentary on the Song of Songs is also suffused with his love of Torah, which he considered to be one of the book's allegorically expressed motifs. The sixty mighty warriors said to surround Solomon's bed, described as 'skilled in battle' (S. of S. 3: 7), are none other than scholars, who fight 'the battle of Torah'. The Tower of David that is referred to—'Your neck is like the Tower of David' (S. of S. 4: 4)—symbolizes the chamber of hewn stone in the Temple, 'from which instruction goes forth, for the Torah protects Israel'. This interpretation is far removed from the plain meaning of the text, and Rashi's proof for it reinforces the

[a] *Mashal*, here translated 'proverb', also means 'parable'.

sense that the interpretation is tendentious: '*Hung with a thousand shields* [S. of S. 4: 4]—The "thousand shields" are like defenders of the thousand, in the manner of "the promise he gave for a thousand generations" [Ps. 105: 8; 1 Chr. 16: 15].'

Chapter 28 of Job is devoted to the virtue of wisdom. According to Rashi, it refers to the Torah, and in commenting on the beginning of the chapter, he notes that the passage is the most precious of all—'Accordingly, I have directed my attention to its study all my life' (on Job 28: 1). It is not clear whether he is there speaking of himself or placing those words in Job's mouth. Later in that chapter, he cites at length and in detail the talmudic account, in *Shabat* 89*a*, of how Satan travelled around the world at the time the Torah was given, asking everyone, including the mighty forces of nature, 'Where is the Torah?' Rashi's purpose was to teach that the Torah is not to be found in the depths of the sea or the heights of the heavens, rather it is given to man, who is obligated to study it. In that same chapter, Rashi also enumerated many of the Torah's praises.

In his liturgical poem 'Torah temimah' (A Perfect Torah), Rashi emphasized the virtues of the Torah, the diligence of its students, their devotion, even in times of famine and deprivation, and the harm to Torah study caused by persecutions. He concluded his plea for redemption by expressing the hope that in the Land of Israel, the 'descendants of the pious colleagues and students' would continue to engage in Torah study and be privileged to probe its deepest mysteries and interpret it properly.[3]

This subject—the place of the Torah in Rashi's interpretative method—is an extremely broad one. Within the confines of this book, I can deal with it only briefly.[4]

### Virtues of the Torah

At the very beginning of his commentary on the Torah, in interpreting the word *bereshit* ('in the beginning' or 'at the beginning of'), Rashi selected *midrashim* that sing the praises of the Land of Israel, the people of Israel, and the Torah. The choice was clearly deliberate: '*In the beginning God created* [Gen. 1: 1, OJPS]—For the sake of the Torah, which is called "the beginning [*reshit*] of His course" [Prov. 8: 22]; and for the sake of Israel, which is called "the first fruits [*reshit*] of His harvest" [Jer. 2: 3].' The people of Israel and the Torah of Israel are the purpose of all creation. Rashi likewise concludes his commentary on Deuteronomy with words of praise for the Torah, which he took to be the referent of the verse 'all the great might' displayed by Moses (Deut. 34: 12). It is hard to see this opening and closing as mere happenstance. Of course, the source of the *midrash* is *Sifrei* on Deuteronomy, but

---

[3]  Rashi, *Liturgical Poems* (Heb.), 21–3.

[4]  For a good treatment of this subject see Rappel, *Rashi's Jewish World-View* (Heb.), 37–43. I have used only some of his material and have supplemented it in a manner consistent with my purpose in the present volume.

*midrashim* abound, and Rashi could easily have selected others. Indeed, *Sifrei* itself previously refers to a different *midrash* that understands the 'great might' to be the plague of the firstborn.

The Torah tells of the wealth of the tribes of Zebulon and Issachar: 'For they draw from the riches of the sea' (Deut. 33: 19). Rashi offers a plain-meaning interpretation ('the sea affords them bounteous wealth'), but he first cites the *midrash* according to which the wealth is given them not for the sake of the money itself but to ensure 'they will have time to engage in Torah'. That, in his view, is the purpose of wealth.

The tendency on Rashi's part to extol the Torah is evidenced most impressively by his frequent use of biblical verses whose plain meanings have nothing at all to do with Torah to glorify and exalt the Torah and to emphasize the virtue of studying it. Dozens of examples appear in his commentaries. Let me note five that illuminate different aspects of this:

1. '*The sixth day* [Gen 1: 31]—He added a definite article to "sixth" at the completion of Creation to say that He conditioned [their creation] on Israel's acceptance of the five books of the Torah.[b] Another interpretation: The sixth day—they are created conditionally and must await the sixth day, that is, the sixth of Sivan, the day set for the giving of the Torah.' Both of these *midrashim* carry the same message: the world exists only by the merit of the Torah, without which all would return to formlessness. Rashi here forsook *Genesis Rabbah*, the source for most of his commentary on Genesis, in favour of *Midrash taṇḥuma* ('Bereshit', 1) and the Babylonian Talmud (*Shab.* 89*a*), in order to select two *midrashim* that suited his purpose.

2. In interpreting the verse 'If you walk in my statutes and keep my commandments, and do them' (Lev. 26: 3, OJPS), Rashi writes: 'Can this refer to fulfilment of the commandments? When it says "and keep my commandments", it already speaks of keeping the commandments, so what does "if you walk in my statutes" require? That you toil in Torah study.' To follow God's statutes means to study Torah. The source for this interpretation is *Sifra*, where the *midrash* is longer. At first blush, it seems that Rashi was moved to interpret this way by the seeming redundancy of the verse, as the *midrash* points out ('it already speaks of keeping the commandments'), but he immediately goes on to interpret the second half of the verse as a command to study Torah: '*And keep my commandments*—Toil at Torah so as to observe and fulfil it.' To interpret 'walk in my statutes' as referring to Torah study seems possible, but to interpret the second part of the verse in the same way seems quite remote from the text, for 'keep my commandments' in its plain sense seems to refer not to study of the

---

[b] The definite article is indicated by the letter *heh*, which has the numerical value of five.

commandments but to their fulfilment. The verse contains three verbs—walk, keep, and do—and Rashi interprets the first two as referring to Torah study. Only his regard for study as the central value in the Jewish heritage can explain his willingness to accept *Sifra*'s interpretation and explain the verse on that basis. His pedagogical inclinations overcome exegetical considerations.

3. 'He had sent Judah ahead of him to Joseph, to point the way before him to Goshen' (Gen. 46: 28). Rashi comments: 'To clear a place for him and show him how to settle there. An aggadic *midrash*: "to point the way [*lehorot*]" [means] to prepare for him a house of study, from which instruction [*hora'ah*] would go forth.' The verse poses no difficulty warranting importation of this *midrash* from *Genesis Rabbah* 95: 3.[5] Why, then, did Rashi cite it and not rest content with the plain meaning? He evidently selected this *midrash* because it provided an opportunity to teach that the first thing one should do when moving to a new location is to take care of Torah study.

4. 'Is Ephraim a darling son unto me? Is he a child that is dandled? For as often as I speak of him, I do earnestly remember him still, therefore my heart yearneth for him' (Jer. 31: 19, OJPS). Rashi first offers a plain-meaning interpretation ('whenever I speak of him') but then adds a *midrash* from *Leviticus Rabbah* 2: 3: 'My words that I placed within him in teaching him my Torah suffice for me to have compassion for him.' In other words, the virtue of the Torah is so great that its study alone suffices to arouse divine compassion for the Jewish people even if they sin. No difficulty in understanding the phrase 'speak of him' caused Rashi to cite the *midrash*. Here, too, he was moved by his pedagogical agenda.

5. As noted, Rashi concluded his commentary on the Pentateuch with words of praise for the Torah that Moses conveyed to the children of Israel. With regard to the phrase 'all the great might' (Deut. 34: 12), *Sifrei* cites two interpretations: it refers either to the plague of the firstborn or, in Rabbi Elazar's opinion, to the giving of the Torah at Sinai. Rashi chose the latter opinion, even though it offers no exegetical (that is, linguistic or contextual) advantage. Indeed, the advantage lies, if anywhere, with the former opinion, for the words 'all the great might' (literally, 'the mighty hand') can readily be linked with the ten plagues, where they appear several times (for example, 'a greater might [literally, 'a mighty hand'] . . . I will stretch out my hand and smite Egypt' (Exod. 3: 19–20)). Rashi's preference for the second interpretation flows from his profound sense

---

[5] The word *lehorot* (from the stem *yod-resh-heh*), as used in the Bible, typically connotes teaching of Torah or providing spiritual guidance, and that, at first blush, might account for Rashi's use of this *midrash*. But the verb also appears in the sense of indicating or giving direction towards an object or a place, as in 'the Lord showed him [*vayorehu*] a piece of wood' (Exod. 15: 25) or 'winking his eyes . . . pointing [*moreh*] his finger' (Prov. 6: 13).

that Moses' work simply cannot be summed up without a reference to the giving of the Torah. And, as noted, it is likely that Rashi wanted to begin and end his commentary on the Torah with words of praise for it.

The foregoing provide only a small sample of the many instances in Rashi's commentary where this phenomenon can be observed.

Further evidence for the pedagogical agenda that Rashi set for himself in dealing with this subject can be found in his repetitions of the same idea. As a general matter, Rashi's commentary is marked by brevity, but he often departed from that style when he spoke in praise of the Torah and of the duty to study it. This tendency is especially evident in his commentaries on Proverbs, Psalms, and the Song of Songs, but it is not limited to those books. A notable example is his use of the word 'today' to teach that one is obligated to review words of Torah every day as if they were newly given to him. Rashi mentions this idea in Exodus (19: 1) and reiterates it four times in Deuteronomy:

1. '[*These instructions*] *with which I charge you today* [Deut. 6: 6]—Let them not be in your eyes as an old royal decree that no one wants to absorb, rather they should be as something new that everyone wants to read.'

2. '[*The commandments*] *that I enjoin upon you this day* [Deut. 11: 13]—Let them be new for you, as if you heard them that very day.'

3. '*The Lord your God commands you this day* [Deut. 26: 16]—Each day they should be new in your eyes, as if you were commanded concerning them that very day.'

4. '*This day you have become the people* [*of the Lord*] [Deut. 27: 9]—Let it seem to you each day that you have just then entered into a covenant with Him.' He does not say here that the verse is referring to the words of the Torah, but his overall message in interpreting the verse was to argue that fulfilling the commandments and studying the Torah constitute the covenant between the people of Israel and God.

Because of his powerful desire to teach people and to instil a particular idea into their hearts, Rashi repeated the same idea four times in one book. This is not exegesis so much as preaching.

The third sort of evidence for Rashi's tendentiousness is his choice of *midrashim* to weave into his commentary. Rashi himself casually attests to his tendency to seek out aggadic *midrashim* that serve his purpose of increasing Torah study on the part of Jews. In interpreting the verse 'But the Lord hath not given you a heart to know or eyes to see or ears to hear, unto this day' (Deut. 29: 3, OJPS), how does he identify 'this day'? He writes:

I have heard that on the day Moses gave a Torah scroll to the children of Levi, all Israel came before Moses and said to him: Moses our teacher, we too, stood at Sinai and received the Torah, which was given to us. Why, therefore, are you giving control over it to the members of your own tribe, who may say to us tomorrow 'it was given to us, not to you'? Moses was happy about that, and in view of that, he said to them 'this day you have become the people', etc. This day I understand that you are bonded to and desire God.

Rashi did not identify the source of this interpretation, but he favoured it over the interpretations in the classical *midrashim* available to him. *Deuteronomy Rabbah* 7: 11, for example, offers five *midrashim* on this passage, and some of them are at least as closely related to the text. Evidently, it was the pedagogical message—praise for the Torah and the Jewish people's love of Torah—that moved Rashi to choose this interpretation. That message was an important one. Its reading of the verses suggests that the ten plagues, the parting of the Reed Sea, and the giving of the Torah—all of them events that the Israelites had witnessed in their youth or had heard about from their parents and that were symbolized by bodily organs (heart, ears, eyes)— were insufficient to instil in them an adequate recognition of God's grandeur. What was effective in doing so was an event that took place at the plains of Moab—their request for the Torah. From Rashi's perspective, the earlier events were ones in which the people had been passive observers (in Egypt and at the sea: 'the Lord will battle for you; you hold your peace' (Exod. 14: 14); at the giving of the Torah: 'when the people saw it, they fell back and stood at a distance' (Exod. 20: 15)). In the struggle over 'ownership' of the Torah, in contrast, they demonstrated involvement almost to the point of rebellion. That involvement is what is depicted in so positive a light.

Rashi believed the people of Israel had been brought out of Egypt solely because they were destined to receive the Torah: 'Should you [Moses] ask by what merit Israel should go out of Egypt, I [God] have something great in connection with this exodus, for they are destined to receive the Torah on this mountain three months after [leaving Egypt]' (on Exod. 3: 12). In general, the episode of the giving of the Torah (Exod. 19–20; Deut. 33) is described in Rashi's commentary in a special light, with respect both to Israel's spiritual exaltation and to God's closeness to them.

Another example is Rashi's interpretation of the verse 'It is a time to act for the Lord, for they have violated Your teaching' (Ps. 119: 126). Rashi first explains it in accordance with its plain meaning as he sees it and then cites the rabbinic *midrashim* that take the verse as authorizing transgression of the Torah's words in certain exigent circumstances 'to make a barrier and a fence for Israel'. But Rashi is not satisfied until he adds: 'I also saw the following aggadic *midrash*: 'A man who is at leisure to stroll around and makes Torah study an occasional activity breaches the covenant, for a man who is at leisure must toil in Torah all hours of the day.' In other words, one who studies Torah only when it is convenient and does not do so regularly is considered to have breached the covenant.

The breach of the covenant mentioned in the admonitions in Leviticus (26: 29) also involves failure to study Torah. That is the root of all evil: 'Here are seven sins;

the first brings about the second and so forth until the seventh. And these are they: failure to study, failure to act, disdain for others who act, hatred of sages, prevention of others [from acting properly], denial of the commandments, denial of the principle [of religion, that is, of belief in God].'

## Study of Torah

Consistent with his pedagogical programme, Rashi devoted much of his writing not only to praise of the Torah but also to praise of its students and its teachers. The three subjects—Torah, teachers, and students—are intertwined and cannot be readily differentiated. Rashi emphasized the blessings conferred by study, as shown in the following examples: 'Just as these winds fortify the grasses and cause them grow, so do words of Torah cause those who study them to grow' (on Deut. 32: 4); a student of Torah turns out to be greatly rewarded, for 'there is nothing empty in Torah, nothing that, if studied, does not grant a reward' (on Deut. 32: 47); 'The reward for the mouths of those who engage in Torah is that they eat well in this world and the principal benefit is preserved for them in the world-to-come' (on Prov. 12: 14); '*If there is anxiety in a man's mind let him quash it, and turn it to joy with a good word* [Prov. 12: 25]—Let him engage in Torah and it will turn the anxiety in his heart to joy and save him from it'. Dozens of other examples could be cited.

Students benefit so much from Torah study that one engaged in teaching Torah can be compared to the student's father: 'This is to teach that anyone who teaches Torah to his friend's son is considered by Scripture to be as if he had fathered him' (Rashi on Num. 3: 1). This idea, whose source is in Midrash, is one that Rashi returned to several times in his biblical commentary. A notable example is in his interpretation of 'And thou shalt teach them diligently to your children [or: sons]' (Deut. 6: 7, OJPS):

These are the students. We find everywhere that students are called 'sons', as it is said, 'You are the children of the Lord your God' [Deut. 14: 1], and it says 'the sons of the prophets that were at Beth-el' [2 Kgs 2: 3, OJPS]. So, too, in the case of Hezekiah, who taught Torah to all Israel and called them 'sons' . . . And just as students are called 'sons', as it is said, 'You are the children [or sons] of the Lord your God', so is the teacher called 'father', as it is said, 'O father, father! Israel's chariots and horsemen!' [2 Kgs 2: 12].

This is not a mere rhetorical trope. In Rashi's opinion, a teacher must feel affection for his students as if they were his sons (on Isa. 8: 19).

Rashi offers a particularly interesting comment on the verse 'It is the glory of God to conceal a matter and the glory of a king to plumb a matter' (Prov. 25: 2). He there appears to express his opinion, based on the *midrash*, on the various objects of study:

*It is the glory of God to conceal a matter*—such as *ma'aseh merkavah* [the mystical account of the divine chariot] and *ma'aseh bereshit* [the mystical account of Creation]. *And the glory of a king to plumb a matter*—When you speak of the glory of kings or the glory of sages who made fences for the Torah and issued various decrees, one should probe and enquire and ask about its reason. But when you speak of *ma'aseh merkavah* and *ma'aseh bereshit* and of the [non-rational] statutes written in the Torah, such as the statutes and other matters which Satan mocks and tries to refute, such as [the prohibitions against] eating pig, planting species together, and wearing wool and linen together, then you should not probe but rather conceal and say it is the king's decree.

In Rashi's opinion, some subjects—*ma'aseh merkavah* and *ma'aseh bereshit*—should not be dealt with at all. Similarly, one should not probe deeply into those matters treated by the sages as (non-rational) statutes (*ḥukim*) or as divine decrees (*gezeirot*), along the lines of the examples he cites, for human beings are not equipped to understand their mysteries. On the other hand, and importantly, a person is obligated to enquire into the bases for rabbinic enactments and into the commandments whose rationales can be determined, for doing so gives honour to God and honour to the sages. He is also referring here to customs and communal enactments lacking explicitly stated reasons. Not only is it permitted to enquire into them, it is proper to do so. In taking that position, Rashi disagreed with some of the German sages of his time, who were concerned that this sort of enquiry might undermine their customs. This is something we have already considered, in connection with Rashi's personality. His stance represented a sort of compromise among the different approaches prevalent at that time—and even more so later—within the Jewish world, especially in Europe.

Rashi believed that one's study should encompass Bible, Mishnah, and *Gemara*; the first two alone did not suffice. After offering a plain-meaning interpretation of the verse 'A lover of money never has his fill of money, nor a lover of wealth his fill of income. That too is futile' (Eccles. 5: 9), Rashi went on to cite a *midrash* from *Leviticus Rabbah* 22: 1 in praise of the study of *Gemara*:

Israel's reward lies in all words of Torah, whether Bible, Mishnah, or *Gemara*... One who has mastered [literally, 'become a king of'] Bible and Mishnah must still toil to acquire *Gemara*, which presents him with instruction on the prohibited and permitted, the impure and pure, and on civil law ... If one has Bible and Mishnah but lacks *Gemara*, what benefit does he have?

This verse presents no difficulty warranting the use of this *midrash*, and there was no reason not to rest content with explicating its plain meaning. It was Rashi's pedagogical agenda that moved him to present a second interpretation.

## How to Study Torah

In his biblical commentary, especially on Proverbs, Rashi considered, among other things, the desirable ways to study Torah. His guidance took the form of words of advice scattered throughout the commentaries rather than an organized set of instructions; nevertheless, the advice he provides, much of it based on rabbinic teachings, tells us a lot about his personality and world-view. A basic prerequisite for Torah study is proper spiritual preparation. One must study lovingly and joy-fully, not intending thereby to gain honour, social standing, or office of any sort: 'Do not say I will study so as to become wealthy, so as to be called "rabbi", so as to gain a reward. Rather, do everything you do out of love, and in the end, honour will follow' (Rashi on Deut. 11: 22).[6] If one studies to 'to make a name for himself', to acquire honour and standing, all he does is invalid (on Prov. 17: 16).

Study must begin at a very early age: 'When the child begins to speak, his father speaks to him in Hebrew and teaches him Torah. If he does not do so, it is as if he buries him' (Rashi on Deut. 11: 19, following *Sifrei*).

It is not enough to love study, for there is a risk it will become routine. One must, therefore, always be enthusiastic about study. As noted earlier, a person should sense each day that something new and interesting has come into his hands, as if the words of Torah were given to him that very day at Mount Sinai.[7]

Even a pre-eminent scholar must remain diligent in Torah study. One who abandons it, thinking he has already learned enough, will eventually be 'deficient in his labour', 'a brother to the master of destruction, namely, Satan' (Rashi on Prov. 18: 9). In his commentary on *Avodah zarah*, Rashi writes: 'It is the way of scholars to begrudge [distraction from] Torah study, so they do not wash their clothes' (on *AZ* 16*b*, *patya ukhema*). He resorts to other harsh words regarding scholars who are not diligent in their studies and do not review what they have learned, as we shall see later in the discussion of scholars.

While studying, one should activate and apply all one's bodily and spiritual powers. Torah should be studied with maximum concentration and through a blend of intellectual and emotional force: 'One's eyes, ears, and heart must be directed to words of Torah . . . for they are as mountains suspended by a thread' (Rashi on Deut. 32: 46). It follows that one should toil while studying Torah, and his study should be for the purpose of observing and fulfilling the commandments and not merely theoretical (on Lev. 26: 14).

One who studies without going into all the pertinent details is considered 'a fraud in his study' and will eventually forget what he has learned. Even though it is proper to organize words of Torah around subjects, one who has difficulty with that sort of organization need not do so (Rashi on Prov. 23: 4 and elsewhere).

Love of Torah will bolster its study: '*A lover of money never has his fill of money* [Eccles. 5: 9]—One who loves Torah will never be satiated with it.' If one studies

---

[6] The principal textual peg for this *midrash* is Mishnah *Avot* 1: 3: 'Do not be as servants who serve the master in order to receive a reward.' On joy, see Rashi on Deut. 32: 2.

[7] Rashi derived this from the word 'today'. See the four extracts above from Rashi's comments on Deuteronomy.

diligently, his '*springs will gush forth* [Prov. 5: 16]—You will acquire students, instruct the public, and gain renown'.

One must have a teacher from whom to learn Torah and wisdom, and one who does so is called 'discerning' (Rashi on Prov. 16: 21). One learns a bit from every instructor, so it is proper to study with several teachers; Rashi based this idea on the verse 'I have gained more insight than all my teachers' (Ps. 119: 99).[c] The printed editions of Rashi's commentary on the Psalms add a statement that studying with many teachers is proper only after one has learned from his principal teacher, but that statement appears in none of the manuscripts and seems to have been inserted by a later copyist who thought it important for a person to learn most of his Torah from a single teacher. An insightful student knows how to draw out the Torah concealed within his teacher (Rashi on Prov. 20: 5). He must study Torah with his teachers and engage in it regardless of economic difficulties, never asking 'How will I make a living?' (on Prov. 22: 19). Rashi himself followed this course in his youth. He believed it insufficient merely to study with a teacher; rather, one must remain with the teacher as much as possible and should attend on scholars. Relying on a statement by the rabbis, he called for 'clinging to scholars' (on Deut. 11: 22) and acted accordingly while at the yeshivas in Germany. He studied with three teachers (two in Mainz and one in Worms) and also heard words of Torah from other sages in those communities. He spoke of his closeness to his teachers, especially Rabbi Jacob ben Yakar. In turn, he drew his own students close, treating them as if they were his sons, as we saw in the discussion of his relationships with his students. His interpretation of the verse 'His eyes are like doves . . . set by a brimming pool' (S. of S. 5: 12) is consistent with his experiences as a student in the German yeshivas and with the world of his time: 'Like doves that wander from dovecote to dovecote seeking food, so do they go from the *beit midrash* of one sage to the *beit midrash* of another sage, seeking tastes of Torah.' A teacher must find ways to endear study to his students: 'When a person suits his words to his student and sweetens his words tastefully, [the student] will take in more' (on Prov. 16: 21).

To learn from a sage is very important—so much so that in the absence of a God-fearing sage, one should 'study Torah with any sage', even a wicked one. In such a case, however, one must be take pains not to be influenced by his ways: 'If your teacher is wicked, do not learn from his deeds' (Rashi on Prov. 22: 17). A teacher, however, must strictly avoid teaching Torah to an unworthy student. Rashi cites a rabbinic *midrash* that compares teaching such a student to idolatry: 'One who gives honour to a fool is not worthy of existing. And our rabbis of blessed memory interpreted it with reference to one who teaches Torah to a student who is not worthy, who is as one who casts a stone in honour of Mars' (on Prov. 26: 8).

---

[c] Thus NJPS. OJPS similarly renders 'I have more understanding than all my teachers.' The Hebrew, however, is often read to mean 'I have learned from all my teachers', and that sense appears to underlie Rashi's point.

Similarly, Rashi interpreted the obscure 'one who sings songs to a sorrowful soul' (Prov. 25: 20) as referring to 'one who teaches Torah to a wicked student, who does not plan to fulfil it'. The act resembles subjecting oneself to the danger of standing on soft earth. It goes without saying that this interpretation is far removed from the plain meaning of Scripture.

A person can learn much from his students as well as from his teachers: 'Much Torah goes forth from students, whose teachers learn from them through rigorous halakhic discussion' (Rashi on Prov. 13: 23);[8] 'For one learns much Torah from one's students' (on Eccles. 4: 8). Students can supplement and sharpen their teacher's ideas. Beyond that, the very need to explain words of Torah to one's students enhances one's understanding. According to Rashi, one must embark on one's studies gradually—first Bible, then Mishnah, and finally *Gemara* (on Prov. 25: 2).

The student must be careful to show honour to his teacher. If he sees the teacher cannot respond adequately to his questions and has difficulty dealing with them, he should avoid embarrassing the teacher by burdening him with questions and should instead seek out another teacher:

*If you have a large appetite* [Prov. 23: 2]—If you are a hungry sort and crave food . . . But our rabbis interpreted it as referring to a student seated before his teacher. If he knows that his teacher will respond to every one of his questions, he should word his questions precisely and pose them, but if not, he should remain silent . . . and leave him and go to a worthy teacher instead of embarrassing [the first teacher] with questions that he does not know how to answer.

One should diligently review material one has already studied, for that provides a foundation for studying new material: 'If you understand the old, you will understand the new' (Rashi on Deut. 11: 3); *'He who tills his land shall have food in plenty* [Prov. 12: 11]—For he constantly reviews what he has studied, so it is never forgotten.' Reviewing what has already been studied is prerequisite to further progress, and one who fails to do so brings about ruin: *'And its stone fence lay in ruins* [Prov. 23: 31]—Thus, one who does not review what he has studied first forgets [even] the highlights and eventually distorts the words of the sages and reverses matters, calling the pure impure and the impure pure and destroying the world.' Rashi especially emphasized the need to devote much attention to the Oral Torah. Following *Sifrei* on Deuteronomy, Rashi interprets the verse 'Be careful to heed all these commandments' (Deut. 12: 28) as referring to the words of the Mishnah, 'which you must be careful to preserve in your belly, so you do not forget them; and if you reviewed them, it is possible you will heed and fulfil them'. In contrast, *'Laziness induces sleep* [Prov. 19: 15]—One who is lazy in his studies will eventually be asked a question about some word of wisdom and will fall asleep.'

---

[8] Cf. the statement of R. Hanina: 'I have learned much from my teachers, more from my colleagues than from my teachers, and from my students more than from all of them' (*Ta'an.* 7a).

One should never be unnerved by the vast scope of the Written and Oral Torah. Contemplating it in its totality can give rise to fears and uncertainties about one's ability to deal with it all. One should set oneself small, measured assignments and proceed like a slowly rising fountain:

*The eyes of the dullard range to the end of the earth*—As he says, there is no wisdom to be found before me, for it is distant; how can I study all thirty chapters of the order *Nezikin*, all thirty chapters of tractate *Kelim*, all twenty-four chapters of tractate *Shabat*. But for a wise person, it is easy. Today he studies two chapters, tomorrow he studies two chapters, and he says: This is how those who came before me have always done it. (Rashi on Prov. 17: 24, following *Song of Songs Rabbah* 5: 8)

A further prerequisite to productive study is that the student be humble, to the point of willingly bearing insults: '*I am small and despised* [Ps. 119: 141, OJPS]—I am self-effacing enough to diminish myself before those who are engaged in Torah, so I can learn.' To that end, one may even isolate oneself from the community and avoid conversation with a friend: 'One who sneaks away from his friend and goes to the *beit midrash* and engages in Torah and is found "must pay sevenfold"; in the end, he will be appointed a judge and issue instructions, for "sevenfold" refers to the Torah' (Rashi on Prov. 6: 35). '*If thou has done foolishly in lifting thyself up* [Prov. 30: 32, OJPS]—If you have lowered yourself for words of Torah, presenting your questions and doubts to your teacher even if you appeared to him to be a mindless fool, in the end, you will be lifted up'; '*If you have been a schemer* [*zamota*], *then clap your hand to your mouth*—If you have placed a muzzle [*zemam*] on your mouth, muzzling it and not asking him all your questions, in the end, when someone asks you a question of halakhah, you will place your hand over your mouth in silence, for you will not know how to answer.'

On several occasions Rashi dealt with disputes among sages, seeing them as a positive phenomenon. He believed disputes could sharpen and illuminate the respective positions, for each side would have to examine its own opinions more carefully in light of its adversaries' comments. As a result of that process, the truth would emerge. '*Like arrows in the hand of a warrior are sons born to a man in his youth* [Ps. 127: 4]—The students that a man raises up in his youth . . . *shall not be put to shame when they contend with the enemy in the gate* [Ps. 127: 5]—Scholars who contend with one another over halakhah appear as enemies of one another.' Rashi emphasized that these disputes were for the sake of Heaven and did not in any way impair the unity of the Jewish people or the love of Jews for one another: '*Only one is my dove, my perfect one, the only one of her mother* [S. of S. 6: 9]—In its assembly. There are many disputes within study halls, but all of them mean to understand the Torah properly and truly.' Additional discussion of modes of study appears below, in the chapter on Rashi's views regarding scholars.

The many examples of praise for Torah and its study that I have cited are only a small sample. Their large number, their repetitiveness, and Rashi's inclusion of them even when they are remote from the plain meaning shows his underlying purpose. That most are derived from rabbinic Midrash in no way weakens their evidentiary force.

## Reasons for the Commandments

The reasons for the commandments was a subject regularly treated by the medieval Spanish commentators and by most of the French commentators who succeeded Rashi, but Rashi himself dealt with it only infrequently. Nevertheless, it would be a mistake to assume that the subject was of no interest to him. Although he did not try to provide detailed rationales for the existence and purpose of specific commandments, he referred several times to the basic idea that the commandments had been given to the Jewish people because of their merit and that their purpose was to enhance the sanctity of the nation and its connection to God. That is especially so with respect to the commandments that, at first glance, raise eyebrows—those whose rationales are not evident and over which the nations of the world express surprise. For example, on the verse 'These are the creatures that you may eat from among all the land animals' (Lev. 11: 2), Rashi writes: '*These are the creatures* [*haḥayah*]—the wording refers to life [*ḥayim*]; because Israel is bonded to God and is fit to be alive, he separated it from impurity and decreed commandments for it, but for the nations of the world, he forbade nothing.' Similarly, he interprets 'You shall be holy people to Me; you must not eat flesh torn by beasts in the field' (Exod. 22: 30) in accordance with *Mekhilta*: 'If you are holy and separated from abominable carcasses and torn animals, then you are Mine; if not, you are not Mine.' Elsewhere, too, he reiterates the idea that the prohibition on eating certain foods is meant to sanctify the people of Israel and separate them from impurity.

That rationale is not unique to the subject of forbidden foods. Rashi explains many commandments—especially those between man and God—as expressions of profound mutual connections between God and the Jewish people. He says as much explicitly in interpreting the verse 'My beloved is mine and I am His' (S. of S. 2: 16):

He asked me to provide for all His needs and commanded only me to observe Pesach, dedicate the firstborn, build a tabernacle, and sacrifice burnt offerings, making no such demands of other nations. *And I am His*—I asked Him, and no other gods, to provide for all my needs.

Rashi cited this *midrash*, from *Song of Songs Rabbah* 2: 34, to emphasize in no uncertain terms the mutuality of the relationship between God and the nation of Israel, a relationship whose clearest expression is the Jews' observance of the commandments. As noted, the specific commandments cited are only illustrative; they imply that all the commandments, especially those between man and God, are likewise expressions of that relationship.

Most of the reasons for the commandments that Rashi cites are from rabbinic sources. He does not offer a structured presentation on the subject, complete with proofs and logical give-and-take. Instead, we find a series of brief references having a common denominator that will be discussed below. Let me offer five varied examples to illustrate his method:

1. **Redeeming the firstborn of a donkey (two reasons).** 'Because the firstborn of the Egyptians are compared to donkeys; moreover, [the donkeys] helped Israel when they left Egypt' (Rashi on Exod. 13: 13, following *Bekh 5b* and *Genesis Rabbah* 96: 5).

2. **Piercing a slave's ear at the door if the slave is unwilling to be freed.** 'Said the Holy One, Blessed Be He: The door and doorpost served as witnesses in Egypt when I passed over the lintel and two doorposts and said: "For the Israelites are My servants" [Lev. 25: 55]. They are not to be servants of servants, yet this one has acquired for himself a master; let him be pierced before them' (on Exod. 21: 6, following *Kid.* 22*b*).

3. **The High Priest's wearing of the breastplate with the ephod.** 'So the Holy One, Blessed Be He, sees the names of the tribes written before Him and recalls their righteousness' (on Exod. 28: 12).

4. **Purifying a leper with the blood of birds.** Because the affliction is retribution for speaking slander, which entails prattle, purification from it requires birds, which constantly prattle in their chirping voices (on Lev. 14: 4).[9]

5. **Sacrificing seventy bullocks during Sukkot.** The seventy bullocks of the festival correspond to the seventy nations, which are diminishing [the number of bullocks declines from day to day during the festival] ... *And lambs*—corresponding to Israel, who are called a lamb; dispersed yet fixed [in number, as the sacrifices] (on Num. 29: 18, following *Suk.* 55*b*).

These five examples constitute about one-third of the instances in which Rashi offers reasons for commandments in his commentary on the Torah. In each case, the reason is only partial, sometimes explaining only one detail of a broader directive, and rarely does it deal with the commandment as a whole. A comparison between his treatment of the commandment to pierce a slave's ear and that of Ibn Ezra can help us appreciate the difference between the ways in which Rashi and other writers approach this subject. Rashi cites the rationale offered by Rabbi Simeon bar Yohai, according to which the ear is pierced against the door and doorpost because it had heard the declaration 'For it is to Me that the Israelites are

---

[9] Cf. Rashi's comment on this in the name of R. Moses Hadarashan on Num. 19: 22.

servants.' Ibn Ezra, in contrast, treats broader questions related to the matter, especially regarding why the Torah portion 'Mishpatim' opens with this topic.

In dealing with the reasons for the commandments, Rashi is entirely dependent on the Talmud and *midrashim*, drawing his explanations from them. One may reasonably ask why he did not add his own explanations and why he did not write about the subject in detail, but these omissions really come as no surprise. Jews were part of the general culture. As we have seen in examining Rashi's interpretative method, the study of philosophy and rational analysis in general gained much more attention in eleventh-century Spain than in Ashkenaz. It was the twelfth-century renaissance that produced a more rational approach to the Bible, classical Greek literature, the Gospels, and nature. This new departure underlay the interest in the reasons for the commandments on the part of Jewish sages in France beginning in the twelfth century.

Rabbi Joseph Kara, Rashi's colleague and student, was one of the first to deal systematically with the reasons for the commandments. This is evident from recently discovered remnants of his commentary on the Torah. The reasons he offers attest to a rational approach that characterizes many elements of his biblical commentary. Rashi's grandson, Rashbam, likewise devoted considerable attention to the subject.

Another explanation for Rashi's reticence about adding his own rationales for commandments, I believe, lies in his conception of the commandments in general as royal decrees not to be questioned. He stressed that idea on several occasions and saw it as a characteristic distinguishing Israel from the other nations of the world. His comments, to be sure, pertain specifically to the non-rational 'statutes' (*ḥukim*) and 'decrees' (*gezeirot*) rather than to the commandments overall (see e.g. Rashi on Lev. 18: 4; on Num. 19: 2), but they represent, as a matter of principle, a perspective that the commandments should be lovingly accepted as they are, in wholehearted devotion to God. Seeking out their reasons might be seen as a rational undertaking in an area where, in principle, reason is better avoided. The willingness of the people of Israel to accept the Torah and its commandments, something the other nations refused to do, constitutes clear evidence of the love between God and Israel. Given that love, the pursuit of reasons for the commandments leaves a bad taste. Earlier in this section, I quoted Rashi's comments regarding forbidden foods and why God imposed those prohibitions only on Israel and not on the other nations. Because Rashi believed the commandments in general symbolized the great love between God and his people, he saw no reason to consider each one's separate purpose. This approach is expressed in his commentary on 'You must be wholehearted with the Lord your God' (Deut. 18: 13): 'Walk with Him wholeheartedly, await Him, do not enquire about the future, but wholeheartedly accept whatever comes upon you, and then you will be with Him and His portion.'

# Prayer

Rashi's comments on the subject of prayer are consistent with his characteristic sensitivity to the sufferings of others and the sufferings of the nation. It is only natural that prayer would rank high in his intellectual and his emotional worlds. The great value he assigned to prayer is evident in his refraining from it while ill, lest the illness prevent him from mustering the proper intention. He instructed others to do the same. One of his foremost students, Rabbi Shemayah, attests that:

[Rashi] would say that an ill person is forbidden to pray, for the weight of his illness distracts his mind and he cannot properly direct his intention while ill. His prayer is limited solely to reciting the Shema.[10]

Only someone who insisted on sharply focused attention during prayer would adopt such a practice when ill. Rashi responded similarly to a question on the subject that had been sent to him, and yet another story evidently reported by Rabbi Shemayah pertains to this:

At times I saw the rabbi [Rashi], when presented with meat . . . or spiced meat or eggs fried in honey, would wash his hands and recite the 'Shehakol' blessing before breaking bread and reciting 'Hamotsi'.[d] The rabbi said to me: I like this more than bread, and I am comfortable to give it its blessing, praising my Creator through the things I like.[11]

As a matter of law, it is preferable first to break bread and recite the blessing for it, which obviates separate blessings over the meat and eggs. But Rashi, moved by his desire to bless and praise God for the food he enjoyed more, would recite the blessing over meat and the eggs before the blessing over bread and the entire meal. Only one who truly cherishes the opportunity to bless God for the good he has done for his creatures would act in this way, demonstrating to others that one reciting a blessing should do so out of profound inner enthusiasm, intending the maximal degree of thinks to the Creator.[12]

In one of his responsa, Rashi wrote that it was not obligatory to recite the 'Kedushah' during the reader's repetition of the 'Shemoneh esreh' ('Nowhere in the Talmud do we find an obligation related to the "Kedushah"'); nevertheless, it should not be recited in the absence of a ten-man quorum because 'it is beloved to us'.[13] His use of the word 'beloved' likewise shows his emotional attitude towards prayer.

Rashi's attitude towards prayer was the result of his understanding of the close and unique relationship between God and his people and of his own sensitive

---

[10] *Tahtsul*, §60; Rashi, *Responsa* (Heb.), ed. Elfenbein, §90.          [11] *Mahzor vitri*, 40.

[12] Although the laws of blessings provide for a blessing recited over something of which a person is very fond, it is not said in this sort of situation, involving a blessing over bread and an entire meal.

[13] Rashi, *Responsa* (Heb.), ed. Elfenbein, §92.

[d] 'Shehakol' is the blessing over meat or eggs; 'Hamotsi' is the blessing over bread.

character. With the end of prophecy, prayer became the foremost mechanism for expressing these relationships. Because God is tied to the Jewish people by bonds of love, cares for them as a loving father, and oversees them at all times, it is only natural that he expect them to express their thanks and loving feelings towards him. It is their mutual love that requires as much: 'One is obligated to thank God on hearing good news', Rashi wrote to explain the words of thanks uttered by Abraham's servant on hearing Rebecca's positive response to the proposal that she accompany him back to Canaan to be married to Isaac (Gen. 24: 52). Rashi's comment, which has a midrashic source, is less an explanation than a judgement regarding proper conduct and an exhortation to his readers to act accordingly.

A verse in Psalms states: 'Deliverance is the Lord's; Your blessing is on Your people! *Selah*' (Ps. 3: 9). The plain meaning is that God's deliverance and blessing are upon Israel, and the other medieval commentators so understood it. Rashi interprets it differently: 'His people are obligated to bless and thank Him for His deliverance.' The place in Rashi's consciousness of the duty to say thank you, and the value he ascribed to it, are evident in his comment on the talmudic statement that 'Israel has affection for troubles' (*Shab.* 13*b*). Rashi's explanation is that once the people of Israel are saved from those troubles, 'the miracle is beloved to them so they mention it in praise of the Holy One, Blessed Be He.' In effect, thanks and praise to God following a rescue are of such great value that the righteous cherish the troubles that give them the opportunity to express their thanks. A plain-meaning explanation of the statement might attribute Israel's affection for the troubles to the ability of suffering to effect atonement for sins.

Prayer can also strengthen love for God and the ties that keep one close to him. When two lovers express their mutual affection, their affection grows. God's expression takes the form of his concern for his people and his readiness to accept the repentance of sinners and forgive their transgressions like a merciful father who takes pity on his son and forgives him. Israel's expression takes the form of prayer. This concept has implications for the ways in which one prays, as discussed below.

Prayer is the principal symbol of Israel, just as the sword is the principal symbol of Esau. In chastising Simeon and Levi for having killed the men of Shechem, Jacob says 'their weapons are tools of lawlessness' (Gen. 49: 5). To interpret the verse, Rashi selects a *midrash* from *Midrash tanḥuma* ('Vayeḥi', 9): 'This craft of murder is stolen property that they possess. It is from the blessing to Esau, it is his craft; and you have unlawfully taken it from him.' Balaam 'exchanged his craft for yours, for [Israel] is victorious only through their mouths, by prayer and petition, and he came and seized their craft to curse them with his mouth' (Rashi on Num. 31: 5); accordingly, they slew him by the sword, which is the 'craft' of non-Jews. What the other nations attain by force and sword, the Jewish people attain by the force of prayer.

Prayer as a uniquely Jewish characteristic was recognized by non-Jews. In the verse 'Lo, a people that rises like a lion, leaps up like the king of beasts' (Num. 23: 24), Balaam describes Israel's might and conquests. Rashi, following the *midrash*, interprets it as referring not to Israel's might but to its prayers: 'When they awaken from their sleep in the morning, they are as mighty as lions in taking up the commandments—wearing a prayer-shawl, reciting the Shema, donning phylacteries.' The verse continues 'it rests not till it has feasted on prey and drunk the blood of the slain', which Rashi similarly interprets as referring to the recitation of the Shema before retiring for the night. Only after presenting these *midrashim* did Rashi offer the plain-meaning interpretation related to Israel's military victories. That sequence reverses Rashi's usual practice of citing the plain-meaning interpretation first and then adding the *midrash*, and the reversal in these instances (both Gen. 49: 5 and Num. 23: 24) is surely no coincidence. It reflects, I believe, his tendency to strengthen his readers' feelings about prayer and raise the esteem in which they hold it. He similarly follows the *midrash* in taking the view that that the spies sent by Moses to Jazer—unlike those sent earlier to the Land of Israel—recognized the value of prayer. The earlier spies had instilled fear in the people, but in the case of Jazer, 'the spies conquered it. They said: we will not act as the earlier [spies] did; we are confident in the ability of Moses' prayer to wage war' (Rashi on Num. 21: 32).

Following the rabbis, Rashi emphasized that prayer was characteristic even of the patriarchs. When the Egyptians pursued the Israelites and caught up with them at the Reed Sea, the Israelites 'cried out' to God. Rashi interprets: 'They took up the craft of their fathers', supporting his opinion that they engaged in prayer. He also commented on the power of prayer in the context of the building of the Tabernacle, suggesting that all the sacrifices and other ritual acts performed by Moses and Aaron were unable to bring down the presence of God; only their prayers succeeded (on Lev. 9: 23).

Also attesting to Rashi's view of the value of prayer is his comment on 'I will make all My goodness pass before you' (Exod. 33: 19). These are encouraging words, urging people in general, and Jews enduring the exile in particular, to avoid giving in to hopelessness and instead to believe in the power of prayer to arouse divine mercy even in the absence of other factors meriting it:

I must teach you the order of prayer, for when you were required to request mercy for Israel, you reminded Me of the merit of the patriarchs. Do you believe that when the merit of the patriarchs is exhausted, there is no more hope? I will make all My goodness pass before you on the rock, while you are in the cave, 'and I will proclaim before you the name Lord' to teach you the order for requesting mercy, even if the merit of the patriarchs is unavailing. Just as you see Me wrapped [in My prayer shawl] and proclaiming the Thirteen Attributes, so shall you teach Israel to do and to say before Me 'compassionate and gracious', for My mercies never end.

It follows from this that the power of Jewish prayer (mentioning 'compassionate and gracious') before God exceeds that of any other factor, including the merit of the patriarchs. The basis for this *midrash* appears in *Rosh hashanah* (17*b*), but Rashi broadens it and adds 'even if the merit of the patriarchs is unavailing', using wording that can invigorate and encourage his readers. The moving description of God wrapped in a prayer shawl teaching Moses the order of the Thirteen Attributes equates prayer to the construction of the Tabernacle's candelabrum, for when Moses was having difficulty understanding the correct design for the candelabrum, God is said to have shown him all the details. Two conclusions follow: prayer requires the investment of great energy, but its power is huge. There is nothing that can help the Jewish people, collectively and individually, as much as turning to God in prayer. Rashi therefore devoted considerable attention in his commentaries to Jewish prayers, which he saw as the principal means for bringing about the redemption of the nation languishing in exile. As already noted, he would sometimes take psalms having a clearly personal character and interpret them as pertaining to the nation overall.[14]

Rashi's basic notion of prayer as an expression of one's love of God and connection to him—a notion grounded in rabbinic thought—has practical implications. Prayer must have the character of a plea, not of a demand pressed by one who is certain he is entitled to mercy. That is so even of the prayers of the righteous: 'Though the righteous may rest [their prayers] on their good deeds, they request from God only a gratuitous gift' (Rashi on Deut. 3: 23); 'One who makes a request should first recite two or three pleas and then make his request' (on Num. 12: 13). Malachi 1: 11 includes the statement 'My name is great among the nations, and in every place offerings are presented unto My name' (OJPS); Rashi comments: 'All prayers offered by Israel at any location are as a pure grain offering to Him.' Rashi is alluding here to the rabbinic idea that prayers are a surrogate for sacrifices, but I also see in his statement a polemic against the nations of the world, especially Christendom. His interpretation is meant to foreclose the possibility, seemingly consistent with the verse's plain meaning, that non-Jewish worship directed to God rather than to idols entails recognition of his greatness. In any case, there is no reference to the motif of purity, and it is clear that Rashi has interjected it on the basis of his own inner world and his desire to teach the Jews to recognize the value of prayer.

No discussion of Rashi's teachings on prayer can ignore his important contribution to the writing and interpretation of liturgical poems. In discussing his personality I referred to sensitivity, and it is only natural that a sensitive person would see liturgical poems, petitions, and pleas as an important medium for recounting the nation's sorrows. His *seliḥot* (penitential prayers), discussed in Chapter 7, may not be among the most poetically inspired of the Ashkenazi liturgical poems, but

---

[14] e.g. Pss. 5: 9, 16: 25; see also the discussion of Rashi's commentary on Psalms in Ch. 5, above.

they attest to his emotional turmoil in the face of his people's suffering at the time. This is especially true of his poem 'Torah temimah', evidently written in the aftermath of the edicts of 1096.

Weighty philosophical questions about prayer occupied a prominent place in the thought of the Jewish sages of Spain and the Muslim lands, who were reared in the philosophical tradition. Rashi, however, does not treat these questions—not in any of his commentaries nor in his halakhic writings. The two principal questions that concerned the philosophical writers were why God needs his creatures' prayers and whether prayer had the capacity to alter God's will. Indeed, the very suggestion that it could appeared to impugn God's dignity. Not having been schooled in a philosophical environment, Rashi did not treat these questions, and this sort of rationalistic thinking would have been out of character. The value of prayer, the call to engage in it extensively, and the discussion of various liturgies and their development were the matters that occupied him.[15]

## Truth and Humility

Rashi's personality was characterized by two qualities that are evident in all his literary works and communal activity: humility and the pursuit of truth. Because they are intertwined, I will treat them together.

At first blush, it may seem surprising to examine the place of humility and truth in Rashi's teachings. The sages repeatedly sing the praises of these qualities, and all branches of the talmudic literature hold them in high esteem: humility in particular is heaped with laurels. How, then, could a later sage, living in the Middle Ages, say anything at all new on these subjects? It is, in fact, difficult to find substantive innovation in Rashi's thinking about the virtues of humility and truth and their place in personal and communal life, and I will not attempt to enumerate the numerous references to humility and truth throughout his writings. Instead, I want to note three principal features that characterize his treatment of these qualities: their central place in his consciousness, his application of them in his dealings with people and his leadership of the community, and, above all, his tendency in his commentaries on the Bible and the Talmud to teach people to adopt these qualities.

Although the place of humility in Rashi's conceptual world has not yet been the subject of scholarly investigation, scholars have noted his personal humility (discussed in Chapter 2). His readiness to battle forcefully on behalf of his opinions and to reject what he thought to be erroneous customs show that his humility was genuine and not the product of personal weakness on the part of a man who sought to curry favour through self-deprecation. Rashi was well aware of the difference

[15] Rashi recognized that the texts of the prayers had been corrupted through the errors of cantors and copyists, and he did not hesitate to correct the wording of a prayer where he thought it was erroneous (see the discussion of Rashi's personality in Ch. 2, above).

between these two sorts of humility, referring to it in his comment on *Arakhin*: '*Humility for ulterior purposes*—He makes himself out to be humble, for he does not wish to chastise him. But that sort of humility is not for the sake of Heaven, but only so the [other] does not hate him' (on *Arakh.* 16*b*, *ki nafak*).[16] The opposite of that trait is 'humility for the sake of Heaven' or 'righteous humility' (Rashi on Ps. 46: 5).

## Humility in Rashi's Consciousness

Clear evidence for the central position of humility in Rashi's thinking is provided by his portrayal of positive figures in the Bible and rabbinic literature as humble even where the biblical or rabbinic texts themselves provide no basis for doing so. Rashi ties a person's righteousness, decency, and virtue to his humility, as if asking whether it was even conceivable that a man of virtue would not be extremely humble. Let me offer just three examples of this phenomenon.

1. **Jotham son of Uziah, king of Judah.** The Talmud cites the following statement by Rabbi Simeon bar Yohai: 'I could exempt the entire world from punishment from the day I was created until this day. Were my son Eliezer considered together with me, [the exemption would run] from the day the world was created until this day. And were Jotham son of Uziah considered together with us, [the exemption would run] from the day the world was created to its end' (*Suk.* 45*b*). Rashi comments: 'Jotham son of Uziah was righteous and more humble than other kings. He had the merit of honouring his father, and of him it was said: "A son honoureth his father" [Mal. 1: 6, OJPS]. For during the entire time his father suffered from leprosy . . . he did not assume the title of king while his father was still alive, and he issued all his judgements in his father's name.' In other words, it was because of his humility that Jotham was considered a man of virtue. Only a few verses are devoted to King Jotham in the books of Kings and Chronicles, where he is described as 'judging the people of the land' [2 Kgs 15: 5; 2 Chr. 26: 21, OJPS]. He also is said to have done 'that which was right in the eyes of the Lord', and his construction activities are mentioned. But none of this provides any basis for Rashi's view that Jotham's righteousness and humility were expressed by his declining to call himself 'king' while he judged the people during his father's incapacity. Nor is there any reason to assume that Uziah had agreed to waive his royal title during his illness, particularly given Jotham's youth during his father's illness and his ascent to the throne after his father's death, when he was 25 years old.[17]

[16] See Rashi on *Arakh.* 16*b*, *ki nafak*, regarding a scholar who, to avoid harming relations with his colleague, spoke deprecatingly of him only after he had left the *beit midrash*. Rashi considered this to be 'humility not for its own sake' (that is, for ulterior purposes).

[17] Cf. *MK* 7*b*; Rashi ad loc.; Tosafot ad loc. Although the Talmud elsewhere states that a prince who has fallen ill with leprosy is removed from office and cites Uziah as precedent (*Hor.* 10*a*), it does not state that Uziah's son Jotham reigned in his place.

Rabbenu Hananel offered a different interpretation of Rabbi Simeon bar Yohai's comment: 'For he received in this world nothing at all of what he was entitled to; for the righteous receive in this world a taste of what is in store for them in the world to come, but Rabbi Simeon, and his son, and Jotham received nothing in this world; accordingly, they had greater merit [in reserve] than other righteous people.'[18] In the commentary on Chronicles erroneously attributed to Rashi, the commentator cites Rabbi Simeon bar Yohai's comment and interprets it yet another way: 'For in all the kings that preceded him and that followed him, some sin is to be found, but not in Jotham' (on 2 Chr. 26: 21, attributed to Rashi). Rashi is atypical in associating Jotham's great merit with his personal humility, and he has no proof for his premise in the plain meaning of the text.

**2. 'Noah was in his generations a man righteous and whole-hearted' (Gen. 6: 9, OJPS).** The Talmud (*AZ* 6*a*) struggles with the meaning of 'righteous and whole' (the Hebrew word rendered 'whole-hearted' literally means 'whole'). At first, it is suggested that 'whole' means he was not only righteous in his deeds but also physically unblemished. The Talmud rejects that interpretation and raises a second possibility closer to the plain meaning: the term describes the magnitude of Noah's righteousness. And what is the meaning of 'whole in his ways', as the Talmud puts it? Rashi interprets it as 'humble and unpretentious'.

It would not have been difficult to suggest a different interpretation. For example, one might distinguish between positive behaviour associated with a person's actions ('righteous in his deeds') and positive personality traits associated with a person's attributes ('whole in his ways').[19] A verse in the book of Psalms in fact treats these qualities as parallel terms: 'The Lord is beneficent in all His ways and faithful in all His works' (Ps. 145: 17). But there is no exegetical rationale for Rashi's interpretation. In his opinion, a perfected man, 'whole in his ways', is one whose learning and good deeds have not made him arrogant; he remains humble and unpretentious even at the height of his greatness. Righteousness without humility is flawed.

**3. The definition of 'righteous people' (*vatikin*).** The Talmud (*Ber.* 9*b*) states in the name of Rabbi Yohanan that 'righteous people' would complete the 'Shemoneh esreh' prayer precisely at sunrise, and a *baraita* is cited that supports his view. But what does the word translated 'righteous persons' mean? Rashi comments: '*Righteous people*—Men who are humble men and love the commandments.' The talmudic passage itself contains no hint of any connection between humility and a love of the commandments that makes one willing to rise early so as to pray at the

---

[18] Rabbenu Hananel on *Suk.* 45*b*.

[19] For example, avoiding anger, speaking favourably of people, not questioning God's ways, and so on.

earliest possible moment. Rashi drew the connection on his own, consistent with his view of the world.[20]

## Truth and Humility as the Grounding for Character Training

Rashi's comment on Proverbs 31: 27 demonstrates the special importance he ascribed to truth and humility as the twin pillars of the Jewish household. The woman of valour is described there as one who, among other things, 'oversees the activities [OJPS: ways] of her household and never eats the bread of idleness'. Rashi comments: 'Within her household she attends to the needs of its members, that they conduct themselves in truth and in modesty.' He uses 'modesty' as a synonym for 'humility'. 'Activities' (or 'ways') encompass a range of character traits including kindness, concern for one's fellow's dignity, refraining from gossip, avoidance of anger, but Rashi selected only two: truth and humility. He did so, I believe, because he regarded these two qualities as the basis for the Jews' moral and conceptual world and way of life. It is difficult indeed to find some exegetical explanation for the selection of specifically these two traits. At first blush, one might associate the choice with the injunction in Micah (6: 8) 'to walk modestly with your God' and with the declaration in Psalms (86: 11) that 'I will walk in Your truth.' In both verses, the verb 'to walk' is associated with humility and truth.[e] Any such association, however, would be far removed from the plain meaning of the text; moreover, Rashi did not cite any of the many other qualities that are similarly associated with the verb 'to walk'. It would have been easy enough to add acting justly or avoiding gossip to the 'ways of her household' that the woman inculcates in the members of her household. Rashi's choice of truth and humility reflects, more than anything else, his own image.

The book of Proverbs teaches that 'the reward of humility is the fear of the Lord, even riches, honour, and life' (Prov. 22: 4, OJPS). The foregoing translation is consistent with the plain meaning of the text, according to which the word rendered 'reward' (*ekev*) means 'on account of' or 'in the wake of'. So read, the verse teaches that on account of his humility, a person will merit other good things: fear of God, wealth, honour, and life. A similar idea appears earlier in Proverbs— 'humility precedes honour' (Prov. 15: 33)—and Rashi there comments, 'humility causes honour to ensue'. Medieval and modern commentators have understood this verse in that way, taking it to mean that humility leads to fear of God. Rashi cites that interpretation but then, surprisingly, suggests a second interpretation, quite distant from the plain meaning: '*The reward of humility*—On account of humility, fear of the Lord ensues. Another interpretation: 'Humility is primary and

---

[20] On the meaning of *vatik* (here translated as 'righteous person'), see *Arukh hashalem*, iii. 259, s.v. *vatik* (one with good qualities, one who is faithful); Ben-Yehudah, *Dictionary* (Heb.), iii. 1273. None of the ancient sources supports Rashi's linking of the term with humility.

[e] The Hebrew verb 'to walk' is from the same root as 'ways'.

fear is subordinate to it, a foothold for it.'[f] The two interpretations are quite different. The first regards humility as the basis for all the other qualities; they are dependent on it, but in no sense is humility the preferred one. On the contrary, the other qualities are built on it, implying that they attain greater heights. The second interpretation, in contrast, treats humility as the highest virtue, greater than all the others that are mentioned, including fear of God. Rashi did not rest content with leaving the point as a clear implication of his comment; instead, he explicitly emphasized that fear was subordinate to humility, a 'foothold' for it. He may have been influenced by talmudic passages (*AZ* 20*b*; *Arakh.* 16*b*) that refer to humility as the quality that is 'greatest of all [human attributes]', but that cannot explain his departure from the plain meaning here. In sum, Rashi took advantage of the opportunity to teach his readers to recognize the overarching importance of humility and urge them to make it a trait of their own.

Rashi's tendency to extol humility and condemn pride and a life of excess and pretentiousness is particularly prominent in his commentary on Ecclesiastes. Commenting on the verse 'One generation goes, another comes, but the earth remains the same forever' (Eccles. 1: 4), he interprets 'the earth' as referring to humble people: 'Who are those who endure? The lowly and humble, who lower themselves to the ground.' Rashi's citing of an interpretation so far removed from the plain meaning says much about his moral world and his pedagogical goals. Similarly, he interprets the verse 'Wherefore I perceived that there is nothing better, than that a man should rejoice in his works' (Eccles. 3: 22, OJPS) to mean 'He should rejoice and sustain himself through the work of his hands, not opening his maw as wide as Sheol with desire and becoming wealthy by acquiring what is not his.'

For the same reason, Rashi links the verse 'A season is set for everything, a time for every experience under heaven' (Eccles. 3: 1) to the verse that precedes it ('to him who displeases, he has given the urge to gather and amass') and interprets it to mean 'let not the one who amasses wealth in vain rejoice, for even if he now possesses it, he will yet be succeeded in ownership by the righteous'. He reads it this way even though the key word 'time' shows quite clearly that the verse is part of the ensuing passage, not the preceding one.

## Biblical Characters as Models of Humility

In portraying their activities, Rashi emphasized the humility of the nation's patriarchs and prophets, and he did so not only when warranted by the plain meaning of the text, but even where the text affords no such warrant. In describing the figure of Moses, Rashi on several occasions mentions his extreme humility, using biblical texts as a foundation for his observations. In his view, Moses' most characteristic quality was humility. A verse in Jeremiah states 'I look: no man is left' (Jer. 4: 25),

[f] This reading plays on the ambiguity of the word *ekev*, which also means 'heel'.

and Rashi comments: 'The merit of Moses, said to be the most humble of men', is no longer available to be drawn on (on Jer. 4: 26).[g]

The Torah tells that Joktan, one of Shem's descendants, had many children (Gen. 10: 25). Rashi writes: 'He was humble, lessening himself;[h] accordingly, he had the privilege of establishing all these families.' The *midrash* appears in *Genesis Rabbah* 37: 25 in a different version: 'Why was he called Joktan? Because he lessened his dealings. And what did he merit? He had the privilege of establishing thirteen families. And if that is so for a lesser person who lessens his dealings, how much more so is it for a great person who lessens his dealings.' Rashi preferred to use the version in *Genesis Rabbah*, where Joktan is described as one who had lessened himself. It is hard to imagine that Rashi did not recognize the tendentiousness of the *midrash* and was unaware that the connection between 'Joktan' and 'small [*katan*]' was based solely on assonance. It appears that Rashi chose this *midrash*, in this version, on account of the pedagogical agenda so evident throughout his commentary.

Abraham and Jacob are likewise depicted by Rashi as models of humility. When God calls to Abraham before the binding of Isaac, Abraham responds 'Here I am' (Gen. 22: 1). Rashi comments: 'This is the response of the pious; it is a term of humility and a term of readiness.' He similarly interprets Joseph's 'Here I am' response to Jacob (Gen. 37: 13; NJPS: 'I am ready'): 'a term of humility and eagerness'.

King David likewise excelled in humility. The Talmud (*Sot.* 10*b*) interprets the psalm superscription 'Of David, a *mikhtam*' (Ps. 56: 1) to mean that '[Tamar's] descendant was David, who was lowly [*makh*] and honest [*tam*] to all.' Rashi comments: '*Lowly*—humble. *And honest*—upright in his ways.'

Another model of humility according to Rashi was the prophet Elijah. He asked Elisha not to accompany him when he crossed the Jordan so that Elisha would not witness Elijah's ascent to heaven 'in a whirlwind' on 'a fiery chariot with fiery horses' (2 Kgs 2: 11). Rashi comments: 'He wanted to deter him because of his humility, so he would not see his assumption' (on 2 Kgs 2: 2). The Bible itself offers no explanation for Elijah's extended efforts to dissuade Elisha from accompanying him to his exalted encounter. Most medieval commentators attributed it to Elijah's concern about the harsh effect it might have on Elisha.

Rashi even associates the messiah with humility, which he believes will be one of his qualities. A verse in Zechariah states: 'Lo, your king is coming to you. He is victorious, triumphant, yet humble, riding on an ass, on a donkey foaled by a

---

[g] The quoted verse refers to 'the man' (*ha'adam*), using the definite article, and the verse describing Moses' humility ('Now Moses was a very humble man, more so than any other man on earth', Num. 12: 3) likewise uses *ha'adam*. Rashi's comment appears to be based on an association of the two references. More broadly, in his comment on the verse in Jeremiah, he says he saw an aggadic *midrash* in which various items mentioned by Jeremiah in this and nearby verses are taken to represent biblical figures— the patriarchs, the matriarchs, Moses, and Elijah—whose merit can no longer be drawn upon.

[h] Literally 'making himself smaller', from the root *kuf-tet-nun*, a play on his name.

she-ass' (Zech. 9: 9). Rashi comments: 'It cannot be interpreted other than as referring to the King Messiah ... *Humble*—One marked by humility. *Riding on an ass*—
This is his quality of humility.'

## Arrogant Biblical Figures

At some points in his biblical commentary, Rashi selects rabbinic *midrashim* that
criticize various biblical characters for their arrogance. The *midrash* presents them
as people forced to acknowledge the error of their pride and the limitations of their
power. The common denominator for all these instances is that the biblical text
itself presents no exegetical difficulty warranting recourse to midrashic literature,
once again demonstrating that Rashi's selection was driven by his pedagogical
agenda. Rashi himself notes that that was his purpose, though he does not explicitly
call on his readers to draw the morals taught by the *midrashim*. The rabbis' interpretations in these cases are far removed from the plain meaning of the text, and it
is evident that they, too, had the didactic purpose of teaching people to avoid acting
with excessive pride. Rashi objected to any mode of expression that might be taken
to indicate arrogance. Some examples follow.

**1.** One of the angels sent to destroy Sodom says: 'For I cannot do anything until
You arrive there' (Gen. 19: 22). Rashi comments: 'That is the angels' punishment
for having said "For we are about to destroy this place", making the action their
own. Accordingly, they could not leave there until they said the matter was not
within their control.'

**2.** Balaam arrogantly presumed that by dint of the power of prophecy given to him,
he could foretell the future ('who obtains knowledge from the Most High'). But
the story of Balaam and his ass implies that his knowledge is limited: 'I did not
know that you were standing in my way', he says to the angel (Num. 22: 34). Rashi
writes: 'This, too, is to disparage him. He is required, against his will, to acknowledge with his own mouth that he, who had boasted of obtaining knowledge from
the Most High, in fact did not know.'

**3.** Even Moses, who was 'a humble man, more so than any other man on earth'
(Num. 12: 3), did not escape Rashi's criticism over a possible hint of arrogance. In
the account of Zelophehad's daughters, the Torah states that 'Moses brought their
case before the Lord' (Num. 27: 5), and Rashi comments: 'The halakhah [to be
applied in the case] was not apparent to him. And he was here paid back for having
taken it upon himself to say "any matter that is too difficult for you, you shall bring
to me" [Deut. 1: 17].' This *midrash* represents an extreme statement of the call to
avoid arrogance, for Moses needed to assure the elders he had appointed as judges
that they should not hesitate to turn to him if they were having difficulty in reaching a decision and that they should not adjudicate solely on the basis of their own

assessment of the case. Nevertheless, he had to be careful about everything he said, lest some scintilla of arrogance escape his lips.

Rashi had no exegetical reason to cite this *midrash* in order to be critical of Moses, who had accepted Jethro's advice that he delegate authority, particularly since he usually was quite wary of criticizing the founders of the nation. The criticism in this instance is far removed from the plain meaning of the text, something of which Rashi no doubt was aware. Only the revulsion he felt at the least bit of arrogance and his desire to educate people to the need for extreme diligence with respect to it can explain his interpretation. He simply could not forgo this pedagogical opportunity.

**4.** The Song of Deborah includes the statement 'Awake, awake, O Deborah! Awake, awake, strike up the chant!' (Judg. 5: 12). Rashi comments: 'Terms of praise, in accordance with its plain meaning; sing mightily. But our rabbis said: Because she took pride in herself and said "Till you arose, O Deborah", the holy spirit departed from her [*Pes. 66b*].' Rashi's first interpretation is straightforward and clear, and he himself characterized it as the plain meaning. Nevertheless, he saw a need to cite the rabbis' critical *midrash*. In this instance, too, Rashi did not hesitate to attack one of the Bible's exalted figures, a prophetess raised up within the nation of Israel.

## Humility and Torah Study

In one talmudic discussion, several *amora'im* contrast the easygoing nature of the sages in the Land of Israel with the sharply argumentative style of the rough-and-tumble Babylonian sages. In so doing, they rely on the verse 'And I took unto me two staves; the one I called Graciousness and the other I called Binders' (Zech. 11: 7):

*Graciousness*—These are the sages in the Land of Israel, who are gracious to one another in [discussing] halakhah. *Binders*—These are the sages in Babylonia, who injure[i] one another in [discussing] halakhah . . . The sages in the Land of Israel who are easy on one another in [discussing] halakhah . . . The sages in Babylonia, who are bitter to one another in [discussing] halakhah. (*San. 24a*)

The Talmud compares the two modes of study without saying anything about how these modes of study affect the study itself. Rashi, in contrast, speaks several times of the important substantive contribution made by the pleasant manner of study in the Land of Israel. He reiterates and emphasizes the blessing of studying in a pleasant and gracious manner, as each scholar yields to his fellow: 'The people of the Land of Israel are at ease together, enquire together, improve one another's words, and the issue is thereby illuminated.' Rabbi Jeremiah, who immigrated from

---

[i] A play on words: 'Binders' translates the Hebrew *ḥovelim*, which can also mean 'injurers'.

Babylonia to the Land of Israel, offered a *midrash* on study in Babylonia: '*He has made me dwell in darkness like those long dead* [Lam. 3: 6]—That is the learning in Babylonia' (*San.* 24*a*). Rashi associated his comment with a mode of study lacking in humility and marked by a competitive argumentativeness that impairs the fruits of study: '*He has made me dwell in darkness*—They are not at ease with one another, and the teaching they receive is doubtful.' In other words, corruption may enter into their transmission and deliberation because of their competitiveness. Pride and unwillingness to concede to the other are responsible for the description of Babylonian study as 'darkness'. But that interpretation is not inevitable, and it is not supported by Rabbi Jeremiah's comment. Here, too, Rashi's interpretation offers a window on his inner world. In his view, pride does more than undermine interpersonal relationships; it also impairs one of Judaism's key values: the study of Torah.

In Rashi's opinion, humility and an atmosphere of collegiality and cordiality not only promote Torah study among scholars but also enhance relationships between teachers and their students. A teacher who conducts himself with humility helps his students develop their ideas freely and unhesitatingly. A forceful, strict teacher, in contrast, will suppress their free creativity. Here, too, Rashi taught the idea on the basis of the talmudic discussion even though humility is not explicitly referred to in the passage. He inferred it from his personal concept of the world and integrated it into his commentary.

The Talmud recounts that Rami bar Hama, though a great and renowned scholar of his time, praised Rabbi Kahana and Rabbi Safra for an observation they had made in his presence. They replied that only because of his good nature had they dared to raise the point with him: 'They said to him: Because of the master's goodness, we say more' (*San.* 41*b*). Rashi offered the following interpretation: 'Because you are good and humble and acknowledge us, we are able to say more . . . If you wanted to object and question, we would know no response.' But the students' comment made no reference to humility, and Rashi added the reference on the basis of his personal view of things. He similarly interpreted a talmudic statement to mean that Resh Lakish dubbed Rabbi Meir 'a holy mouth' out of humility, even though that trait is not mentioned in the talmudic comment at issue (Rashi on *San.* 24*a*, *vetoḥnan zeh bazeh*). In all of these passages, Rashi praises study that is pursued in humility, love, and affection, going beyond what can be found in the Talmud's own discussion. And, as discussed earlier in connection with his *beit midrash*, an examination of his relationships with his students shows that he practised what he preached in this area.

Rashi's great esteem for humility and its influence on literary creativity is likewise evident at other points where he discusses relationships among scholars; let me note only one. His comment on the discussion in *Shabat* of letter shapes manifests his sense that one should engage in Torah with great humility. There is a statement there that the Torah was given with 'a nod of the head', which Rashi interprets as 'with trembling and extreme humility'. There is no linguistic or substantive basis for that interpretation. In connection with the form of the letter *tsadi*, he wrote: 'A proper person should be bent and humble, and he will end up being straight and erect in the world to come' (Rashi on *Shab.* 104*a*, *bimenod rosh*).

## The Value of Truth

At dozens of points in his commentaries, Rashi deals with the subject of truth. His treatment of it resembles his treatment of humility: he selects biblical and rabbinic statements in praise of truth and builds them into his own grand structure. His consideration of truth, however, is less original than his consideration of humility, so I will here cite only some highlights.

We have already seen, in our discussion of the verse 'she oversees the activities [OJPS: ways] of her household' (Prov. 31: 27), that Rashi set truth at the pinnacle of the hierarchy of values that mark the Jewish home. The woman of valour must instil this attribute, more than any other, into the members of her household.

Rashi frequently emphasized the importance of truth in a court of justice: 'Every judge who sits in judgement in accordance with the highest degree of truth for even one hour is considered by Scripture to have engaged in Torah study the whole day and to have become a partner of the Holy One, Blessed Be He, in the work of Creation' (on Exod. 18: 13). That *midrash* appears in *Shabat* (10*a*) and *Mekhilta*,[21] but neither of those sources includes the reference to having 'engaged in Torah study the whole day'. Rashi added the point to reassure judges that the time they invest in careful pursuit of the genuine truth in a case is not considered to their detriment as time spent away from Torah study. It was this pedagogical purpose that moved Rashi to cite a *midrash* for which there was no exegetical need, and there is a considerable degree of contrivance in linking the *midrash* to the biblical comment that Moses was engaged in judging 'from morning to evening'.

Because his purpose was to educate people to appreciate the value and importance of justice, Rashi declined to adopt the usual rabbinic interpretation of 'God stands in the divine assembly; among the divine beings [OJPS: the judges] he pronounces judgement' (Ps. 82: 1). Instead, he interprets the verse as an admonition to judges: God is standing there 'to see whether they judge truthfully'. He concludes his interpretation of the psalm with a request that God 'arise and cut off those crooked judges in Israel'. In interpreting the verse 'By justice a king sustains the land, but a fraudulent man tears it down' (Prov. 29: 4), Rashi sets the truthful judge, by virtue of whom the world endures, as a foil to the unfit judge, whose pride brings about its destruction: 'If he is a truthful judge, he will sustain the land. And *a fraudulent man* is one who is not deliberate in judging.' Other medieval interpreters understood the term here rendered 'fraudulent man' differently.

---

[21] 'Yitro', 2: 22 (Venice, 1545, col. 4).

Rashi even saw a possibility that the Bible referred to the truthful judge as a 'king': '*The king seated on the throne of judgement* [Prov. 20:8]—This may be interpreted as referring to the Holy One, Blessed Be He, and it may be interpreted as referring to truthful judges.' The Psalms declare that truth helps the king triumph over his enemies, a point that Rashi reiterates: '*Teach thee* [Ps. 45: 5, OJPS]—The Torah and the words of truth in which you engage will teach you military tactics so your right hand will do wondrous things . . . And in reward for that Torah, the nations will fall before Israel.' In the next verse, he ties the king's ability to terrify the enemy and maintain his sovereignty expressly to the truthfulness alluded to in that verse, even though the plain meaning of the text requires no such link. The insistence on truth will also benefit the Jewish people overall: '*Mercy and truth are met together* [Ps. 85: 11, OJPS]—Let Israel be speakers of truth, and mercy will meet them from the Heavens.'

Israel's redemption likewise depends on the attribute of truth. In the absence of truth on Israel's part, God will not redeem them: '*And so redress is turned back* [Isa. 59: 14]—Our vengeance against our enemies depends on the Holy One, Blessed Be He, and His *vindication stays afar*. Why? Because [*truth*] *stumbles in the public square*, and when truth is weakened on earth, neither do righteousness and justice come from Heaven.'[22]

## Between Truth and Humility

Although truth and humility are the two values to which Rashi assigned pride of place, they sometimes come into conflict with each other. In at least one such case, Rashi favoured humility. The Talmud reports in the name of the *amora* Samuel that scholars may 'alter their words' and depart from the truth with respect to three matters. One of the three is *masekhet* (literally: tractate); Rashi explains it as a case in which a scholar is asked '"Do you have a particular tractate ordered at your fingertips [that is, in your memory]?" Even if he has it ordered, he should respond "No", and doing so reflects the attribute of humility' (Rashi on *BM* 23*b*, *bemasekhet*). In other words, an erudite person may disavow his erudition in order to avoid the appearance of arrogance.

Rashi's interpretation of Samuel's statement is not at all universally adopted. The tosafists, for example, explain the permitted departure from truth on a utilitarian basis unrelated to concern about arrogance. The concern raised there is that the questioner's purpose is to harass the sage by testing his erudition on the tractate in question; to avoid that harassment, the sage may alter his words: '[The questioner] having come to test his knowledge, he is permitted to alter and say "I have not learned this".'

---

[22] This wording appears only in some manuscripts (see Rashi, *Parshandata*, ii. 128); cf. Rashi on Zeph. 3: 5: '*Every morning doth He bring His right to light* [OJPS]—He judges with the highest degree of truth', that is, the Holy One, Blessed Be He, helps the judge to issue a truthful judgment; see also Rashi on Zech. 7: 7.

Rashi's position on Samuel's comment is especially noteworthy in comparison to some of his other Talmud interpretations. As a general matter, he refuses to assume that one of the sages might have uttered an untruth even where it might be permissible to do so. At the beginning of *Pesaḥim*, for example, in a passage already discussed in Chapter 2, the sages speak in praise of a person who avoids conveying bad news directly and instead alludes to it indirectly, allowing the listener to infer what happened. To illustrate, they cite the news that the parents of the talmudic sage Rav had died. To convey that information to Rabbi Hiya (who also was related to Rav's parents), Rav used indirect hints. When asked by Rabbi Hiya whether his father was still alive, Rav replied 'Mother lives.' When asked whether his mother was still alive, he replied 'Father lives' (*Pes.* 4a). Rashi explains:

*Mother lives*—Couched in the interrogative, that is, since you're asking about my father, ask about my mother . . . and he [Rabbi Hiya] understood on his own. And some say: Rav gently responded, referring to a person about whom Rabbi Hiya had not asked, so he would infer the situation in general. But it is difficult for me to say that Rav's mouth would utter any falsehood.

Because the love of truth was Rashi's guiding light, deeply instilled in his consciousness, his thoughts, and his deeds, he found it very hard to accept the possibility that an eminent sage like Rav could utter a falsehood—even in special circumstances where the halakhah permits a departure from the truth. I see no contradiction between this and his position regarding the *masekhet*, for the two cases can be distinguished. Knowledge of a tractate is limitless, and denying one knows a tractate is not an express falsehood of the sort arguably uttered by Rav. That distinction may account for Rashi's divergent interpretations of the two cases.

## Summary

Rashi had a broad understanding of the meaning of humility. As he conceived of it, the attribute required more than the mere avoidance of arrogance. A humble person also had to be patient and had to accept lovingly and submissively whatever life offered, torments included. One who is 'whole in his ways' is 'humble and patient', rejoicing in fulfilling the commandments and carrying out God's directives energetically and unhesitatingly (Rashi on *Zev.* 116a, *tamim bedarko*; cf. on Gen. 37: 13). Rashi defined Moses' humility in precisely those terms: '*Moses was a . . . humble man* [Num. 12: 3]—unpretentious and patient'.

Humility pertains to all areas of life, and its blessing is likewise comprehensive and inclusive. Its reward is great, for individual and community, in this world and the next. It also makes an important contribution to Torah study, and Rashi frequently speaks of the humility of the sages, especially their ability to overcome the argumentative competitiveness that is motivated by (among other things) pride. 'A fit person' must also be a humble one.

According to Rashi, the patriarchs and other national leaders acted in a humble manner, and that conduct will likewise characterize the King Messiah. As a rule, Rashi did not expressly call on people to treat the humility of these exalted figures as a model, but that was clearly his intent, as evidenced primarily by the *midrashim* he selected. Moreover, God himself is marked by humility, a motif also explicitly presented by the sages. At the very beginning of his commentary on the Torah, in the description of Creation, Rashi selects a *midrash* that describes God as humbly seeking the angels' advice about creating man. And he expressly notes the didactic aspect of the episode, which conveys a message about proper conduct: '*Let Us make man* [Gen. 1: 26]—Even though they did not assist Him in His creative acts and [the use of the plural verb] opens the door to rebellion [against monotheism], Scripture was not deterred from teaching proper conduct and the attribute of humility; namely, that a great one takes counsel with and seeks permission from a lesser one.' The *midrash* is found in *Genesis Rabbah* 8: 8.

It is no wonder, then, that Rashi opposed the practice of awaiting the return of 'important people' who had stepped out of the synagogue before continuing with the prayers: to do so would be an affront to the dignity of the other worshippers. (I noted this earlier, in the discussion of Rashi's personality.) Especially noteworthy in this context is the instruction that one should shun a person 'of little accomplishment' who acts 'arbitrarily and pretentiously' as a pious person. Rashi so ruled because he regarded arrogance as a serious sin.

These many and varied sources suggest that humility occupied a central place not only in Rashi's conceptual world and private life but also in his practice of communal leadership. As noted, he saw no contradiction between complete humility and vigorous pursuit of truth: indeed, these two attributes, though sometimes pointing in opposite directions, coexisted within him in perfect harmony.

## Human Dignity

Rabbi Shemayah, Rashi's student, offers evidence of his teacher's sensitivity to human dignity. As a matter of halakhah, mourners are not to be comforted during the intermediate days of a festival.[j] But Rashi found it difficult to witness a person's suffering and not offer comfort. He therefore found a way to provide comfort by expounding on words of Torah: 'But it was difficult for the rabbi [Rashi] to sit silently [with the mourner], for what comfort is there in silence? So he would begin to speak to the mourner with words of consolation.'[23] That attitude also provides the background for his stance regarding people who had been forced to convert, as we shall see. Because of the importance to him of human dignity, he objected, as

---

[23] Rashi, *Responsa* (Heb.), ed. Elfenbein, §189. Cf. *MK* 19*b*.

[j] The intermediate days of a festival partake of the joy of the festival even though labour is not forbidden.

just mentioned, to interrupting the prayer service to await the return of one who had left the synagogue, even if the person who had left was a prominent and distinguished man. This sensitivity was a prominent feature of his personality. Another clear example is provided by his concern not only for the welfare of a woman who had been mistreated by her husband but also for her dignity. Rashi's comments on that episode—to be discussed below in connection with his teachings on women— show the emotional turmoil and distress it caused him. It is no wonder, then, that his commentaries on the Bible and the Talmud likewise manifest his interest in educating people to have regard for the essential human dignity of others.

In interpreting the Creation story, Rashi emphasized humanity's exalted status, regarding mankind as the crown of Creation, for whose sake and honour everything else had been created. Scripture there states: 'And no grasses of the field had yet sprouted, because the Lord God had not yet sent rain upon the earth and there was no man to till the soil' (Gen. 2: 5). Rashi comments: 'And why had He not sent rain? Because there was no man to till the soil and no one to recognize the benefit of rains, but when man came and knew that [rains] were needed by the world and prayed for them, they came down and trees and vegetation grew.' The idea is a basic one, grounded in rabbinic statements, and Rashi reiterated it elsewhere. His concern for human dignity is evident also in the account of the creation of woman. Rashi cites the talmudic statement (*San.* 39*a*) that when God created her, he caused Adam to fall into a deep sleep 'so he would not see the cutting of the flesh from which she was created, which would have humiliated her before him' (on Gen. 2: 21). For that reason, Rashi likewise objected to understanding the clause 'and he shall rule over you' (Gen. 3: 16) to mean 'he shall govern you'. He narrowed the interpretation considerably and declined to cite *midrashim* that impaired a woman's dignity—a subject to which I shall return in Chapter 10, where I discuss the status of women. Rashi repeatedly refers in his commentary to man's creation in the image of God as the rationale for taking pains to avoid affronts to man's dignity (e.g., Exod. 20: 23). This warning runs like a thread through Rashi's oeuvre and is not really anything new, for it is a central motif of rabbinic sources too. Let me offer a few examples that will illustrate his use of his commentaries as a tool for educating people to be meticulous in this area, especially with respect to avoiding any embarrassment of one's fellow.

## Shame and Human Dignity

At the beginning of his comments on Deuteronomy, Rashi observes that Moses emulated Jacob and rebuked the Israelites only at the end of his life; he adds that there are four reasons why that is the proper way to act. The first two reasons, which pertain to concern for human dignity, are expressly stated but the other two, unrelated to human dignity, are merely alluded to. In citing this example in my methodological introduction at the beginning of Chapter 8, I suggested that Rashi had cited the first two reasons for pedagogical purposes: they implicitly teach that one should avoid any affront to others.

A similar instance is God's telling Aaron and Miriam to step away from Moses while he rebukes them for their complaint about Moses' wife, Zipporah (Num. 12: 5). Rashi cites two explanations. First, only a portion of a person's praise is to be spoken of in the presence of a person, and God's words of rebuke to Aaron and Miriam incorporate uncommonly effusive praise for Moses. Second, God did not want Moses to hear his reprimand to Aaron, lest Aaron be embarrassed and shamed. As in the first instance, a person's dignity is to be taken into account even when the person has sinned and deserves rebuke. Rashi begins his comment with a non-exegetical exhortation: 'It is a fortiori so that a human being ['flesh and blood'] should not show anger at his fellow without informing him of his offense' (on Num. 12: 9). Even anger at another is forbidden unless the reason for the anger is conveyed; it is reasonable to assume that the explanation and clarification may diminish hatred among people.

Shame is a central motif in the story of Joseph and his brothers. Rashi repeatedly emphasizes the brothers' sense of profound shame over what they had done and the extent to which Joseph, concerned about their dignity, tried to deflect that shame, especially when revealing his identity to them: 'He could not bear to allow the Egyptians to stand near him and witness his brothers' shame' (on Gen. 45: 1). The brothers were frightened of him not because they thought he might injure them but 'on account of shame' (on Gen. 45: 3). To teach the great harm caused by shame, Rashi notes that '[Joseph] saw them drawing back and said, "Now my brothers are abashed" and called to them with gentle entreaties' (on Gen. 45: 11). The brothers were silent because 'from the beginning they had been ashamed before him' (on Gen. 45: 15). 'Because they were abashed, he was worried that they might quarrel en route about their having sold him' (on Gen. 45: 24). Rashi even attributed Joseph's transfer of the Egyptian populace from city to city—a step taken to subject the populace to Pharaoh's rule under a sort of feudal regime (Gen. 47)—to his desire to avoid shaming his brothers. He transferred the populace so the brothers' situation would not be unusual: 'so they would not call them exiles' (on Gen. 47: 21). Rashi's selection of *midrashim* here likewise had a clear pedagogical purpose.

An additional example of Rashi's pursuit of his pedagogical agenda can be found in the passage related to the altar. The Torah requires that the structure providing access to the altar be a ramp rather than a staircase, so 'that your nakedness may not be exposed upon it' (Exod. 20: 23). Rashi comments:

On a staircase, you are required to take wide steps . . . In any case, widening one's steps is almost tantamount to uncovering one's nakedness, and it shames them. *And one may reason a fortiori* [emphasis added]: If the Torah forbids shaming these stones, which lack the consciousness to perceive any affront, because they are needed and should not be treated disdainfully, how much more so [does it forbid] shaming your fellow, who is made in the image of your Creator and resents being shamed.

The a fortiori reasoning is not exegetical; it is, rather, a Midrash-based exhortation to diligence in protecting human dignity.

Rashi also finds a moral, with elements of exhortation, in the story of Judah and Tamar:

She did not want to embarrass him and say he had made her pregnant; instead [she said, the father is] 'the man to whom these belong'. She thought: If he confesses on his own, [good]; but if not, let them burn me but I will not embarrass him. *On this basis, they said*: It is better that one be cast into a furnace than that one embarrass one's fellow publicly. (Rashi on Gen. 38: 25, emphasis added)

Up to 'I will not embarrass him', Rashi is writing as an exegete; from there on, he is a pedagogue. In the Talmud, the lesson is formulated as 'that one cast oneself into a fiery furnace' (*Sot.* 10*b*). Rashi alters the wording to read 'that one be cast' so that the comment be appropriate for the words 'as she was being brought out'.

Additional evidence for Rashi's pedagogical purpose appears in his comments on the proclamation, issued when an army is being raised, about the men who are exempt from military service. He cites the remarks of Rabbi Yosi the Galilean, who sees a deliberate order in the sequence of exemptions: those who have built a house, planted a vineyard, or betrothed a woman are mentioned first in order to protect the dignity of those who are exempt because they have sinned:

Rabbi Yosi the Galilean says ['fearful' as a ground for exemption means] fearful of sins he has committed. And for that reason, the Torah associated his exemption with that related to a house, a vineyard or a woman, so as to cover for those who are exempted because of sins they committed, so it is not evident that they committed sins. One who sees him returning will say: perhaps he built a house, planted a vineyard, or betrothed a woman. (Rashi on Deut. 20: 8)

Here, too, the Torah protects the dignity even of sinners. We might have regarded the shame caused to a sinner as a sort of atonement for the sin, but human dignity is so exalted a trait that it overcomes even atonement.

## Slander

Rashi used various biblical texts as the basis for exhortations against slander: some dealt directly with the subject while others are connected to it only through *midrashim*. The Torah recounts that Joseph brought evil reports about his brothers to their father (Gen. 37: 2), and several *midrashim*, including some in *Pirkei derabi eli'ezer*, say that Joseph's reports were true, not false, and that his purpose was the positive one of trying to deter his brothers from sinning. Although Rashi's comments suggest he sometimes favoured these *midrashim*, he nevertheless sharply criticized Joseph and wrote of the severe, quid pro quo punishments he suffered:

Anything evil that he observed in his brothers, Leah's sons, he would report to his father: that they ate limbs torn from living animals or that they demeaned the sons of the concubines, calling them slaves who were suspected of improper sexual activities. And he was punished for all three: [for Joseph's charge that they ate from a living animal, the brothers] slaughtered a kid when they sold him and did not eat it while it was alive; for the charge of calling their [half-]brothers slaves, Joseph was sold as a slave; and for his stories about their illicit sexual activity, 'his master's wife cast her eyes [upon Joseph]'.

A similar fate befell Moses, who raised the concern that when he arrived in Egypt, the Israelites would not believe that he was God's emissary, sent to redeem them. The Torah recounts that his hand became leprous as a sign of the authenticity of his mission. But according to Rashi—here following the *midrash*—it was also a punishment for his having 'slandered' the people and having suspected that they would not believe him; 'accordingly, he was afflicted with leprosy, just as Miriam was [so] afflicted because of slander'. When Moses complained that 'before long [the Israelites] will be stoning me' (Exod. 17: 4), God impatiently asked him, 'Why have you spoken ill of my children?' All of these *midrashim* have a clear pedagogical bent. It is hard to see them as explications of the plain meaning of the text, and Rashi selected them to advance his underlying purpose.

At times, Rashi did not rest content with interpreting the story and instead made use of a talmudic source to add an express exhortation against slander. The punishment imposed on Miriam, who had joined with Aaron in speaking against Moses, led Rashi to conclude that 'if Miriam, who did not intend to demean Moses, was nevertheless punished, [it is true] a fortiori [that] one who intends to demean his fellow [will be punished]' (on Num. 12: 1). And he reiterated the point in commenting on the verse 'Remember what the Lord your God did to Miriam' (Deut. 24: 9): 'If you want to be cautioned how to avoid being afflicted with leprosy, do not speak slander. Remember what happened to Miriam, who spoke [slanderously] against her brother and was afflicted.'

The leper is required to dwell in isolation outside the camp. Rashi comments: 'And our rabbis said: Why is [leprosy] different from all other impurities, requiring those afflicted with it to dwell in isolation? Because by his slander he separated man from wife or man from his fellow, he, too, should be separated' (on Lev. 13: 46). Only rarely did Rashi note reasons for commandments, and even more rarely in his commentary on the Torah did he introduce a *midrash* with the words 'and our rabbis said'. I believe he here departed from his usual practice in both respects in order to give the comment added weight. And not by mere chance did he discuss the matter at length in explaining the purification ritual for the leper:

Because the affliction is retribution for speaking slander, which entails prattle, purification from it requires birds, which constantly prattle in their chirping voices. *And cedar wood* [Lev. 14: 4]—Because the affliction is the result of arrogance. And *crimson stuff and hyssop*—What is his remedy so he might be healed? Let him lower himself from his arrogant stance and be like a worm[k] and like hyssop.

The Torah states: 'Cursed be he who strikes down his fellow countryman in secret' (Deut. 27: 24). Rashi comments: 'It is speaking of slander', an interpretation having its source in *Pirkei derabi eli'ezer* 53. Rashi favoured this *midrash* over others because it served his pedagogical purposes.

An additional—and, in my view, especially forceful—example appears in Rashi's explanation of the place-name Rithmah, the only one of the forty-two places mentioned in Numbers 33 whose name Rashi interprets. In his view, it is not a place-name at all but a nickname given to the place 'on account of the spies' slander'. The proof for that premise is extremely remote from the plain meaning and provides powerful evidence that Rashi's underlying purpose was to educate people to recognize the effects of slander—in this instance, a change in how a geographic place is referred to. Rashi wanted to emphasize that slander leaves a negative impression even on a person's physical environment, as I have discussed in detail in the methodological introduction to Chapter 8.

# Peace and Factionalism

Peace in its broadest sense occupied an important place in Rashi's world. It is a central subject in his oeuvre, clearly spoken of in his commentaries on the Bible and Talmud, treated even more forcefully in his responsa, and evident in his actions as a community leader. At first blush, the subject seems to be one about which little new can be said; it was broadly treated and effusively praised in the Bible, the Talmud, and the *midrashim*, and 'peace' (*shalom*) is said to be one of the divine names. The sages even assigned it a literary unit of its own: *Perek hashalom* in the tractate *Derekh erets zuta*. Nevertheless, Rashi was able to stake out a position even on this subject.

## The Meaning of Peace

The meaning assigned to peace in Rashi's teachings provides evidence of its important place in his conceptual world. Peace is not merely a passive state, the absence of war or enmity between nations and people. It is, rather, a state in which love and brotherhood prevail among people and actions are taken to bring people closer together. Rashi sees that as the ideal to be aspired to in human relationships in general and in relationships among Jews in particular. The basic notion of 'what's mine is mine and what's yours is yours'[24] is a destructive one. Rashi included within the

---

[24] Mishnah *Avot* 5: 1: 'That [attitude] is the average characteristic. But some say: It is the characteristic of Sodom.'

[k] The term rendered as 'crimson stuff' is *sheni tola'at*, literally, 'crimson of a worm', referring to the creature from which crimson dye was derived.

concept of peace good deeds performed out of gratitude to one's fellow, along with actions that express closeness and love among people. This broad view of peace characterizes Rashi's approach in his biblical commentary and all his literary works. Let me cite three of the many examples that could be offered.

1. In his commentary on the Talmud, Rashi provides the following interpretation of the verse 'for I have taken away my peace from this people' (Jer. 16: 5, OJPS): 'And what is peace? The [acts of] kindness and mercy that they had regularly performed' (on *BB* 10a, *ki asafti*). Peace includes interpersonal love and compassion.

2. To interpret the verse 'let the mountains bear peace to the people' (Ps. 72: 3, OJPS), Rashi writes: 'And what is the peace that the mountains bear? When they are fruitful, people are not stingy, and a man calls to his fellow [to join him] under his vine and under his fig-tree.' In other words, economic blessings forestall interpersonal jealousy and cause people to host their friends lovingly. Here, too, peace is taken as an expression of love and friendship among people.

3. The Talmud states that the verse 'He hath redeemed my soul in peace so that none come nigh me' (Ps. 55: 19, OJPS) is meant to teach that the time of public prayer is a 'time of favour' (*Ber.* 8a). Rashi comments: '*Hath redeemed . . . in peace*—One who engaged in words of peace, that is, Torah, as it is said, "All her paths [are] peaceful" [Prov. 3: 17]; and acts of kindness are likewise peace, for by doing a physical act of kindness for his fellow, he comes to recognize that he loves him, and that brings about brotherhood and peace.'[1] Not only did Rashi broaden the concept of peace and tie it explicitly to brotherhood and to Torah; he even used his commentary to exhort people to do acts of kindness for one another so as to increase love.

## Love of Peace and Pursuit of Peace

Rashi's love of peace and his regard for it as a value of the highest order are further evidenced by his references to it even where Scripture does not mention it explicitly. In some of those places, he speaks in praise of peace more as a preacher than as an exegete, which also demonstrates his profound attachment to the idea. He took advantage of opportunities to integrate into his commentary *midrashim* that speak in praise of peace. A few examples:

[1] It is noteworthy that NJPS does not refer to 'peace' in any of these verses. It follows its regular practice of using a different word to translate *shalom* in each place, so as to capture the individual meaning more precisely, but it thereby loses the shared meaning. OJPS, in contrast, refers to 'peace' and reflects the shared meaning, and it is the shared meaning to which Rashi appears to be responding. His broad sense of 'peace' is quite consistent with the biblical view, since the word *shalom* has all these different shades of meaning.

**1.** In interpreting the verse 'And from there the Lord scattered them over the face of the whole earth' (Gen. 11: 9), Rashi cites the midrashic expression of surprise over the fact that the generation of the dispersion (following the building of the Tower of Babel) was not wiped out as had been the generation of the flood. He replies:

The generation of the flood were quarrelsome robbers, and therefore they were wiped out. But these [the generation of the dispersion] practised love and friendship towards one another, as it is said, they 'had the same language and the same words'. You thus learn that disputes are despised and peace is great.

Rashi's comments are derived from *Genesis Rabbah*, but their formulation there is different:

The generation of the flood were immersed in robbery; accordingly, no remnant of them survived; but these [these generation of the dispersion], because they loved one another, 'had the same language and the same words'; accordingly, a remnant survived.[25]

Rashi preserved the substance of the *midrash* but reworked its style to emphasize the value of peace even more. He therefore expressly added, in characterizing the generation of the flood, the reference to internecine quarrels—something only hinted at in *Genesis Rabbah*. Instead of the *midrash*'s statement 'that they loved one another', Rashi wrote that they 'practised love and friendship towards one another'. Passive love is insufficient; there is a need in addition for actions that express it ('practised'). Rashi's express conclusion that 'You thus learn that disputes are despised and peace is great' likewise does not appear in *Genesis Rabbah*. He added it because his goal was to educate people to love peace.

**2.** In interpreting the verse 'Then he became king in Jeshurun when the heads of the people assembled, the tribes of Israel together' (Deut. 33: 5), Rashi offers two possibilities:

*King in Jeshurun*—The yoke of his sovereignty is upon them whenever their heads assemble. Another interpretation: *Assembled*—When they gather together in a single coming together and there is peace among them, he is their king; that is not the case when there are disputes among them.

Both interpretations are based on *Sifrei* on Deuteronomy. Although the version in *Sifrei* is longer than Rashi's, the primary message—praise for peace and disdain for conflict—is not stated there expressly but only alluded to:

When Israel are in agreement below, his great name is extolled on high, as it is said, 'Then he became king in Jeshurun'. When? When the heads of the people are assembled. And an assembly is only of the heads of the people, as it is said, 'Take all the chiefs of the people' [Num. 25: 4, OJPS].[26]

---

[25] *Genesis Rabbah* 38: 5.    [26] *Sifrei* on Deut. 33: 5.

The version in *Sifrei* reads 'are in agreement'. Rashi modified the wording and added 'and there is peace among them'. God is king over Israel only if both unity and peace prevail among them. Rashi's pedagogical purpose is advanced by the change, and to emphasize that purpose even more, Rashi added express words of disdain for conflict. Moreover, the very addition of a second interpretation for which there is no exegetical need ('another interpretation') evidently serves the same purpose.

**3.** In interpreting the verse 'it was You who established equity' (Ps. 99: 4), Rashi writes:

You established compromise and peacemaking among people when You said 'When you see the ass of your enemy lying under its burden [you must provide assistance].' And who can see his enemy showing him kindness without being moved to embrace and kiss him!

The source of the comment, in *Midrash tehilim*, contains a broad description of the peace and brotherhood that are attained through fulfilment of the commandments:

*You established equity*—Said Rabbi Alexandrei: You established righteousness in Your world. If a person has a dispute with his fellow, he goes to court with him and they accept what the court determines and make peace; hence it says, 'You established equity.' If a person sets out on the road and sees his fellow's ass lying under its burden, he extends a hand and helps him rebalance the load. They go to an inn and he says so-and-so loves me, and here I thought he hated me. They immediately begin speaking to each other, and peace comes to prevail between them.[27]

The midrashic source speaks of a righteous judgement, but Rashi alters it to speak of compromise—a core value in his teachings and one on which he believes human relations should be based. Compromise can do more than judgement to enhance love and brotherhood among people, even though judgement may be preferable from the perspective of justice. As we shall see, Rashi held consistently to this position. Another interesting change introduced by Rashi pertains to the effects of helping an enemy. The *midrash* says that helping an enemy leads to peace. A parallel text in *Midrash tanḥuma* states that compromise leads to love between the two former enemies. Not content with that, Rashi added 'being moved to embrace and kiss him'. It is hard to see the change as mere happenstance; more likely, it is deliberate and reflects a clear pedagogical purpose. Rashi preached greater closeness among people.

**4.** In interpreting the verse 'Their heart is divided; now they shall bear their guilt; He will break down their altars' (Hos. 10: 2, OJPS), Rashi writes:

*Their heart is divided*—From Me. *Now they shall bear their guilt*—That is what will break

---

[27] *Midrash tehilim* on Ps. 99: 3, ed. Buber, 212a. This *midrash* has a parallel in *Midrash tanḥuma*, 'Mishpatim'.

down their altars, destroy . . . Another interpretation, following an aggadic *midrash*: great is peace, for even though Israel be idolaters, if there is peace among them, Satan does not accuse them . . . But conflict is hated, as it is said 'Their heart is divided; now they shall bear their guilt'—Satan has an opportunity to accuse.

Rashi, like the *midrash*, sees the beginning of the verse as a conditional clause: if conflict and hatred prevail among them (that is, 'their heart is divided'), they are held guilty in judgement, but if peace prevails, they will be exonerated in all cases. There can be no doubt that Rashi recognized the great distance between the plain meaning of the text and the aggadic *midrash* he cited as a second possibility, and that is why he noted the midrashic nature of the comments. Nor is there any flaw in the first interpretation that warrants introduction of a second. Why, then, did Rashi suggest the second interpretation? Almost certainly, he was motivated by his pedagogical purpose of promoting peace and denigrating conflict—the purpose that runs like a scarlet thread through his entire oeuvre. That Rashi dealt with the subject dozens of times shows the degree to which it coursed through his veins and occupied a central place in his consciousness.

Among the qualities that characterize a righteous person are his efforts on behalf of peace and his ability to promote it among people. In interpreting the verse 'The lips of the righteous know what is pleasing' (Prov. 10: 32), Rashi writes: 'They know how to please and appease their Creator and know how to please people and instil peace among them.' It goes without saying that the word translated 'pleasing' (*ratson*) need not be interpreted as Rashi suggests and, even more so, that there is no need for both of the interpretations he offers. It appears that his goal of teaching people to love peace and pursue it is what moved him to suggest the second interpretation.

## Between Peace and Truth

In some instances, Rashi faced a dilemma that required him to choose between peace and truth, both values he strongly affirmed. At the beginning of *Pesaḥim*, for example, the sages speak in praise of people who avoid reporting bad news and convey it only through indirect allusions that allow the listener to infer the events in question.

An interesting example is provided by Rashi's description of certain actions taken by the talmudic sage Hillel. The Mishnah reports a dispute between the House of Hillel and the House of Shammai regarding certain sacrifices—burnt offerings and peace offerings—when brought to the Temple on a festival day:

The House of Shammai say: They bring peace offerings, but do not lay their hands upon them, but not so burnt offerings. And the House of Hillel say: They bring peace offerings and burnt offerings and lay their hands upon them. (Mishnah *Bets.* 2: 4)[28]

[28] According to the House of Shammai, the prohibition against laying hands on the sacrificial animal's head on a festival day follows from the prohibition against making use of an animal on the festival. Accordingly, they rule that the laying of hands should take place on the eve of the festival.

The *Gemara* states:

It happened that Hillel the Elder brought his [beast for a] burnt offering to the Temple courtyard to lay his hands upon it on a festival day. Students of Shammai gathered round him and said to him: What is the nature of this beast? He said to them: It is a female, and I have brought it for a peace offering. He wiggled its tail for them and they went on their way. (*Bets. 20a*)

Hillel did not speak the truth to the students of the House of Shammai, for he said the animal was being brought for a peace offering rather than a burnt offering. He even 'wiggled' its tail so they would think it was a female, and a female may not be brought as a burnt offering. He deceived them doubly, in both word and deed. Rashi explains that he acted in this manner to avoid a quarrel: 'Because of Hillel's great humility, he would depart [from the truth] for the sake of peace.' In other words, Rashi judged Hillel's action favourably even though he had not spoken truthfully. What is the difference in principle between this case and the one cited earlier from *Pesaḥim*, where Rashi wrote that he found it difficult to imagine that Rav would allow a falsehood to pass his lips, even though he had done so in order to avoid violating the halakhah? Why was it not equally difficult for Rashi to imagine that Hillel the Elder would allow a falsehood to pass his lips? It is not as if potential excuses were unavailable in Rav's case. Rashi could have found a way, had he so chosen, to account for Rav's words without interpreting them as a falsehood.[29] The difference appears to arise out of the different circumstances of the two cases. In contrast to what happened in the other case, Hillel here departed from the truth for the sake of peace. He was attempting to avoid an intense argument with the students of the House of Shammai that might have even brought about a physical attack on him. The sages had already determined that it was permissible to depart from the truth for the sake of peace, but Rashi's repeated emphasis on that point in his commentaries is noteworthy, given his overall attitude regarding truth.

Rashi supported the idea of compromise, a position consistent with his devotion to peace and his advocacy of peace even, on occasion, at the expense of truth. He thereby followed the sages, who saw compromise in a positive light and favoured it over a legal verdict,[30] even though a verdict would be preferred from the perspective of pristine truth. Rashi adopted that position and often preached on behalf of compromise, despite his extremely high regard for truth and his placement of it at

[29] As he did, for example, in the case of Jacob, who misled his father Isaac in order to secure his blessing. Jacob says, 'I am Esau, your firstborn' (Gen. 27: 19); Rashi, following the *midrash*, glosses 'I am he who brings you [food], and Esau is your firstborn.'

[30] This is so from a jurisprudential perspective as well: 'R. Simeon ben Gamaliel says: A verdict [requires] three [judges] but a compromise [requires] two. And the force of a compromise is stronger than that of a verdict, for if two issue a verdict, the litigants can change their minds, but if two arrive at a compromise, the litigants cannot change their minds' (*San. 5b*; see Rashi ad loc.; Tosafot ad loc.).

the pinnacle of his value system. The Torah instructs the Israelites to 'do what is right and good in the sight of the Lord' (Deut. 6: 18) and Rashi comments: 'This refers to compromise, going beyond what the law requires.' Rashi uses the word translated 'right' (*yashar*) (from which the word for 'equity', *meisharim*, is derived) to speak favourably of compromise in other places too. He takes the verse 'It was you who established equity' (Ps. 99: 4) as referring to 'compromise and causing peace to prevail among people'. He similarly finds a reference to compromise in 'execute the judgement of truth and peace in your gates' (Zech. 8: 16, OJPS). Judgement, to be sure, is based on law and truth, but if we want to bring about peace among people, compromise should be preferred to it. Rashi similarly interprets the term *meisharim* ('agreement') in Daniel 11: 6 to mean 'a peaceful compromise'.

In considering Rashi's character in Chapter 2, I noted several cases referred to in his responsa that provide extremely powerful evidence of his struggle against factionalism and his pursuit of peace. His responsa related to converts from Judaism—forced and otherwise—likewise manifest these qualities, something to be discussed further in the next chapter.

CHAPTER TEN

# Society

## Scholars

### Their Virtues and their Suffering

Rashi greatly honoured scholars, considering them to be the most exalted of men. They ensure the continued existence of the world, which is based on the study of Torah and observance of its commandments. We have already seen, in connection with Rashi's adulation of the Torah, how deeply ingrained this idea was in his consciousness. He recognized that the scholars bore much of the brunt of leadership in the Jewish communities of the time, and he believed it was their strength and steadfastness that ensured the continuation of Jewish life in the diaspora. But his writings make clear that he had more than this practical aspect in mind and that he contemplated an idealized world in which Torah was the value shared by all people, and the bearers of Torah—that is, the scholars—occupied a central place: 'Scholars, to whom the Holy One, Blessed Be He, gives eyes with which to illuminate the world' (Rashi on S. of S. 5: 12, following *Song of Songs Rabbah* 5: 9–11).

This attitude in itself is not novel, for the various genres of rabbinic literature contain hundreds of statements in praise of scholars and their teachings. But Rashi does more than merely reiterate an accepted idea; his comments flow from a profound inner conviction regarding the great merit of scholars and attest to his desire to persuade others to adopt this attitude themselves. Three principal objectives can be identified in Rashi's writings on the matter: (1) encouraging scholars to remain steadfast in dedicating all their might and energy to Torah study, despite the difficulties they confront in doing so; (2) promoting affection for scholars on the part of all people; and (3) suggesting how scholars should study, a subject treated in Chapter 9. Two sorts of evidence clearly attest to these objectives: biblical verses that are interpreted with reference to scholars even where that is not their plain meaning and generalizations as to the merits of scholars that are drawn on the basis of isolated details. Let me offer two examples, one from his biblical commentary and one from his talmudic commentary.

The first example appears in the commentary on Psalm 45. In its plain sense, the psalm has nothing to do with scholars. It offers blessings to the king of Israel and his consort, evidently from the city of Tyre, on the occasion of their marriage. That understanding is supported by numerous verses in the psalm, which sing the praises of the king on his wedding day and describe him as a man perfect in body, attributes, and deeds. He excels in his beauty, his might, and his victories over his enemies; in addition, he speaks the truth and he pursues justice. In the psalmist's words, 'You are fairer than all men ... Gird your sword upon your thigh, O hero ... Your arrows [are] sharpened ... peoples fall at your feet ... the consort stands at your right hand, decked in gold of Ophir.' Later, the poet addresses the queen ('O Tyrian lass'), asking her to forsake her foreign origins and be faithful to the king: 'Take heed, lass, and note, incline your ear; forget your people and your father's house, and let the king be aroused by your beauty; since he is your lord, bow to him' (Ps. 45: 11–12). The poet likewise expresses the wish that the king's sons carry on his reign.

That is how most commentators, traditional as well as modern, have understood the psalm. They disagree only as to whether the king in question is David, Solomon, or Ahab. Rashi, however, takes a different tack. Disregarding even the *midrashim* in *Midrash tehilim*, he instead interprets the entire psalm as a paean to the virtues of scholars:

*For the leader; on* shoshanim.[a] *Of the Korahites. A* maskil. *A love song* [Ps. 45: 1]—This song was established in honour of scholars, for they are as gentle as lilies, as pleasant as lilies, and as suffused with good deeds as lilies are moist ... A song of praise for them, *to make them beloved to people and make their Torah beloved to them* [emphasis added]. I sing this song, which I established and created, to one who is fit to be a king.

Why did Rashi deviate from the plain meaning of the text? It is true that his basic idea—that scholars are as kings—can be grounded in the Talmud and that several *midrashim* from *Shabat* 63a, which speak in praise of scholars, are based on verses in this psalm. But that does not adequately respond to the question. First, the Talmud there refers not to the psalm as a whole but only to four phrases, all taken from verse 5. Second, Rashi knew well how far removed his interpretation was from the plain meaning of Scripture. He greatly expanded upon the four *midrashim* in the Talmud and used the opportunity to interpret the entire psalm as dealing with scholars and their teachings. At many points in his commentary, he disregards *midrashim* of this sort, which rely on scriptural phrases; and his promotion of them here, and his application of them to the psalm as a whole, show that he had an agenda: to depict the sage (and not the king) as the chosen personage. According to Rashi's line of interpretation, the military terminology ('gird your sword', 'your arrows [are] sharpened', 'peoples fall at your feet') refers to the wars of Torah. When he speaks of the king's beauty, the psalmist is referring to the sage's Torah, for the sage, in contrast to others who 'engage in transitory labours', engages in the

[a] The meaning of *shoshanim* is uncertain in this context. It usually means 'lilies'.

eternal Torah and issues proper halakhic rulings. The Torah of scholars brings blessings not only to them but to all Israel: 'In reward for the Torah, nations will fall before Israel.'[1] The sage's throne is eternal because his rulings are true. The description of the king's magnificent palace (Ps. 45: 9) refers, in Rashi's view, to the sage's place in Paradise, and he interprets the poet's call for the Tyrian lass to accept the king's authority as a request for the congregation of Israel to heed words of Torah: '*Take heed* [Ps. 45: 11], O congregation of Israel and see the right path; *incline your ear* to Torah; and *forget your people*—the nations among whom you are raised.' Rashi concludes with words of encouragement for sages, whose suffering and humility during their lifetimes will redound to their merit in the future: '*All glorious is the king's daughter within the palace* ... [Ps. 45: 14, OJPS]—They on whom all glory depends, namely, the assembly of the king who conducted themselves with humility, will now find their garments more important than the golden embroideries of high priests.'

The second example comes from Rashi's comments on the death of Aaron's sons. Moses instructs Aaron and his two remaining sons not to mourn the deaths of Nadab and Abihu (Lev. 10: 1–7), lest they thereby desecrate their exalted office. He adds: 'But your kinsmen, all the house of Israel, shall mourn the burning that the Lord has wrought' (Lev. 10: 6). Rashi comments: '[We learn] from this that the woes of scholars are borne by all, to mourn over them.' A generalization of this sort does not appear in the rabbinic texts, and Rashi inferred it from the Talmud's account of the scholars' efforts to comfort Rabbi Ishmael on the death of his two sons:

Our rabbis taught: When Rabbi Ishmael's sons died, four elders went in to comfort him—Rabbi Tarfon, Rabbi Yosi the Galilean, Rabbi Eleazar ben Azariah, and Rabbi Akiba. Rabbi Ishmael spoke first and said: His sins are many, his mourning has laid him low, he burdened his rabbis one time and a second. (*MK* 28*b*)

That is, Rabbi Ishmael justified, on the basis of his sins, the divine verdict that took the lives of his two sons, and he expressed his regret at having imposed on his friends (whom he respectfully calls 'his rabbis') the burden of comforting him twice. The four sages comforted him and denied that coming was a burden, for they were obligated to do so on the basis of four biblical precedents. The first sage, Rabbi Tarfon, mentioned the deaths of Aaron's two sons:

Rabbi Tarfon answered and said: *But your kinsmen, all the house of Israel, shall mourn the burning.* Can we not reason a fortiori? If it is so [that everyone mourns] for Nadab and Abihu, who performed only a single commandment, as it is written 'Aaron's sons brought the blood to him' [Lev. 9: 9], how much more should it be so for Rabbi Ishmael's sons? (*MK* 28*b*)

---

[1] The quotation above follows the manuscripts. As a result of censorship, many printed versions read 'worshippers of idols will fall before Israel' instead of 'nations will fall before Israel'.

On the basis of this *midrash*, Rashi came to the general conclusion that all Israel must mourn the sorrows that befall scholars. Rabbi Tarfon's homily, of course, is subject to challenge. In the biblical case, we are speaking of the high priest Aaron, whose two sons died while performing their assignment in the sanctuary, and it is only natural that Aaron's exalted status, the unique circumstances of his sons' deaths, and, most of all, the inability of Aaron and his remaining sons to mourn without defiling their priestly sanctity would warrant the request that all Israel mourn 'the burning'. Disregarding these distinctions, Rashi used Rabbi Tarfon's words to formulate a general principle. Moreover, from an exegetical perspective, Rashi had no need to interpret the verse in Leviticus this way, for everyone can understand why, in the special circumstances of that case, all Israel were asked to mourn for Nadab and Abihu. The rule that Rashi established here was the product of his pedagogical interest in instructing the Jews about the exalted status of scholars.

The emphasis Rashi placed on the difficulties and suffering faced by scholars and his tendency to offer them words of encouragement warrant further enquiry. Both themes, to be sure, appear in talmudic literature; but the considerable space Rashi devotes to them, and his use of them in connection with biblical verses unrelated in their plain meaning, shows his tendentiousness here. For example, on the verse 'The heart alone knows its bitterness' (Prov. 14: 10), he comments: 'His struggles and his labour as he toils in Torah; accordingly, *no outsider can share in its joy*—when he receives his future reward.' The context suggests the verse has nothing to do with scholars and how they study, and Rashi clearly recognized as much. In the Talmud, too, the verse is interpreted in a manner closer to its plain meaning (*Yoma* 83*a*).[2] But Rashi's clear goal was to fortify scholars so they would diligently pursue their studies even if their economic situation was unstable, for they would ultimately gain honour.

The second possible interpretation Rashi proposes for the verse—it praises the Jewish people, who suffer under the yoke of exile—is likewise tendentious: 'Another interpretation: *the heart alone knows its bitterness*—[this refers to] Israel, who are bitter in their exile and are killed for the sanctification of God's name; *and no outsider can share in its joy*—in the future.'

Rashi's desire to lift the spirits of scholars is evident too in his interpretation of 'the crown of the wise is their riches' (Prov. 14: 24, OJPS). He comments: 'they are rich in Torah'. Why did Rashi interpret the word 'riches' in a manner different from its plain meaning? Use of the plain meaning would have been at odds with the effort to bolster the community of scholars. If riches are the proper crown for scholars, what would that mean for the scholars of Rashi's time—himself included—many of whom could barely earn a living? Rashi often emphasized that

[2] In this passage, R. Ashi infers from the verse that a person who asserts that his medical condition requires him to eat on Yom Kippur is to be believed even if one hundred people dispute his claim.

the scholars' reward is being withheld until the future, when all will honour them, even those who had previously demeaned them (on Prov. 13: 4; 13: 13; 14: 10). It is quite likely that the economic difficulties suffered by the scholars of Rashi's time, who wandered from community to community in order to study, are what moved Rashi to offer this interpretation. In his liturgical poetry, too, Rashi spoke of the difficulties encountered by scholars and of their dedication in the face of those difficulties:

> They who dwell in *batei midrash* / in the sorrow of exile,
> Probing your mysteries / in all cities and towns.
> Toiling in the chambers of your words / your sages and scribes,
> And valuing your wares / over trade in silver and gold.
> Bound up in study/ both young and elderly,
> To aggrandize Torah and exalt it / never departing from the study hall . . .
> In hunger and thirst / and all their deprivations.[3]

At dozens of points in his commentaries, Rashi refers to the virtues of scholars and to their way of life, following in the path of the talmudic literature's extensive consideration of the subject. In most of these cases, his comments have no grounding in the plain meaning of the biblical verses. Ten of his observations follow:

1.  One who serves scholars is as one who 'serves before the Shekhinah':[c] commenting on the verse 'And the child did minister unto the Lord before Eli the priest' (1 Sam. 2: 11, OJPS).

2.  Where there are no scholars, proper halakhic rulings are not issued: commenting on the verse 'If there are no oxen, the crib is clean [that is, empty]' (Prov. 14: 4).

3.  A scholar who declines to teach Torah to others deserves to be censured and cursed; in contrast, a scholar who teaches 'acquires[d] souls, for he teaches them the right path, and they belong to him as if he had acquired them' (Rashi on Prov. 11: 26–30).

---

[3]                              Rashi, *Liturgical Poems* (Heb.), 22.[b]

[b] The translation makes no attempt to replicate the rhyme or metre of the original.

[c] The divine presence.

[d] The words translated 'acquires' and 'acquired' might also be rendered 'creates' and 'created'. The Hebrew verb stem is *kof-nun-heh*, which can have both meanings. As noted earlier, 'acquire' is more frequent in rabbinic Hebrew and 'create' is more frequent in biblical Hebrew. The ambiguity here may be deliberate, reflecting Rashi's comment on Gen. 12: 5, which refers to 'the persons they had acquired in Haran'. The verb there translated 'acquired'—from the root *ayin-sin-heh*—can also mean 'created'. The sense of 'acquire' is largely limited to biblical Hebrew. Rashi there comments that the plain meaning is indeed 'acquire', but he first cites the midrashic understanding that attributes to Abraham the creation of these people by virtue of his having taught them.

4. Among the obligations borne by scholars is to foster peace among people (on Prov. 12: 18).

5. Torah must be studied for the purpose of observing and fulfilling the commandments, not to gain fame and honour (on Prov. 17: 16). Torah should not be taught to a wicked student who has no intention of fulfilling the commandments (on Prov. 25: 20; 26: 8).

6. Torah study is sacred labour, and a scholar who leaves his studies 'is lazy in his work' and untrue to his task (on Prov. 18: 9).

7. Through Torah study, a man gains many friends (on Prov. 19: 6). Rashi uses this motif twice: in both cases, his interpretation is remote from the plain meaning of the verse.

8. It is proper for a scholar to teach Torah to others gratis, even if he himself is required to pay for his studies (on Prov. 23: 23). If he is named to a position of communal leadership, he should be sure 'to carry them [his constituents] in his bosom and guide them' with care (on Prov. 27: 27).

9. Every person, and especially a scholar, should show that he craves words of Torah (on Prov. 27: 7).

10. In the future, the other nations will restore to the scholars the funds that they extorted from the Jews: commenting on 'and the guards of the fruit' (S. of S. 8: 12).

Being a scholar entails not only privileges but also duties that must be diligently carried out. On the verse 'Declare to my people their transgression, to the House of Jacob their sin' (Isa. 58: 1), Rashi comments: '*Declare to my people their transgression*—these are the scholars, whose inadvertent misdeeds are transgressions, for a scholar's inadvertent act is considered to be intentional. *To the House of Jacob their sin*—these are the common folk, whose intentional actions are considered inadvertent.' In other words, it is because the scholars are close to God (they are called 'my people') that God holds them to a higher standard, treating more strictly every departure from the right path. In contrast, God is willing to forgive the common folk even for their deliberate transgressions.

The theme appears even in Rashi's interpretation of the verse 'Like a gold ring in the snout of a pig is a beautiful woman bereft of sense' (Prov. 11: 22). He takes the verse as referring to 'a scholar who strays from the right path', who is called 'a pig'. A scholar must be especially concerned about his dignity when he is in the company of common folk. If he acts in a way that seems to be flawed, he thereby desecrates God's name, for one who sees him will say 'the Torah is not pleasing' (Rashi on *Meg.* 28a, *mesani'ai*). A scholar who does not expound the Torah before the members of his community and fails to prevent them from sinning is destined to be held to account (on Eccles. 10: 11).

Rashi weaves into his biblical and talmudic commentaries various words of advice to scholars on the proper modes of study. I dealt with some of these in Chapter 9, in discussing the Torah and its study.

## The Righteous Person

Rashi treats the righteous person (*tsadik*) separately from the scholar. He appears to use the term to denote a person of excellent qualities, one who acts righteously, and not necessarily one who devotes his entire life to study. Several examples bear that out.

Noah's son Shem is depicted by Rashi as a righteous person, hence the placement of his name before those of his brothers Ham and Japhet (on Gen. 5: 32, following *Genesis Rabbah* 26: 3). His father Noah is likewise referred to in the Torah as a 'righteous person', but Rashi seeks out the flaws in his character, so he can say that only Abraham and his progeny, and especially Jacob and his progeny, possess perfect attributes. The prayer of righteous people is powerful, capable of transforming God's attribute of justice into that of mercy, and an entire generation can be saved by the merit of a righteous person (Rashi on Gen. 8: 1). Thanks to Job, all his contemporaries were protected (on Num. 14: 9). All of history is directed towards the welfare of the righteous. The actions of Pharaoh's butler and baker were divinely directed so that everyone would be preoccupied by them and lose their interest in Potiphar's wife's accusations against Joseph (on Gen. 40: 1). The merit of the 'wholly righteous' is so great that they have no need for a sign of the covenant such as the rainbow (on Gen. 9: 12). A banquet attended by a righteous person has unique value (on Gen. 21: 8).[4] The reward for a righteous person's actions is sometimes delayed for many generations; because of Judah's outstanding actions, for example, his descendants in the time of the monarchy were privileged to lead comfortable lives (on Gen. 49: 9).

'The death of the righteous is as difficult for God as the day on which the tablets were broken' (on Deut. 10: 7). The righteous do not invoke their good deeds when they ask God to help them and their contemporaries; 'they ask of God only a gratuitous gift, and that is because of their humility' (on Deut. 3: 23).

On occasion, the righteous receive their reward only in the world to come. Rashi interprets the text 'a faithful God, never false' (Deut. 32: 4) as conveying that idea, and it follows that he saw it as a central element of Jewish belief.

Women, too, are included among the righteous of the age and contribute to its protection: 'Why is the passage about Miriam's death juxtaposed with the passage about the red heifer? To teach you that just as offerings provide atonement, so does the death of the righteous provide atonement.' It should come as no surprise,

---

[4] On the basis of a *midrash*, he writes in similar terms of a scholar's presence at a banquet: 'One who enjoys a banquet attended by scholars is like one enjoying the glow of God's presence' (Rashi on Exod. 18: 12).

therefore, that Miriam merited 'death by a kiss', even though the Torah does not suggest it as it does in the cases of Moses and Aaron (Rashi on Num. 20: 1).

Some of these quotations regarding the righteous can certainly be applied to scholars too, especially the comment that the day of their death is as difficult for God as the day on which the tablets were destroyed. That comparison makes sense only if one sees the righteous person as a scholar replete with Torah, similar to the tablets on which the Decalogue was written. But other statements, primarily those pertaining to Noah, to Miriam, and, especially, to Job, show that Rashi drew a fundamental distinction between a scholar and a righteous person. The former excels in Torah; the latter, in good deeds.

## Community Leaders

### Virtues and Obligations

In his commentary on the Torah, Rashi cited rabbinic *midrashim* that emphasize the duties of community leaders and the ingratitude they are shown. Leaders must guide the nation 'calmly and tolerantly' (on Exod. 6: 13). He infers this from the words 'and gave [Moses and Aaron] a charge unto the children of Israel' (Exod. 6: 13, OJPS). After interpreting the passage in accordance with its plain meaning ('He commanded them with respect to the Israelites'), Rashi adds the aforesaid *midrash*. Because he does this type of thing consistently, using tendentious *midrashim* of this sort in other places too, it is fair to assume that his selection was deliberate and that this is how he viewed the role of the leader. For example, he interpreted the verse 'Give Joshua his instructions and imbue him with strength and courage' (Deut. 3: 28)—a statement made in anticipation of Joshua receiving the mantle of leadership—as referring to 'the effort and the burdens and the quarrels'. He thought this was the reality that could be expected by a fit leader, who had to be prepared for difficult tasks and ingratitude. He interpreted '[the seventy elders] shall share the burden of the people with you' (Num. 11: 17) in a similar vein: 'he imposed on them the condition that they assume the burden of My children, who are burdensome and insubordinate'. As if that were not enough, Rashi added, in accordance with *Sifrei* on Numbers, that Moses from the outset imposed on those seventy elders the condition that they be prepared to assist him in leading the community, 'even if they stone and shame you' (on Num. 11: 12). They must be ready to suffer all of this as part of their role. It is hard to attribute Rashi's selection of these *midrashim* to mere happenstance. The verses themselves offer no support for this interpretation, and I believe Rashi's choice of *midrashim* was tendentious, reflecting his goal of preaching to Jewish leaders in all generations.

It is not enough that the leader be ready to toil, suffer, and absorb insults and curses; he must always lead the nation to war and stand at its head. In interpreting

God's comment to Moses that Joshua 'shall go across at the head of this people' (Deut. 3: 28), Rashi writes, following *Sifrei*:

If he go across at their head, they shall acquire [the Land], but if not, they shall not acquire it. And so one finds that when [Joshua] sent some of the nation to [fight against] Ai, and he stayed behind, the men of Ai struck them down, etc.; and when he fell on his face [in prayer], He said to him 'Get thee up' [Jos. 7: 10]. But the written version of the text [*ketiv*] reads 'Arise, go'—you are standing in place and sending My sons to war; why are you [praying]? Did I not say to Moses your master that if [you] go across, they go across, but if not, they do not go across?

In other words, even though Joshua was engaged in prayer on behalf of the people, God chastised him. In time of war, the leader must be at the head of the army and nowhere else. Rashi comments to similar effect on the verse 'who shall go out before them' (Num. 27: 17):

Not in the manner of the kings of the other nations, who remain in their homes and send their soldiers off to war; rather, as I [Moses] did in going to war against Sihon and Og, as it is said, 'Do not fear him' [Num. 21: 34], and in the manner of Joshua, as it is said, 'Joshua went up to him and asked him, "Are you one of us or of our enemies?"' [Jos. 5: 13], etc. And so, too, of David it is said: 'For he went out and came in before them' [1 Sam. 18: 16, OJPS], he went out at their head and came in at their head.

Leaders are forbidden to relax or be angry. They must dedicate themselves on behalf of the people and share their sorrows (Rashi on Exod. 35: 27; 37: 1; on Num. 7: 1–2; 31: 21). Because leaders are forbidden to be angry, Rashi interpreted the verse 'And Moses was very wroth' (Num. 16: 15, OJPS; the object of Moses' wrath is Korah and his band) as an expression of sorrow rather than anger.[e]

Notwithstanding all the suffering and injustice, Rashi encourages worthy people to assume the mantle of office: '*Bring them* [Num. 11: 16]—Entice them with words [such as] "fortunate are you that you have been appointed to be officials over the children of God".' When God tells Moses to appoint Joshua his successor, he says, 'Take thee' (Num. 27: 18, OJPS), and Rashi again comments: 'Entice him with words: fortunate are you that you are privileged to lead the children of God.' Again, a few verses later: '*He took Joshua* [Num. 27: 22]—he enticed him with words, telling him the reward to be given to the leaders of Israel in the world to come.' In other words, the hard labours of the leaders of Israel will be rewarded. Their lot today is insults, sorrow, and toil, but in the world to come, they will receive their reward.

The reiteration of these motifs, the citation of *midrashim* most of which lack any grounding in the plain meaning of the verses, and the difficulties faced by community leaders in Rashi's time (to be discussed below) all support the premise that Rashi's interpretations incorporate a tendentious element, suited to the needs of the time.

---

[e] NJPS translates 'aggrieved', suggesting that its view of the plain meaning is closer to Rashi's than to that of OJPS.

# Moses as the Ideal Leader

Rashi devoted a lot of attention to the figure of Moses, far more than the Torah itself. He did so for two reasons: to justify Moses' actions and portray him as the ideal leader, but also to criticize the Israelites' ingratitude towards him. He selected rabbinic *midrashim* that served those purposes, sometimes adding comments of his own. Through these *midrashim*, he depicted Moses as a man who 'turned his eye and his heart' to Israel's suffering, and he justified, among other things, Moses' killing the Egyptian who had struck an Israelite, his relationship to his wife, Zipporah, and his attitude towards Korah and his band. Along with these *midrashim*, however, Rashi collected others that raise serious misgivings about Moses and describe the people's feelings of animosity towards him. It is easy to understand the inclusion of *midrashim* of the first sort, which express praise for Moses and his actions, for Moses was the man who received the Torah and transmitted it to Israel; who took them out of Egypt; and who, in his pleading at the time of God's anger, declared his willingness to give his life for Israel. The Torah itself emphasizes Moses' positive qualities, first among them his humility.[5] The *midrashim* of the second type are quite surprising, however. What led Rashi to disregard dozens of positive *midrashim* about Moses and choose several very harsh ones that describe the nation's animosity towards him? Let me offer one example. On the verse 'How can I bear unaided the trouble of you, and the burden, and the bickering' (Deut. 1: 12), Rashi writes:

If Moses went out [of his home] early, they would say: Why did the son of Amram see fit to go out? Perhaps he is not able to think clearly in his home. If he went out late, they would say: Why did the son of Amram see fit not to go out? What do you think: he is sitting and taking evil counsel and plotting against you.

In presenting this *midrash*, from *Sifrei*, Rashi uses literary devices to emphasize numerous negative features, beginning with the reference to 'the son of Amram' instead of 'Moses' and ending with the direct address of 'what do you think?' That Rashi chose to cite this *midrash*, in its original, hyperbolic wording, warrants explanation, for the biblical text itself provides no support for this reading. The verse 'How can I bear unaided the trouble of you, and the burden, and the bickering' simply describes the heavy yoke borne by a leader (trouble, burden, bickering), but the word 'burden', to which Rashi linked his comment, does not lend itself to this interpretation. Understanding the word in this way would appear to be at odds with

---

[5] Rashi, following the *midrash*, criticizes Moses for his angry responses to the Israelites' complaints, responses that a leader is not permitted to indulge in (see on Exod. 4: 6; 17: 5). He also criticizes Moses' appointment of Joshua to lead the army that goes to war against the Amalekites, but in the very same context he praises Moses for sitting on a stone during that battle while raising his arms to encourage the Israelite fighters: 'And he did not sit on a pillow or a cushion, for he said, "Israel are in distress; I, too, will be with them in their distress"' (on Exod. 17: 12).

Rashi's well-known declaration that he would cite only *midrashim* that are well suited to the text.

The rather shocking contrast between the depiction of Moses as the exemplary model of a dedicated leader and the scorn directed towards him by the Israelites—a contrast made even sharper in the *midrashim* Rashi selected—raises the possibility that Rashi made deliberate use of this motif, intending thereby to emphasize the difficulties that would face a Jewish leader, and the high degree of devotion that would be required of him, because of the factionalism and disputatiousness that have always marked the Jewish community. Rashi knew of this factionalism—and the toll it took on a leader—not only from the sources but also from his personal experience. The difficulties of leading the Jewish communities in northern France and Germany during the eleventh century provided him with plenty of real-life examples of the situations portrayed in Midrash. Even the sages Rashi thought of most highly, such as Rabbenu Gershom and Rabbi Simeon ben Isaac ben Abun, found it difficult to assert their authority over the community of Mainz. In one of the *seliḥot* he composed, Rabbi Simeon described the scorn and ridicule directed at him and the leadership generally at the time. The picture that emerges from the communities of northern France, particularly Rashi's community of Troyes, is even harsher, as I recounted in Chapter 1. It is not surprising that Rabbi Simeon compared his opponents to Korah and his band, who rose up against Moses.[6]

Rashi, who recognized both the magnitude of the difficulties faced by the leaders and the importance of their work for Jewish autonomy and for the very existence of the Jewish diaspora communities during the Middle Ages, set out to strengthen their hand. He believed that they were duty bound to act with humility and to work with all their might for the good of their flock but also that their work was sacred. He admonished them not to be disheartened by the objective difficulties they faced or by the ridicule and personal affronts directed at them, for that was Moses' lot too, and God will fully reward them in times to come.

I have no unambiguous proof for my position on this, but it is supported by Rashi's selection of the *midrashim* I mentioned in preference to others on the same biblical texts that appear in the sources. At one point, Rashi even offered Moses as the model for sound community leadership. The Torah records that before his death, Moses asked God to appoint a proper leader for the people. Rashi comments: 'This is to declare the praise of the righteous, who, [even] when they depart the world, set aside their personal needs and deal with the needs of the community' (on Num. 27: 15).

Notwithstanding the many difficulties that confront the leader, he is obligated, in Rashi's opinion, to have an understanding of the inner nature of each and every member of his community. On the verse 'Let the Lord, the God of the spirits of all flesh, set a man . . . who may go out before them' (Num. 27: 16–17, OJPS), Rashi

---

[6]  See Grossman, 'Offenders and Violent Men in Jewish Society in Early Ashkenaz' (Heb.).

writes: 'Said [Moses] before him: "Master of the Universe, the ideas of each and every individual are evident and known to you, and one does not resemble another. Appoint for them a leader who will accept each and every one in accord with his ideas."' In what follows, Joshua is described as 'a man in whom is spirit' (Num. 27: 18), and Rashi comments: 'As you asked, for he will be able to deal with the spirit of each and every one.' In other words, the leader must have profound psychological understanding. This interpretation is not consistent with the text, especially insofar as it treats 'a man in whom is spirit' as meaning a man able to understand the spirit of others. It is remote not only from the plain meaning of the text but also from the measure of 'fitness' (*ofan*) on which Rashi based his choice of *midrashim*. He nevertheless selected it because of the great importance and contemporary significance of the idea.

In considering this issue, we cannot lose sight of the fact that Rashi himself was a community leader. Given the harsh controversies he was called upon to resolve, he was well aware of the difficulties of leading a community. The principal challenges that confronted him involved peacemaking between the families that struggled for control of the local community and that competed with one another because of their differing economic interests. I have already discussed this in Chapter 2, in the sketch of his biography.

## Forced and Voluntary Converts from Judaism

A central dilemma that confronted Jewish sages and communities in eleventh-century Christian Europe was that of the attitude to be taken towards those Jews who converted to Christianity, either under compulsion (*anusim*) or voluntarily (*meshumadim*). The number of Jews who underwent conversion at the time is generally understated in the scholarly literature. Some abandoned Judaism because of socio-economic pressure and some because of the influence of Christian propaganda; and conversion, whether voluntary or compelled, was a problem the Jewish communities of the time had to deal with. Evidence of the powerful pressure exerted by Christian propaganda and of the concern about conversion appears in the Jewish–Christian polemical literature written in France at the end of the eleventh century and throughout the twelfth and in the Jewish biblical interpretations of the time.

Jewish society struggled with the question of how to treat people who had converted—a question having both halakhic and social implications. Should they be seen as non-Jews for all purposes, to the point of prohibiting consumption of their wine? Was a Jewish bill of divorce needed to free a convert's wife from the status of 'married woman', enabling her to remarry? Or was the husband's very act of conversion enough to sever the bond between him and his wife, since he was now a 'non-Jew', and a purported marriage between a Jew and a non-Jew lacks any halakhic recognition?

Another dilemma involved the treatment to be accorded the *anusim*, who had converted to Christianity under compulsion, and those who had converted voluntarily but later repented and returned to the Jewish fold. To understand Rashi's position on this important issue, it must be compared to the position taken by other great sages in Germany and France at the time, especially Rabbenu Gershom. The earliest surviving halakhic question from the Troyes community deals with this subject, and it was posed to Rabbenu Gershom. The immediacy of the issue in the Ashkenazi communities is evidenced by the fact that Rabbenu Gershom enacted remedial legislation specifically for the purpose of preventing affronts to those who had converted but then returned to Judaism:

One of [the group] then jumped up and mentioned to him that he had been sullied with the waters of apostasy. And another arose and said to the first: Be silent and do not mention that, for [a ban] has been decreed against doing so . . . And now it is known that Rabbenu Gershom so decreed, that anyone who mentions [the earlier apostasy of one who has returned] is to be banned in perpetuity.[7]

One who referred to another's former apostasy could be subjected to so harsh a punishment—permanent banning—only in a society in which mentioning an act of apostasy was both common and painful, causing injury not only to the former apostate but also to the honour of his family. The apostasy made reintegration of the returnee into the Jewish fold more difficult as a social matter and greatly impaired the marital prospects of the returnee's children. In his responsum, Rashi questioned whether Rabbenu Gershom had, in fact, imposed so harsh a ban, whether he 'altered the severity of other imprecations and barriers [to transgression] as practised in recent times, using the wording of an oath, and also whether he decreed that this shameful act not be mentioned to the returnee himself or also to his succeeding generations . . . thereby ruling more severely than existing practice'.[8] Rabbenu Gershom had two principal purposes: to make it easier for apostates (voluntary or compelled) to return to the Jewish fold and to avoid impugning their honour once they returned. This is evident also in his responsum regarding a *kohen* who had converted and then returned to Judaism. Rabbenu Gershom permitted him to participate in the priestly blessing of the congregation and to be called to the Torah as a *kohen*:

It is already written by his prophets: 'Turn back to Me and I will turn back to you' [Mal. 3: 7], and since he has returned, God has accepted him and assents to have His blessing conveyed by him. And so we have no proof from Scripture or from the Mishnah that he should be disqualified. Rather, there is support from Scripture and from the Mishnah [for the view that] he should not be disqualified . . . In addition, it turns out that [by disqualifying him] *you weaken the hands of penitents*. And were you to say he should not ascend

---

[7] *Taḥtsul*, §21.        [8] Ibid.

the platform [to bless the congregation], he might say 'woe to me for that shame, woe to me for that dishonour', and he would be deterred from repenting.[9]

But another responsum on this matter attributed to Rabbenu Gershom is entirely different: 'Rabbenu Gershom replied to the Troyes community [which had enquired about] the status of a *kohen* who had converted, and he replied to them that it is not proper for that *kohen* to ascend the platform [to bless the congregation] or to read first from the Torah, for he had committed an act of idolatry in the way that idolatry is practised.'[10] This directive by Rabbenu Gershom appears on the face of it to run counter to his position on converts noted above. But a closer examination of the responsum, including its various manuscript parallels, shows that the question sent to him from Troyes involved a *kohen* who had converted voluntarily rather than under compulsion, and that is why Rabbenu Gershom ruled strictly in his case. A *kohen* who had been compelled to convert and then repented, he believed, should be permitted to bless the congregation and be called to the Torah as a *kohen*, but one who had converted of his own will was disqualified in both respects, even after repenting and returning. This distinction drives home even more the harsh reality in which conversions were compelled, and the desire to help the victims of that reality to return is quite understandable. That this tragedy affected the family of Rabbenu Gershom himself, and perhaps that of his friend Rabbi Simeon ben Isaac, shows the harsh effects of persecutions at the time.

Other sages in Germany and France at the time took the same approach as Rabbenu Gershom, including Rabbi Joseph Tov Elem, Rabbi Judah Hakohen, and Rabbi Eliezer the Great, as did somewhat later sages, including Rabbi Simhah of Speyer. The Babylonian geonim and their followers, however, took a different course in their rulings. They treated apostates, including those who repented and returned to the Jewish fold, very severely. Maimonides, for example, expressly ruled as follows:

A *kohen* who worshipped stars [that is, idols], whether under compulsion or unintentionally, even if he repented, may never again raise his hands [to bless the congregation] . . . Similarly, a *kohen* who apostasized and became an idolator, even if he returned, may never again raise his hands.[11]

In their quite different rulings, Rashi and Maimonides rely on the same passage in the Talmud (*Men.* 109*a*).

If the early Ashkenazi sages struggled with this issue, those who followed them, in the late eleventh and early twelfth centuries, did so even more. By then, the number of *anusim* had become very large, thanks to the edicts of 1096. In his ruling, Rashi followed the path of Rabbenu Gershom and his students, urging that

---

[9] *Mahzor vitri*, 90, emphasis added.          [10] Gershom Me'or Hagolah, *Responsa*, §5, p. 60.
[11] Maimonides, *Mishneh torah*, 'Laws of the Priestly Blessing', 15: 3; id., *Hagahot maimuniyot* ad loc.; Tosafot, *Men.* 109*a*, *lo yeshameshu*.

the *anusim* be treated as Jews who had not sinned at all and that their honour not be impugned:

[The question related to] whether one must avoid the wine of *anusim* until they had stood by their repentance for a lengthy time and their repentance had become widely known and evident . . . And the rabbi [Rashi] replied: God forbid one avoid their wine and embarrass them, for his heart was not in any libation he had poured for idolatry . . . And when they took it upon themselves to return to fear our God, they are considered to be fit.[12]

Rashi's basic premise was that 'the hearts of all the *anusim* were directed towards Heaven'. And even one who had converted of his own free will but then repented should be brought back into the community and not demeaned.

Rashi found support for his approach in the Mishnah, which rules that priests who had served in the Temple of Onias in Egypt were not to serve in the Jerusalem Temple. That statement allows for the inference that they were disqualified only from service in the Temple but not from other priestly roles. Moreover, those priests are there characterized as 'disfigured', and a disfigured priest, though disqualified from service in the Temple, is permitted to bless the congregation (unless the disfigurement is in his hands, which are raised when the blessing is given). Rabbi Meir of Rothenberg (Maharam, *c.*1215–93) likewise took a lenient position and ruled that such a priest should not be encouraged to bless the congregation, but if he has nevertheless ascended the platform to give the blessing, he should go ahead and do so without interference.

But the approach to the matter taken by the sages of Germany and France was not based solely on their analysis of the talmudic passage. It followed also from their historical reality and from an inclination to make it easier for *anusim* to return to the Jewish fold.

What, though, of Rashi's attitude towards one who converted and did not return? Rashi considered five real-life issues related to the convert's status, issues that gained considerable attention in the Jewish communities of Germany and France of the time: marriage ('if one who converted voluntarily betroths a woman, the betrothal is valid'); levirate marriage and *ḥalitsah* (the ritual that obviates marriage to the levir and frees the woman to marry someone else) ('a woman whose levir is a convert requires *ḥalitsah* [before she can marry someone else]'); lending on interest ('it is forbidden to take interest from a Jew who has converted . . . and he is considered only to be a Jew who had converted and sinned'); inheritance ('his relatives are entitled to the assets and are fit to inherit, for we do not find that the rules of inheritance are inapplicable to the wicked'); and wine ('his wine is considered to be *yayin nesekh* [and therefore forbidden], for he is suspected of idolatry').

Rashi thus took a consistent approach to the halakhic status of Jews who had

---

[12]   Rashi, *Responsa* (Heb.), ed. Elfenbein, §168.

converted. His basic premise was that the act of conversion did not have the effect of divesting the convert of his status as a Jew. The contrary ruling with respect to *yayin nesekh* is clear and simple, for, as a practical matter, one who engages in idolatry may dedicate his wine to his god, and that is unaffected by the person's having previously been Jewish.

Rashi based his rulings on the first three issues listed above on the talmudic dictum that 'although he sinned, he is still a Jew'. In these decisions, Rashi's interpretation differed from that in the basic ruling in the Talmud (*San. 44a*). His ruling on the fourth issue, inheritance, is probably based in principle on that rule. Some saw his rationale here as an expression of moderation and tolerance; in fact, however, his ruling on levirate marriage entails stringency rather than leniency, as Jacob Katz has noted:

> Locating a levir who had left the community and motivating him to grant *ḥalitsah* to his Jewish sister-in-law must have posed vast difficulties, and Rashi was certainly not unaware of them ... He rejected the ruling of the geonim with respect to levirate marriage when the levir had converted, even though it is almost certain that those who argued against him must also have relied on the policy, applied in the context of withheld divorces, that leniency was called for so that the levir's sister-in-law could be married to another. If Rashi nevertheless rejected the geonic ruling, it is only because he wanted to avoid any breach in his principle that the convert was considered to have remained a Jew in all respects.[13]

## The Status of Women and their Place in Society and the Family

Rashi devoted considerable attention to protecting the honour and rights of women, probably more than any other medieval Jewish sage. To be sure, even he could not break completely free of the prejudices against women that were so widespread in ancient and medieval times, but his efforts on behalf of their rights are clear. The subject is a wide-ranging one, and confines of space require that I limit myself to some key points.[14]

### Woman as 'a seed given of God'

Malachi addresses those who have returned to Zion from exile and reproves them for having abandoned their wives and taken non-Jewish wives (Mal. 2: 10–16). The passage contains the one biblical appearance of the term *zera elohim* ('a seed given of God', OJPS; NJPS: 'godly folk'): 'Because the Lord hath been witness between

[13] Katz, *Halakhah and Kabbala* (Heb.), 261–2.
[14] The subject is an important one, for it sheds light not only on Rashi's view of the specific issue, but also on his confrontation with the reality surrounding him and on his innovativeness and daring. For a more detailed discussion, see Grossman, 'Rashi's Teachings Concerning Women' (Heb.).

thee and the wife of thy youth, against whom thou hast dealt treacherously, though she is thy companion and the wife of thy covenant. And not one hath done so who had exuberance of spirit! For what seeketh the one? *A seed given of God* [emphasis added]. Therefore take heed to your spirit and let none deal treacherously against the wife of his youth' (Mal. 2: 14–15, OJPS). Rashi comments:

*Not one hath done so*—The Holy One, Blessed Be He, [created both] Adam and Eve at the beginning . . . *For what seeketh the one?*—The first one in the couple [the husband] seeks to find some transgression with which he can accuse his wife, his partner, *she being a seed given of God* [emphasis added]. Why does he accuse her, disparaging her?! *Therefore take heed to your spirit and let none deal treacherously against the wife of his youth*—Your spirit.[15]

Rashi's brief comments here attest to the high esteem in which he held women and the institution of marriage. I am unaware of any other traditional, medieval Bible commentator who followed his lead and built so solid a structure. In Rashi's view, God created both Adam and Eve, and it follows that women, too, are 'a seed given of God', with all that implies for the image of woman. Many medieval Jewish sages interpreted this powerful expression as referring to the progeny that a man hopes for. The children are the 'seed given of God', but the attainment of that goal does not justify treachery to a Jewish wife and exchanging her for a non-Jewish wife. Rashi, however, proposes a different interpretation, according to which the woman herself is the 'seed given of God'. Most of the later printed editions emend the wording, changing 'she being a seed given of God' to 'he being a seed given of God': that is, it is the husband, who is the seed given of God.[f] But the manuscripts show that 'she' is the correct reading, as the context also suggests: 'he being . . .' would make no sense following 'his partner'. Had Rashi meant to refer to the man, he would have placed the idea of the 'seed given of God' earlier in the sentence, linking it to the 'the first one in the couple'. He did not explain the concept conveyed by regarding woman as 'a seed given of God', but the context makes plain that it provides a basis for demanding that the husband treat his wife decently and honourably.

It is also possible that Rashi's interpretation might be tied, albeit in a somewhat far-fetched way, to the Jewish–Christian polemic of the time, in which Rashi played an important part. But even if that is so, it does not at all change the foregoing view of Rashi's attitude towards women.

## Creation: Two Attached Bodies

The *midrashim* offer three interpretative views of the *tsela* ('rib') from which the first woman was formed. The first takes it to refer literally to one of Adam's ribs, as it would in modern Hebrew; the second takes it to mean a tail; and the third

---

[15] MS Vienna 23, fo. 199*b*, and also other reliable manuscripts; cf. Rashi, *Parshandata* (Heb.), i. III.

[f] The change in Hebrew is very slight, from *shehi* to *shehu*.

understands it to signify that man and woman were created as two complete bodies that were connected to each other and then separated.[16] Rashi selected the third option: '*He took one of his ribs* [Gen. 2: 21]—One of his sides, as in "the . . . side wall of the Tabernacle" [*tsela hamishkan*, Exod. 26: 20]. This is as they said: they were created with two faces.' Rashi relied here on the wording of Scripture, but it is hard to imagine that he was unaware of this interpretation's conceptual significance with respect to the place of woman in the cosmos, and it seems to be no mere happenstance that he included the reference to their being 'created with two faces'. In any case, his selection had considerable influence on the place of woman in the ideological world of Jewish sages. The biblical account of creation had given rise to many demeaning comments about women, but they fell by the way, one and all, in the wake of this interpretation.

Confirmation that Rashi's choice of interpretation was deliberate and not merely a matter of language can be found in his absolute disregard for the many negative comments about women that appear in the midrashic literature. Her creation from one of Adam's ribs was a central axis of *midrashim* that tended to disparage her. Especially noteworthy is the *midrash* in *Genesis Rabbah* that follows immediately after the one noted earlier about woman being created from one of Adam's sides: it tells of Satan being created together with the woman.[17] Rashi selected the first *midrash* and entirely disregarded the second.

Medieval Jewish commentators used the biblical account of creation and the *midrashim* disparaging women to bear out their predisposition to prove women's inferiority. Man was created first, his body from the earth and his spirit from God ('He blew into his nostrils the breath of life' (Gen. 2: 7)). Not only was woman created later than man, but she was created from his rib, demonstrating that she was secondary and man primary. Had there been true equality between man and woman, creation would have followed a different course. Moreover, woman is described from the outset as 'a fitting helper for [man]', again suggesting that he is primary and her role is merely supportive. This negative view is common to all three monotheistic religions. But these ideas do not appear in Rashi's interpretations of the creation narrative. He cites not one of the *midrashim* that disparage women, and it is hard to see that as mere coincidence.

## The Sin in the Garden of Eden

The woman's sin of seducing Adam in the Garden of Eden caused her to be viewed negatively by many religious thinkers, Jewish and Christian alike. Christians portrayed Eve as a sinful woman, a foil for the pure and innocent Mary. Jewish sages held Eve responsible for the expulsion of Adam from the Garden of Eden, for his

---

[16] See e.g. *Ber.* 61*a*; *Eruv.* 18*a*; *Genesis Rabbah* 8: 1 and Theodor-Albeck's additional notes, including *androgenos bera'am* (p. 55).          [17] *Genesis Rabbah* 17: 6.

need to labour to produce food for himself and his family, and even for his descent from the higher spiritual status he held before sinning. In the context of Eve's punishment, the Torah says: 'Yet your urge shall be for your husband and he shall rule over you' (Gen. 3: 16), a verse that many medieval Jewish sages interpreted as evidence of the husband's right to dominion over his wife. Some went so far as to portray the relationship as involving the wife's servitude to her husband. In Maimonides' view, 'he shall rule over you' is not descriptive but imperative: the husband is required to exercise dominion over the wife, and that is God's will on account of her sin in the Garden.[18] Radak comments: '*And he shall rule over you*—Commanding you however he wishes, *as a master to a slave*.'[19] So, too, Nahmanides: 'He keeps her as a maidservant . . . he should command her entirely at his will.'[20] Rabbenu Bahya ben Asher likewise used the word 'slave' in describing the relationship between Adam and Eve, concluding: 'and that she shall want to be enslaved to him . . . such that the husband will be her ruler and commander'.[21] In contrast to all of these, Rashi interpreted 'Yet your urge shall be for your husband and he shall rule over you' to refer to one thing only, namely, conjugal relations between husband and wife, and there alone does the husband have preferential status: '*Yet your urge shall be for your husband*—Regarding sexual relations, but you, nevertheless, do not have the insolence to ask it of him verbally. Rather, *he shall rule over you*—he initiates it, not you. *Your urge*—your desire' (on Gen. 3: 16).

Rashi's interpretation, which confines the woman's punishment for the sin in the Garden to one area only—the husband's greater rights with regard to conjugal relations—negated in all other respects the view of the spousal relationship as one of master and servant, entailing the husband's overall dominion over his wife. The husband's 'rule' ('and he shall rule over you') is expressed only in his initiation of conjugal relations. To be sure, this interpretation—like most of Rashi's interpretations of the Torah—can be grounded in the rabbinic literature, but that in no way weakens its force. He could have chosen any of the many other *midrashim* that were available to him, and the biblical text provides no basis for preferring the interpretation he proposed. Rashi well understood the great force implicit in the clause 'and he shall rule over you', and he set out to negate it in his commentary and to narrow greatly the scope of the husband's dominion over his wife.

## Marriage as Covenant

In one of his responsa Rashi voices his view of the nature of marriage and the force of the bond and commitment it forges between husband and wife. In his usual way, he does not outline his position systematically; rather, he integrates it into a halakhic analysis of the husband's duty to care for his wife even if she becomes ill

---

[18] Maimonides, *Guide of the Perplexed*, iii. 8 (trans. Pines, p. 431).
[19] See *Mikra'ot gedolot haketer*, Gen. 3: 16, emphasis added.
[20] Nahmanides on Gen. 3: 16.      [21] Rabbenu Bahya on Gen. 3: 16.

after the wedding. The question posed to Rashi involved a husband who wanted to divorce his wife without paying her the settlement specified in the marriage contract (*ketubah*) on the grounds that the wife, at the time of the wedding, had a sort of facial blemish that she had concealed with cosmetics. The husband argued that the marriage was invalid, essentially a fraudulent transaction. Evidence reaching Rashi contradicted the husband's claim regarding the blemish, and Rashi ruled against him. But he did not rest content with the halakhic analysis and ruling and used the opportunity to admonish the husband angrily:

And the man showed his actions to be wicked, showing himself not to be of the seed of Abraham our father, whose way was to act mercifully to all people, and certainly *to his own flesh with whom he had entered into a covenant* [that is, his wife]. For if he had tried to draw her near as he had tried to distance her, he would have been taken by her grace . . . and how fortunate he would have been had he been privileged to gain her and, through her, to acquire the life of the world to come . . . And it is harsh on the house of our Father in Heaven when one bears witness against the wife of his youth.[22]

Rashi's comments suggest he saw marriage as a 'covenant'—a term that, as used in the Bible, is religiously and emotionally fraught. God is the witness to the existence of this covenant and is even a participant in it. In Rashi's view, Judaism requires the husband not only to honour his wife but also to live with her in love and companionship, and one who treats his wife in this way enjoys great reward. Rashi evidently relies on the verse that describes a wife as 'thy companion and the wife of thy covenant' (Mal. 2: 14, OJPS) and her abandonment as an act of treachery.

Particularly interesting is Rashi's observation that if the husband had acted properly towards his wife he would have been privileged 'through her to acquire the life of the world to come'. This novel idea does not appear in Midrash, the Talmud, or the writings of other medieval Jewish commentators. The sages spoke of several questions that a man is asked after his death, but they do not include the manner in which he treated his wife.[23] Nor do the sources provide any precedent for Rashi's idea that a man acquires the life of the world to come by virtue of his good relationship with his wife. It appears that Rashi saw this as a result of the covenant entered into by the couple, in which, as noted, God, too, takes part. This idea that God's presence dwells with the couple and that God is the third partner in the marital covenant appears in rabbinic pronouncements.[24] Evidently, Rashi inferred from this covenant that each member of the couple who preserves the

[22] *Taḥtsul*, §40, emphasis added.

[23] 'When a man comes to be judged, he is asked: Were you faithful in your commercial dealings? Did you set aside specific times for Torah study? Did you procreate? Did you anticipate salvation? Did you wisely debate the law? Did you draw sound inferences?' (*Shab.* 31a).

[24] *Kid.* 30b; *Nid.* 31a. On the idea that marriage is a sort of covenant between the partners, see also, among others, Eliezer of Beaugency, *Commentary on Ezekiel and the Twelve Prophets* (Heb.), 215; Isaac b. Judah Abrabanel on Mal. 2: 14.

institution of marriage merits God's blessing, and anyone who violates it will be held to account for doing so.

## The Positive Image of Women in Rashi's Biblical and Talmudic Commentaries

As noted, Rashi generally avoided citing *midrashim* that disparaged women in his commentary on the Torah. He did, however, cite *midrashim* that spoke in praise of them. For the most part, these *midrashim* pertain to the Israelites' difficult experiences during their enslavement in Egypt and wanderings in the wilderness. It was the women who maintained the continuity of the Jewish nation in Egypt, making every effort to go on bearing children even though the Egyptians were throwing their sons into the Nile. They donated their most precious jewels to the construction of the Tabernacle, a contribution that God regarded as especially important:

*The mirrors of the women who performed tasks*—The Israelite women possessed mirrors that they looked into while adorning themselves, and they did not withhold even those from their donation to the Tabernacle; but Moses considered them repugnant, for they were used for [fostering] the evil impulse [that is, to make the women attractive to their husbands]. The Holy One, Blessed Be He, said to him: Accept them, for these are more beloved to Me that any others . . . and the laver was made from them, for it was used to bring peace between a man and his wife by providing the water to be drunk by a wife whose husband suspected her and brought her to be subject to the ordeal [of the *sotah* ritual]. (Rashi on Exod. 38: 8, following *Midrash tanḥuma*, 'Pekudei', 9)

The women's great love for the Land of Israel saved them from the sin of the spies and the ensuing punishment. In contrast to their husbands, they were privileged to enter the Land: '*But among these there was not a man* [Num. 26: 64, OJPS], and so on—But the women were not subject to the decree related to the spies, for they loved the Land.' Most of the Jewish women mentioned in Scripture are depicted in a favourable light in Rashi's commentaries: they include the four matriarchs (Sarah, Rebecca, Leah, and Rachel), Jochebed, Miriam, Achsah daughter of Caleb, Deborah, Hannah, Samson's mother, Abigail, Ruth, and Esther. That said, there remains some doubt about whether these and other positive accounts allow us to draw inferences about the place of women in Rashi's teachings. The doubt flows not simply from Rashi's profound attachment to Midrash, for his choice of *midrashim*, as often noted, tells much about his own approach, especially when the choice is not grounded in the wording of the biblical text. Rather, what we may have here is a characteristic feature of Rashi's biblical commentary in general, namely, his tendency to speak favourably of the ancestors of the Jewish people. It follows that one cannot necessarily draw, from his favourable comments about biblical women, any inferences specifically related to his attitude towards the Jewish woman. There are instances, however, in which such inferences may be drawn, and I will note only two examples.

The Bible recounts in a negative light the actions of Caleb's daughter Achsah, who induced her husband to ask her father to give her a desirable parcel of land ('she induced him [*vatesitehu*] to ask her father for some property' (OJPS: 'she persuaded him to ask of her father a field'), Jos. 15: 18; Judg. 1: 14). The term *hasatah* ('inducement', 'persuasion') in various forms appears in the Bible sixteen more times, each with pejorative overtones suggesting seduction. Nevertheless, Rashi chose to interpret the word in Achsah's case to refer simply to taking counsel, as in Targum Jonathan. That is, he understands it to mean that Achsah took counsel with her husband Othniel about the best way to ask her father for the field. It is hard to imagine that Rashi was unaware of this clear departure from the plain meaning of the verse. Evidently, his interpretation grew out of his desire to portray Achsah in a positive light.

The second example involves Hannah, whom Rashi consistently portrays more positively than he does Eli, the judge and leader. The favourable image is conveyed at least in part by the plain meaning of the text itself, and it appears in the Talmud (*Ber. 31b*). Rashi, however, systematically paints a positive picture of Hannah throughout her dialogue with Eli and goes beyond the Talmud in treating her more favourably than him. Like the Talmud, he places in Hannah's mouth words of admonition and perhaps even disdain for Eli ('you yourself have shown that the holy spirit does not dwell upon you to tell you that I am not drunk with wine'). But he goes further, attributing to her words of apology for the admonition ('because she had spoken harshly to him, she went back and apologized'). There is no support for this in the talmudic *midrashim*, and the interpretation even runs counter to Rashi's comment on the Talmud. It appears that Rashi wanted to describe Hannah as a perfect woman in all respects.

Rashi's tendency to depict Jewish women in a positive light is evident also in his commentary on the Talmud. Two examples will suffice. *Menaḥot* (110a) cites Rabbi Huna's homily on the verse 'Bring my sons from afar and my daughters from the end of the earth' (Isa. 43: 6): '*My sons*—These are the exiles in Babylonia, who are level-headed, like sons. *My daughters*—These are the exiles in other lands, who are not level-headed, like daughters.' The plain meaning is that sons are 'level-headed', that is, reasonable and deliberate in their actions and decisions; daughters, in contrast, are not so. That is the dichotomy implied by Rabbi Huna's words. Rashi slightly changes this interpretation to avoid saying that women are not at all level-headed; he writes that 'males are more level-headed than women' (on *Men.* 110a, *kevanim*).[25] Both sexes are level-headed, but males are more so. The difference between the sexes in this regard is merely quantitative.

The Talmud also cites the words of the tanna Rabbi Yosi: 'Throughout my life, I have never called my wife "my woman"; rather, I have called her "my house"' (*Shab.*

---

[25] See also Ahdut, 'Status of the Jewish Woman in Babylonia' (Heb.), 37.

118*b*; *Git.* 52*a*). Rashi interprets Rabbi Yosi's comment to mean that the woman is the primary component of the household. The *amora* Samuel, meanwhile, states that for reasons of modesty, 'one does not at all ask a woman about her health'; Rashi comments, 'but one may ask the master about the health of the mistress' (on *BM* 87*a*, *al yedei ba'alah*). The tosafists were stricter than Rashi, ruling that it was permitted only 'to ask where a particular woman was, but to ask even her husband about her health is forbidden'. Note particularly that Rashi refers to the wife as 'the mistress' (*hageveret*). In one of his responsa, he calls Bellette, the sister of Rabbi Isaac ben Menaham, 'the mistress'. Only one who regards the woman as the primary component of the household can call her 'the mistress'—a term used in the earlier literature to refer to wealthy women who kept maidservants in their households.[26] In a similar vein, Rashi's interpretations of allusive or obscure stories in the Talmud tend to depict women as dominant figures.

## Marital Relationships

At several points, Rashi considers the proper relationship between husband and wife. As noted, he saw marriage as a covenant whose signatories are not only the husband and wife but also God, a concept having various practical consequences. In the responsum discussed earlier, Rashi demanded that the husband treat his wife, whose face had become disfigured by previously unseen wounds, 'with mercy and honour'. He likewise regarded it as an act of treachery for a husband to divorce a wife simply because she had aged and he wanted to marry a younger woman, even if he sought various pretexts for the divorce (on Mal. 2: 12–16).

A husband who treats his wife with suspicion and lack of trust undermines the family unit. Suspicion in particular leads the wife to bear a grudge against her husband and to act treacherously towards him. The Talmud tells of Paphos ben Judah, whose suspicion that his wife might betray him led him to lock her in the house whenever he went out:

Rabbi Meir would say: just as there are various ways of relating to food, so are there various ways of relating to women. There is a sort of man who, if a fly falls into his cup, tosses it out and does not drink, and that is the quality of Paphos ben Judah, who would lock up his wife when he went out. There is also a sort of man who, if a fly falls into his cup, tosses out [the fly] and drinks, and that is the quality of the usual man, [whose wife] speaks with her brothers and her relatives and he allows her to do so. And there is a sort of man who,

---

[26] The Mishnah recounts a 'great remedial measure' adopted by the sages in the women's court of the Temple on the evening following the first day of the festival of Sukkot. Aviad Hacohen has called my attention to the fact that Rashi interprets the 'great remedial measure' in an original way, reflecting his attitude towards women. The purpose of the measure, he says, was not merely to separate men and women during that evening's festivities (the *simḥat beit hasho'evah*) but also to provide women with a better vantage point for viewing them. See Rashi on *Suk.* 51*b*, *vehikifuha gezuztera*: 'So that women could stand there during the *simḥat beit hasho'evah* and observe, and this was the great remedial measure that the Mishnah teaches was adopted every year.'

if a fly falls into his bowl, squeezes the fly and eats the food, and that is the quality of a wicked man, whose wife goes out with her head uncovered and weaves in the market place and has her garment open on both sides and bathes with people. (*Git.* 90*a*)

The Talmud depicts Paphos's action as odd but says nothing of the risks inherent in it. In contrast, Rashi comments that the action is not only odd but also risky: 'When he goes out of his house to the marketplace, he locks the door in her face so she cannot speak with anyone, and *this is unseemly* [emphasis added], for it causes enmity to come between them, as a result of which she betrays him.' In other words, Rashi believes 'locking the door' is much worse than merely useless: it actually undermines the relationships between husband and wife and leads to treachery against the husband. Trust and fairness in marital relations, not suspicion and excessive caution, are the guarantors of mutual faithfulness. Rashi's comment is not essential for an understanding of the talmudic passage and has no basis in the talmudic text. It is, rather, an interpretative supplement that reflects Rashi's personality. He included it, among other reasons, in order to teach people to avoid excessive strictness and suspicion, which are likely to undermine the peacefulness of the household.

## Levirate Marriage as Voluntary

The importance of love and mutual esteem in Rashi's thinking can be inferred from his ruling that a woman may not be compelled to enter into levirate marriage and that any objection she may raise against it will be accepted and result in the use of *ḥalitsah* instead. Levirate marriage, to be sure, is a venerable commandment, highly valued in the Bible, the Talmud, Midrash, and the writings of medieval Jewish sages. It was practised in Germany and France during the eleventh and twelfth centuries, and it was likewise accepted in Spain and other centres of Judaism at the time. A woman who declined a levirate marriage without good cause was regarded as rebellious and denied her marriage settlement. Rabbi Judah Hakohen, the student of Rabbenu Gershom and a leader of the Mainz community following his death, ruled, however, that a woman was not to be compelled to enter in marriage to her levir. He argued against pressing a woman into submission by delaying *ḥalitsah* and counselled that, if necessary, the levir be deceived into granting it, but he objected to compelling *ḥalitsah*, for it had to be the product of the levir's free will. He characterized that as not only his personal position but 'something I received from my teachers'.[27] His principal teacher was Rabbenu Gershom, and his comment thus seems to preserve evidence of the practice in Germany during the first half of the eleventh century.

Rashi believed that if the woman declined to enter into the levirate marriage, it was permitted to deceive the levir into granting *ḥalitsah* by promising him a sum

[27] Kupfer, *Responsa and Rulings* (Heb.), §§141, 143.

of money and then not delivering it. If the levir maintains his refusal to grant *ḥalitsah*, moreover, he is compelled to do so. This ruling on Rashi's part provided extremely valuable support to the woman. Contemporary sources show that in many cases, a levir would use a woman's desire for *ḥalitsah* as an opportunity to extort money and other valuables from her. Rashi's ruling explicitly differed from the accepted practice in eleventh-century Germany—something he well knew from his studies there—which would not compel an unwilling levir to grant *ḥalitsah* to a woman who wanted to decline the levirate marriage.

There was another significant step that Rashi took on behalf of women. The Talmud cites Rabbi Eleazar ben Azariah's statement that if a woman 'becomes subject to levirate marriage to one afflicted with boils, she is not bound [to be married to him]' (*Yev.* 39*b*). Rashi greatly expanded that ruling, determining in his commentary on the Talmud that 'afflicted with boils' is merely illustrative and that the category encompasses not only physical defects but 'any pretext she may offer for her words [of refusal]'. Let the excuse be what it may, but if a woman declines levirate marriage, the levir is to be compelled to grant *ḥalitsah* and pay her marriage settlement (Rashi on *Yev.* 39*b*, *tenan hatam*). Rashi's principal innovation here is his affirmation of two principles: a woman has the right to decline levirate marriage, and, in so doing, she has the right to compel the levir to grant her *ḥalitsah* and pay her marriage settlement.

Rashi's position was highly innovative, and it was not without reason that many medieval and modern Jewish sages came out against it. Rashi's own great-grandson, Rabbi Isaac ben Samuel of Dampierre (Ri, twelfth century), one of the greatest of the tosafists, disagreed with him. The plain meaning of the talmudic text is that the reference to boils as the factor warranting compulsory *ḥalitsah* was no mere coincidence. It is a harsh, possibly contagious, skin disease, of a sort likely to disrupt family life. It is difficult to see it as an illustration for any sort of claim that a woman might raise in order to justify her refusal to enter a levirate marriage and her desire to compel the levir to grant *ḥalitsah*.[28]

What impelled Rashi to rule this way? He was well aware of his ruling's great practical significance, and he linked it to the Talmud's words in order to ground it in the sources. Moreover, it was not his usual practice to issue halakhic rulings in his commentary on the Talmud. He did so primarily with respect to issues of contemporary importance that were the subject of disagreement among the sages.

Rabbi Levi ben Jacob ibn Habib (Ralbah, *c*.1483–1545), a Spanish exile and the greatest of the Jerusalem sages at the beginning of the sixteenth century, believed

---

[28] Maimonides inferred from this example that only physical flaws could provide warrant for a woman's refusal to accept levirate marriage (*Mishneh torah*, 'Laws of Levirate Marriage', 2: 14; see also *Ket.* 75*a*). R. Isaac b. Samuel raised a serious objection against Rashi's position, arguing that 'afflicted with boils' is one of the flaws warranting compulsory divorce, and the sages seem to have selected the example with this in mind. See Isaac of Vienna, *Or zarua*, pt. 1, §638.

that Rashi offered this ruling, which manifests a high degree of consideration for women, for personal reasons, inasmuch as he was the father only of girls: 'I have found no one who takes [Rashi's] side. Evidently the Rabbi, may his memory be for a blessing, as the father of daughters, took their side on all things, and perhaps for that reason he added a compulsory aspect to *ḥalitsah* in a way unlike any other decisor.'[29] But Jacob Katz has already noted that it is hard to attribute a ruling of this sort to a biographical detail of Rashi's private life. In his view, with which I agree, it was the improved standing of women in the Ashkenazi communities of that time that brought about the ruling. I believe, however, that the ruling must be viewed from a broader perspective.

The sources show the harsh lot faced by women in Ashkenaz who became widowed and subject to levirate marriage. Attaining *ḥalitsah* entailed numerous difficulties, including extortionate demands. To make matters worse, the weak communal leadership in tenth- and eleventh-century Germany and France was reluctant to assert their authority over recalcitrant levirs. The latter declined to heed the community's rulings and dragged out the *ḥalitsah* process for years in order to extort additional monies from the widows. Rashi was well aware of this situation and felt compelled to help the widows. He therefore ruled that any pretext they might offer for declining levirate marriage would justify compelling *ḥalitsah* and requiring full payment of the marriage settlement specified in the *ketubah*.

### Attitude towards Divorce

Throughout the mishnaic, talmudic, and medieval periods, Jewish sages were divided in their view of divorce. Was it a fundamentally improper action, to be taken only in cases of adultery or other particularly obnoxious conduct (*ervah*), or was it a step that might be taken in any situation in which relationships between the spouses go awry?[30] Deuteronomy 24: 1 reads: '[If] a man takes a wife and possesses her, [and] she fails to please him because he finds something obnoxious [*ervat davar*] about her, and he writes her a bill of divorcement, hands it to her, and sends her away from his house.' In his commentary, Rashi cites *midrashim* from *Sifrei* and the Talmud (*Git.* 90*b*) that harshly disparage the divorced woman in whom 'something obnoxious' is found, portraying her as a wicked woman who ought to be divorced; if her husband fails to do so, he is destined to despise her. But in his comments on Malachi, Rashi describes at length the transgression of those who returned to Zion following Cyrus's declaration, who took foreign wives in addition to their devoted Jewish wives whose external appearance had suffered as a result of their having endured the yoke of exile. He speaks with great emotion of the exploitation and treacherous treatment of women: '*And him that covers his garment with violence* [Mal. 2: 16]—Is it at all proper that you spread your garment over

---

[29] Levi b. Habib, *Responsa* (Heb.), §36.
[30] On this difference of opinion, see Grossman, *Pious and Rebellious*, 232–9.

her to maintain her as your wife, but violence is spread over the garment, for in your heart, there is hatred for her and you constantly mock and distress her?' That said, he concludes by citing the opinion of the sages in *Gitin* 90*a–b*, that a husband who hates his wife ought to divorce her. None of this, however, tells us of Rashi's position on divorce in principle, which he regarded, except in cases of 'something obnoxious', as a negative act.

As noted, Rashi expressed considerable anger towards a husband who wanted to divorce his wife on the grounds of facial wounds. He described such a man as one 'who is not of the seed of Abraham our father', one who breaches a covenant entered into by the spouses at their wedding. Divorce resulting from a husband's negative attitude towards his wife partakes of a transgression against God ('and it is harsh on the house of our Father in Heaven'[31]). The uncharacteristically severe way in which Rashi refers to the husband demonstrates not only his angry response to the case but also his fundamental attitude towards divorce. Marriage is a covenant, and the husband therefore may not breach it without some persuasive reason. The idea of marriage as a covenant, with all the significance attached to the concept of covenant in the Bible, is a pillar of Rashi's thought.

At the same time, Rashi showed that he understood the position of women who did not want to continue to live with their husbands and therefore sought a divorce. He accepted the remedial decree instituted by the Babylonian geonim in 651 CE, which determined that a husband should be compelled to issue a divorce to a wife who requests it. In his view, however, the wife in such a case is not entitled to receive her marriage settlement.[32] This was an issue on which twelfth-century Jewish sages differed. The most prominent and renowned generally opposed maintaining the geonic ruling that made it possible for a woman to compel her husband to issue a divorce.

## Women and the Commandments

The sages of Rashi's time struggled mightily with the question of whether a woman could recite a blessing over the performance of a 'time-bound positive commandment'. The Talmud rules that women are exempt from 'all time-bound positive commandments' (*Ber.* 20*b*); that is, commandments associated with set times during the course of the day or the year. The rule excluded women from the performance of many positive commandments and, as a practical matter, removed them from the circle of those who were subject to the commandments that gave Jewish religious life its flavour. The commandments at issue included donning phylacteries, reciting the Shema morning and evening, dwelling in the sukkah, and hearing

---

[31]  *Taḥtsul*, §40.

[32]  That is the implication of his comment on *Ket.* 63*b*, *la kaifinan lah* ('rather, he gives her a bill of divorce, and she leaves the marriage without her marriage settlement'); see also Meir of Rothenburg, *Responsa* (Heb.), ed. Rabinowitz, §946; ed. Bloch, 135*a*.

the sound of the *shofar*. Another rule, which forbade women to read publicly from the Torah lest their doing so be an affront to the dignity of the community (*Meg.* 23*a*), had the effect of distancing women from an important component of religious activity in the synagogue. One who believes in the sanctity of the Torah but is not permitted to recite a blessing over it or to read from it may feel herself to be cut off from one of the most emotionally charged elements of sacred service. Accordingly, Jewish women in Germany struggled for the right not only to fulfil these commandments voluntarily, but also to recite a blessing over them—even though there was a serious halakhic concern that such a blessing would be 'wasted', for it would be recited in accordance with a commandment a woman was not obligated to fulfil.

At some point after 1050, Rabbi Isaac Halevi—Rashi's teacher and the head of the yeshiva in Worms—ruled that women should be permitted to recite these blessings:

Rabbi Isaac Halevi ruled that we do not prevent women from reciting a blessing over *lulav* and sukkah . . . If she wants to submit to the yoke of the commandment, she is free to do so, and we do not protest her action . . . And since she is fulfilling the commandment, it is not possible [to do so] without a blessing.[33]

Rashi's second teacher, Rabbi Isaac ben Judah, the head of the yeshiva in Mainz at the time, ruled similarly. But Rashi, following the tradition of the Babylonian Talmud (as he usually did), forbade it.

The sages' numerous struggles with this issue at the end of eleventh century and the beginning of the twelfth show that there was no single early and clear tradition on it. They therefore relied not on precedents set by earlier rabbis but on their own understanding of the relevant talmudic passages. Does Rashi's opposition allow us to infer from it anything about his position in principle regarding the place of women in fulfilling the commandments? That is doubtful. Certainly, he was not prepared to allow a woman to recite the blessing associated with performance of a commandment she was not obligated to fulfil, as two of his pre-eminent teachers had ruled she might, but it is almost certain that he did not do so out of any fundamental concept regarding the place of women in fulfilment of the commandments. More likely, he did so because of his basic practice of ruling in accordance with the Babylonian Talmud and of displacing on its account even ancient practices long accepted in Ashkenaz. He took this approach with respect to other matters, and it is fair to assume that he did likewise here.

The account of Rabbi Eliezer ben Nathan, who lived and worked in Mainz during the first half of the twelfth century, suggests that it was the women in Ashkenaz who took the initiative and began to recite blessings over time-bound positive commandments. The sages acquiesced in their wishes and actions and sought to come up with a halakhic grounding for them. Rabbenu Tam's comments

[33] *Maḥzor vitri*, 413–14 and parallels.

likewise imply that he saw this as a custom that developed in Ashkenaz, which he then decided to accept and maintain: 'And Rabbenu Tam likewise explained that women recite a blessing over time-bound positive commandments, for it was their custom to perform and fulfil them.'[34]

This ruling is inconsistent with the practice in the talmudic period and at odds with the view of the Babylonian geonim and the early Spanish sages. Maimonides, too, took a different view: 'Women and slaves who want to wrap themselves in a fringed garment do so without a blessing. And so, too, regarding the other commandments from which women are exempt. If they want to perform them without reciting a blessing, they are not stopped.'[35] The ruling has its source in the basic principle affirmed by the Babylonian geonim and early Spanish sages that 'one who recites a blessing that is unnecessary takes the name of God in vain; and it is as if he is swearing falsely and it is forbidden to respond to him by saying "Amen".'[36] A blessing recited by a woman is in the category of 'a blessing that is unnecessary', and the principle is thus invoked. The ruling follows from the discussion in the Babylonian Talmud, and not without reason did Rashi forbid the blessing, following his usual practice of deferring to the Babylonian Talmud even if it ran contrary to local custom. Nor is it happenstance that the Spanish sages, who likewise assigned priority to the Babylonian Talmud, believed that women should not be permitted to recite a blessing over a time-bound positive commandment.

It follows from the foregoing that this issue, notwithstanding its great importance for a woman's place in society and for her self-image, in no way implies that Rashi devalued either the intellectual skills of women or the seriousness of their intentions and feelings with respect to fulfilling the commandments. His position was determined not by the personality or education of women but only by the talmudic ruling. Rashi occasionally deviated from the conclusion implied by the Babylonian Talmud—especially in the matter of levirate marriage, discussed earlier—but he did not do so routinely.

More problematic is Rashi's ruling that one may not rely on a woman's pre-Passover search for and removal of leaven and that a woman may attest only that the head of the household has performed the search. The Babylonian Talmud states explicitly that one may rely on a woman's search, since the commandment is a matter of rabbinic, not biblical, law: 'All are trustworthy with respect to removal of leaven—even women, even slaves, even minors' (*Pes. 4a–b*).

What does the term 'trustworthy' mean? Can one rely on a search conducted by a woman, or may one only accept her testimony that the search was carried out by a man? Early and later sages struggled with the question. Rashi explained that one may not rely on a woman's conduct of the search but only on her 'testimony on

[34] Mordecai ben Hillel Hakohen [the *Mordecai*] on BT *Shab.*, §286; see also Tosafot on *Eruv. 96a*, *dilma*.

[35] Maimonides, *Mishneh torah*, 'Laws of Fringes', 3: 9.          [36] Ibid., 'Laws of Blessings', 1: 15.

the fourteenth [of Nisan] that its owners had searched the previous evening' (on *Pes.* 4*a*, *ne'emanin al bi'ur ḥamets*). In contrast, Maimonides permitted a woman to search for leaven herself: 'All are fit to search, even women, slaves, and minors.'[37] The dispute is attributable not solely to the vagueness of the Babylonian Talmud's wording, but also to the Jerusalem Talmud's statement on the matter, which has important implications for the image of women in general:

All are trustworthy with respect to removal of leaven, even women and even slaves. Rabbi Jeremiah in the name of Rabbi Zeira: The wording here is not 'even women'; women themselves are reliable because they are painstaking [*atsilot*] and they examine each and every little bit. (JT *Pes.* 1: 5; 27*b*)

Rashi occasionally made use of the Jerusalem Talmud. He may have been familiar with the foregoing passage but may have interpreted *atsilot* to mean 'lazy' (*atseilot*) and therefore ruled that they could not carry on the search of leaven on their own.[g] More likely, however, his interpretation resulted from the wording of the Babylonian Talmud and the context in which it appears. With regard to the fitness of women to slaughter animals for food, the passage reads: 'All may slaughter and their slaughtering is fit' (Mishnah *Ḥul.* 1: 1); the formulation here, however, is 'all are trustworthy with respect to removal of leaven', not all 'may remove' or 'are fit' to remove. Rashi therefore interpreted the statement to mean that a woman is trustworthy with respect to her statement that others searched, but not with respect to her own searching. In the talmudic passage, moreover, the words are cited as evidence that the search for leaven was properly performed.

## A Negative Perception: The Matter of *Tseniut*[h]

In one central area of Rashi's teachings—that of *tseniut*—women are depicted in a negative manner. Here, Rashi accepted the rabbinic position, frequently reiterated in the Talmud and *midrashim*, that 'women's minds are frivolous' and they are easily seduced; accordingly, their husbands and society at large must strictly enforce their *tseniut*. The idea appears in Rashi's commentaries on both the Bible and the Talmud. Not by happenstance did Rashi choose to cite in his commentary on the Torah the midrashic comments in *Midrash tanḥuma* ('Vayishlaḥ', 6) that disparage Dinah, the daughter of Leah, who went out 'to visit the daughters of the land' (Gen. 34: 1): it was her going out that, in effect, resulted in her being raped.

---

[37] Ibid., 'Laws of Leavened Bread and Matzah', 2: 17.

[g] The translation of JT *Pes.* 1: 5 understands the adjective in a positive sense, as required by the context.

[h] *Tseniut* is often translated as 'modesty', but it connotes more than that English word might suggest, encompassing a range of halakhot and customs related to conduct, attire, and interaction between men and women. The full range of meanings is not readily represented by any one English word; accordingly, the transliterated Hebrew word will be used.

Rashi took a similar position in interpreting a verse in Ecclesiastes: '*One man among a thousand have I found; but a woman among all those have I not found* [Eccles. 7: 28, OJPS]—My soul sought a fit woman, but I did not find one, for all they all are of frivolous mind.' Accordingly, he believed, it was necessarily to enforce women's *tseniut* strictly. Later, Rashi cites the *midrash* declaring that in the wake of the first woman, 'harm came into the world' (on Eccles. 7: 29). His comment is based on a *midrash* (*Ecclesiastes Rabbah* 7: 49), as he himself there acknowledges, but he selected or disregarded *midrashim* insofar as they were suited to his agenda. Nor may it be argued that this interpretation was selected because it accords with the verse's plain meaning, for Rashi often disregarded that plain meaning. (The phenomenon is especially prominent in his commentary on the Psalms, where he often carried on his polemic against Christological interpretation of Scripture in particular and against Christianity in general, as described in Chapter 5.) And it is a fact that other medieval sages softened the harsh import for women of 'a woman among all those have I not found'.

Similarly, in interpreting 'You shall not tolerate a sorceress' (Exod. 22: 17), Rashi cites the rabbinic statement that the Torah refers expressly to a woman, even though the same law applies to a male sorcerer, because sorcery is more common among women.

The great value Rashi assigned to *tseniut* in general is evident in his comments on Proverbs 31: 27. It is said of the 'capable wife' that 'she oversees the activities of her household'. Rashi interprets this to mean that the woman makes sure to educate the members of her household regarding truth and *tseniut*.

That said, one should not overstate the concept of *tseniut* in Rashi's teachings or compare it to the limitations imposed on women, in the name of *tseniut*, by some Jewish sages in Muslim lands. The Muslim tradition insisted strongly on the *tseniut* of women and limited their freedom of movement. It is against that background that one must understand the statements by some Jewish sages in Muslim lands who praise women who confine themselves to their homes: 'A husband should prevent his wife from [going out often] and should not allow her to go out more than once a month or several times a month, as may be needed, for there is nothing more beautiful for a woman than to remain in the recesses of her home.'[38]

Rashi's understanding was very different. Notwithstanding his great concern about the *tseniut* of women and his worries about their 'frivolity of mind', he imposes no limitations on their movements. The questions posed to him tell of women who maintained strong personal ties to feudal officials and visited their homes, and Rashi accepted that as routine and understandable. One questioner even mentioned that his mother-in-law was friendly with the officials in her area.[39]

Of particular interest is Rashi's interpretation of the incident of Beruriah

---

[38] Maimonides, *Mishneh torah*, 'Laws of Marriage', 13: 11.      [39] *Taḥtsul*, §30.

referred to in the Babylonian Talmud (*AZ* 18*b*). The Talmud first recounts that Rabbi Meir, Beruriah's husband, used guile to redeem her sister, who had been imprisoned in a brothel. Fearful of how the Romans would react, he was compelled to flee from the Land of Israel to Babylonia. It then offers another explanation for his fleeing, referred to as 'the incident of Beruriah', but it does not even hint at what that incident might have been. Rashi explains:

She once mocked the rabbinic statement that 'women are frivolous of mind'. [Rabbi Meir] said to her: By your life, you will end up acknowledging their statement. He directed one of his students to test her [by inducing her] to sin. He pleaded with her for many days, until she acceded. But when she found him out, she strangled herself. And Rabbi Meir fled in shame.

This comment poses several significant difficulties that are beyond the scope of this study. The North African Rabbi Nissim ben Jacob of Kairouan had a different interpretative tradition,[40] and I believe, consistent with that tradition, that Rabbi Meir fled to Babylonia together with his wife because of his concern that the Romans would harm her just as they had harmed all the members of her family. But the central issue here is not the historical truth about why Rabbi Meir fled to Babylonia; it is, rather, Rashi's attitude towards women as expressed in this interpretation. The story he reports seems to have reached him through some interpretative tradition, albeit one that is unknown. What is absolutely clear, however, is that Rashi did not invent it himself. Our inability to uncover the source of Rashi's interpretation or to determine what of his own he may have added to it makes it very difficult to use this interpretation to characterize his personality, and that is true of other stories he includes in his commentary when the Talmud itself contains only an allusion to the episode, as we shall see below. But the fact that Rashi cites the story without attributing it to his teachers or to some literary source available to him, and his account of how Beruriah's mockery of the rabbinic statement that 'women are of frivolous mind' led to her downfall, support the premise that Rashi in fact agreed with the rabbinic statement.

It may be that the author of the legend from which Rashi drew his interpretation opposed the study of Torah by women and therefore selected this strange story, but I have my doubts about that. It seems more likely that the purpose of the narrator was to show how hard it was for a woman, even one who excelled in Torah and action, to withstand the seductions of a man. Beruriah sinned even though she had studied Torah, but not on account of the study itself.

In *Maḥzor vitri*, Rashi's students cited Rashi's ruling regarding prayer in the synagogue by a menstruating woman. The Talmud contains no hint of a prohibition

[40] In his book *Ḥibur yafeh mehayeshu'ah*, R. Nissim b. Jacob tells how Beruriah and R. Meir fled to Babylonia together because of their fear of the Roman authorities. It follows that the story of her suicide lacks any basis at all.

against a menstruating woman praying in the synagogue, but some circles, following *Baraita denidah*,[i] began to act more strictly in that regard, even forbidding a menstruant from entering the synagogue. Some saw it as a genuine prohibition, given the concept of the synagogue as a holy place similar to the ancient Temple; others saw it as a praiseworthy purity custom; still others entirely denied the existence of any such ban.[41] Rashi's words on the subject are not unambiguous:

There are women who refrain from entering the synagogue during their menstrual days, but they need not do so. For what is the reason for doing so? If it is because they believe the synagogue is like the Temple ... but if it is not like the Temple, they can enter ... You have learned that it is not like the Temple, and they can enter. Nevertheless, it is in any event a place of purity, and they are acting properly [by not entering].[42]

This statement is internally contradictory. Rashi rejects entirely their not entering the synagogue, yet he ends by praising their action. It may be that the conclusion is in the nature of advice to go beyond the letter of the law, that is, to act more strictly than the law requires in order to maintain a higher level of purity. Another possibility is that the conclusion does not embody Rashi's own words and was added by his student and secretary Rabbi Shemayah, who committed Rashi's halakhot to writing.

## A Father's Feelings for his Sons and Daughters

In his comments on *Shabat*, Rashi seems, on the face it, to manifest a negative attitude towards women. Sons are described as more beloved to their fathers than daughters. According to Mishnah *Shabat* (6: 9), on the sabbath, 'sons may go out into the public domain carrying knots'. The *Gemara* asks why the passage refers specifically to sons and not to daughters and explains that the reference is to knots that are tied for medical reasons: 'a son, who longs for his father, takes a strap from a right sandal and ties it on his left one'. Rashi there explains that the Talmud is speaking of a medicinal contrivance, for a son 'longs for his father and cannot part from him. But this medicinal contrivance is not pertinent to females, for the father does not show them the affection at the outset that would cause them to long for him' (on *Shab.* 66*b*). In other words, the great affection shown by the father to his sons when they are children results in their being so bound to him that there is reason for concern about their health when they part. The knots are a contrivance to prevent that. The concern does not apply in the case of daughters, for the father

---

[41] See Dinary, 'Desecration by a Menstruant' (Heb.); id., 'The Impurity Customs of the Menstruant Woman' (Heb.); Ta-Shma, 'Exclusion of a Menstruant in Early Ashkenaz' (Heb.).

[42] *Maḥzor vitri*, 606.

[i] *Baraita denidah* is a work on ritual purity whose provenance and dating are a matter of debate; it may have been known to the geonim. It adopts an uncompromisingly strict position on matters of ritual purity and imposes various limitations on the activities of menstruating women.

from the outset does not show them enough affection to generate such powerful bonds.

Rashi—himself the father of daughters—seems to be saying that his feelings of affection for them were less than they would have been had they been sons. But the preference for sons is inherent in the structure of the talmudic passage. Whatever its meaning, this fundamental distinction, whose source is in the Talmud, cannot be denied, even if the 'knots' are interpreted in some other way.

## The Perception of Women in the Stories in Rashi's Commentary on the Talmud

Rashi's commentary on the Talmud cites numerous stories, some of them dealing with talmudic allusions to obscure episodes. About half of these stories involve women. Rashi interpreted the stories and described the incidents alluded to.

Louis Landau examined the stories appearing in Rashi's commentary, focusing primarily on their literary character. He identified two prominent features of the stories that deal with women: (1) the women in Rashi's commentaries are dominant and active and (2) most are described in a negative light.[43]

Landau credibly assumed that the account of women as dominant was influenced by the socio-economic realities of the time. But it must be noted that the same picture appears in a book written in North Africa a generation before Rashi's commentary—*Ḥibur yafeh mehayeshu'ah* by Rabbi Nissim ben Jacob. There, too, women figure quite prominently, playing active and dominant roles in most of the stories and not appearing merely as 'someone's wife'. That is the case, too, in *Megilat aḥima'ats*, written in Italy in 1054, and in the stories appearing in the comments on *Ta'anit* and *Nedarim* attributed to Rashi, though not actually written by him. In Jewish and non-Jewish society alike, folk stories typically assigned a prominent place to women, because of their great importance in family and social life, even if their place is concealed somewhat for reasons of modesty in various literary sagas written by men. In any case, I find it hard to attribute the prominence Rashi assigns to women and his portrayal of them as active players to the fact that he was the father only of daughters.

Even less certain is the meaning of the apparent negativity identified by Landau in Rashi's depictions of women. It is unlikely that the negative accounts of many of the women mentioned in the stories in Rashi's commentaries say anything about the place of women in his teachings. These are not Rashi's original interpretations; they are, rather, interpretative traditions that he received from his teachers. Moreover, he expressly states in some cases that the stories are taken from *Sefer hashe'iltot* or from a 'legend' available to him. Landau himself believed that the stories were earlier traditions that Rashi inherited. It follows that only the formulation of the stories, not their substance, can tell us anything about Rashi's personality,

[43] Landau, 'Rashi's Stories in the Babylonian Talmud' (Heb.).

and there are doubts even about the formulations. As long as we lack the texts of the sources on which Rashi drew, we cannot compare Rashi's versions of the stories to them and ascertain what Rashi added on his own and what he changed.

Even more, most of the obscure talmudic stories related to women appear in contexts requiring a negative interpretation of the women's actions. Let me offer just one example, the story of Yohani bat Retivi.

The Talmud lists hypocritical women who present a righteous appearance though acting wickedly but challenges the significance of the list by noting that there are women whose actions have made them exemplars of piety and observance of commandments. It goes on to explain that the remarks about wicked women (as below) refer only to women like Yohani bat Retivi, but it tells us nothing about her nature. Rashi describes her as a sorceress who posed as a righteous woman but used her sorcery to impair the ability of women to bear children. Landau includes this story in his list of those that cast a 'negative light' on the image of the woman. But given the course of the talmudic discussion, was it at all possible for Rashi to present her in a 'positive light'? The similar interpretation offered by Rabbi Nissim ben Jacob in *Ḥibur yafeh mehayeshu'ah* shows that we are dealing here with an early interpretative tradition that reached both writers. If we remove from Landau's list the interpretations wrongly attributed to Rashi and those in which the talmudic passage allows for no alternative to a negative depiction of the woman, we are left with no basis for accusing Rashi of depicting women negatively in his interpretations of the talmudic stories. In my view, this literary form—interpretations of obscure talmudic stories—contains nothing that can shed light on Rashi's attitude towards women or their place in society.

# PART IV

# POSTSCRIPT

# Between Innovation and Conservatism

T HIS BOOK MIGHT have been entitled *Rashi: Revolutionary or Conservative?* In some ways, however, a better title would have been *Rashi: Between Innovation and Conservatism*. The title would reflect the fact that in the circumstances of Rashi's time, some of his innovations can be regarded as effecting a pedagogical or cultural revolution. In this final chapter I want to sum up, in highly abbreviated form and sometimes only allusively, the innovations that Rashi introduced. They have been referred to throughout this book, but by collecting them in one place we can use them to shed more light on Rashi's personality from this important perspective and on the reasons for his innovativeness. More than 150 years ago, Simon Bloch characterized Rashi as an innovator, but his observations did not receive the attention they deserved—either because he wrote in flowery Hebrew or because he was speaking of the innovation entailed in the very idea of writing commentaries that adhered to the plain meaning:

Therefore only an extremely exalted man, who does not restrain his spirit from breaking new paths with his mind, not always following those who have come before him since time immemorial . . . he is a sage and a daring man who dwells in the higher realms and is raised above the few exalted ones in each generation. These are men of valour, of priceless worth, who themselves forged a new mind and new spirit within God's Torah. Two [such men] have been born to us by our nation, they being Rashi and Rabbi Abraham ibn Ezra, of blessed memory . . . The former was entirely unprecedented in his energetically brief interpretations and explanations, which used only a very few words to interpret for us in accord with the plain meaning and grammatical usage.[1]

To declare Rashi an innovator in his talmudic commentary is a bit of an overstatement, for Rabbenu Gershom in Germany and Rabbi Hananel ben Hushiel in Kairouan, North Africa, preceded him. Even if their commentaries were not of the same quality as Rashi's, we cannot say that Rashi introduced substantive innovations. There is, however, a degree of innovation in the attention he devoted to interpreting the Bible and liturgical poems, in the breadth of his interpretative

---

[1] Zunz and Bloch, *Life of Rashi* (Heb.), introduction, 3*a*.

effort, and in the very transformation of the interpretative genre into the central intellectual activity within the Jewish society of his time—at first in France and Germany and ultimately beyond them. The Babylonian geonim made only limited use of the interpretative genre, primarily in the late tenth and early eleventh centuries. For hundreds of years, the Babylonian geonim avoided writing commentaries on the Bible or the Talmud, and I have elsewhere considered in detail the reasons for that reluctance.[2] Rashi's abundant and comprehensive use of this literary genre, encompassing various sorts of ancient sources, shows his desire to bring those sources not only to the world of the scholar but also to the world of the 'average', 'educated' Jew. I have described this activity as flowing from a sense of mission and a democratic world-view, in contrast to the conservative, somewhat elitist, attitude that characterized the yeshivas of the Babylonian geonim. Once the sources are interpreted, they can be independently approached by anyone wanting to do so. The Babylonian geonim were very much afraid that this sort of approach would result in erroneous interpretations, which could be avoided only by studying with a teacher. It also is possible that they were trying to maintain their hegemony.

In calling Rashi a revolutionary and an innovator, however, I am referring to various important aspects of his career that were not considered by Zunz, Bloch, or others. His four most important innovations are in the area of education:

**1. Openness and willingness to accept Torah teachings from all the Jewish centres in Europe and the Muslim lands, including Babylonia, the Land of Israel, Italy, Germany, Provence, and Spain.** I refer here to interpretative, grammatical, and halakhic traditions alike. The degree of openness becomes evident when it is compared to the suspicion and exclusivity that prevailed at the time in Spain and Germany, each centre taking a stand against the traditions of the others. I considered the point in Chapter 3, when I discussed Rashi's *beit midrash*. Let me illustrate it here with the correspondence between the Ashkenazi sages and their Spanish counterparts regarding the wording of the marriage ceremony.[3] The dispute among the various sages related to how the conclusion of the betrothal blessing should be formulated, and the letters are estimated to date from the last quarter of the eleventh century. At the time, fierce debates raged in Germany and, to a lesser degree, in northern France, regarding the force of various customs. The divergence of customs within the Ashkenazi communities during the second half of the eleventh century was particularly great, primarily because the Jews living there had come from various places. It was there and then that the first book directed

---

[2] Grossman, 'The Relationship between the Social Structure and Spiritual Activity of the Jewish Communities in the Geonic Period' (Heb.).

[3] Simha Assaf examined the exchange of letters between these centres as preserved in *Sefer shibolei haleket* ('The Exchange of Responsa between Spain and Franco-Germany' (Heb.)).

primarily towards collecting the various customs was written. In writing to the Spanish sages, the questioners expressly note that 'some in our locale conclude [the betrothal blessing] with "Blessed are you, Lord, Who sanctifies His people Israel through the wedding canopy and marriage", and some conclude "... Who sanctifies His people Israel".' Later, the writers reply to the Spanish sages: 'Know that we will not depart [from our custom] and will not deviate to the left or to the right from the custom of our predecessors, the geniuses.'

The Ashkenazi sages did not refer to their teachers as 'geniuses' lightly.[a] They used the term elsewhere as well, and it is not a mere rhetorical flourish. It conveys their great esteem for their teachers. In any case, the declaration—that they will not deviate to the left or to the right —attests powerfully to their devotion to their local custom.

**2. Critical analysis.** As one devoted to and guided by truth, Rashi felt committed to critiquing what he believed to be erroneous interpretations and rulings, and he conveyed that commitment to his students—who, in turn, did not hesitate to critique their master's teachings. At the beginning of the eleventh century, Rabbi Elijah ben Menahem of Le Mans justified his claim to lead the communities of northern France on the basis of his ties to Rabbi Hai Gaon, describing himself as Rabbi Hai's heir and as one selected for the role by divine Providence. At the end of that century, Rashi—a modest, humble, and unpretentious man, with no distinguished family connections—succeeded by dint of his achievements in elevating the centre in France to its pinnacle. And yet Rashi's closest students, who spoke of him with great warmth and esteem as one 'whose actions are all for the sake of Heaven', allowed themselves to disagree with him forcefully and energetically. That is the background for the changes in Rashi's commentary on the Torah made by Rabbi Shemayah and for Rashbam characterizing Rashi's comment on Exodus 2: 2 as a 'falsehood'. We can assume that Rashbam envisioned his grandfather forcefully arguing with his own teachers as he pursued the truth and characterizing as 'falsehood' some erroneous words in the prayer book about setting aside the priestly gifts (see Chapter 2). Rabbenu Tam, another of Rashi's grandsons, likewise sometimes disagreed forcefully with his grandfather, and his approach is typical of that taken in Rashi's own *beit midrash*, reflecting Rashi's spirit and method. It was no mere happenstance that twelfth-century northern France was where students were permitted to open *batei midrash* near those of their teachers, and new standards were thereby set for relations between teachers and students. Rabbi Isaac ben Samuel, Rashi's great-grandson, played a major role in this change, which seems to have been—though we lack conclusive evidence—the natural efflorescence of the seeds of openness planted by Rashi two generations earlier.

---

[a] *Geonim*: here used in its generic sense rather than as the title given to the heads of the Babylonian yeshivas.

**3. Encouragement of literary production by students while they were still students.** This was an important change. Rabbenu Gershom was the first to set out on this course, but it was Rashi who brought it to its pinnacle. In Chapter 3, I listed Rashi's students' works. They wrote interpretative works on the Bible, the Talmud, the Midrash, and the liturgical poems; halakhic monographs; prayer books; treatises on grammar and astronomy; rabbinic biographies; and other works. The list is remarkable for both its length and its variety. There is almost no area of interest to Jewish medieval sages that Rashi and his students did not deal with: the exceptions are philosophy and medicine, which had not yet penetrated Ashkenaz. If we compare this varied output with the literary activity in *batei midrash* elsewhere in the Jewish diaspora of the time, including Germany and Spain, the phenomenon emerges as even more amazing with respect to both the number of writers and the broad and varied scope of their works. Rashi's students spoke of his involvement in their varied literary activity, and it is hard to imagine these impressive developments having taken place without his encouragement and guidance.

**4. Attitude to custom.** Rashi assigned priority to the Babylonian Talmud, limiting the force of local customs that originated in Italy, the Land of Israel, or other centres or whose origin was unclear. Notwithstanding his affection for local custom, he generally declined to allow it to prevail over the Talmud. As noted in the discussion of Rashi's image in Chapter 2, he erased with his own hand the accepted wording for blessings within his community because it was at odds with the wording implied by the Talmud and because he took account of economic needs. All of these steps were meant to make life easier for the members of his community.

In his willingness to abrogate some customs, Rashi took an independent path at odds with those of his contemporary Ashkenazi sages, especially in Mainz. As noted, the sons of Makhir, who described the situation in the German yeshivas at the end of the eleventh century, adhered to local custom and declined not only to change it but even to look into its origins. To illustrate, let me cite Rabbi Nathan ben Makhir's harsh response to a sage who had asked him to explain the origins of a particular custom followed when writing a *ketubah*: 'he reproved him, [asking] why he needed to examine the custom of holy communities [followed] since the days of the holy ones'.[4] He even attacked, in scathing terms, those who would change the customs in Mainz, Rashi included, characterizing them as 'foxes' (for a discussion of Rashi's stance, see Chapter 2).

We see here two diametrically opposed intellectual worlds. One, represented by Rashi, saw the Babylonian Talmud as the basis for halakhic rulings and was prepared, through the use of a rational approach, to abrogate local customs in favour of the Talmud and even to alter the ancient formulation of blessings. The other, followed in Germany and especially in Mainz, regarded local custom as sacred. An

---

[4] *Sefer ma'aseh hage'onim*, 55.

instructive example is the practice of concluding one of the blessings in the 'Shemoneh esreh', during the ten days of penitence, with the words *hamelekh hamishpat*. In a responsum to Rabbi Nathan ben Makhir of Mainz, Rashi explained that the use of that erroneous wording, instead of *melekh hamishpat*,[b] was nothing more than the result of poor articulation on the part of prayer leaders that had made its way into the formulation of the prayer.[5] This rationalistic approach lies at the basis of much of what Rashi did. Instructing his students and the populace at large to seek the underlying truth and reject, on that basis, revered local customs was a significantly revolutionary stance, especially in the context of the Jewish communities of Ashkenaz at that time.

Rashi's innovativeness in this area should be viewed against the background of accepted practice in Germany, which exerted considerable influence on the French communities of the time. Rabbi Joseph Tov Elem and Rabbi Elijah ben Menahem had already begun the process of bringing the legacy of the Babylonian geonim to the Jewish communities of Christian Europe. They drew on and were influenced by the Babylonian tradition much more than were the German sages. The extensive adherence of the French sages to the Babylonian Talmud and to the literary and halakhic output of the Babylonian geonim continued into the second half of the eleventh century. The pre-eminent expression of that trend was Rashi's interpretative and halakhic work, followed by that of his students, the leaders of the Jewish communities in northern France. As noted in Chapter 3, Rashi's students recognized the importance of these innovations on Rashi's part and referred to him as 'the great teacher'.

Rashi was also innovative in the area of style and language. As mentioned earlier, Isaac Avinery found that Rashi coined more than one thousand new Hebrew words. He also developed a new method for analysing Hebrew grammar, something most recently examined by Chanoch Gamliel. Both of these areas were considered in Chapter 5.

Rashi's use of biblical interpretation in the service of polemic against the Christians can also be seen as innovative. The subject has been considered extensively at several points in the book, particularly in Chapters 4 and 5. The use of the Bible for polemical purposes reached its peak only in the twelfth century, but Rashi opened the path for it—especially in his comments on the Song of Songs, Psalms, Isaiah, and the Twelve Prophets—and cleared the way for those who followed him.

A somewhat innovative social phenomenon that indirectly influenced the character of the French *beit midrash* in contrast to the German was the marginalization

---

[5]   Rashi, *Responsa* (Heb.), ed. Elfenbein, §18.

[b]   *Melekh hamishpat* means 'the king of justice'. *Hamelekh hamishpat* is grammatically impossible and seems to be a corruption, as Rashi suggests, yet it remains the prevalent reading in Ashkenazi prayer books to this day.

of family lineage as the key factor in yeshiva and society. With the one exception of Rabbi Jacob ben Yakar, all the known great sages of the Mainz yeshiva before 1096 were descendants of only five distinguished families. In those times, the sons of these distinguished families had exclusive rights to head and teach in the yeshiva. The situation was similar, if less extreme, in Worms, where certain families had standing in the community and the yeshiva analogous to that of the leading families in Mainz. The importance of family lineage within the Jewish community as a whole can be seen in the deference with which prominent sages addressed the offspring of distinguished families even if they were young.

Rashi's academy knew nothing of these practices. He himself was not of distinguished lineage, and it is fair to assume that he would never have been named head of the yeshiva had he remained in Mainz (or even Worms). In France, too, there are accounts of dynastic sages during the two generations preceding Rashi, but there is no evidence of an etiquette of deference or of the integration of political and spiritual leadership in the community in Rashi's time. Moreover, Rashi's character placed him at a far remove from the ambience of distinguished families, and he instituted no etiquette of deference or domination within his yeshiva. It is ironic that he himself became, through no desire of his own, the founder of a dynasty that led the French Jewish communities for several generations and, over time, gained even higher esteem than the distinguished families in Germany.

Rashi's innovations brought great benefits. It is impossible to imagine the development of the Jewish centre in northern France in Rashi's generation—and, even more, in the ensuing one—without the openness, the critical thinking, and the creativity that he encouraged. These factors guided and fostered the continuation of many forms of creativity in France and beyond. Rashi's fundamental approach, which saw truth alone as providing direction to literary productivity, underlies the work of the tosafists. The tosafists, to be sure, originated in Germany, not France, and they began to flourish as early as Rashi's last days, without any ties to his commentary on the Talmud, but it was that commentary that provided a powerful impetus to their continued work.[6] It goes without saying that Rashi's commentaries exerted great influence on the future development of Jewish biblical and talmudic interpretation. Even those who did not adopt his methods used his commentaries as a point of departure for their own enquiries.

## Innovation and Mission

At the start of this book I posed an important question about the study of Rashi's character and work: what moved him to act as a revolutionary and an innovator in education and intellectual creativity when doing so would appear to be diametrically at odds with his character? What impelled him to build an academy based on

[6] See Grossman, 'The Origins of the Tosafot' (Heb.).

active creativity by students and on broad openness, and what led him to write a comprehensive commentary on the Bible marked by all the qualities discussed above?

I believe Rashi himself provided the answer to these questions. In his typical fashion, as a man of great humility, he concealed his response and did not speak of it explicitly, but it can be uncovered from allusions in his biblical and talmudic commentaries. The matter deserves detailed analysis, and I can deal with it here only in a highly abbreviated way. Rashi offered the following description of the style, in literary and community matters, of his teacher, Rabbi Isaac Halevi, the head of the Worms yeshiva: 'Our rabbi Isaac Halevi placed matters in his heart and disseminated them at a time when they were gathered in.'[7] Rashi was here alluding to a *baraita* in *Berakhot*, in which the following statement is attributed to Hillel the Elder: 'In the time of those who gather in, disseminate; in the time of those who disseminate, gather in.' Rashi there interprets:

*In the time of those who gather in*—The sages of the time do not transmit Torah to the students. *Disseminate*—You, teach the students. *In the time of those who disseminate*—The great scholars of the age transmit Torah. *Gather in*—You, do not assume control of them, and one honours Heaven, too, by practising the attribute of humility. (Rashi on *Ber.* 63a, *bishe'at hamakhnisim*)

Rashi believed that, in Hillel's view, worthy people were duty-bound to assume the responsibility of teaching Torah publicly if the sages of the age were not doing so. But if others were teaching, they should refrain from doing so and instead practise 'the attribute of humility', for the sacred work of teaching Torah in public was already being done by others. It is the Torah that should occupy the centre of their world, and not their own honour and personal status. Rabbi Isaac Halevi was the central figure in the establishment of the Worms yeshiva during the second half of the eleventh century. He played a crucial role in transforming it into an effervescent and productive Torah centre, to the point of becoming a competitor to the grand yet conservative yeshiva in Mainz. If Rashi saw Rabbi Isaac Halevi as one who was concerned about spreading Torah and who 'disseminated when [others] gathered in', he would certainly apply the same judgement to his own work in northern France, a centre that in his day was inferior in its knowledge of Torah.

In his comments on Ecclesiastes 10: 11, Rashi explicitly stated that a scholar must teach and propound Torah before his community. If he fails to do so, he will ultimately be held to account. The difficult circumstances that prevailed in northern France in Rashi's time—the lack of great scholars, ignorance on the part of wide segments of society, and intense social discord—moved him to take on the heavy burden of transmitting Torah publicly and leading the community.

Rashi's sense of mission drew on two additional sources: the influence of

---

[7] *Sidur rashi*, §174.

Hillel's image and the religious polemic with Christianity. In the Talmud, Hillel is described as one who was concerned about the dissemination of Torah in the Land of Israel during a difficult time: 'Earlier, when Torah was forgotten in Israel, Ezra went up from Babylonia and established it. It was again forgotten, and Hillel the Babylonian went up and established it' (*Suk.* 20*a*). Hillel and Rashi shared character traits, first and foremost humility. Hillel was prominently marked by his humility, as the Talmud states: 'Let one always be humble, like Hillel' (*Shab.* 30*a*). Another quality they had in common was their pursuit of peace. They shared similar fates: it is told of Hillel that he studied Torah in extreme poverty, and, as we saw in Chapter 2, Rashi did so too ('For a lack of food and clothing were as a millstone around my neck, ruining the time I spent studying with my teachers'). Despite Hillel's extreme humility and miserable poverty, he devoted all his strength to Torah study. It is only natural that Hillel's statement would have great influence on Rashi in particular.

The other important source on which Rashi's sense of mission drew was, as we have seen, Jewish–Christian polemic. In his comments on the Song of Songs, Rashi mentioned the heavy responsibility borne by Jewish sages in religious debates with learned non-Jews who sought to destroy the foundations of Jewish faith and entice Jews into abandoning their Judaism:

*I say: Let me climb the palm* (S. of S. 7: 9)—I take pride in you amidst the heavenly hosts, for I am raised and sanctified through you in the lower reaches, for you sanctify My name amongst the nations . . . That you not be enticed after the nations, *and that the good and wise amongst you stand by their faith and respond to those who would entice you* [emphasis added], so that the lesser ones amongst them learn from them.

'The good and the wise' of Israel are duty-bound to know how to respond to the enemies ('those who would entice you') and must make sure that their arguments can provide an example for 'the lesser ones'. Later in that passage, Rashi writes: 'Take care with your responses, so they are like good wine.' This assignment, which Rashi saw as obligatory for Jewish sages, was something he kept in mind and that preoccupied him. He was witness not only to the force of the religious polemic in his time, given the enticements offered by the Christian Church, but also to harsh persecutions. It is no wonder, therefore, that he saw himself as obligated to write a biblical commentary in which he could use scriptural verses and *midrashim* not only to spread Torah publicly but also to neutralize Christian propaganda.

## How Did Rashi Attain his Historic Status?

No other Jewish sage since the time of the Talmud has attained Rashi's degree of fame and esteem. As noted in Chapter 2, as early as the twelfth century, Rabbi Eliezer ben Nathan, a pre-eminent German sage, described him as one who 'stabilized the world', and in the thirteenth century, Nahmanides, in Spain, called him 'the lamps of the pure candelabrum'. From that point on, he acquired rare honorific titles in both Christian and Muslim lands. His commentary on the Torah—the first Hebrew book to be printed—became the subject of hundreds of supercommentaries, and works of that sort continue to be produced in a manner not seen in connection with any other text written by a Jewish sage. Beyond that, numerous folk legends grew up around him and talismanic powers to save people from difficulties came to be attributed to him. No man in the last millennium and a half of Jewish life has been judged so favourably by history.

In Chapter 4, I considered the influence of Rashi's commentary on the Torah and examined some of the reasons for it. I cited various opinions by scholars who had dealt with the spread of his commentary and its extraordinary influence, and I enumerated what I take to be the five principal factors underlying the phenomenon. They apply with equal force to the present subject—Rashi's fame in general—and need not be listed again. Let me mention, however, an additional point of interest with respect to his historical stature, namely, the attitudes of earlier and later writers. (By 'earlier writers' I mean the medieval and early modern Jewish sages; the 'later writers' are those of the past two hundred years, since the Enlightenment movement made its way into the Jewish world.) The earlier writers mainly devoted their attention to Rashi's intellectual output and lauded his great contribution to the interpretation and study of ancient sacred texts.[8]

The later writers gave a central place in their explanations of Rashi's fame to 'external aspects' of his commentary and personality. They cited his humility, the clarity of his language, and his warm style, characteristics they regarded as emotionally attractive. Dozens of comments along these lines are preserved in the literature, and I will make no effort to list them here, presenting only two by way of illustration. One is by a prominent scholar, Ephraim E. Urbach; the other is by a poet, Samson Meltzer.

Urbach deals with the extraordinary esteem in which Rashi has been held, and, after ascertaining that it exceeds even that assigned to Maimonides, he lists personal qualities as a weighty factor. More than that, he goes on, anyone who reads Rashi is taken, at least a bit, by those lofty qualities. Meltzer, in his ballad 'Ashirah lerashi', speaks of love for Rashi's personality and associated it with his warm style and the sense of innocence and purity that characterizes him. I quoted some of Meltzer's lines as the epigraph for this book.

What accounts for the difference between the assessments by the earlier and the later writers? Evidently, the Enlightenment of the eighteenth century played a role in this development. The evaluation by the early writers was the product of eminent sages whose literary activity and study was centred on the Talmud, and

---

[8]  Statements of that esteem are collected in Rosenthal, 'Rashi and Maimonides in the Perspective of History' (Heb.); Maimon (ed.), *Rashi* (Heb.); Avinery, in the introduction to *Rashi's Palace* (Heb.), and in the works of many other scholars.

these sages by their nature focused their attention on the scholarly aspects of Rashi's life and work. The later writers, in contrast, include academic scholars, intellectuals, and students of language and poetry, inspired and guided by the Enlightenment. They examined Rashi's career from a broader perspective and through a sociological and psychological lens. It is only natural that people with their learning and outlook would focus on examining Rashi's personal world, his character traits, and his literary style.

There may well be some truth to the assumption by Samson Bloch, one of the first to study Rashi's life, that Rashi's humility was the fundamental factor responsible for his great fame. Bloch is not the only one to make that suggestion, and other scholars have trodden the same path. This is not an explanation based on rational analysis. Bloch described Rashi as one 'like whom none may be found among all the great ones of Israel from the time we became a people . . . And so, just as Hillel, because of his humility, merited having the halakhah determined in all cases in accord with his view (JT *Suk.* 3*c*), so did our rabbi—whose commentaries and rulings have adorned all Israel since they first became diadems for their heads—merit fulfilling the words of the sage: before honour, humility'.[9]

If there is anything to that assumption, it should be broadened to include Rashi's openness, that is, his affinity for numerous, sometimes opposing, traditions. The sages of blessed memory associated openness with the preference afforded the House of Hillel over the House of Shammai: 'Why did the House of Hillel merit having the halakhah determined in accord with their view? Because they were easygoing and humble, studying both their own words and those of the House of Shammai. And not only that, but they even set the words of the House of Shammai before their own' (*Eruv.* 13*b*). As noted in Chapter 2, Rashi set truth and humility as his foremost concerns. These two qualities coexisted within him in wondrous harmony, and he based his teachings on them. They are the foundation for his accomplishments and his blessed oeuvre and from them grew his fame and his preeminence.

---

[9] Zunz and Bloch, *Life of Rashi* (Heb.), introduction, 3*b*.

# Bibliography

ABRAHAM BEN AZRIEL, *Sefer arugat habosem* [commentaries on liturgical poems], ed. Efraim E. Urbach (Jerusalem, 1963).

AGUS, IRVING A., *Responsa of the Tosaphists* [Teshuvot ba'alei hatosafot] (New York, 1954).

AHDUT, ELIYAHOU, 'The Status of the Jewish Woman in Babylonia in the Talmudic Era' [Ma'amad ha'ishah hayehudiyah bebavel bitekufat hatalmud], doctoral dissertation, Hebrew University (Jerusalem, 1999).

AHREND, MOSHE, 'Clarifying the Concept of "Plain Meaning of the Text"' (Heb.), in Sara Japhet (ed.), *The Bible in the Light of its Interpreters: Sarah Kamin Memorial Volume* [Hamikra bire'i mefareshav: sefer zikaron lesarah kamin] (Jerusalem, 1994), 237–61.

—— 'Rashi's Method of Explaining Words' (Heb.), in Zvi Aryeh Steinfeld (ed.), *Rashi Studies* [Rashi: iyunim biyetsirato] (Ramat Gan, 1993).

—— 'Rashi's Torah Commentary' (Heb.), *Maḥanayim*, 68/3 (1993), 92–108.

*Alilot devarim, Otsar neḥmad*, 4 (1864), 179–95.

APTOWITZER, VICTOR, *Introduction to Sefer Rabiah* [Mavo lesefer ravyah] (Jerusalem, 1938).

—— 'On the History of Rashi's Commentaries on the Talmud' (Heb.), in Yehudah Leib Maimon (ed.), *Rashi* [Sefer rashi] (Jerusalem, 1956), 286–321.

*Arukh hashalem* [talmudic dictionary], ed. Alexander Kohut, 8 vols. (Vienna, 1878–92; photo-offset, 1970).

ASSAF, SIMHA, 'The Exchange of Responsa between Spain and Franco-Germany' (Heb.), *Tarbiz*, 8 (1937), 162–70.

AVINERY, ISAAC, *Rashi's Palace* [Heikhal rashi], new edn., 2 vols. (Jerusalem, 1980–5).

*Avot derabi natan*, ed. Shneur Zalman Schechter (Vienna, 1887).

AZULAI, HAYIM JOSEPH DAVID (HIDA), *Shem hagedolim* [bibliography of Hebrew works] (Livorno, 1774).

BAER, YITZHAK, 'Rashi and the Historical Reality of his Time' (Heb.), *Tarbiz*, 20 (1949), 320–32.

BANITT, MENAHEM, *Rashi, Interpreter of the Biblical Letter* (Tel Aviv, 1985).

BENEDIKT, BENJAMIN ZE'EV, 'On Rashi's Halakhic Decisions in his Talmud Commentary', in Zvi Aryeh Steinfeld (ed.), *Rashi Studies* [Rashi: iyunim biyetsirato] (Ramat Gan, 1993), 21–5.

BEN-YEHUDAH, ELIEZER, *Dictionary* [Milon], 17 vols. (photo-offset, Jerusalem, 1980).

BERGER, DAVID, *The Jewish–Christian Debate in the High Middle Ages* (Philadelphia, 1969).

—— 'On the Image and Destiny of Gentiles in Ashkenazic Polemical Literature' (Heb.), in Yom Tov Assis et al. (eds.), *Facing the Cross: The Persecutions of 1096 in History and Historiography* [Yehudim mul hatselav] (Jerusalem, 2000).

—— 'Three Typological Themes in Early Jewish Messianism: Messiah Son of Joseph, Rabbinic Calculations, and the Figure of Armilus', *AJS Review*, 10 (1985), 141–64.

BERLINER, ABRAHAM, 'On the History of Rashi's Commentaries' (Heb.), in *Selected Writings* [Ketavim nivḥarim], 2 vols. (Jerusalem, 1949), ii. 179–226.

CATANE, MOCHÈ, *Foreign Words in Rashi's Writings* [Otsar hale'azim] (Jerusalem, 1984).

—— *Life in Rashi's Time* [Haḥayim biyemei rashi] (Jerusalem, 1997).

—— 'Le Monde intellectuel de Rashi: Les Juifs au regard de l'histoire', in Gilbert Dahan (ed.), *Mélanges en l'honneur de Bernhard Blumenkranz* (Paris, 1985), 63–85.

COHEN, GERSON D., 'Esau as Symbol in Early Medieval Thought', in Alexander Altmann (ed.), *Jewish Medieval and Renaissance Studies* (Cambridge, Mass., 1967), 19–49.

COHEN, JEREMY, *Living Letters of the Law: Ideas of the Jew in Medieval Christianity* (Berkeley, 1999).

CONFORTE, DAVID, *Kore hadorot* [seventeenth-century history of Jewish sages since the talmudic period and their literary output, written in Cairo], ed. David Cassel (Berlin, 1846).

DAHAN, GILBERT, 'Un dossier latin de textes de Rashi, autour de la controverse de 1240', in Zvi Aryeh Steinfeld (ed.), *Rashi Studies* [Rashi: iyunim biyetsirato] (Ramat Gan, 1993), French section, pp. xv–xxix.

—— GÉRARD NAHON, and ELIE NICOLAS (eds.), *Rashi et la culture juive en France du nord au moyen âge* (Paris, 1997).

DAN, JOSEPH, 'Rashi and the Merkabah', in Gabrielle Sed-Rajna (ed.), *Rashi 1040–1990* (Paris, 1993), 259–64.

DARMESTETER, ARSÈNE, and DAVID S. BLONDHEIM, *Les Glosses françaises dans les commentaires talmudiques de Rashi*, 2 vols. (Paris, 1929–37).

DINARY, YEDIDYA, 'Desecration by a Menstruant and Ezra's Enactment' (Heb.), *Te'udah*, 3 (1983), 17–35.

—— 'The Impurity Customs of the Menstruant Woman: Sources and Development' (Heb.), *Tarbiz*, 49 (1980), 302–24.

ELIEZER B. NATHAN OF MAINZ (RABAN), *Sefer even ha'ezer* [halakhic work], ed. Solomon Zalman Ehrenreich (1927; repr. Jerusalem, 1975).

ELIEZER OF BEAUGENCY, *Commentary on Ezekiel and the Twelve Prophets* [Peirush al yeḥezkel veterei asar], ed. Samuel Poznański (Warsaw, 1913).

EPSTEIN, JACOB NAHUM, 'Rivan's Commentaries and the Commentaries of Worms' (Heb.), *Tarbiz*, 4 (1933), 11–33, 153–92.

*Exodus Rabbah* (Heb.), ed. A. Sha'anan (Jerusalem, 1984).

FLEISCHER, EZRA, *Hebrew Liturgical Poetry in the Middle Ages* [Shirat hakodesh ha'ivrit biyemei habeinayim] (Jerusalem, 1975).

FLORSHEIM, YO'EL, *Rashi on the Bible in his Commentary on the Talmud* [Rashi lamikra beferusho latalmud], 3 vols. (Jerusalem, 1981–9).

FRAENKEL, YONAH, 'Liturgical Poems and Commentary: Aggadic Sources in Rashi's Commentary on the Torah' (Heb.), *Iyunei mikra ufarshanut*, 7 (2005), 475–90.

—— *Rashi's Methodology in his Exegesis of the Babylonian Talmud* [Darko shel rashi beferusho latalmud habavli] (Jerusalem, 1975).

FREIMANN, AHARON, "'Let Them Be Shamed'" (Heb.), *Tarbiz*, 12 (1941), 70–1.

—— 'Manuscript Supercommentaries on Rashi's Commentary on the Pentateuch', in

American Academy for Jewish Research, *Rashi Anniversary Volume* (New York, 1941), 73–114.

FRIEDMAN, SHAMMA, 'Rashi's Talmud Commentary: Annotations and Editions' (Heb.), in Zvi Aryeh Steinfeld (ed.), *Rashi Studies* [Rashi: iyunim biyetsirato] (Ramat Gan, 1993), 147–75.

GAMLIEL, CHANOCH, *Linguistics in Rashi's Commentary* [Rashi kefarshan ukhebalshan] (Jerusalem, 2010).

—— 'Syntactical Issues in Rashi's Commentary' [Tefisot tahbiriyot beferush rashi latorah], doctoral dissertation, Hebrew University (Jerusalem, 2003).

GELLES, BENJAMIN J., *Peshat and Derash in the Exegesis of Rashi* (Leiden, 1981).

*Genesis Rabbah*, ed. Judah Theodor and Chanoch Albeck, 3 vols. (Berlin, 1912–36; repr. with corrections Jerusalem, 1965).

GERSHOM ME'OR HAGOLAH, *Responsa* [Teshuvot rabbenu gershom me'or hagolah], ed. Solomon Eidelberg (New York, 1955).

GINZBERG, LOUIS, *Geonica*, 2 vols. (New York, 1909).

—— *Legends of the Jews*, 2nd edn., 2 vols. (Philadelphia, 2003).

GOLDBERG, BER, *Hofes matmonim* [early sources related to the geonim, Rashi, Ibn Ezra, etc.] (Berlin, 1845).

GOLDSCHMIDT, DANIEL (ed.), *Order of Selihot According to the Polish Rite* [Seder selihot keminhag polin] (Jerusalem, 1965).

GROSS, ABRAHAM, 'Spanish Jewry and Rashi's Commentary on the Pentateuch' (Heb.), in Zvi Aryeh Steinfeld (ed.), *Rashi Studies* [Rashi: iyunim biyetsirato] (Ramat Gan, 1993), 27–55.

GROSSMAN, AVRAHAM, 'The Beginning of the Tosaphot' (Heb.), in Zvi Aryeh Steinfeld (ed.), *Rashi Studies* [Rashi: iyunim biyetsirato] (Ramat Gan, 1993), 57–68.

—— *The Early Sages of Ashkenaz* [Hakhmei ashkenaz harishonim], 2nd edn. (Jerusalem, 1989).

—— *The Early Sages of France* [Hakhmei tsarefat harishonim], 3rd edn. (Jerusalem, 2003).

—— 'Erets Yisra'el in the Thought of Rashi' (Heb.), *Shalem*, 7 (2002), 15–31.

—— 'Offenders and Violent Men in Jewish Society in Early Ashkenaz and their Influence upon Legal Procedures' (Heb.), *Annals of the Institute for Research in Jewish Law* [Shenaton hamishpat ha'ivri], 8 (1981), 135–52.

—— *Pious and Rebellious: Jewish Women in Medieval Europe*, trans. Jonathan Chipman (Waltham, Mass., 2004).

—— '"Proselytizing Redemption" in the Teachings of the Early Ashkenazi Sages' (Heb.), *Zion*, 59 (1994), 325–42.

—— 'Rashi's Commentary on Psalms and Jewish–Christian Polemic' (Heb.), in Dov Rappel (ed.), *Studies in Torah and Education: Jubilee Volume for Professor Moshe Ahrend* [Mehkarim betorah uvehinukh: sefer yovel leprofesor moshe arend] (Jerusalem, 1996), 59–74.

—— 'Rashi's Teachings Concerning Women', (Heb.), *Zion*, 70 (2005), 157–90.

—— 'The Relationship between the Social Structure and Spiritual Activity of Jewish Communities in the Geonic Period' (Heb.), *Zion*, 53 (1988), 259–72.

GROSSMAN, AVRAHAM, 'Social Structure and Intellectual Creativity in Medieval Jewish Communities (Eighth to Twelfth Centuries)', in Isadore Twersky and Jay M. Harris (eds.), *Studies in Medieval Jewish History and Literature*, 3 vols. (Cambridge, Mass., 2001), iii. 1–19.

—— and BEN-ZION KEDAR, 'Rashi's Maps of the Land of Israel and their Historical Significance' (Heb.), *Igeret*, 25 (2003), 26–9.

GRUBER, MAYER I., 'Light on Rashi's Diagrams from the Asher Library of Spertus College of Judaica', in id. (ed.), *The Solomon Goldman Lectures* (Chicago, 1993), vi. 73–85.

HAILPERIN, HERMAN, *Rashi and the Christian Scholars* (Pittsburgh, 1963).

HALAMISH, MOSHE, and AVIEZER RAVITZKY (eds.), *The Land of Israel in Medieval Jewish Thought* [Erets yisra'el bahagut hayehudit biyemei habeinayim] (Jerusalem, 1991).

HALIVNI, DAVID WEISS, 'On the Identity of the Commentary on Ta'anit Attributed to Rashi' (Heb.), *Sinai*, 44 (1959), 23–5.

—— *Peshat and Derash* (New York, 1991).

HALLAM, ELIZABETH M., *Capetian France, 987–1138* (London, 1980).

HALPERIN, DAVID, *The Faces of the Chariot: Early Jewish Responses to Ezekiel's Vision* (Tübingen, 1988).

HAVLIN, SHELOMO ZALMAN, *Manuscripts of Rashi's Commentary on the Talmud* [Kitvei hayad shel peirush rashi al hatalmud] (Ramat Gan, 1988).

HAYIM PALTIEL B. JACOB, *Peirush hatorah* [commentary on the Torah], ed. Isaak S. Lange (Jerusalem, 1981).

HEIDE, ALBERT VAN DER, 'The Longer Variants in Rashi's Commentary on the Torah', in Gabrielle Sed-Rajna (ed.), *Rashi 1040–1990* (Paris, 1993), 419–26.

*Ḥumash meḥokekei yehudah* [rabbinic Bible], ed. Judah Leib Karinsky (1907; repr. Benei Berak, 1961).

IBN KASPI, JOSEPH, 'Commentaries on the Book of Proverbs (Two Versions)' (Heb.), in *Asarah kelei kesef* [essays], ed. I. H. Last (Pressberg, 1903), i. 5–132.

ISAAC B. JACOB CANPANTON, *Darkhei hatalmud* [talmudic methodology], ed. Yitzhak Shimshon Lange (Jerusalem, 1981).

ISAAC OF VIENNA, *Or zarua* [halakhic work] (Zhitomir, 1862).

JAPHET, SARA, *The Bible in the Light of its Interpreters: Sarah Kamin Memorial Volume* [Hamikra bire'i mefareshav: sefer zikaron lesarah kamin] (Jerusalem, 1994).

*Josippon* [medieval historical narrative of the Second Temple period], ed. David Flusser, 2 vols. (Jerusalem, 1978–80).

JUDAH B. ELAZAR, *Minḥat yehudah* [kabbalistic biblical commentary], ed. Hazoniel Touitou (Ramat Gan, 2004).

KALATZ JUDAH, *Mesiaḥ ilmim* [supercommentary on Rashi and others] (Jerusalem, 1955).

KAMIN, SARAH, *Rashi: Plain Meaning and Midrashic Understanding of the Text* [Rashi: peshuto shel mikra umidrasho shel mikra] (Jerusalem, 1986).

KANARFOGEL, EPHRAIM, *Peering Through the Lattices* (Detroit, 2000).

KARA, JOSEPH, *Commentaries on the Early Prophets* [Peirushei rabi yosef kara linevi'im rishonim], ed. Simon Eppenstein (Jerusalem, 1973).

KATZ, JACOB, *Between Jews and Gentiles* [Bein yehudim legoyim] (Jerusalem, 1961).

—— *Halakhah and Kabbala* [Halakhah vekabalah] (Jerusalem, 1984).

*Kol bo* [collection of ritual and civil laws] (Naples, 1590).

KUPFER, EFRAIM (ed.), *Responsa and Rulings by the Sages of Germany and France* [Teshuvot ufesakim me'et ḥakhmei ashkenaz vetsarefat] (Jerusalem, 1973).

LANDAU, LOUIS, 'Rashi's Stories in the Babylonian Talmud' (Heb.), *Eshel be'er sheva*, 3 (1986), 101–17.

LATTES, ISAAC B. JACOB, *Sha'arei tsiyon* [history of the rabbinic tradition], ed. Shlomo Zalman Havlin (Jerusalem, 1992) (bound with Meiri, *Seder hakabalah*).

LEIBOWITZ, NEHAMA, 'Rashi's Use of Midrash in his Commentary on the Torah' (Heb.), in id., *New Studies in the Book of Exodus* [Iyunim ḥadashim besefer shemot] (Jerusalem, 1970), 495–524.

—— *The Study of Biblical Commentators* [Limud parshanei hatorah uderakhim lehora'atam] (Jerusalem, 1975).

—— and MOSHE AHREND, *Rashi's Commentary on the Torah: Studies in his Method* [Peirush rashi latorah: iyunim beshitato] (Tel Aviv, 1990).

LEVI B. HABIB (RALBAH), *Responsa* [Teshuvot] (Venice, 1565).

LIPSCHUETZ, ELIEZER M., 'Rashi' (Heb.), in id., *Writings* [Ketavim], 3 vols. (Jerusalem, 1947), i. 9–196.

LURIA, SOLOMON B. JEHIEL (MAHARSHAL), *Responsa* [Teshuvot rabi shelomoh luria] (Lublin, 1574).

*Maḥzor vitri* [halakhic-liturgical composition by Simhah b. Samuel of Vitry], ed. S. Horowitz (Nuremberg, 1923).

MAIMON, YEHUDAH LEIB (ed.), *Rashi* [Sefer rashi] (Jerusalem, 1956).

MAIMONIDES, MOSES, *The Guide of the Perplexed*, trans. Shlomo Pines (Chicago, 1963).

—— *Letters* [Igerot harambam], ed. Isaac Shailat (Jerusalem, 1987).

MALACHI B. JACOB HAKOHEN, *Yad malakhi* [methodology of the Talmud and codifiers], ed. Isaiah Pick (Berlin, 1852).

MARCUS, IVAN G., 'Rashi's Historiosophy in the Introductions to his Bible Commentaries', *Revue des Études Juives*, 157/1–2 (1998), 47–55.

MARGALIOT, MORDECAI, *Halakhot of the Land of Israel from the Genizah* [Hilkhot erets yisra'el min hagenizah] (Jerusalem, 1974).

MARMORSTEIN, ARTHUR, 'An Italian Sage and Decisor' (Heb.), *Dvir*, 2 (1924), 213–43.

MEIR OF ROTHENBURG (MAHARAM), *Responsa* [Teshuvot], ed. M. A. Bloch (Prague, 1895).

—— *Responsa* [Teshuvot], ed. N. N. Rabinowitz (Lemberg [Lvov], 1860).

MEIRI, MENAHEM B. SOLOMON, *Seder hakabalah lerabenu menaḥem hame'iri* [historical survey of the sages and their works], ed. Shlomo Zalman Havlin (Jerusalem, 1992) (bound with Lattes, *Sha'arei tsiyon*).

*Mekhilta de rabi yishma'el* (Venice, 1545).

MELAMMED, EZRA ZION, 'Rashi's Commentary on the Bible' (Heb.), in id., *Bible Commentators* [Mefareshei hamikra, darkheihem veshitoteihem] (Jerusalem, 1978), 353–447.

MELTZER, SHIMSHON, 'Ashirah lerashi', in id., *Poems and Ballads* [Shirot ubaladot] (Tel Aviv, 1960), 19–24.

*Midrash mishlei*, ed. Burton Visotzky (New York, 1990).

*Midrash tehilim*, ed. Solomon Buber (Vilna, 1891).

*Mikra'ot gedolot haketer* [rabbinic Bible], ed. Menahem Cohen, 8 vols. (Jerusalem, 1992–2003).

MIRSKY, AHARON, 'Rashi and Menahem's *Mahberet*' (Heb.), *Sinai*, 100 (1987), 579–86.

MONDSCHEIN, JOSHUA, 'Rashi and Mysticism' (Heb.), *Zefunot*, 11 (Nisan 1991), 108–9.

NAHMANIDES (RAMBAN), *Commentary on the Torah*, trans. and ed. Charles Chavel, 5 vols. (New York, 1971).

NEUBAUER, ADOLF, 'Collectaneen', *Monatschrift für Geschichte und Wissenschaft des Judentums*, 36 (1887), 498–506.

—— (ed.), *Mediaeval Jewish Chronicles and the Events of History* [Seder hahakhamim vekorot hayamim], vol. i (Oxford, 1888).

NISSIM BEN JACOB, *Hibur yafeh mehayeshu'ah* [collection of Hebrew folk-tales], ed. Hayim Ze'ev Hirschberg (Jerusalem, 1970).

NOAM, VERED, 'Early Textual Traditions in Rashi's Editorial Comments on the Talmud' (Heb.), *Sidra*, 17 (2001–2), 109–50.

OVADIA, A., 'Rashi on the Torah and his Interpreters' (Heb.), in Yehudah Leib Maimon (ed.), *Rashi* [Sefer rashi] (Jerusalem, 1956), 543–69.

PENKOWER, JORDAN, 'The End of Rashi's Commentary on Job: The Manuscripts and the Printed Editions', *Jewish Studies Quarterly*, 10 (2003), 18–48.

POZEN, RAFAEL, 'Targum from Sinai' (Heb.), *Sidra*, 15 (1999), 95–110.

POZNAŃSKI, SAMUEL, *Introduction to the French Biblical Interpreters* [Mavo al hakhmei tsarefat mefareshei hamikra], 2nd edn. (Jerusalem, 1965).

RABBENU TAM, *Sefer hayashar*, i: *Novellae on the Talmud*, ed. Simon Solomon Schlesinger (Jerusalem, 1974); ii: *Responsa*, ed. Shraga Ferdinand Rosenthal (Berlin, 1898).

RABBINOVICZ, RAPHAEL NATHAN, *Dikdukei soferim lemasekhet pesahim* [textual variants of tractate *Pesahim*], 2nd edn. (Jerusalem, 1960).

RACHAMAN, YOSEFA, *Rashi's Aggadah* [Agadat rashi] (Jerusalem, 1991).

RAPPEL, DOV, *Rashi's Jewish World-View* [Rashi: temunat olamo hayehudit] (Jerusalem, 1995).

RASHI, *Commentary on Ezekiel 40–48*, ed. Abraham J. Levy (Philadelphia, 1931).

—— *Commentary on Joshua and Judges* [Yehoshua–shofetim im peirush rashi], ed. Mordecai Leib Katzenellenbogen (Jerusalem, 1987).

—— *Commentary on Mo'ed katan* [Peirush rashi lemasakhet mo'ed katan], ed. Ephraim Kupfer (Jerusalem, 1961).

—— *Commentary on the Torah* [Rashi al hatorah], ed. Abraham Berliner (Berlin, 1867; 2nd edn., Frankfurt, 1905; photo-offset, Jerusalem, 1962).

—— *Complete Works* [Rashi hashalem], 6 vols. (Jerusalem, 1986–2003).

—— *Liturgical Poems* [Piyutei rabi shelomoh yitshaki], ed. Abraham M. Haberman (Jerusalem, 1941).

—— 'On Job' (Heb.), ed. Abraham Shoshana, in *The Book of Job in Rashi's Beit Midrash* [Sefer iyov mibeit midrasho shel rashi] (Jerusalem, 2000), 19–73.

—— 'On the Song of Songs' (Heb.), ed. Y. Rosenthal, in *Samuel K. Mirsky Jubilee Volume* [Sefer yovel lishemu'el kalman mirski] (New York, 1958), 130–88; repr. separately (New York, 1959).

—— *Parshandatha: Rashi's Commentary on the Prophets and the Writings* [Parshandata: vehu peirush rashi al nakh], ed. I. Maarsen, i: *The Twelve Prophets* (Jerusalem, 1930), ii: *Isaiah* (Jerusalem, 1933), iii: *Psalms* (Jerusalem, 1936).

—— *Responsa* [Teshuvot rashi], ed. Israel Elfenbein (New York, 1943).

—— *Responsa* [Teshuvot rashi], ed. Menahem M. Kasher (Jerusalem, 1925).

RICHÉ, PIERRE, *Écoles et enseignement dans le Haut Moyen Age* (Paris, 1979).

ROSENTHAL, JUDAH, 'Rashi and Maimonides in the Perspective of History' (Heb.), in id., *Studies and Texts in Jewish History, Literature and Religion* [Meḥkarim umekorot] (Jerusalem, 1967), 117–25.

SADAN, JOSEPH, 'Polemics as Religious and Literary Writing' (Heb.), in Hava Lazarus-Yafeh (ed.), *Muslim Authors on Jews and Judaism* [Soferim muslemim al yehudim veyahadut] (Jerusalem, 1996), 37–58.

SAMBARI, JOSEPH, *Sefer divrei yosef lerabi yosef sambari* [seventeenth-century chronicle of Jewish history under Muslim rule], ed. Simon Shtober (Jerusalem, 1994).

SAMUEL ELIEZER HALEVI EDELS (MAHARSHA), *Novellae* [Ḥidushei halakhot va'agadot maharsha] (Hanau, Germany, 1716).

SCHAPIRO, YISRAEL, 'Interpreters of Rashi on the Torah' (Heb.), *Bitsaron*, 1 (1940), 426–37.

SCHNEERSON, MENACHEM MENDEL, *Principles of Rashi's Torah Commentary* [Kelalei rashi beferusho al hatorah], ed. Tuvia Blau, based on discussions with the author (Kefar Habad, 1991).

SCHWARZFUCHS, SIMEON, *History of the Jews in Medieval France* [Yehudei tsarefat biyemei habeinayim] (Tel Aviv, 2001).

*Seder olam* [midrashic chronology from the creation of the world to the Bar Kokhba Revolt], ed. Dov Ber Ratner (New York, 1966).

SED-RAJNA, GABRIELLE (ed.), *Rashi 1040–1990* (Paris, 1993).

*Sefer ha'oreh* [collection of halakhic rulings by Rashi and other sages compiled by Rashi's students], ed. Solomon Buber (Lvov, 1905).

*Sefer hapardes* [collection of halakhic rulings by Rashi and other sages compiled by Rashi's students], ed. Hayim Ehrenreich (Budapest, 1924).

*Sefer ḥasidim* [twelfth-century ethical treatise by R. Judah Hahasid], ed. J. Freiman (Frankfurt am Main, 1924).

*Sefer haterumot* [code of Jewish civil and commercial law by Samuel b. Isaac Sardi] (Salonika, 1596).

*Sefer ma'aseh hage'onim* [rulings and customs of the Babylonian geonim and early Ashkenazi sages], ed. Abraham Epstein (Berlin, 1910).

SHAPIRA, AMNON, 'Rashi's Twofold Interpretations (*Peshuto* and *Midrasho*): A Dualistic Approach?' (Heb.), in Sara Japhet (ed.), *The Bible in the Light of its Interpreters: Sara Kamin Memorial Volume* [Hamikra bire'i mefareshav: sefer zikaron lesarah kamin] (Jerusalem, 1994), 287–311.

SHAPIRA, NOAH, 'On Rashi's Technical and Technological Knowledge' (Heb.), *Korot*, 3 (1963), 145–61.

SHERESHEVSKY, ESRA, *Rashi: The Man and his World* (New York, 1982).

SHOCHETMAN, E., 'On the Custom of Giving Gifts to Poor Non-Jews on Purim' (Heb.), *Sinai*, 100 (1987), 852–65.

*Sidur rashi* [collection of halakhic rulings by Rashi and other sages compiled by Rashi's students], ed. Solomon Buber and Jacob Fraiman (Berlin, 1912).

*Sifrei on Deuteronomy* (Heb.), ed. Louis Finkelstein, 2nd edn. (New York, 1969).

SOKOLOW, MOSHE, 'The Text of Rashi's Commentary on Job' (Heb.), *Proceedings of the American Academy of Jewish Research*, 48 (1981), Hebrew section, 19–35.

SOLOVEITCHIK, HAYM, 'Can Halakhic Texts Talk History?' (Heb.), *Netu'im*, 9 (2002), 9–50.

—— *Halakhah, Economics, and Self-Image: Pawnbroking in the Middle Ages* [Halakhah, kalkalah, vedimui-atsmi: hamashkona'ut biyemei habeinayim] (Jerusalem, 1985).

—— *Their Wine: Trade in Non-Jewish Wine and the Evolution of Halakhah in the Practical World* [Yeinam: saḥar beyeinam shel goyim, al gilgulah shel halakhah be'olam hama'aseh] (Tel Aviv, 2003).

SONNE, ISAIAH, 'On the Textual Criticism of Rashi's Commentary on the Torah' (Heb.), *Hebrew Union College Annual*, 15 (1940), 37–56.

STEINFELD, ZVI ARYEH (ed.), *Rashi Studies* [Rashi: iyunim biyetsirato] (Ramat Gan, 1993).

SUSSMAN, JACOB, 'The Study Tradition and Textual Tradition of the Jerusalem Talmud: An Enquiry into the Textual Versions of the Jerusalem Talmud, Tractate Shekalim' (Heb.), in Samuel Re'em (ed.), *Researches in Talmudic Literature in Honour of the Eightieth Birthday of Saul Lieberman* [Meḥkarim besifrut hatalmudit leregel melot shemonim shanah lesha'ul liberman] (Jerusalem, 1983), 12–76.

*Taḥtsul: teshuvot ḥakhmei tsarefat velotir* [responsa of the sages of France and Lorraine], ed. Joel Müller (Vienna, 1981).

TAITZ, EMILY, *The Jews of Medieval France: The Community of Champagne* (London, 1995).

TA-SHMA, ISRAEL, *Early Franco-German Ritual and Custom* [Minhag ashkenaz hakadmon] (Jerusalem, 1992).

—— 'Exclusion of a Menstruant in Early Ashkenaz' (Heb.), in id., *Ritual, Custom and Reality in Franco-Germany, 1000–1350* [Halakhah, minhag umetsiut be'ashkenaz, 1000–1350] (Jerusalem, 1996), 280–8.

—— *Talmudic Commentary in Europe and North Africa* [Hasifrut haparshanit latalmud be'eiropah uvitsefon afrikah], 2 vols. (Jerusalem, 1999–2000).

*Torat ḥayim* [rabbinic Bible: Pentateuch], ed. Mordecai Leib Katzenellenbogen (Jerusalem, 1992).

TOUITOU, ELAZAR, 'Evolution of the Text of Rashi's Commentary on the Torah' (Heb.), *Tarbiz*, 56 (1987), 211–42.

—— *Exegesis in Perpetual Motion: Studies in the Pentateuchal Commentary of Rabbi Samuel ben Meir* [Hapeshatot hamitḥadeshim bekhol yom: iyunim befeirushav shel rashbam latorah] (Jerusalem, 2003).

—— 'From Exegesis to Ethics: The Torah's World-View According to Rashi's Commentary' (Heb.), in Sara Japhet (ed.), *The Bible in the Light of its Interpreters: Sarah Kamin*

*Memorial Volume* [Hamikra bire'i mefareshav: sefer zikaron lesarah kamin] (Jerusalem, 1994), 312–34.

—— 'Rashi's Use of Rabbinic Midrash' (Heb.), *Talelei orot*, 9 (2000), 51–78.

URBACH, EPHRAIM E., 'How Did Rashi Merit the Title *Parshandata*?', in Gabrielle Sed-Rajna (ed.), *Rashi 1040–1990* (Paris, 1993), 387–93.

—— 'Rabbinic Homilies on Non-Jewish Prophets and on the Account of Balaam' (Heb.), *Tarbiz*, 25 (1956), 272–89.

—— *The Tosafists* [Ba'alei hatosafot], 4th edn., 2 vols. (Jerusalem, 1980).

WEISS, ISAAC HIRSCH, 'Life of Rabbi Solomon bar Isaac' (Heb.), *Beit talmud*, 2 (1882), 33–40, 65–73, 129–38, 161–72, 193–206.

WEST, MARTIN L., *Textual Criticism and Editorial Technique Applicable to Greek and Latin Texts* (Stuttgart, 1973).

WOLFSON, ELLIOT, 'Mysticism of the Ashkenazi Pietists' (Heb.), in Michal Oron and Amos Goldreich (eds.), *Masu'ot: Ephraim Gottleib Memorial Volume* [Masu'ot: sefer zikaron le'efrayim gotlib] (Tel Aviv, 1994), 131–85.

YASSIF, ELI, 'Rashi Legends and Medieval Popular Culture', in Gabrielle Sed-Rajna (ed.), *Rashi 1040–1990* (Paris, 1993), 483–92.

YUVAL, ISRAEL JACOB, *Two Nations in Your Womb: Perceptions of Jews and Christians in Late Antiquity and the Middle Ages*, trans. Barbara Harshav and Jonathan Chipman (Berkeley, 2006).

ZAFRANI, DAVID, 'On "Repeated Commentary" in Rashi's Commentary on the Torah' (Heb.), *Beit mikra*, 161 (2001), 224–45.

ZAHARI, HAYYIM, *Rashi's Sources: Halakhic and Aggadic Midrash in his Commentaries* [Mekorot rashi: midreshei halakhah ve'agadah befeirushav], 17 vols. (Jerusalem, 1993–4).

ZUNZ, LEOPOLD, and SIMSON BLOCH, *Life of Rashi* [Toledot rashi] (Warsaw, 1862).

# Index of Scriptural References

# Index of Rabbinic References

# General Index

woman of valour 231
*see also* adultery; divorce; *ḥalitsah*; marriage
Worms, yeshiva in 37, 44, 55, 56 n. 7, 140–1,
  147–8, 294
  damage during pogroms 23, 53
  Meir ben Samuel at 63–4, 141, 159, 206
  Rashi at 15–18
  teachers at, *see* Isaac Halevi; Solomon ben
    Samson of Worms

## Y
Yakar ben Makhir, R. 68 n. 25
*yayin nesekh, see under* wine
yeshivas, medieval 16

libraries 18
  *see also under* Babylonia; Mainz; Speyer;
    Worms
'Yiru eineinu', recitation of 36
Yohanan, R. 186, 230
Yosi the Galilean, R. 243, 254, 273–4

## Z
Zechariah 200
Zeira, R. 281
Zelophehad's daughters 118–20, 234
*Zevaḥim* 45, 61
Zion, return to 123
Zipporah 106, 24